Toward Managed Peace

This Book Belongs To:

WILLIAM A. NAVAS, Jr.

Other Books by the Author

A National Policy for the Oil Industry (1948)

Planning for Freedom (1959)

The Sovereign Prerogative (1962)

Law, Power, and the Pursuit of Peace (1968)

Peace in the Balance (1972)

The Ideal in Law (1978)

*Report of the President's Task Force
on National Communications Policy,
E. V. Rostow, Chairman* (1968)

Editor, *Is Law Dead?* (1971)

EUGENE V. ROSTOW

Toward Managed Peace

The National Security Interests of the United States, 1759 to the Present

YALE UNIVERSITY PRESS
NEW HAVEN AND LONDON

Designed by Sally Harris, Summer Hill Books,
Weathersfield, Vermont.
Set in Times Roman type by
Rainsford Type, Danbury, Connecticut.
Printed in the United States of America by
Vail-Ballou Press, Binghamton, New York.

This work is based in large measure on
research and study conducted while the
author was serving as Distinguished
Visiting Research Professor of Law and
Diplomacy at the Institute for National
Strategic Studies, National Defense
University. Accordingly, reproduction in
whole or in part is hereby granted for any
purpose of the university or the U.S.
government.

Library of Congress Cataloging-in-Publication
Data

Rostow, Eugene V. (Eugene Victor), 1913–
    Toward managed peace : the national security
interests of the United States, 1759 to the
present / Eugene V. Rostow.
        p.   cm.
    ISBN 0-300-05700-8
    1. United States—Foreign relations. I. Title.
E183.7.R748   1992
327.73—dc20   92-24550
                                                    CIP

A catalogue record for this book is available from
the British Library.

The paper in this book meets the guidelines
for permanence and durability of the Committee
on Production Guidelines for Book Longevity
of the Council on Library Resources.

10 9 8 7 6 5 4 3 2 1

To the students of my seminar at the National Defense University,
who helped shape this book, with gratitude

Contents

PART III   The Age of Truman and Acheson, 1945 to the Present

Preface

This book came into being through a lucky combination of circumstances. As I approached compulsory retirement at Yale in 1984, my family and I naturally discussed possible alternatives for my working future. For some years, I had been increasingly absorbed by foreign affairs, and I had written and spoken widely on the subject, both as professor and as practitioner. We concluded that the most congenial and appropriate final act of my career would be to attempt a systematic reexamination of the field, and to write a series of three books about some of its main problems. The focus of all three books would be that of any other social study, the many-sided relationship between ideas and events: in this case, the experience of the United States with war and other international relations, and the aspirations of our culture for the just ordering of those relations.

This is the first of the three books in the projected series. It seeks to define the national security interests which our foreign policy should be designed to protect. My conclusion is that the supreme interest of the United States is the effective functioning of the system of world public order as a system of peace. For our time, the operational principles of the state system are defined by the Charter of the United Nations, which echoes the just war tradition of the world's prevailing moral code and the lessons we have drawn or failed to draw from our national experience in "the great external realm." The Charter can become a decisive influence on the behavior of states only if it is supported by a favorable balance of power maintained by the political and military influence of the dominant states. Despite our national myths to the contrary, the United States has always been an integral part of the state system, first as an intended target of some of the larger states, then as a secondary but increasingly important participant in world affairs, and finally as a superpower—for the moment, at least, the only superpower.

If that definition of the national interest is accepted, it follows that the second book of the series should deal with aggression, the most fundamental and most important problem of the state system, and the distinction in international law between aggression and self-defense. And the third should examine the ways in which Congress and the President, separately and together, make decisions in the realm of foreign policy. That book will be written from the perspective of American Constitutional law.

In 1984, the National Defense University, which is part of the Department of Defense, had recently been reorganized, in order to put more emphasis on the development of its research and post-graduate programs. To assist in that effort, I was in July 1984 appointed Distinguished Visiting Research Professor of Law and Diplomacy at the university. Appointed for two years, I was kept on for six, the statutory maximum for the post. Most of this book, therefore, was written at the National Defense University. Its ideas were tried out in a seminar I conducted there every year, and in lectures and conferences during this period at other senior military institutions, civilian universities, think-tanks, and conferences on foreign affairs both at home and abroad. While the book inevitably borrows a few pages here and there from some of the publications which resulted from these activities, most of it is freshly minted. I can hardly claim, however, that it reveals much change in my outlook since I began to struggle with foreign policy problems many years ago. On the other hand, I have never before undertaken to review our diplomatic history in the light of the questions I am trying to answer here, so that Part II is entirely new, and Parts I and III are largely new.

The experience of living and working at the National Defense University proved to be exceptionally stimulating and agreeable both for me and for my wife. The authorities graciously allowed us to rent a splendid apartment in a Victorian mansion at Fort McNair, where the university is located. The house is haunted by the ghost of Marie Surratt, who was tried in the building where we lived, and hanged just outside for her part in the conspiracy to assassinate President Lincoln. Living on the post meant that we were readily available to students and colleagues. Thus we had an unusually good opportunity to share in many aspects of the life of the university, and to gain some insight into military life as well. It was our first taste of a military atmosphere, however atypical, and both my wife and I found ourselves impressed and attracted by what we learned. We have come to know, like, respect, and appreciate many of the people we met at the university. Some we admire immoderately. And we made a considerable number of friends.

I wish to thank some of those particularly responsible for our happy sojourn at the National Defense University: Undersecretary Fred C. Ikle, the prime mover, and Deputy Secretary William Howard Taft IV, who helped in many ways, both intellectual and admininstrative; General Richard D. Lawrence, USA; Lieutenant General Bradley C. Hosmer, USAF; and Vice Admiral John A. Baldwin, USN, the presidents of the university under whom I served; ambassadors L. Bruce Laingen, Robert H. Miller, and Walter E. Stadtler, the vice-presidents during my time; Major General Albin G. Wheeler, USA, Commandant of the Industrial College of the Armed Forces, who shared Mrs. Surratt's ghost and much besides, both at Quarters 21 and elsewhere; Dr. John Endicott, the director of the Institute for National Strategic Studies, my guide, sponsor, colleague, and friend in many aspects of the venture; Dr. Frederick T. Kiley, the creative director of the National Defense University Press, and the warm and colorful staff he has brought together; and Lieutenant Colonel A. D. Rogers, USA, legal adviser to the president of the university, and a superb lawyer, tactician, and master of the bureaucratic art, who solved a number of delicate problems with imagination and panache. The last sections of this book were completed at the United States Institute of Peace. I thank Ambassador Samuel W. Lewis, president of the institute, an old and admired colleague in the State Department, for his help and support.

Thanks are also due to Oxford University Press for permission to quote at some length in Chapter 10 from Lord Devlin's book *Too Proud to Fight: Woodrow Wilson's Neutrality* and to Maurice Temple Smith, Ltd., for permission to quote in Chapter 4 from Sir Michael Howard's *War and the Liberal Conscience.* Passages in Chapter 16 appeared earlier in my chapter in *Gorbachev's USSR: A System in Crisis,* edited by Uri Ra'anan and Igor Lukes (London and New York: Macmillan and St. Martin's Press, 1990); in my lecture and article "Why Is It So Hard to Negotiate with the Russians?" (6 *Pace L. Rev.* 1 [1985]); in my lecture "Morality and Pragmatism in Foreign Policy," delivered on 12 November 1984 at the University of Texas at Dallas; and in my lecture "From the Finland Station," delivered on 18 February 1983 at the Fletcher School of Law and Diplomacy. The epigraph to Chapter 12 is from a book by my second son, Nicholas.

Finally, I thank Anne Cushman, my devoted and skillful secretary, and Jan Hietala, an editor at the National Defense University Press, who helped prepare the manuscript in its final stages, for infinitely valuable assistance. Special thanks are due to Cynthia Wells, senior production editor at the Yale University Press, a perceptive, punctilious, and sympathetic editor, who went over the text with a currycomb, and improved it immeasurably.

E.V.R.

Peru, Vermont
June 1992

Surely none of us wish to see Bonaparte conquer Russia, and lay thus at his feet the whole continent of Europe. This done, England would be but a breakfast; and, although I am free from the visionary fears which the votaries of England have effected to entertain, because I believe he cannot effect the conquest of Europe; yet put all Europe into his hands, and he might spare such a force to be sent in British ships, as I would as leave not have to encounter, when I see how much trouble a handful of British soldiers in Canada has given us. No. It cannot be to our interest that all Europe should be reduced to a single monarchy.—Thomas Jefferson, letter to Thomas Lieper, 1 January, 1814

PART I

By Way of Conceptual Framework

Introduction

A friend recently asked me why the United States cannot live as Switzerland does, peacefully governing itself, and doing business with everybody. "Why do we have to get involved in messy and disagreeable problems all over the world?" he asked. "Why can't we concentrate on what we do best—business and industry, and the development of our country—what we did so well before the First World War?" Our first reaction when Gorbachev came to power in 1985 and announced "the end of the Cold War" was the thought, widely repeated, that now we can bring the troops home and resume our natural foreign policy of isolationism.

I have heard or read the question, or its equivalent, hundreds if not thousands of times from students and colleagues; from the earnest, troubled people who crowd around the speaker after a lecture; from readers, friends, and critics. Since our withdrawal from Vietnam, the rapid growth of the Soviet nuclear arsenal, and now the stunning collapse of the Soviet state, the question has been put with increasing insistence all across the American political spectrum. Indeed, it is no longer a question but an assertion: an advocacy of American retreat from the foreign policy the United States has pursued since the Second World War. The proponents of withdrawal imagine that such a retreat would permit the United States to escape down the rabbit-hole of history to the golden age of isolation and neutrality they fondly suppose America enjoyed during most of the nineteenth century. Those who urge retreat never specify how far we should retreat, and each member of the party has a different reason for advancing the thesis. The chorus of voices urging American isolation from the troubles of the world is stronger than it has been since the thirties.

This book attempts to answer my friend's question, which weighs heavily on every American mind. It is a rumination, an essay, not a treatise. Its subject is the national interest of the United States in world politics—more precisely, the national security interests of the United tes, the interests for which we should fight, if necessary, in the turbulent political and military environment we know today and must anticipate for tomorrow. Its argument is that the supreme security interest of the United States—the interest most worth fighting for—is an organized and effectively enforced system of general international peace: not a world order of Utopian perfection, but one in which the phenomenon of war is kept within tolerable limits by the cooperation of the states which constitute the world community, and especially of the major powers, or at least a decisive number of them.

Every American would agree that the influence of the nation should be deployed abroad only in behalf of what is loosely called the national interest. But from the eighteenth century to this day, there has been no agreement among Americans about what the national interest is. There are easy cases: defending the frontiers and rescuing citizens in distress abroad, for example, although there is sometimes controversy even about rescuing Americans being mistreated in foreign countries. But if one attempts to go beyond the obvious, one finds himself in a fog which never clears.

Some who speak and write about American foreign policy berate its principal spokesmen and practitioners as hopelessly naive because they cannot commit themselves exclusively to the robust creed of "power politics," but insist on talking about the spread of liberty and democracy, the protection of the weak against the strong, the promotion of human rights, and above all about "the rule of law." For reasons rooted in the nature of our culture and our history, however, most Americans have found such criticism morally repulsive. Luckily, our conditioned reflexes are considerably more realistic than our vocabulary for talking about the problems of our foreign policy. Still, what we think does sometimes affect what we do. It is true that we have survived and indeed flourished despite the fact that we have never achieved a coherent and universally accepted theory of our foreign policy. Yet, in our hazardous world, it would be foolhardy to assume that we can expect to do so indefinitely.

In this context, I fully agree with Lord Carrington's judgment that the greatest weakness of the democratic alliance systems is that they lack a shared vision of what they want to accomplish in world politics. In no realm is the admonition of the Book of Proverbs more pertinent: "Where there is no vision, the people perish: but he that keepeth the law, happy is he."

The difficulty is that there can be no Western grand strategy until the American people define the national interests of the United States and agree on the foreign and security policies required to defend them. While Soviet programs of expansion all over the world were moving forward, the reason for this conclusion was obvious, though by no means easy to accept: the security of the United States required at an absolute minimum that Western Europe, Canada, Mexico, Japan, China, and a number of other critical states and areas be kept free of Soviet control. Unfortunately, none of those states and areas, singly or in combination, could protect itself against the Soviet Union without the full backing of United States conventional and nuclear forces. Western Europe, China, and Japan could surely defend themselves against the pressure of Soviet expansion if the instruments of military power were still purely conventional. Without American backing, however, those states and regions could not successfully confront Soviet nuclear power, and therefore could not use their conventional forces. They would perforce yield. The countries grouped around the United States for security purposes therefore are not American protectorates or imperial dependencies in any sense. The United States and the nations associated with it in security coalitions are indispensable to each other: not overlord and vassals, but true partners. Whether this logic will continue to be applicable if the Russian and the other successor states to the Soviet Union give up both the capacity and the ambition for expansion remains to be seen. Despite the changed rhetoric of Soviet and Russian official statements, the Gorbachev years, at least, did not accomplish either a reduction of the Soviet military budget or a full liquidation of Soviet imperial policy in Europe, Asia, Latin America, or the Middle East. The long campaign of Soviet expansion, which has its roots in five hundred years of Russian history, may be coming to an end as this book is being finished. We can be certain, however, that other problems of the same character will emerge as the structure of world politics changes. Indeed, some are already visible on the horizon.

To clarify the goals of American and Western foreign policy is thus a task of primordial importance and urgency. It is also a task of quite special difficulty. While the principal problems of our foreign and security policy are intellectual, and cannot be solved without intellectual effort, they are not exclusively intellectual, and cannot be solved by intellectual effort alone. Our emotional defenses against the reality behind problems of grand strategy are formidable and tenaciously held. Like other nations, we have demonstrated our capacity for wishful thinking, self-deception, and denial, to say nothing of indecision and irrationality.

Part I of this book, the first three chapters, sets out the principal ideas needed to define the national security interests of the United States and to formulate a policy for protecting them.

Chapter 1 attempts to discriminate among the many strands in the American conception of the national interest, distinguishing between the security interests of the United States as a state among the states, and its ineradicable sense of mission as a prophet of liberty and democracy. It focuses on two concepts which are usually treated as antithetical: power and law. And it seeks to demonstrate that the most fundamental security interest of the United States is to achieve and maintain a pluralist system of world public order, based on a balance of power and regulated by law. No army has ever gone into battle behind banners emblazoned with the words "Long live the balance of power." I submit, however, that there is no more legitimate reason for a democracy to fight.

The second and third chapters introduce the key analytical tools used in developing the argument of the book—the notion of the state system and the legal concepts of peace and war.

American statesmen, like most of their fellow citizens, are possessed by one of the strongest passions of the American culture, its commitment to the role of law in the social process. We are people of the Book. At the deepest level, we believe—correctly—that peace is the highest and most vital security interest of the United States. And we have learned from our history with peculiar vividness that the notion of peace is a legal concept which can be summed up in the much-abused phrase "the rule of law." As Professor Ralph Goldman has said, "No cops, no law. No law, no peace."

It is the argument of this book that power and law are not alternative ways of analyzing the life of societies—domestic or international—but two sides of the same coin. Law is unintelligible outside its social matrix, and the restraint of mores—that is, of customs having the force of law—limits the behavior of states even when the society of nations is in a condition of near-anarchy. The abiding question of policy, in my view, is not whether international society is governed by international law—by definition, it is and must be—but whether that law is or can be made just law and generally fulfilled.

1

On War and Peace

The world of war is not a fully comprehensible, let alone a morally satis-
factory place. And yet it cannot be escaped, short of a universal order in
which the existence of nations and peoples could never be threatened.
There is every reason to work for such an order. The difficulty is that we
sometimes have no choice but to fight for it.—Michael Walzer

It is axiomatic that the government of the United States should send
troops to risk death only in order to defend the security interests of
the nation as it perceives them. John Quincy Adams' famous maxim
is a moral imperative for every modern democracy, and especially for
the United States. In response to enthusiasts who would have had the
vulnerable infant republic defy the great powers of Europe and rush
to the aid of revolutionaries in Europe and South America, Adams
wrote:

> America, in the assembly of nations, since her admission among
> them, has invariably, though often fruitlessly, held forth to them
> the hand of honest friendship, of equal freedom, of generous re-
> ciprocity. She has uniformly spoken among them, though often to
> heedless and often to disdainful ears, the language of equal liberty,
> of equal justice, and of equal rights. She has in the lapse of nearly
> half a century, without a single exception, respected the independ-
> ence of other nations while asserting and maintaining her own. She
> has abstained from interference in the concerns of others, even
> when the conflict has been for principles to which she clings, as to
> the last vital drop that visits the heart. . . . Wherever the standard
> of freedom and Independence, has been or shall be unfurled, there
> will her heart, her benedictions and her prayers be. But she goes

The epigraph for this chapter is taken from Michael Walzer, *Just and Unjust Wars* (New
York: Basic Books, 1977), 327.

not abroad, in search of monsters to destroy. She is the well-wisher to the freedom and independence of all. She is the champion and vindicator only of her own.[1]

But Adams, who was surely one of the three greatest American secretaries of state, and perhaps the greatest, also pointed out that while policy does not change, circumstances do. The purpose of this book is to examine the "changes in circumstance" which have occurred since 1776, and what they imply about the future of our foreign policy.

Obviously, the United States of Adams' time, a small, weak appendage of the European state system, faced security problems entirely different from those confronting it at the end of the twentieth century. Nevertheless, the security concerns of the nation, then and now, can be described by the same words: to make the world safe for American democracy at home, that is, to safeguard the territorial integrity and political independence of the United States, and to protect its citizens, its commerce, and its other interests abroad. Hans Morgenthau defines "the hard core" of the national interest as "the identity of the nation," that is, its physical, political, and cultural survival. How a state may prudently protect that interest depends on the political environment and on the national necessities which limit the choice of ends and means by all the actors on the stage.[3] Obviously, the task of vindicating the "freedom and independence" of the United States today has implications which would have startled the Founding Fathers, proud and optimistic as they were about the future of the nation they had created.

For most of the nineteenth century, the United States had what C. Vann Woodward once called "free security."[4] We were a ward of the Concert of Europe, reasonably safe within its equipoise, protected by British diplomacy and the British fleet as well as by our own exertions. The reality was not so simple nor so idyllic as Professor Woodward's comment may imply. There were moments of danger when Britain and France were tempted to prevent the United States from becoming too big and too strong, and during the Civil War only the

[handwritten margin note: Us + UK for edsie life until missiles and now other even more]

---

1. An address delivered at the request of the Committee of Citizens of Washington, 4 July 1821 (Washington, D.C.: Davis and Force, 1821), 28–29.

2. Samuel Flagg Bemis, *John Quincy Adams and the Foundations of American Foreign Policy* (New York: Alfred A. Knopf, 1949), 572.

3. Hans J. Morgenthau, *Dilemmas of Politics* (Chicago: University of Chicago Press, 1958), chap. 4, passim, particularly pp. 65–66.

4. C. Vann, Woodward, "The Age of Reinterpretation," *American Historical Review* 66 (October 1960): 1, 2–8; the address was reprinted with some revision as chapter 4, "The Age of Reinterpretation," in C. Vann Woodward, *The Future of the Past* (New York: Oxford University Press, 1989).

Union victories at Gettysburg and Vicksburg restrained them from moving decisively in that direction. But our foreign policy problems before 1914 were far less threatening than they are today, and the European balance of power worked—usually—to our advantage.

The Eurocentered state system of the nineteenth century is gone, however, and the state system which has succeeded it is precarious and unstable. The magnetic field of world politics has profoundly changed. It is no longer regulated by the prudent rivalries and ultimate co-operation of four or five Christian European powers. Europe has lost the power to conduct the world's orchestra. If the orchestra is to be led in behalf of civilization and democracy, the United States has to lead it.

And it must be an orchestra. Between 1815 and 1914, foreign intervention seriously threatened the United States only during the Civil War. Since 1914, however, except for the few transient years of the American nuclear monopoly at the end of the Second World War, the United States has never had the power to defend its security single-handedly. From its beginning in 1776, the United States, like nearly all nations throughout history, could assure its safety only through tacit or open alliances. The relative power of the United States is declining and will continue to decline in the world of Behemoths and Leviathans we perceive looming up in the future. For as far ahead as we can foresee, however, the United States cannot escape from the task of directing the quest for peace. The evidence to support this proposition will be reviewed in Part III. For present purposes it can be summarized in these terms:

Between 1945 and 1990, at least, world politics has been dominated by a Soviet thrust for overwhelming power and the coming together of other states in association with the United States to resist this attempt. The Soviet—or now the Russian—drive for expansion will not go on forever; such phenomena always come to an end. In fact, Yeltsin may be abandoning that ambition or facing the fate of Kerensky. On the other hand, the sensational proclamations of Gorbachev and Yeltsin may turn out to have been purely tactical maneuvers. Until events justify another hypothesis, the United States must assume that after an interval of economic recovery, Russia, at least, may well resume the course of expansion the Soviet Union pursued since 1917. Indeed, the Russian Empire followed much the same policy for more than five hundred years before the Bolsheviks seized power. The Soviet campaign was based on ideological claims and military strength, and especially on the menace of its nuclear arsenal, which has not yet icantly declined. The idea of Russian expansion in the ideology of the Russian people seems almost instinctive.

The Soviet Union was not of course the only state which has engaged in or supported aggression since the Second World War. But its program of expansion based on the illegal use of force has been on a larger scale than that of other aggressor nations, and has more deeply threatened the stability of the state system as a whole. Even if the successor states of the Soviet Union visibly become peaceful and cooperative members of the society of nations, that fact alone would not allow us to dismantle our armed forces and withdraw from world politics. There can be no expectation that even a pacific Russian Federation would give up its nuclear arsenal. There can therefore be no way to assure the security of the United States and its allies without an adequate American nuclear force, with all that entails. And the restless shifts in the balance of power which have characterized every period of human history will surely continue, creating new problems for the United States in their turn.

By an accident of history, only the United States could provide a deterrent counterweight to the Soviet nuclear arsenal and therefore to the Soviet thrust for dominion. If the United States should falter in the foreign policy effort it has undertaken since 1947, it would lose the capacity to vindicate its own freedom and independence, in John Quincy Adams' sense of those words. In order to assure its survival, that is, "to secure the Blessings of Liberty to ourselves and our Posterity," in the language of the Constitution, America must renew its leadership of the regional coalitions required to achieve and maintain both a stable balance of power in international politics and a world order based on that balance of power—as nearly as may be, a world order of independent states living together peacefully, in accordance with the rules of law necessary to their cooperation.

This conclusion can be explained in the vocabulary of President Wilson or of Sir Halford Mackinder. Mackinder was a British geographer and theorist of power, a Liberal M.P., and head of the London School of Economics. His writings have been the most distinguished and influential force in the modern literature of the subject.[5] Mackinder's argument derives from his map of world politics, first published early in the century and later developed by Nicholas Spykman and others. The political and military implications of Mackinder's map are

5. Edward Mead Earle, Introduction, in *Democratic Ideals and Reality: A Study in the Politics of Reconstruction,* by Halford J. Mackinder (1919; reprint, New York: Henry Holt, 1942), xxi.

different now than when he put it forward. Planes and missiles can fly over the Arctic ice, submarines can navigate under it, and naval vessels are at risk—as the Falkland Islands conflict showed—as never before. But the map remains an indispensable tool of analysis.

If one looks at the globe as a whole—and in defining American security, no lesser perspective is possible—one sees that 9/12ths of its surface is occupied by the oceans and 2/12ths by what Mackinder called the World Island—Europe, Asia, and Africa, connected by land and backed by the Arctic Circle, which in Mackinder's day was unassailable. Britain, Japan, and the Americas occupy 1/12th of the earth's surface, and should be viewed as satellite islands off the coast of the vastly larger World Island. In 1919, when Mackinder published his most important book, 14/16ths of the world's population lived on the World Island— the single continent made up of Europe, Asia, and Africa; 1/16th in Great Britain and Japan together; and 1/16th on the American continent and the smaller islands. These proportions had changed a little by 1978, the last year for which I have been able to find the relevant statistics. In that year 13/16ths of the world population lived on the World Island, a drop of about 6 percent; the share of Great Britain and Japan in world population had fallen about 2 1/2 percent, to 0.6/16th; and the percentage of the world's population living in the Americas and the other islands had risen 8.5 percent, to 2.4/16ths.

What Mackinder called the Heartland of the World Island—the great central patch of Asia and Europe extending from the Arctic shores of Siberia to Persia and Baluchistan and from the Pacific coastal regions of Asia to the larger part of Germany—has until recently been inaccessible from the sea. As Catherine the Great once remarked during a period of diplomatic tension between Russia and Great Britain, "Let Pitt send his ships to Moscow." The Heartland area constitutes an enormous center of power from which military forces have attacked the coastal regions of Asia and Europe (the Rimlands, in Mackinder's terminology) since the beginning of time, and, the islands like Great Britain, Japan, and the Americas as well.

The moral of this history is by no means a matter of merely antiquarian interest. Russia today is still outflanking Norway, showing great interest in Iceland, and directly threatening Iran and Baluchistan. A brilliant American student of strategy once said Russia should never be allowed to go south of the line between Tehran and Kabul. Russia has by no means lost interest in Afghanistan, and has forces in Indochina, putting pressure on China and Japan. Even more important, has it abandoned, or only suspended, its enormous efforts to its central strategic goal, the separation of Europe from the United States, and the neutralization of Europe, and therefore of Japan and China as well?

Those who have attempted to view history in this perspective have seemed to disagree about the relative importance of sea power and land power in the wars and diplomacy of the past. Equally, they seem to disagree today about the relative significance of air power and nuclear power as compared to the older forms of land and sea power. Some advocates of sea power have undoubtedly exaggerated the military value of blockades and of economic warfare more generally, just as the enthusiasts for air power and nuclear power have made excessive claims in their turn.

Nonetheless, the main positions in the literature of strategy are easily reconciled. Sea power is of immense utility in enabling the Island and Rimland powers to prevent any one power from dominating the Heartland and thus achieving hegemony. But the bases of sea power are sometimes vulnerable to attack from the land, as Singapore was captured in World War II. And to be significant, sea power must be amphibious; its purpose is not to control the fishes, but to project military power on land. The defeat of the Spanish Armada did not end Spain's thrust for dominance in Europe; Elizabeth I had to fight with allies on the Continent to achieve that end, as her successors did against different aspirants for hegemony in the times of Marlborough, Wellington, and both the world wars of this century. Similarly, for all the immense importance of air power as an adjunct to land and sea operations, it has not become an independent dimension of warfare, while the principal function of nuclear weapons thus far has been political, in controlling the use of nonnuclear weapons.

Given modern technology in transportation, communication, and war, the military potential of the Eurasian-African land mass is even more overwhelming than it was in the past, should it be brought under the control of a single power bent on conquest. Western and Central Europe have formidable military resources; despite its social and economic troubles since 1988, Russia is stronger than ever before; and Central Asia is no longer the home only of nomad horsemen armed with spears or old rifles. China is modernizing; Japan is, of course, extremely powerful; and India, rapidly industrializing, will be a great power within a generation.

For the United States, an island state like Britain and Japan, the first problem of national security is therefore to help prevent the emergence of a decisive aggregation of power in Europe, Asia, or the Middle East. We fought in two world wars during this century to keep Germany from achieving a position of dominance in Europe, and the Western allies united in NATO have prevented the Soviet Union from attaining the same goal. It is this imperative which makes Central Europe such an important pivot in the geography of power, and the independence of Poland, Czechoslovakia, Hungary, Yugoslavia, Bulgaria, and Rumania therefore so critical to the security of the West. In 1962, President Kennedy told the Soviet Union that there could be no peace between our peoples until the Soviet Union carried out the promise of free elections in Eastern Europe that it had made at Yalta and Potsdam. The considerations lying behind that judgment will remain valid indefinitely.

Our security interests in the Pacific Basin and the Middle East are exactly parallel. As President Nixon and Chou En-lai declared in their Shanghai communiqué of 1972, the United States and China are agreed in opposing "any hegemonic power in Asia." Despite intense Soviet pressure, Japan later acceded to that declaration: a classic instance of Island and Rimland powers combining to deter the strongest land power of the day from gaining ascendancy. This was the strategic consideration for which we fought the Korean and Vietnam wars. It justified our interest in the Philippines, Taiwan, the ASEAN states, and of course the island nations of the South Pacific.

The Western Allies followed Mackinder's advice after the First World War when they partitioned the Russian and the Austro-Hungarian Empires and created the Baltic States and the states of Eastern Europe as a buffer, a *cordon sanitaire,* between Russia and Germany. Twenty years later, however, the Western Allies—or at least the British and the Americans—forgot Mackinder's analysis, and allowed Poland, Czechoslovakia, Austria, and the rest of Central Europe to be overwhelmed by Hitler.

The policy we have followed since the Second World War should be adapted to changing circumstances, but it must be continued. This conclusion is required both by our most earthy, pragmatic, and fundamental security interests as a nation and by the most compelling moral principles of our culture. It is commonplace to suppose that morality and what is often called realpolitik, or power politics, represent opposing principles for the conduct of foreign relations. But the circumstances of modern life—and especially the nuclear weapon—require morality and power politics to join hands. The paradox is not so shocking as it may appear. This is by no means the first time that democratic ideals have been reinforced by the reality of military power.

This, in brief, is why we cannot live as Switzerland does today.

Neutrality in international politics and law is not a status which a state can choose alone. It is based on international agreement. The neutrality of Switzerland rests not only on the valor of the well-trained Swiss citizen army but on treaties which all the major powers have an equal interest in respecting. The United States has far too much specific gravity to be accepted as a neutral by an international community dominated by a hostile power or a hostile combination of powers. If we should proclaim our neutrality in such an environment, the dominant states would assume we might change our minds later, and would act accordingly. The neutrality legislation of the thirties did not protect us against Pearl Harbor and Hitler's declaration of war, and the treaty guaranteeing the neutrality of Belgium turned out to be "a scrap of paper" in 1914.

James Madison stated the point with classical force and precision in No. 41 of the Federalist Papers. He was addressing the anxiety of those who opposed the new Constitution because it did not prohibit standing military forces in peacetime. The question was indeed difficult, Madison wrote, but the answer was not in our hands: "How could a readiness for war in time of peace be safely prohibited, unless we could prohibit in like manner, the preparations and establishment of every hostile nation? The means of security can only be regulated by the means and the danger of attack. They will, in fact, be ever determined by these rules, and by no others. It is in vain to oppose Constitutional barriers to the impulse of self preservation."

In identifying international peace as one of the moral principles of free societies, one should distinguish "peace" from what are loosely called "human rights." Of course the United States and other civilized societies should always encourage the universal acceptance and legal protection of human liberty, insofar as they can do so without intervening in the domestic affairs of other states. In the nature of things, they must; they do; and they will, unless they are cowed into a posture of ignoble silence on the subject by their fear of offending the leadership of states where human liberty is not respected. As Samuel Flagg Bemis once said, the love of individual liberty "set the tone and gave color to the activities of our countrymen at the beginning of our nation. . . . These freedoms of the individual are the values for which the United States has stood throughout its history in the shifting configurations of power and politics in the world of nations."[6]

---

6. Samuel Flagg Bemis, *American Foreign Policy and the Blessings of Liberty, and Other Essays* (New Haven, Conn.: Yale University Press, 1962), 2.

But international peace is something quite different from antipathy to tyranny and barbarism. To recall the language of the United Nations Charter, peace can be defined only as an effectively enforced rule of respect for the territorial integrity and political independence of all states, large and small, socialist or capitalist, democratic or nondemocratic. In a world of states based on diverse social and political systems, the rule of peace is essential to the possibility of their coexistence.

The concept of peace within the international state system is discussed in Chapter 2. All that needs be said here is that the focus will be on the nature of peace within the only contemporary system of world order which can be imagined as historically possible and, indeed, the only system of world order compatible with our national character: an open and pluralist system of independent nation-states. The United States will never have an appetite for imperial power; the idea goes against the grain of our political character, and has never been sustained by our politics. In any event, imperial aspirations would be beyond our capabilities even if, in a feverish moment, we entertained them.

The kind of state system with which we are concerned here has been evolving for the last two centuries, first as the world order managed by the Concert of Europe between 1815 and 1914, and more recently as the less tightly organized system brought together under the Covenant of the League of Nations and the Charter of the United Nations. To improve that system and fulfill its aspiration for peace is not simply the most desirable foreign policy for the United States, its allies and associates, and other nations committed to peace; in the age of nuclear weapons, it is an inescapable necessity as well.

When Alfred Nobel invented dynamite, he thought the new explosive would make the prospect of war so terrible that the nations would at last accept the necessity for peace. If reason and the instinct for self-preservation have not lost all their influence in human affairs, the menace of nuclear weapons and other modern weapons of high technology should finally bring about the realization of Nobel's dream. But they have not done so yet. While the nuclear weapon has not been fired in anger since 1945, several hundred international wars have taken place; millions of people have been killed, wounded, and driven into exile by war; and cities and societies without number destroyed.

The greatest risk of nuclear war is through escalation from conventional war. No one can be confident that the taboo against the use of nuclear weapons which has lasted since 1945 will be effective indefinitely; nuclear threats have been made on a number of occasions since

1945. Thus far, they have all been respected, but no one can say that will always be the case. Nuclear weapons may fall into the hands of irrational political leaders or terrorists. And nuclear weapons may be fired and may trigger nuclear escalation under the pressures of a crisis or a conventional war, if the crisis involves a nuclear power, or a nonnuclear power which obtains a few nuclear weapons in some obscure bazaar of the world arms market. The political and military leaders who attempt to manage crises or conduct conventional wars are fallible human beings. Policy must not rest on the assumption that they will forever resist the temptation to use nuclear weapons or other weapons of mass destruction in circumstances of extreme tension—for example, in the confusion of a war they are losing. The world has, after all, witnessed the repeated use of chemical and biological weapons by the Soviet Union and its client-states at intervals since the Yemen War of 1967, despite the universal revulsion against them. And these appalling weapons were not employed in great crises, but as cold-blooded experiments in minor colonial wars against Third World peoples. These risks are by no means confined to great powers and their proxies. In order to prevent nuclear war it is therefore necessary to prevent all international war, as the American Conference of Catholic Bishops said in their important pastoral letter on the morality of the nuclear weapon in 1983.[7]

II

The method of this book is historical. I do not conceive of history as the antonym of theory. On the contrary, any version of the past necessarily requires and applies a theoretical view of the process of social change, in terms of which the evidence is selected and marshalled to test, modify, or discard the tentative theory. The memory of the past is an inescapable part of the present and future of every social organization. Part II is therefore reviews some critical junctures of our diplomatic history in order to isolate and clarify the factors which define the national interest of the United States.

There is another reason, a compelling psychological and political reason, for approaching the task in its historical perspective. The common American perception of our nineteenth-century experience in for-

7. See George Weigel, *Tranquilitas Ordinis: The Present Failure and Future Promise of American Catholic Thought on War and Peace* (New York: Oxford University Press, 1987), 257–85.

eign affairs is still an immensely powerful part of the national outlook. The popular understanding of Washington's Farewell Address and the Monroe Doctrine has the force of a commandment. That this perception is largely mythical does not weaken its influence. In their hearts, nearly all Americans believe that the natural and rightful role of the United States in world politics is one of isolation and neutrality, living at peace in a Western Hemisphere carefully insulated from the wickedness and corruption of Europe and Asia. The power of this belief is so great that the principal problem of American foreign policy, in my experience, is a conflict between our collective unconscious and the realities of life in the late twentieth century.

The historian invariably writes with the problems of his own age in mind. Those problems dominate his mind, and dictate both his frame of reference and his choice among premises. What has dominated my mind in writing this book is the conviction that the diplomatic and military policies we adopt and carry out during the next decade will determine whether the United States can survive as a nation worthy of its heritage. I have faith that the nation which met the ordeal of the Civil War will prevail in the struggles which it confronts today. The challenges of the late twentieth century are every bit as threatening as those which faced the United States after Fort Sumter. And they are novel challenges, requiring thought and action for which our educational system has prepared us badly. One thing is certain: these challenges will not be overcome by faith alone. Works also are needed.

III

By summarizing my thesis in this way, I do not intend to suggest that security is the only interest of the nation in the functioning of international society, and that the armed forces are the only instrumentality of its foreign policy for safeguarding security. Every nation has many interests beyond security in the external world: cultural and economic interests; interests of sympathy and antipathy based on kinship, history, ideology, and religion; and interests of other kinds as well—interests in travel, sport, and food, for example, and in the international communion of learning. Chancelleries, foreign offices, and embassies work hard and long both on the issues of policy arising from the interplay of these interests and on the inevitable episodes of friction to which they give rise. Sailors are arrested and students run out of money, usually in remote and exotic places. Great battles are fought with words and paper when companies try to buy, sell, or invest abroad and confront resistance. Repression, injustice, and tyranny have always aroused the indignation of democratic peoples, and especially of Americans. I hope they always will. When such conditions develop abroad, they often enlist the active concern of the American people, or of groups among them, and sometimes affect the foreign policy of the United States, at least in detail.

But these strands in the fuller definition of our national interest will not be examined here for a simple reason: they are necessarily subordinate to the nation's primordial concern for its security, that is, for its political independence and the integrity of its territories. And security is a question not of ideology or economics or human rights but of power and the customs of international society governing the use of power. We were right, I should contend, to make common cause with the Soviet Union during the Second World War, and we are right to make common cause with China today, despite the totalitarian character of their governments. Unless the world balance of power is preserved, and the national security of the United States thereby protected, it will be impossible for us to pursue our economic, cultural, and humanitarian interests abroad in comparative freedom, or to indulge our extranational enthusiasms at all. In any event, the national security of the United States in the late twentieth century is a matter sufficiently complicated and sufficiently important to merit separate consideration.

Throughout the centuries, Americans have always had great difficulty in articulating their perception of what national security requires. We embrace contradictory principles with equal fervor and cling to them with equal tenacity. Should our foreign policy be based on power or morality? Realism or idealism? Pragmatism or principle? Should its goal be the protection of interests or the promotion of values? Should we be nationalists or internationalists? Liberals or conservatives? We blithely answer, "All of the above."

Living with unresolved contradictions is not of course a psychological phenomenon peculiar to the realm of foreign policy. And it is not a shortcoming confined to Americans. The social psychologists label the condition "cognitive dissonance." Kenneth Clark, talking about the tension between custom and aspiration in the field of race relations, called it "moral schizophrenia," which is a good deal more somber and realistic as a definition of the syndrome. In the conduct of a nation's foreign policy, as in the conduct of its race relations, the price of error can indeed be death.

Our failure to achieve a coherent and realistic way of thinking about the national interest in world affairs is a serious obstacle to rational and sustained policymaking. It means that we often act on the basis of instinct rather than thought, and have to cope with crises instead of preventing them. The pairs of words I have just listed—liberal and conservative, nationalist and internationalist, and the others—have all sorts of resonance for other purposes, but they have no meaning in the realm of foreign policy. Foreign policies can be prudent or imprudent, wise or foolish, too active or too passive, realistic or unrealistic. But they cannot be "liberal" or "conservative," "nationalist" or "internationalist."

With the rise of social history, economic history, intellectual history, and cultural history, the role of politics and war in the process of history has been relatively neglected. Political and diplomatic history is often regarded as old-fashioned, if not reprehensible and reactionary. And military history is viewed by many as beyond the pale. This is a strange form of myopia to become fashionable in an age whose social, economic, moral, intellectual, and cultural life has been dominated by politics and war.

In his mordant and delightful book *The Art of War,* written in 500 B.C., Sun Tzu spoke of war as "a matter of vital importance to the State; the province of life or death; the road to survival or ruin."[8] No American can doubt the truth of Sun Tzu's insight. We cannot suppose that the French helped us in our Revolutionary War because the Bourbon king was a republican at heart and favored the idea of revolution. And we know that the Civil War was settled irrevocably on America's haunted battlefields and in the foreign offices of Europe through an immense military and diplomatic effort conjured from the soul of the nation by the genius of Abraham Lincoln.

This book seeks to demonstrate that the basic national security interest of the United States for the indefinite future is parallel to that which burdened Great Britain for at least four centuries: the task of helping to achieve and maintain a reasonably stable balance of power within which Britain could be free and independent. The long contest among the forces of order, hegemony, and anarchy in Europe involved Great Britain in many wars. The relationship between the United States and the Soviet Union between 1945 and the day before yesterday was like that between Great Britain and the nations which bid for dominion in Europe between the sixteenth and the twentieth centuries—Spain in

8. Sun Tzu, *The Art of War,* trans. Samuel B. Griffith (London: Oxford University Press, 1963), 63.

the age of Philip II and Elizabeth I, France from the time of Louis XIV to Napoleon, and Germany in the first half of this century. No doubt the central concerns of American security policy will change in the future as they have changed in the past. In this era, however, the Soviet—and now the Russian—attempt to escape from the restraints of the balance of power has been and, in another form, may remain the principal problem of American foreign policy.

The Soviet Union has been dissolved, and given way to a number of successor states. Has Russia yet abandoned its imperial ambitions? One day it will surely do so, under the pressures of defeat, collapse, boredom, and the gradual realization that the goal is costly, immoral, and impossible to achieve in the modern world. For one or another of these reasons, the other imperial powers have long since accepted this conclusion, and settled down to the humdrum life of trade and peace. As this manuscript is being prepared for the printer, the West is agog with hope that perhaps Yeltsin has indeed foresworn the policy of expansion which Russia conducted for five hundred years. Perhaps he has. It is a consummation devoutly to be desired. What is certain, however, is that if Russia should retire from its imperial role, the task of helping to maintain the equilibrium of the state system will continue to require active and sometimes costly efforts by the United States for the indefinite future. In their turn, Spain, France, Turkey, Germany, Sweden, and Holland each sought a degree of power which made their neighbors uncomfortable. History may be coming to an end in an Hegelian sense. The jostling response of states to changes in the balance of power shows no sign of disappearing, however. Nor is it yet clear that Yeltsin and his policy will prevail in the internal life of the Russian state.

The task of protecting the security of the United States is like that of Britain throughout the four hundred fifty years between Elizabeth I and Elizabeth II in another sense as well. At no point during the period between the two Queens Elizabeth was Britain as strong as her chief rivals, or her rivals in combination. As was noted earlier—and the point bears emphasis, because American pride resists it—the United States is not strong enough and cannot make itself strong enough to protect its security interests in world politics by its own efforts alone. Our dependence on alliances and coalitions will necessarily continue in the years ahead as the magnetic field of world power changes again.

Churchill characterized the role of war in international politics in his life of Marlborough:

If anyone in 1672 computed the relative forces of France and England, he could only feel that no contest was possible; and the apparent weakness and humiliation of the pensioner island was aggravated by the feeble, divided condition of Europe. No dreamer, however romantic, however remote his dreams from reason, could have foreseen a surely approaching day when, by the formation of mighty coalitions and across the struggles of a generation, the noble colossus of France would lie prostrate in the dust, while the small island, beginning to gather to itself the empires of India and America, stripping France and Holland of their colonial possessions, would emerge victorious, mistress of the Mediterranean, the Narrow Seas, and the oceans. Aye, and carry forward with her, intact and enshrined, all that peculiar structure of law and liberty, all her own inheritance of learning and letters, which are to-day the treasure of the most powerful family in the human race.

The prodigy was achieved by conflicting yet contributory forces, and by a succession of great islanders and their noble foreign comrades or guides. We owe our salvation to the sturdy independence of the House of Commons and to its creators, the aristocracy and country gentlemen. We owe it to our hardy tars and bold sea-captains, and to the quality of a British Army as yet unborn. We owe it to the inherent sanity and vigour of the political conceptions sprung from the genius of the English race. But those forces would have failed without the men to use them. For the quarter of a century from 1688 to 1712 England was to be led by two of the greatest warriors and statesmen in all history: William of Orange, and John, Duke of Marlborough. They broke the military power of France, and fatally weakened her economic and financial foundations. They championed the Protestant faith, crowned Parliamentary institutions with triumph, and opened the door to an age of reason and freedom. They reversed the proportions and balances of Europe. They turned into new courses the destinies of Asia and America. They united Great Britain, and raised her to the rank she holds today.[9]

Churchill could have said as much for the younger Pitt, Wellington, Nelson, and Castlereagh, who, a century later, achieved another hundred years of British ascendancy on the foundation William and Marlborough had laid. In the name of the tradition these great men

---

9. Winston S. Churchill, *Marlborough: His Life and Times* (New York: Charles Scribner's Sons, 1933), 1:82.

fortified, Churchill excoriated their feeble successors who governed Britain in the decades before 1914 and 1939. Their weakness was primarily responsible for the failure to prevent the two world wars which ended a century of general progress towards peace and social improvement, and, by weakening the taboos of civilization, opened the door to the horrors of Communism and Fascism.

IV

People often imagine that diplomacy is a stylized game like chess, arcane yet rational. This is not the case and never was the case. International politics is politics in every sense of the word—a highly emotional process in which dreams, images, and gusts of passion are often more important than the calculus of costs and benefits. An effective foreign policy must take all these motivations for action into account as they affect the making of decisions at different times and in different circumstances.

Diplomacy has many peaceful ways for bringing influence to bear in order to resolve conflicts. Peaceful methods are usually effective unless the conflict has generated or released emotional forces which make it inaccessible to reason. When that happens, armed conflict can only be deterred by the calm and sobering deployment of sufficient force. And sometimes deterrence fails, in which case the nation must be prepared either to prevail or to surrender interests it regards as important, perhaps even vital. In the end, therefore, even the most conciliatory foreign policy will be impotent unless it is backed by credible force. There is no escaping the military dimension of history. Frederick the Great once said that diplomacy without arms is like music without instruments. In the same mood, George Kennan remarked, "You have no idea . . . how much it contributes to the general politeness and pleasantness of diplomacy when you have a little quiet armed force in the background. People who otherwise are very insulting and very violent become just as pleasant:—why, they couldn't be nicer if they belonged to the same golf club and played golf together every Sunday morning."[10]

From on high, it must seem absurd to settle international disputes by armed combat. But it remains the fact that the international state

10. From a 1946 lecture at the National War College, quoted in Barton Gellman, *Contending with Kennan: Toward a Philosophy of American Power* (New York: Praeger, 1984), 126–27.

system functions in the shadow of fear and anger which strain the psychological barriers against violence. In this respect, the international order is not different from that of domestic society. No people, however gentle, civilized, and well disposed, has ever succeeded in living harmoniously together without the help of a police force and ultimately of an army to see to it that the norms of its law are generally fulfilled. In the international community, warfare and the threat of warfare between states is still the decisive factor in international affairs. There is no way to protect the national security of the United States by peaceful means alone. As the Russian proverb has it, "If you act like a sheep, you will soon find a wolf."

The wolf is an appropriate symbol for the ultimate task of governance both in the society of nations and in the domestic society of every state: the achievement of order through the control of the aggressive instinct. Order can be the order of the cemetery, imposed by the iron fist of tyrants, or the tranquil order of civilization, embodied in laws which all help to make, and most people obey. As Freud said, particularly in *Civilization and Its Discontents,* what distinguishes a civilization from other cultures is that a civilized community diverts the aggressive instinct into useful channels within a social structure of ordered peace: into sport and work, art and business competition, public service and the quest for justice, rather than giving a free field to murder, cruelty, massacre, and aggressive war. For the individual, Freud wrote, the discontents of civilization arise from the restraints which even a liberal community must impose on the aggressive instincts of its members in order to survive as a society and become a civilization. The history of mankind is therefore the record, at the psychological level, of an endless struggle between the forces of evil in every human personality and social aggregation (the death wish) and those of love and creativity, man's equally strong impulse to fulfill the vision of goodness which Freud identified with Eros and St. Paul.

Of course all periods of history are not equally unstable, nor does every state live in fear of sudden attack even in eras of turbulence. War has become unthinkable in the relationship of many states—Canada and the United States, for example, or Great Britain and France. Obviously this was not always the case. But it is the case today. The possibility of war does not enter into the diplomatic calculations of such pairs or groups of states, even when their relations are difficult and contentious.

But the occurrence of war or the menace of war in any part of the world puts pressure on the state system as a whole, especially in modern times. The society of nation-states is much smaller than it used to be, more interdependent, more volatile, and more vulnerable. In the nineteenth century the formation of Germany and its development as a vigorous, militaristic, and outward-thrusting empire spread fear among the other powers. This fear in turn led to a reorientation of European alliances and alignments, and finally to a breakdown of the system. The expansion of the Soviet Union since 1945 and its highly militarized, secretive, and deceptive foreign policy have had a comparable effect in our own times.

Immense transformations in the state system have occurred in this century. And new flows of change are remaking world politics. The European empires which drew the globe into a single political, economic, and social system during the eighteenth and nineteenth centuries have all dissolved, save only the Russian, and the Soviet empire is now breaking up in its turn. More than a hundred new states have come into being as a consequence, many weak and ineffective in attempting to master the secrets of modern government. Their weakness is a temptation for predators. Japan and a number of smaller Asian states have become supremely successful participants in the capitalist economy which is the dynamo of modern international economic life. They are active participants as well in the social and political life of the world community. China is emerging as a modern state after more than a century of frustration and stagnation. If successful in that effort, it is bound to become a portentous factor in world affairs. India, a huge country, is rapidly becoming a major industrial power. Within the Islamic world, a revolt against modernity threatens both its potentialities for progress and in many cases the peace itself. Whether the model of modernity, the creed of Sadat and Atatürk, will prevail in Islam over the savage impulses of the Ayatollah Khomeini is one of the most critical issues of the next century. Until 1991, at least, the Soviet Union pursued an even more ambitious program of expansion than Russia under the Czars, and its influence is now felt far beyond the Russian borders of 1914 or the Soviet borders of 1939. The United States is no longer a province of Europe on the periphery of world politics but an indispensable element in the equation of world power. And the entire process of historical change occurs within the inexorable matrix of demographic trends which must in the end dominate events.

Moreover, technological revolutions succeed each other at an accelerating pace, transforming the military and political significance of weapons and of distance—even of the sea itself. A wise French minister of finance once remarked that what the world needed most was a trade union of finance ministers to suppress the scientists. The seismic effect of war anywhere is now felt everywhere, even when war occurs between small Third World states recently liberated from the constraints of the European imperial system.

Nor has there been in modern history a shortage of states governed by leaders in the grip of demonic ambition, like France under Napoleon, Germany and Japan during the first half of the twentieth century, and the Soviet Union in its turn. Such leaders and their ilk in smaller countries dream for a season of grandeur and power, or become the armed prophets of ideas which ignite holy wars for revenge, national glory, or the exaltation of the true faith.

In trying to think about war and peace it is important also to recall—often—that in the literature of history and social science some important causes of change are almost completely ignored: the prevalence of stupidity, folly, and cowardice, for example, and of illness and other commonplace human weaknesses, to say nothing of chance. Governments are rarely staffed only by brilliant, balanced, and decisive leaders at the height of their powers. How much does history owe to the weakness of President Buchanan? The hardening of President Franklin Roosevelt's arteries? President Wilson's stroke? Hitler's insanity? Or the failure of France to find a Clemenceau in 1940?

The pressures of war and the fear of war cause general anxiety throughout the state system, even when governments believe the war of the moment to be safely encapsulated. Wars have a tendency to spread. Since 1914, and at an accelerating rate since the 1960s, war has become an ever more persistent and ominous element in world politics. War is probably a more pervasive factor in social and political life today than at any time since the seventeenth century. That trend shows no sign of abating. Even when individual or collective self-defense is effective, wars challenge the structure of the state system and the patterns of custom which have been evolving for nearly two centuries to govern it.

Inevitably, the growing weight of war in international affairs increases the role of passion, instinct, fear, hatred, and irrationality in world politics. The decision to wage war is always a psycho-social phenomenon beyond the reach of computer printouts and the working papers of accountants. The decision of the United States in 1861 to put down the secession of thirteen southern states remains a psychological mystery. Most people at the time would have accepted the right of the states to secede as constitutionally plausible, despite Chief Justice Marshall's eloquent opinions to the contrary. Respected leaders of Amer-

ican public life, and especially some leading abolitionists, advised the
government "to let the erring sisters go." They regarded the notion
that the United States is an indissoluble union not of states but of people
as metaphysics carried to the point of mysticism.[11] But events after Fort
Sumter, guided by Lincoln's extraordinary intuition and will, were dominated, as Admiral Mahan once wrote, by forces no one knew were
there, the passion for the Union in the North, and in the South by the
strong loyalty to the gospel of States' rights, feelings which had been
"wrought into the very being" of the people, "quietly and unmarked,
like the slow processes of nature."[12] Conditioned reflexes which few
could articulate or explain vindicated the concept of Union as the indispensable basis for the glorious American future in which all believed.

Comparably powerful emotional feelings have been of importance
in the genesis of every war. Thucydides put first among them the
fear of the growing power of a rival—the instinct for self-preservation,
alerted by the fear that unless the state which feels threatened strikes
out immediately, it will lose all control over its destiny. Wars often
begin with a call to honor in the face of what are perceived as
humiliations, like the German attack on "plucky little Belgium" in
1914, a major factor in the British decision to go to war. This attack
violated a treaty to which both Germany and Great Britain were
parties. And it touched an extremely sensitive nerve. Britain had
fought repeatedly over the centuries to prevent a strong power from
controlling the mouth of the Scheldt River, from which Britain could
easily be attacked.

Similarly, the emotional reaction against unrestricted German submarine warfare, in which many civilians were killed, was an important
catalyst of the American decision to enter the First World War in 1917.
And after Pearl Harbor, it never seriously occurred to any American
that there might have been a diplomatic alternative to war. Nearly thirty
years later, at an Oxford seminar in philosophy, an American raised
the question whether it might have been morally preferable, from the
point of view of the greatest good for the greatest number, to negotiate
after Pearl Harbor rather than to fight. There was an ominous growl
from a number of the participants, led by a group of Australians—an

11. See Edmund S. Morgan, *Inventing the People: The Rise of Popular Sovereignty in
England and America* (New York: W. W. Norton, 1988), 263–87.
12. Alfred Thayer Mahan, "The Possibilities of an Anglo-American Reunion" (July
1894), reprinted in Mahan, *The Interest of America in Sea Power, Present and Future* (1897;
reissued Freeport, N.Y.: Books for Libraries Press, 1970) 107, 114–115; and idem, *From Sail
to Steam: Recollections of a Naval Life* (New York: Harper and Brothers, 1907; reprinted;
New York: De Capo Press, 1964), 87.

unprecedented event for an Oxford seminar. The question was not pursued.

Nor should one ignore the power of ancient elements in the creed of all cultures: respect for valor, self-sacrifice, and skill in war, and the appeal of heroism and indeed of combat itself. However strongly individuals may hate to admit it, Horace's verse, "Dulce et decorum est pro patria mori," still stirs the heart.[13] As Holmes once said, a flag is more than a piece of bunting. When Germany went to war in 1914, even so cosmopoliton an artist as Thomas Mann felt inspired by the release of patriotic emotion, and the men marched off to the trenches from all the countries of Europe, the British Dominions, and later from America as well in a mood of elation.

In acknowledging that emotional forces are of great importance in the bringing wars about, I do not mean to suggest that it is always irrational to go to war or that all wars are a tragic mistake, settling nothing. Most systems of morality agree that wars of self-defense are just, and concentrate on developing methods of conciliation that might be used to settle international disputes. The American Civil War settled many things, and settled them for the best. No other procedure could have achieved the same results. The United States remained a unitary state, able to meet the challenge of the twentieth century as a world power, and did not disintegrate into a quarrelsome collection of impotent regional republics. Slavery was abolished then rather than later. And the balance between national and local authority in the American federal system shifted, giving greater influence to the national spirit and to the national ideals which are its source. Wise statesmanship should have prevented both world wars, and surely the cause of civilization would have been better served if those wars had been prevented. Once diplomacy had failed, however, it was preferable that they be fought and won, for all the tragedy and trauma they brought. The Allied victories in both wars prevented Germany from gaining overwhelming power, destroyed Hitler, Mussolini, and Japanese militarism, and hastened the end of European imperialism.

Finally, it is important to recall that the taboo against war in Western culture has become so strong that it can be overcome only by the conviction that there is literally no alternative. Careful and repeated studies indicate that something like a third of the soldiers in British and

13. "Sweet and fitting it is to die for the fatherland."

American armies will not shoot to kill a human being they can see.[14] They join their fellows in the other tasks of war. They march with them and share their sufferings. But they cannot fire at a visible human being. The prevalence and intensity of these convictions constitute a guaranty, so far as the Western nations are concerned, that war will not be undertaken lightly or recklessly.

14. S. L. A. Marshall, *Men against Fire: The Problem of Battle Command in Future War* (New York: William Morrow, 1947), 50–54.

2

The State System: The Balance of Power and the Concept of Peace

As through the long ages of geology, movements of the earth's land masses have wrought compelling changes in the number and configuration of the continents, in their identity, in their climate, and in the creatures living on them, so throughout the history of international relations, changes in the balance of power have affected the configuration, number, identity, and policy of nations and their peoples in the shorter period of human history. Governments have had to adapt themselves to such geopolitical alterations or sink amid the strife of nations—Samuel Flagg Bemis

The idea of the state system is the basic analytical tool used in this book. The modern notions of war and peace and of all the stages of interstate rivalry between these poles are ways of characterizing the hostile behavior of states toward each other within the system in times of general peace. The writers on international law use a variety of words to define and classify actions taken by a state to remedy forceful breaches of international law: limited and partial wars of self-defense, reprisals, retorsions, low-intensity and covert warfare, psychological and economic warfare, and other terms. It is more realistic to view them as forms of forcible self-help along the spectrum between peace and full-scale, general, and notorious war. The rules which are necessary to the cooperation of states within the system regard such self-help as permissible if "reasonable," that is, if there is no peaceful way of resolving the conflict, and if the hostile action is proportional to the offense and not more severe than is necessary to eliminate the offense. The idea of the state system is thus the predicate for our notions of war and peace, and should be examined first.

The epigraph for this chapter is taken from Samuel Flagg Bemis, *American Foreign Policy and the Blessings of Liberty, and Other Essays* (New Haven, Conn.: Yale University Press, 1962), 2–3.

The phrase *state system* denotes the network of customary practice which prescribes how the business of the world community is conducted: how trade, travel, and political life are carried on; how states deal with each other; and how disagreements among states or their citizens are settled—or not settled, as the case may be. One of the most common illusions of ordinary life is that the state system within which we live is a permanent feature of international politics—as permanent as geography or the quest for power. The historical fact is altogether different. While the state system, like other social institutions, has enormous inertia, it is as fragile as a stage set, changing radically from generation to generation in form and sometimes in substance, at least insofar as the balance among its component elements is concerned. Sometimes the international use of force on a large scale is a nearly constant factor in international affairs; during such periods men perceive the external world as a nightmare of brute force, mitigated somewhat by transitory arrangements for cooperation under conditions of anarchy or near-anarchy. In more tranquil times, men dare to contemplate the possibility that man's aggressive instincts can be tamed or at least controlled; that the shifting patterns of cooperation and rivalry characteristic of balance of power regimes can be institutionalized as more stable and predictable programs of concerted policymaking and action among the dominant powers; and that on such a foundation peace may become more than an interval of armistice in the life of the society of nations. For the last two hundred years, at least, diplomatic history has been a counterpoint of these themes.

There has always been tension between the idea of the state as an independent unit of government and the state as a component of a larger grouping—an empire; a federation; a league; a pattern of feudal relations or of relations among ruling families; an alliance; or an embracing commonwealth like Christendom, Catholicism, Islam, Socialism, Capitalism, or Democracy. From the heydays of the Persian, Greek, and Roman empires to modern times, that tension has been palpable. Depending upon the condition of world politics, the model for interstate relations has varied from one of tight central control, at one extreme, to that of nearly complete state autonomy or "sovereignty," at the other. The kingdoms which constituted the Persian Empire of Cyrus and Darius were held together under a loose and enlightened rein. Similarly, Roman proconsuls and satellite monarchs had considerable discretion in governing their provinces, although they could always summon legions from Rome if needed. The empire of Charlemagne was less effectively controlled, and its component parts quarreled and even went to war with each other almost as often as the states which constituted the Communist bloc. A great deal of modern diplomatic and military history concerns the gradual decline of the Turkish, Spanish, Austro-Hungarian, British, French, and Portuguese empires, and the fears and appetites to which these long cycles of disintegration gave rise. The same reactions are evident in contemporary politics, in the Soviet attempts to take control of territories which formerly belonged to the British, French, Dutch, Belgian, or Portuguese empires and of states whose independence was once guaranteed by the European balance of power, and then, as the tide turned, in the diminution or withdrawal of these pressures with the disintegration of the Soviet Union and the end of the Warsaw Pact.

For the past four centuries, the autonomous, or sovereign, state has been in the ascendant, as empires and dynasties became unitary states or weakened and disappeared. On the other hand, shifting patterns of alliance have been familiar, and smaller states continue to gravitate naturally to the protective shadow of larger ones, becoming buffers, neutrals, or allies in collective security arrangements like NATO or the agreements established by the security treaties between the United States and Japan, South Korea, and many other countries. The relationship between the Soviet Union and its satellites and client-states was different of course in quality, but it too is a familiar and recurrent feature of history. While it functioned, the Soviet security system constituted an alternative form of world public order—alternative, that is, to the open, pluralist system contemplated in the United Nations Charter.

II

Throughout history, one of the driving forces determining the shape and quality of the state system has been the set of impulses usually called the balance of power. It is the oldest, most familiar, and most important idea in the theory and practice of international relations. The instinct behind the concept is simplicity itself: never allow a potential adversary to become too strong, if you can possibly help it. The chief corollary of this precept is equally simple: if you can't help it, know your place and behave accordingly. The principle applies as much to the domestic organization of societies and the states which try to govern them as it does to their external affairs. But usage generally confines the term *balance of power* to the international realm. In talking about the internal affairs of states, terms like *pluralism* and *separation of powers* are commonly used to identify aspects of the same idea.

The balance of power is a pejorative phrase in the American language. Like many British, Canadian, Australian, Dutch, and Swedish people—and unlike the French, Germans, Italians, Japanese, and Russians—Americans talk about international affairs in a vocabulary dominated by the rhetoric of liberty and human rights. We are fond of telling each other that our ancestors crossed the stormy seas not only to worship as they pleased, but to escape the wicked wars of princes and their senseless game of power politics.

It is difficult to understand why the phrase *balance of power* has such a bad name in the United States. The American social order and Constitutional system are surely the supreme examples anywhere of the balance of power principle at work. What else does federalism mean; or the relative independence of the executive, legislative, and judicial branches in our national and state governments; or the antitrust laws; or the diversified structure of the American banking system? No people has a deeper and more stubborn distrust of concentrated power in every realm than the American people. And none is more committed to the idea of equal opportunity and the broad diffusion of social power as the key to personal freedom. Indeed, we carry our checks and balances to such a point as sometimes to imperil our capacity to act at all.

Yet from the time of Tom Paine to that of Woodrow Wilson, Franklin D. Roosevelt, and their successors, American writers and politicians have disparaged the notion that the balance of power should be the lodestar of our foreign policy. America, they have said over the years, is something more than just another great power. It should stand for something nobler than naked power in world affairs.

Of course America does stand for something more than naked power in world affairs. The human and political meaning of American history is a vital part of modern civilization. Washington, Jefferson, and Lincoln, are figures in a universal pantheon. But the United States is also a state among states. First as colonies of Britain and then as a nation, the United States has always been an integral part of the balance of power process. When politicians take office in the American government, they behave as practitioners of power politics with conviction and often with skill. For the fact is that however Americans talk about foreign policy, the actual foreign policy of the United States, like that of any other nation, has been a series of conditioned reflexes responding to actual and prospective changes in the world balance of power. Normally, such responses are unexplained, or explained in misleading terms, not because the true reasons for action are being concealed, but because they are self-evident both to actors and to witnesses. Neither group is schooled to think or speak in a mode of analysis appropriate to the implicit reality. Thus, the United States explained that it went to war in 1917 to "protect the freedom of the seas" and "to make the world safe for democracy," not to prevent a German victory over Russia and Western Europe, and thus protect the balance of power on which the independence of the United States depends.

The idea of the balance of power denotes action, not thought primarily, although thought surely helps. The principle expresses itself mainly in dynamic patterns of reaction to danger or opportunity, as danger and opportunity are perceived by statesmen and public opinion alike. The statesmen may be brilliant or stupid, timid or confident in the exercise of responsibility, farsighted or myopic, belligerent or conciliatory, reckless or prudent, wise or foolish. They may be capable of leading and instructing public opinion, or its helpless victims. They may reassure or alarm their own people and their allies and adversaries, spread tranquillity or fear; act with conviction and authority, or, on the contrary, sound an uncertain trumpet.

The diplomacy of the American Revolution was a dazzling example of balance of power policy at its most effective. The revolutionaries took astute advantage of the crises preoccupying the European governments at the time to find support for their cause in France, and in the Netherlands, Spain, and Russia as well. That support was not based on enthusiasm for republicanism or for the precedent of successful revolution against legitimate monarchs, but on the state interests of each country in the brutal, cynical, and cutthroat maelstrom of European politics. Only in Great Britain itself was there important political support for the new American government based on political principle and deep feeling for the rights of "fellow Englishmen." As Samuel Flagg Bemis, the dean of American diplomatic historians, once remarked, during the fifty years of diplomatic turbulence which began with the American Revolution, the "natural statesmen" who led the United States knew how to turn Europe's distress to America's advantage.

The other side of the coin of power politics is equally vivid. Throughout history, the emergence of a strong, belligerent, and ambitious power has stimulated the states which felt threatened by its diplomatic style and the prospect of its expansion to come together in new alliances to curb and if necessary to defeat the aspirant for primacy.

In the magnetic field of world politics, past animosities and even past wars count for little. Britain and France, rivals and enemies for centuries, became allies against Russia in the Crimean War and succeeded in keeping Russia out of the Mediterranean for a hundred years. Later, when Europe faced the German bid for mastery, France and Russia joined forces, and in the end Britain associated itself with their effort— hesitantly and equivocally, and too late to head off the war. With the benefit of hindsight, it is apparent that a policy of supporting France during the Franco-Prussian War of 1871 would have served Britain's interest and the general interest better than the policy of neutrality which Britain in fact pursued.

Similarly, the rise of Germany and the character of German policy toward the end of the nineteenth century led Russia and Great Britain to suspend their rivalry in Asia in order to cooperate against Germany in Europe. Since 1945, Germany and Japan have become allies of the United States and other recent enemies not only because the democratic forces within their cultures have come to dominate their public life, but because they perceive the expansion of the Soviet Union as a mortal threat. And no American of this generation, despite the national predilection for a foreign policy of ideological purity, has had the slightest difficulty in understanding why it was desirable for the United States to ally itself with Stalin in order to defeat Hitler and later to cooperate with Communist China as a counterweight to the outward thrust of Soviet power. Some foreign observers were surprised by the popularity in the United States of President Nixon's response to the Chinese overture for a Sino-American reconciliation in 1972. They thought that only a conservative Republican President could have accepted such a proposal. They were wrong, however. America would have welcomed China's crossing the aisle under any circumstances.

The moves and countermoves which characterize the balance of power process can be stabilizing or destabilizing, depending on the many variable elements of each situation. Forms of cooperation among nations necessarily give some structure to the state system while they last, though their duration is variable. The Portuguese alliance with Great Britain, for example, was signed in 1703 and is still in effect. On the other hand, Stalin's pact with Hitler in 1939 made the Second World War inevitable, and the Soviet Union's association with the United States, Great Britain, France, and the other Western Allies in the Second World War did not even survive until hostilities were brought to an end in 1945.

When the main participants are firmly convinced that their interests will be better served by preserving the balance of power rather than by attempting to escape from its restraints, a balance of power policy can function as a stabilizing factor in the international community, and as a curb on war. Clausewitz identified the balance of power as the force which obliged even excellent generals and kings like Gustavus Adolphus, Charles XII, and Frederick the Great, at the head of armies just as excellent, "to be content to remain at the general level of moderate achievement" rather than pursue the glory of Alexander. The states of Europe were becoming larger and more integrated. The recognition of their shared interests tended to restrain their ambitions. "Political relations, with their affinities and antipathies, had become so sensitive a nexus that no cannon could be fired in Europe without every government feeling its interest affected. Hence a new Alexander needed more than his own sharp sword: he required a ready pen as well. Even so, his conquests rarely amounted to very much."[1]

A stable and successful balance of power system should in time give rise to habits of behavior and expectations which convince each state that its highest national interest is to preserve and strengthen the system. The achievement of such convictions, and of the belief that other states share them, is the necessary condition which would permit a balance of power system to become a system of enduring peace.

III

Peace is a complex idea, involving far more than the absence of hostilities. It can be defined as a condition of society characterized by the expectation of general obedience to law. The concept of peace and the concept of law are inseparable. Arbitrary power may maintain order in society for a time without the regularities of law, but peace is beyond its reach. While the concept of law pervades society too completely to be held for long by a single definition, in its simplest sense law *is* the system of peace—an alternative both to tyranny and to anarchy, a way of resolving social conflicts through procedures all perceive as fair, and in accordance with rules which express the community's sense of justice. Both within societies and among the states which constitute the society of nations, peace under law implies a certain quality of social relationships such that no person within the domestic order, and no state within the international order, need seriously fear violence from his fellows.

1. Carl von Clausewitz, *On War,* ed. and trans. Michael Howard and Peter Paret (Princeton, N.J.: Princeton University Press, 1976), bk. 8, chap. 3, p. 590.

Peace is a matter of degree. We consider a domestic society to be at peace even if it contains a number of practicing burglars or pick-pockets and there are a few brawls on Saturday night, and occasional assaults, or even murders. The most peaceful societies endure periods of social turbulence from time to time—strikes or other demonstrations which become riots, or outbursts of protest which involve disorder. Phenomena of this kind are not necessarily evidence of disintegration in the harmony of custom and values which constitutes the society and is the source of its law. More often they are signals warning authority that the law on the books has fallen behind the pace of change in men's minds and spirit—that its ideas no longer correspond to the prevailing code of social justice, and that change in the formal law is needed to restore a climate of general acceptance of law.

But no statement can be considered a norm of law unless it is effectively enforced—that is, unless the political system responds to a breach of the purported norm by genuinely attempting to enforce it. Thus, in every functioning state the statute against murder is a true norm of law, although murders still occur and not all murderers are captured and punished. A proposition can be considered a legal norm even if it is not universally respected and enforced, but it cannot be considered a norm of law if respect and enforcement are the exceptions rather than the rule.

In the perspective of history, there are two rival models for peace within the state system—the Roman model and that of the world order between 1815 and 1914, the most peaceful period international society has known since the zenith of the Roman Empire. These models have great power over the human mind, although they represent brief interludes in the long chronicle of recorded history.

Pax Romana and the Pax Britannica of the nineteenth century were altogether different kinds of peace. The peace of Rome was achieved by military dominion within the boundaries the empire could bring under its control. It was embodied in a highly developed system of law which respected the customs of the peoples of the empire and which imperial authority normally enforced through the institutions of vassal states. The system of order achieved for a century by the Concert of Europe, on the other hand, was a system of genuinely independent states drawn into a pattern of relative harmony based on a balance of power and managed by the leading states of the time in accordance with precepts of prudence and restraint they all accepted. Great Britain was the ultimate arbiter of the balance of power for that system. The international law of the time, generally respected, was enforced by the courts and governments of individual states rather than by international bodies, although special international tribunals were established to resolve particular controversies. But aggressive war had not yet been condemned by international law, and controversies raising serious risks of war were dealt with by diplomacy dominated by the influence of the leading powers, or a decisive number of them—diplomatic influence, be it said, backed by a willingness to use force.

Will the state system of the future be a Pax Sovietica or a Pax Russica based on Soviet or Russian dominion? After the startling events of 1989, 1990, and 1991, not very likely, even when Russia and Ukraine have modernized their economies. A Pax Americana modeled on the nineteenth-century system as it has developed since 1914, with the United States fulfilling Britain's nineteenth-century role? Will new combinations, now only dimly perceived as possibilities—an alliance of China and Japan, for example, or one between Russia and the European Community, or between Russia and Germany alone—become dominant factors in the working of the state system? Or will it resemble no earlier model but continue as a muddle of turbulence somewhat limited by the menace of nuclear weapons and other weapons of mass destructions? After all, mankind has managed to survive under conditions of mild or extreme anarchy for most of its time on earth.

IV

As a question of political theory, how should one characterize the international order of modern states—the international order we perceive and experience every day? Is it a system in any recognizable sense of the word—a civil society as Hume and Locke conceived civil society— or simply a congeries of nations living in a Hobbesian state of nature where clubs are trumps, and each citizen goes to bed at night wondering whether there will be a nuclear Pearl Harbor before morning?

There are two common answers to the question. Writers in the tradition of Hobbes, like the pioneering American scholar Nicholas J. Spykman, who wrote and taught during the thirties and forties, take the view that

> nations which renounce the power struggle and deliberately choose impotence will cease to influence international relations either for evil or for good and risk eventual absorption by more powerful neighbors. . . . The international community is a world in which war is an instrument of national policy and the national domain is the

military base from which the state fights and prepares for war during the temporary armistice called peace. In terms of that location, it must conduct its military strategy in war time, and in terms of that location, it should conduct its political strategy in peace time.[2]

Much as I admire Hobbes and Spykman, whose pathbreaking book is a modern classic, they deal with only half the story. They assume that the pattern of history can never change and that the lust for power is its only driving force. And they dismiss as illusory the well-meaning efforts of writers and statesmen to enforce peace in international affairs. It is not difficult to understand their outlook against the background of the prolonged wars which convulsed and devastated their times. And in many instances they are fully justified in dismissing preachments of peace as hypocrisy or self-deception. But I prefer the broader and more dynamic view of history expounded by Montesquieu, who emphasized the central role of law in society both as governor and as aspiration.

In this context, the word *law* means nothing more complex than the pattern of behavior and of social relationships which a society seeks to protect, and to restore when it is disturbed, and the pattern of behavior and of social relationships it hopes to achieve in the future— a prediction, to borrow Holmes' famous phrase, of what its judges and other lawmakers will in fact do. For the purposes of this essay, in dealing with international affairs the word *law* denotes the pattern of behavior and of relationships among the states, peoples, and other institutions of international society which that society deems right and tries to achieve and sustain.

The laws of society, Montesquieu saw, are determined, like the laws of the physical universe, by the nature of things, and not by the command of a sovereign. And those laws change over time, in response to experience refracted through the spirit of the society's law, which also evolves as the moral code of the society evolves. Historical change is the principal subject of Montesquieu's masterpiece, *De l'esprit des lois*. For Montesquieu, the course of history and the growth of the law are shaped more by ideals than by any other causal factors. The spirit of a society's law, in his view, is its moral essence, what Cicero called the "concordia" of a society, the small body of shared values which determine its character and the direction of its development. In the vocabulary of contemporary culture, Montesquieu's "spirit of the laws" could be called the superego of a society, or its conscience. There is

2. Nicholas J. Spykman, *American's Strategy in World Politics: The United States and the Balance of Power* (1942; reprint ed., Garden City, N.Y.: Doubleday, 1970), 446–47.

always tension between the aspirations of society and its customs. But in Montesquieu's view of the social process, unlike Hobbes', it is not a priori impossible for aspirations to prevail over custom, that is, for men to achieve improvement in the substance of law.

The international law governing finance and commerce; the recognition of citizenship, marriage, and divorce; navigation; piracy; the status of travelers and diplomats; and comparable problems has long been enforced quite uniformly as part of the domestic law of each state. It is "law" in every sense of the word, comparable in its substance, predictability, and mode of growth to the law applicable within a state. More recently, international procedures for enforcement have been established by agreement among states—procedures of arbitration and of international adjudication. There has been an explosion of international law in response to the exponential growth of international trade, travel, and finance. The growth of these branches of law has affected both the international law governing private transactions and that regulating the policies of governments in the fields of economics, telecommunications, transportation, environmental protection, fisheries, forestry, and many other realms where international cooperation has been found to be necessary or desirable. There is a network of international agreements, regular conferences, and international agencies governing or at least harmonizing many aspects of policy in these areas on a reasonably consistent basis. Thus the indispensable signs directing motor traffic on the roads of nearly all countries are identical, and almost independent of language, pursuant to international agreement.

Is there, can there also be, a generally accepted and effectively enforced body of public international law dealing with the legitimacy and conduct of warfare, the status of neutral states, the treatment of prisoners and civilians in time of war, and cognate issues?

3

The Quest for Peace, from the Congress of Vienna to the United Nations Charter

A Europe in which the rights of everyone resulted from duties for all was something so strange to the statesmen of the old regime that the Revolutionary and the Napoleonic Wars, lasting a quarter of a century and the most formidable yet seen, were required to impose the idea upon them and demonstrate its necessity. The attempt to give Europe an elementary organization at the Congress of Vienna and in the Congresses which followed was a step forward, not a return to the past. In the eighteenth century such progress was only one of the beautiful theories of philosophers. As the year 1789 approached, it began to insinuate itself into the minds of various political leaders, particularly in France, but they were considered dreamers. The great majority of the rulers of Europe, confounding this design with the chimera of perpetual peace, continued to consider it as the ultimate in paradoxes.—Albert Sorel

Starting with the Treaty of Westphalia, which brought the Thirty Years' War to an end in 1648, more and more men began to believe, as philosophers, theologians, and idealists had long urged, that international law could embrace the phenomenon of war and indeed that it was already beginning to do so. They wrote of the international community as a society of nations which were independent but bound together. What made the nations a society was not the command of an imperial ruler but a web of custom and shared aspiration and of law based on those shared customs and shared aspirations. The European nations and their colonies were united by another and supremely important influence, that of the Christian religion. Until recently, the word *Christendom* was often used to identify the European nations and their progeny around the world as a special community.

Writers of this persuasion considered the normal condition of in-

The epigraph for this chapter is taken from Albert Sorel, *Europe under the Old Regime*, trans. Francis H. Herrick (1885; reprint ed., Harper Torchbooks, 1964), 3–4.

ternational society to be one of peace. Peace, they thought, was or should be a system, a legal system based on a balance of power and governed by the norms necessary to the coexistence and cooperation of the states within it. In such a society, states would be "sovereign"— that is, independent, and free to govern themselves as they wish; aggressive warfare could be effectively forbidden; and hostilities would be confined to what the Catholic Church had long called "just war," limited and proportional military actions of self-defense in times of general peace.

The treatises on international law written by the great scholars of the seventeenth and eighteenth centuries—Grotius, Vattel, Vitoria, and the others—distinguished two conditions of international society, the state of war and the state of peace. This classification remains fundamental to international law and international politics.

The state of war was to be formally initiated by a public declaration of "full, general, and notorious" war. Originally, such declarations were made by heralds. Under international law, the state of war contemplates the unlimited use of force by the belligerents, tempered only by humanitarian traditions and conventions, such as they were at the time. The enemy states were not obliged to confine hostilities to the area where a violent action precipitated the war—if there was such an episode—but could bring force to bear wherever they thought it might be effective, and in whatever measure they deemed essential or simply desirable to that end.

Moving the state system from a condition of peace to one of war was considered to be an historic prerogative of sovereignty. The notion that it might be "illegal" for a state to initiate a state of war had not yet emerged. The commencement of full-scale war has many legal consequences. Diplomatic relations are broken and diplomats withdrawn. The belligerents and their citizens become "enemies" of one another, subject to severe restrictions, including internment or expulsion. Enemy property could be sequestered or even condemned, and trading with the enemy or communicating with its citizens forbidden. States which do not wish to participate in the war as belligerents may declare their neutrality and assume the rights and duties prescribed by the laws and customs of neutrality—in itself always a contentious matter.

Customary international law recognized the propriety of limited uses of force internationally in peacetime if they involved self-defense against breaches of international law of a forceful character. The classic writers on international law accepted that practice as inevitable, and were agreed that such episodes did not require declarations of war nor did they bring about a state of war. Both the customary international law and the law of the United Nations Charter in contemporary times acknowledge the legality of the use of force not only in self-defense but also in collective self-defense, that is, the case in which a second state comes to the aid of a state being attacked from abroad, or of one engaged in suppressing an internal rebellion or in restoring order after a riot or a natural disaster. This latter category includes the protection of citizens exposed to illegal acts of force or unusual dangers while abroad.

The books of Grotius, Vattel, and Vitoria did not of themselves produce a radical change in the behavior of nations. It took another terrible and prolonged period of general war, that of the French Revolution and the First French Empire, to transform the conception of peace from a philosopher's dream into a working rule of thumb for statesmen, perhaps for a time even a norm of international law.

The idea that peace is a condition to be achieved by the deliberate efforts of diplomacy is one of the major achievements of modern civilization. In earlier centuries, at least since the fall of Rome, peace had been viewed as a rare blessing, brought about for brief periods by the lucky conjuncture of wise princes and a balance of power. But the men who dominated the Congress of Vienna in 1815—Castlereagh, Czar Alexander, Talleyrand, and Metternich—took a giant step. They did not restore the ancien régime. It was gone. They created a new system of international order, a mutation of the old one, deeply influenced by the experience of war and, as well by the changes which had transformed the moral and intellectual climate of Western civilization. They realized that the state system was not and could never be a self-regulating mechanism like the solar system. The magnetic attraction and repulsion of states and the ambitions of their rulers could not always be relied upon to maintain a balance of power and to resolve embittered and highly emotional disputes. The system of world public order could preserve or restore the peace only if the leading powers, or a decisive number of them, cooperated actively with each other to that overriding end. Thus in the sixth article of the Treaty of Vienna the leading powers of the time declared:

> To facilitate and to secure the execution of the present treaty, and to consolidate the connections which at the present moment so closely unite the four Sovereigns for the happiness of the world, the High Contracting Parties have agreed to renew their meetings at fixed periods, either under the immediate auspices of the Sov-

ereigns themselves or by their respective Ministers, for the purpose of consulting upon their common interests, and for the consideration of the measures which at each of these periods shall be considered the most salutary for the repose and prosperity of nations and for the maintenance of the peace of Europe.[1]

The statesmen of Vienna, dancing to the tunes of Kant, Gibbon, and Grotius without realizing it, set in motion the development of a new code of values about the use of force in international relations— one occasionally stated but even more influential when unstated—and a new pattern of diplomatic practice. As a result of their work and that of their most important successors during the nineteenth century, those values became admonitions and precepts, then habits, then mores, and then rules of law in the most practical sense, governing the minds and therefore the behavior of men. Despite the setbacks of the period since 1914, the principles of the Concert of Europe remain the essence of the policies which the nations profess to accept today.

During the nineteenth century, treaties and changes in customary practice began to bring many aspects of the use of force by one nation against another into the realm of international law: the treatment of prisoners of war, for example; the use of certain weapons deemed particularly repulsive; the law of military occupation; and the protection of civilians in time of war. Peace itself—that is, the prohibition of the international use of force except in cases of self-defense—remained beyond the perimeters of the possible, but nonetheless progress in the direction of such a rule was made. Military actions not justifiable as self-defense came to be scrutinized in the perspective of law; complaints about such actions were lodged in the course of diplomacy, in arbitrations, and even in courts. In a number of striking instances a state was held liable for an illegal use of force by its own military or by armed bands operating from its territory, or even for negligence in failing to prevent its territory from being used for actions which harmed other states: assassinations, for example.

Between 1815 and 1914, the nations of Europe accepted the principle of collective responsibility for the effective functioning of the state system and its relatively peaceful adaptation to great tides of change— the rise of nationalism; the formation of the modern states of Germany and Italy; the revolution in technology; and the absorption of Asia, Africa, and the Middle East into a Eurocentered world order. As a

---

1. Quoted in Carsten Holbraad, *The Concert of Europe: A Study in German and British International Theory, 1815–1914* (London: Longman, 1970), 1.

society, the European state system fell far short of modern Western ideals of justice, although it did take the lead in the abolition of slavery. But it assured the world a reasonably peaceful order—one far more peaceful, at any rate, than the order the world has known since the lights went out in August 1914. Furthermore, that period of peace proved to be an environment congenial to social progress in every realm and to a flowering of learning and the arts.

The leading states consulted each other about threats to the peace, often through their ambassadors, occasionally at the level of heads of government or foreign ministers meeting at congresses. Both large and small powers recognized a responsibility to limit their ambitions and concert their influence in the interest of sustaining the system of peace. So far as war itself was concerned, the goal of policy was not to abolish war but to confine it. It was taken for granted that political compromises should be found for disputes, and that force should be used only as a last resort. When wars came, their goals were limited; they did not involve the destruction of states or of societies. In the end, wars were smothered in diplomacy. As two British historians conclude: "For the most part the great powers respected each other's status: they were accustomed to a great-power system, and strove to maintain it. There was a constant and conscious fear that its demise would bring untold disasters to them all. This was perhaps the most permanent consequence of Napoleon's bid for the mastery of Europe."[2]

The great Talleyrand, to whom so many witty remarks were attributed, is supposed to have made the point more acidly. After the Napoleonic war, he said, "the statesmen of Europe were intelligent enough not to go to war with each other, but too stupid to agree."

The nineteenth-century diplomatic apparatus of Europe was the model for the ideas and institutions of the League of Nations and the United Nations. Of course the Concert of Europe functioned imperfectly, and of course in retrospect one can note episodes which weakened the confidence of each member state in the effectiveness and unity of the group: the Crimean and Franco-Prussian wars, particularly. Despite nearly a century of relative success, no head of government could be certain that a new regime of peace had completely replaced the old environment of unlimited national rivalries. The French Revolution and its appalling aftermath reminded every statesman that the dream of universal empire after the style of Alexander and Caesar could still

2. F. R. Bridge and Roger Bullen, *The Great Powers and the European State System, 1815–1914* (New York: Longman, 1980), 2.

menace the life of all states and all people. Therefore no country dared to dispense with the armaments and alliances with which it hoped to deter wars, or at least win them if diplomacy failed.

After Sarajevo, the British foreign minister, Sir Edward Grey, invoked the machinery of conciliation which had defused so many crises during the preceding century. This time the diplomacy of concert was swept aside. The consensus for peace broke down under the pressure of Germany's ambition. And after the First World War the attempt to restore and improve the European Concert on a world scale under the League of Nations was stillborn. The United States was paralyzed by its interpretation of Washington's counsel of neutrality and the memory of a century of prosperity as a neutral behind the wall of the British fleet. In the grip of its isolationist fantasies, it refused to join the League of Nations and to participate in world politics. The Soviet position was equivocal and isolated. Great Britain and France—particularly Great Britain—were uncertain about their ability to head off Hitler's bid for dominion in Europe and the broader ambitions of the Axis powers. Stopping Germany and Japan at the same time was beyond the capacity of Britain and France. Britain, France, and the United States alike could not bring themselves to believe that quarrels and aggressions in what is now called the Third World really mattered. As a consequence, they made the same mistake they had made before 1914: they allowed the momentum for war to build up in Asia and Africa and then to overwhelm the European state system, which collapsed once more under the strain.

II

It has been characteristic of the modern state system since the late eighteenth century that every major breakdown of international peace has been followed almost instinctively by an international effort to restore the system and improve it. Sir F. H. Hinsley, the most perceptive student of the subject, considers this to be one of the most important features of contemporary world politics, marking it off from its predecessors: "After every war since the end of the eighteenth century—1815; after the wars of 1854 and 1871; in 1918; and again in 1945—the states have made a conscious and concerted effort, each one more radical than the one they had made before, to reform the international system in ways that were calculated to enable them to avoid another conflict."[3]

3. F. H. Hinsley, "The Modern Pattern of Peace and War" (Lecture 1 in the lecture

The Charter of the United Nations was adopted in 1945, as the hostilities of the Second World War sputtered out and those of the Cold War ominously intensified. Soviet diplomats said later that if the San Francisco Conference had been delayed even a year, the Charter would never have been signed. But on the surface, at least, the Charter conforms to the pattern Professor Hinsley describes. Driven once more by revulsion against war, the nations moved radically to re-establish the state system. The United States and its West European allies were the leaders in the movement, but political opinion throughout the world favored a return to a stronger and more determined League of Nations. The United States was convinced that Wilson had been right in 1919 in urging the United States to join the League, and it sought to make amends to his ghost.

Both the ends and the means to be pursued under the Charter differed somewhat from those of the League Covenant and the Vienna system. They were modified, naturally enough, in the light of the failures and shortcomings of the League as they were perceived at the time. International cooperation in managing the state system was to be continuous, not a matter of occasional conferences and congresses. The Security Council was entrusted with primary responsibility for keeping the peace and endowed with extraordinary powers for carrying out that mission. The special obligation of the great powers for assuring peace was recognized in their Security Council veto. The General Assembly was established as a diplomatic meeting place and center for debate. It has no substantive legislative power, but its recommendatory resolutions have influence—sometimes a good deal of influence. The International Court of Justice took over the work of the Permanent Court of International Justice, a League institution, under a revised statute. A vast family of United Nations specialized agencies began to proliferate all over the world in almost every field of governmental endeavor—health, finance, trade, environmental protection, international law, atomic energy, cultural development, agriculture, and many others. The list is astonishing, and there is no sign that the growth of the United Nations bureaucracy has come to an end. And the League experiment of attempting to create an independent international civil service under a Secretary General of high prestige was continued.

As Clive Parry comments,

> The institutionalization of the pattern of international order in, first, the League, and more latterly the United Nations and the

---

series "The Decline and Fall of the Modern International System," 1980), 6. See also idem, *Power and the Pursuit of Peace* (Cambridge: Cambridge University Press, 1963).

many lesser international agencies so-called, has made men aware that the system of States has a constitution of a sort and that its operation has a legal character giving expression to its phenomena in shapes and concepts long familiar within the State—in such shapes as contract or treaty, wrong or delict, and such concepts as obligation, illegality, and even criminality. This awareness, however, is of very recent growth.[4]

Parry remarks that even so enlightened a statesman as Sir Edward Grey lived in "almost total ignorance of the legal character of the international order—or to put it bluntly, the plain fact that nations no less than men are ruled by law and are so ruled at all times."[5]

Parry's insight is entirely justified. Nations generally conform to patterns of behavior which constitute the living law of international society—the law as it exists at the moment—whether their leaders are conscious of the fact or not. The minds of Sir Edward Grey and his contemporaries were programmed to function in the style of Pitt and Castlereagh, as that style had evolved under the influence of Canning, Palmerston, Disraeli, and Salisbury. They recognized aggression as a threat to the security and well-being of all nations, and did their best to contain and deter it, in accordance with what they often called "the public law and system of Europe." But in their intellectual universe, aggression was still a legal prerogative of sovereignty. They had a different understanding, in Parry's words,

towards the relation of law and policy from that now apparently— it is perhaps necessary to emphasize the word apparently—prevailing, because there then obtained a different legal notion of the central problem of policy, namely war. . . .

. . . the international law of the time condoned, even enhanced, war. This being the case, its elaborate rules on other topics, including the precise manner of carrying out war, were inevitably prejudiced and to a degree necessarily trivial and illogical.[6]

The most radical innovation of the United Nations Charter is its flat prohibition of war, except for purposes of individual or collective self-defense and the implementation of Security Council "decisions"— that is, its rare resolutions given a binding legal character under Article

4. Clive Parry, "Foreign Policy and International Law," in *British Foreign Policy under Sir Edward Grey,* ed. F. H. Hinsley (Cambridge: Cambridge University Press, 1977), 90.
5. Ibid.
6. Ibid., 91.

25 of the Charter. The movement to outlaw war had been gaining ground in the moral universe of the West for a long time. The League Covenant approached the problem but did not grapple with it. The short "cooling-off" period prescribed by the Covenant is not, after all, the same as a prohibition. The Kellogg-Briand Pact of 1928, signed by almost all states, seemed to be an empty rhetorical gesture. It declared that war was not a permissible instrument of national policy, but did not distinguish between aggression and self-defense, and provided no machinery for making its ambiguous writ effective. In 1945, the Charter formally proclaimed that a new legal rule against aggressive war had been born and created the Security Council primarily to enforce it.

Whether the provisions of the United Nations Charter that attempt to make international aggression illegal are in fact norms of the living law of the international community, or accepted aspirations for its future development, or on the other hand, no more than idle fancies and deceptive rhetoric, is the overarching political question confronting every nation today.

Article 1 of the Charter sets out the four "purposes" which constitute the goals of the institution: (1) to maintain peace and security; (2) to develop friendly relations among nations based on the principle of the equal rights of states and the self-determination of peoples; (3) to achieve international cooperation in solving international problems of an economic, social, cultural, or humanitarian character; and (4) to be a center for harmonizing the actions of nations in attaining these common ends.

Article 2, specifying the "principles" in accordance with which the organization and its members should act in pursuing these purposes, provides in subparagraph 3 that all members shall settle their disputes by peaceful means and in subparagraph 4 that all members "shall refrain in their international relations from the threat and use of force against the territorial integrity or political independence of any state, or in any other manner inconsistent with the Purposes of the United Nations."

Article 51, the mirror image of Article 2(4), states that "nothing in the present Charter shall impair the inherent right of individual or collective self-defense if an armed attack occurs against a Member of the United Nations, until the Security Council has taken measures necessary to maintain international peace and security." Under Article 24, the member states agree that in carrying out its primary responsibility for maintaining international peace and security the Security Council acts on their behalf: that is, the states delegate to the Security Council an important aspect of their sovereignty. And in Article 25 the members agree to accept and carry out the "decisions" of the Security Council made in order to achieve this end. The term *decisions* is contrasted throughout the Charter with the word *recommendations,* which refers to pronouncements not binding on states. Thus the Security Council usually "calls upon" states to do or refrain from doing something. It is rare for it to "decide." In the realm of policy, the General Assembly cannot make binding decisions, but only recommendations.

Taken together, these articles constitute the fundamental architectural structure of the state system posited by the Charter—the obligation to settle disputes by peaceful means and the prohibition of aggression, qualified by the caveat that nothing in the Charter impairs the historic sovereign rights of a state to defend itself or get help in its defense from other states unless and until the Security Council acts effectively to restore and maintain the peace. Nominally, these articles transfer extraordinary peacekeeping powers to the Security Council, and at the same time reaffirm the inherent right of states to defend themselves and help other states to do so.

The juxtaposition of these propositions brings out the essential dilemma of the Charter system. The United Nations is an association of states deemed to be sovereign for purposes of voluntary peaceful cooperation in seeking to fulfill principles of justice they all say they accept. At the same time, it is an organization founded to keep the peace, and confers on the Security Council and especially on its permanent members powers which if used would reduce the historic sovereignty of all states except the permanent members themselves. Since that derogation of sovereignty concerns the most important power of a state—its inherent right of self-defense—it is of capital importance and severity. As an exception to the general rule of state sovereignty, lawyers would say that it should be narrowly and strictly construed. The more so, given that the preferential treatment of the permanent members of the Security Council may not be quite what it appears to be: as France and Great Britain discovered during the Suez Crisis of 1956, some permanent members are more equal than others.

If the world delineated by the Charter were the real world, the law governing the international use of force would not be difficult to summarize. But the Charter is a legislative act superimposed on the real world—an attempt through positive law to change custom and state practice with regard to the international use of force. The customary law, which regarded the power to make war as a sovereign prerogative of states, has the momentum of immemorial usage behind it; the tension between the Charter and the older habits of warmaking at will is what would be expected in any serious attempt to change an important part of customary law—the bold experiment of the Fourteenth Amendment to the Constitution of the United States, for example, adopted in 1868 and not fully effective even yet.

PART II

America's Diplomatic Apprenticeship, 1776–1941

Introduction

The revulsion of American opinion against our entry into the First World War did serious damage to the American view of the external world. Through a series of political decisions greatly influenced by Wilson's arteriosclerosis, the President's proposal that the United States make a security treaty with France and Great Britain disappeared without a trace, and the Senate failed to accept his recommendation that the United States join the League of Nations. Isolationist Republican presidents were elected in 1920, 1924, and 1928. The nation was perceived as having embraced the idea of returning to what it supposed was "normalcy" in foreign policy, after the aberration of a "foreign" war. To the American mind during the period between the two world wars, and to many American minds since that tragic interlude, the normal posture of the United States in world politics—and the only policy a virtuous and patriotic citizen can support—is one of nearly hermetic isolation from the political life of the world community. People of this persuasion did not quite recommend that the United States follow the classic examples of isolationist Japan, Tibet, and Yemen. But they urged that our role in world affairs be confined to commerce, which they thought made for peace; to preaching the universal recognition of human liberty; and to setting a good example for less noble people and states.

In order to justify this modern heresy, the advocates of American isolationism had to reinterpret American diplomatic history, and transform Washington's Farewell Address into a pernicious myth. Washington's famous message outlined an intelligent national strategy of aloofness and neutrality for the future he could foresee, and carefully excepted the course America might need to follow in the event of great convulsions of the state system or a fundamental change in its structure. Washington never intended his warning against "entangling alliances" (apart from the treaty with France, which was then still in effect) to become a Mosaic commandment, designed to endure unchanged forever.

Neither President Washington nor his successors before Harding were isolationists in any conceivable modern sense of the word. On the contrary, they took for granted the necessity of swimming in the sea as it was. The Americans had succeeded in the Revolutionary War not only through their grit, endurance, and military skill, but through alliances with France, Spain, and the Netherlands, and a diplomacy of playing the game of power politics with insight and energy. Between 1783 and 1830, the United States took full advantage of Europe's troubles to enlarge and consolidate the nation, and develop the institutions of its unity. For the rest of the century the United States participated actively in world politics as a neutral, judiciously shifting its support from one great power to another, closer at most times to Great Britain than to any of its rivals, but independent nonetheless, and unceasingly busy in Europe, the Mediterranean, the Far East, and Latin America. In the early years, when the United States was a tiny, weak country on the margin of world politics, there was no alternative to the policy of neutrality; any other course would have been suicidal. Later, during the nineteenth century, neutrality proved to be a wise and useful posture which gave America elbow room in fulfilling its Manifest Destiny. Through a series of well-conceived treaties, a restrained and determined diplomacy backed by force, and the Mexican and Spanish-American wars, the United States became a great nation, spanning the continent and controlling the naval approaches to its territory both in the Atlantic and the Pacific. The process of American continental expansion was made possible by the fact that the great powers of Europe kept the larger political environment reasonably stable and were deterred by the Anglo-American Monroe Doctrine from attempting to gain new colonies or spheres of influence in the Western Hemisphere.

Gradually Europe as a polity lost both the capacity and the will to preserve the worldwide political equilibrium. It could have retained its leadership for some time if it had mustered up the insight and wisdom to rise above the passions which exploded into the tragedy of the First World War. But in key governments, above all in Germany, statesmen of vision were lacking, and catastrophe came. Kipling sensed the approaching change in his *Recessional,* written in 1897, when on the surface the old order had never seemed so glorious and all-powerful:

> Far-call'd our navies melt away—
>   On dune and headland sinks the fire—
> Lo, all our pomp of yesterday
>   Is one with Nineveh and Tyre!

When the Concert of Europe broke down in 1914, and finally collapsed in 1939, the United States intervened almost by conditioned reflex to help restore the balance of power. It has taken longer, however, for the United States to accept the implications of these events. After Germany and its allies were defeated in 1918, it required more than twenty years of debate and another world war to convince America that Wilson had been right after all—that a prudent concern for the national security compelled it to participate in rebuilding a worldwide state system on the foundation of a balance of power, and in managing that system in accordance with the rules of state practice necessary to its peaceful functioning.

That conviction acquired institutional shape and momentum during the administration of President Truman, which outlined and began to develop the foreign policy the nation has pursued ever since, sometimes well and sometimes badly, but always adequately.

The purpose of Part II is to review certain key aspects of American diplomatic experience before 1941 in order to identify the forces and ideas which dominated its development, and thus set the stage for Part III, dealing with the period since the Second World War and with the future.

4

From Sea to Shining Sea:
America's Conception of Its Foreign Policy

Does not the United States of America occupy such position towards the great colonial nations of Europe, England, France, Russia, and Spain, that not only their colonial relations, but their European relation to each other, have become to us, matter of prime importance, and if so what are the principles, which should guide the foreign policy of the government in its present or future connection with these great empires? What is to be the practical interpretation of that declaration of Canning, more significant in its meaning than even he comprehended: "That he had called the new world into existence, to redress the balance of the old."

If, then, the government of the United States, stands in such intimate relation to the colonial empires of the world, has it not a direct interest in their relation to each other; has it not a right to be heard in all matters touching their mutual power? Is it not time, that by some distinct and unequivocal manifestation, it should declare its intention to participate in the counsels of the world? There is but one principle upon which American intervention in the international relations of Europe can be justified, but that so wide as to cover almost any interference: and it is this, that wherever the changes among European powers are such as to modify the respective weight of its colonial empires, we are directly interested in the resulting balance of power.—William Henry Trescot

The notion that Americans were a new breed, and that America was something more than a group of British colonies, emerged early in the colonial period. It was noted by travelers and writers even in the seventeenth century, and is a frequent theme in the books, pamphlets, letters, diaries, and speeches of the eighteenth century both in America and in Europe.

Throughout the colonial age in America, communication between

The epigraph for this chapter is taken from William Henry Trescot, *A Few Thoughts on the Foreign Policy of the United States* (Charleston, S. C.: John Russell, 1849), 8–9, 14.

the colonies and Great Britain was easier and more active than communication among most of the colonies themselves. There was an important international trade both in raw materials and in manufactured goods. Americans went abroad to study, to travel, and to do business. And immigrants poured into the colonies on an astonishing scale as part of the vast and restless migration of peoples—and armies—which marked the transformation of Europe from a regional polity, focused on the Mediterranean, into a worldwide political system embracing first the Atlantic basin and then the basins of the Pacific and the Indian oceans as well. The trickle of migration which began with the heroic voyages of exploration of the fifteenth and sixteenth centuries became a flood which still continues—the greatest and most sustained movement of peoples known to history. The immigration to America is a notable and important part of that extraordinary process.

Despite the difficulties of seventeenth-and eighteenth-century communication among the British colonies on the Atlantic coast of North America and their strongly developed direct ties to England, a sense of American nationality was being forged. For this purpose, *America* and *Americans*—sometimes they were called *Anglo-Americans*—referred to the British colonies along the coast from Georgia to Massachusetts, which then included Maine, and the vast wilderness to the west. After it was founded in 1749, Nova Scotia was generally counted in this conception of America, and there was an active relation between Nova Scotia and New England, but there was a certain distance as well. Nova Scotia did not join the Revolution in 1775–76, and many American Tories migrated there after 1776. Most of Canada was French until 1763, when French Canada became British under the Treaty of Paris, which ended the Seven Years' War. Florida belonged successively to Great Britain and to Spain until 1819, when the United States acquired it from Spain as part of the general settlement known as the Transcontinental Treaty. Before that time, the border between Florida and the British colonies and then the United States was unsettled and turbulent, and there was a consciousness of threat from that quarter as there was from French Canada.

The northern and southern boundaries of America as a geographic notion were thus blurred. Certainly Canada, Florida, and the French and Spanish territories beyond the Mississippi were a preoccupation, but the thrust of American settlement was largely directed westward until much later: first beyond the Alleghenies, then to the Mississippi, and later to the El Dorado of the Far West.

After the restoration of the Stuarts in Britain in 1660, and throughout the eighteenth century, British policy was a significant catalyst in overcoming the separateness of the colonies and developing the notion of America as a political entity, or at least a nascent political entity. The officials who had to finance the military and administrative costs of empire naturally tried to get as much help as they could from the colonies. The regulation of colonial trade and navigation was one of their favorite methods for accomplishing this goal, and it was applied to the American colonies as a group. In accordance with the principles of mercantilism, Britain confined a considerable part of American navigation and trade to British citizens, and imposed a series of taxes on imports and exports to supplement its direct regulation. The heavy financial burden of the Seven Years' War increased the pressures of taxation in America. It was the general conviction in the eighteenth century, even among economists, that the near-monopoly of trade with its American and West Indian colonies was an important source of British prosperity and naval power.

Britain's American colonies were also pawns in the wars and other conflicts of European politics during the late seventeenth and eighteenth centuries, and were involved in a series of wars between Great Britain and the Netherlands, France, and Spain. Bounded by France on the north and in the west, and by Spain in the south, the colonies were vulnerable both to attack by armies and to raids by Indian tribes armed and incited by the French or the Spanish. Of these contests, the prolonged effort of Great Britain and its allies to contain and defeat France's attempt to achieve dominion in Europe was by far the most important. It involved four wars—the War of the League of Augsburg, which we call King William's War (1689–1697); the War of the Spanish Succession, or Queen Anne's War (1702–13); the War of the Austrian Succession, or King George's War (1745–48); and the Seven Years' War, known in American history as the French and Indian War (1756–63). For all these wars, as well as many Indian wars throughout the colonies, the royal governors and the colonial legislatures had to raise money, troops, and supplies to supplement the activities of the British forces. The colonists were directly interested in the wars. Their lives and fortunes were at stake. Furthermore, they were always skeptical, and often acutely dubious, about the efficacy of the British military. So the formation of colonial militias and regiments began early. And in the larger campaigns some formations—the Royal Americans, for example—included citizens from several colonies. Such campaigns required cooperation among the colonies and the movement of militias far beyond the boundaries of their home colonies.

By the time of the Seven Years' War, the colonies had grown in population and in political and economic strength, and the British government pursued an ambitious policy of involving them in the prosecution of the war, which culminated in the defeat of Montcalm by Wolfe and the conquest of French Canada by Great Britain. To this end, the British government actively encouraged closer ties among the colonies. The cooperation among colonial political leaders in this period led directly to the Committee on Correspondence and other organizations which became the political sinews of the Revolution. The Albany Congress of 1754, called by the British Board of Trade, came up with a plan for colonial union into a single governmental unit within the British Empire—a federation of the colonies with its own president and council, which would have some taxing power, and powers over defense and negotiation with the Indians. The colonies rejected the plan, but it helped prepare the way for the future.

On the military side, Washington and many other American soldiers in the Revolutionary War received their first military training in the campaigns of the French and Indian War. Colonial troops fought with Wolfe in the assault on the Heights of Abraham in 1759. And France's humiliation over the loss of the war, and particularly the painful loss of French Canada, was one of the main factors which led it to help and sometimes to incite the American insurgents as the Revolution approached.

The implications for America of the British victory were universally understood. After describing the mixed feelings with which England received the news of the fall of Quebec, in which Wolfe died, Parkman writes:

> New England had still more cause of joy than Old, and she filled the land with jubilation. The pulpits resounded with sermons of thanksgiving, some of which were worthy of the occasion that called them forth. Among the rest, Jonathan Mayhew, a young but justly celebrated minister of Boston, pictured with enthusiasm the future greatness of the British-American colonies, with the continent thrown open before them, and foretold that, "with the continued blessing of Heaven, they will become, in another century or two, a mighty empire," adding in cautious parenthesis "I do not mean an independent one."[1]

1. Francis Parkman, *Francis Parkman's Works,* vol. 13, *Montcalm and Wolfe,* ed. Fron-

He read Wolfe's victory aright, and divined its far reaching consequence. As Green said, "With the triumph of Wolfe on the Heights of Abraham began the history of the United States."[2]

When the time came to make peace, whether Canada should be restored to France was a major issue, hotly debated both within the British government and in the pamphlets and press of England and America. The elder Pitt thundered for a Carthaginian peace, which would make it impossible for France to revive as a major power. And many pointed out, in Parkman's words, that "the British colonists, if no longer held in check by France, would spread themselves over the continent, learn to supply all their own wants, grow independent, and become dangerous. . . . Choiseul [the French foreign minister at the time] warned Stanley [the British ambassador in Paris] that they 'would not fail to shake off their dependence the moment Canada should be ceded.'"[3]

Franklin undertook to answer these common arguments. The colonies were so jealous of each other, he said, that they would never unite against England. "If they could not agree to unite against the French and the Indians, can it reasonably be supposed that there is any danger of their uniting against their own nation, which it is well known they all love much more than they love one another?" Such an outcome, he concluded, was not merely improbable but impossible, unless they were treated with "the most grievous tyranny and oppression," like the bloody rule of "Alva in the Netherlands."[4]

Victorious from India and Africa to the West Indies and Canada in a far-reaching war against France and Spain for maritime and colonial ascendancy, Britain decided on a mild peace, and the Treaty of Paris restored Cuba to Spain, left France a considerable presence in the West Indies, and, for the time being, transferred Florida to Great Britain, and New Orleans and the Louisiana Territory to France's Bourbon ally, Spain.

In the nineteenth century, the consciousness of America's Manifest Destiny was the driving force in Americans' perception of themselves and of the commonwealth they were creating. The importance of their

---

tenac (Boston: Little, Brown, 1906), 169–70.

2. John Richard Green, *History of the English People* (New York: George Munro, 1880–81), vol. 4, book 9, p. 31.

3. Parkman, *Montcalm and Wolfe,* 250.

4. Benjamin Franklin, *Interest of Great Britain in Regard to Her Colonies* (London, 1760); quoted in Parkman, *Montcalm and Wolfe,* 251.

idea of America, then and now, cannot be exaggerated. It dominated the key formulations of the American approach to all questions of public policy, and particularly to problems of foreign policy, when America became a nation. And in the end the sense of America as a nation was the strongest element in the spirit which drove the North to fight for four tragic, weary years between 1861 and 1865 in the largest and most costly war of the century.

How much of the North American continent was embraced in the idea of Manifest Destiny? So far as the northern and southern boundaries of America were concerned, the answer was never clearly stated, and only emerged from historical experience. Certainly there was much talk about annexing Canada, which diminished gradually during the nineteenth century, and disappeared when Canada became a self-governing dominion in 1867. And there was always reluctance about contemplating the annexation of territories of predominantly Spanish, or Spanish and Indian, background, and of offshore territories. What is certain, however, was the appeal of the notion of "America from sea to shining sea"—the drive to fill up the vast area of the continent inhabited only by Indians, and, in California, Texas, Arizona, and New Mexico, by small Spanish populations.

The American national personality and character have been profoundly influenced by the British nonconformist tradition, especially by the outlook of small groups of Puritans who were persecuted and denied religious freedom in England. Colonial America was Britain upside down, Cromwell's England transplanted to the wilderness—a largely British population, but a British population mainly belonging to the dissenting Protestant denominations, not to the Church of England or the Roman Catholic Church. These Congregationalists, Presbyterians, and Quakers—and, later, Methodists, Baptists, and other dissenting Protestants—felt, and felt strongly, that their ancestors had not crossed the ocean in small, leaky ships, fought the Indians, and cleared the forest for gain, or for gain alone, but for a higher purpose, a purpose they thought divine. They were a people with a mission, "an almost chosen people," in Lincoln's revealing phrase. They had come on "their errand into the wilderness" primarily to practice a life of religious virtue. Their commonwealth was not to be like the others, dedicated to wealth and power, but a Utopian community, something new under the sun, a temple on the hill, devoted to peace and to safeguarding "the blessings of liberty," in the language of the Constitution, for themselves and their posterity. The most important motives which led Englishmen to seek a new future on the North American continent, Felix Gilbert wrote, were "material advantages and utopian hopes."[5] The colonists who founded Connecticut came from Massachusetts, not from England. They decided to establish their own heaven on earth in the virgin forest because, in their view, the Massachusetts Bay Colony was being corrupted by a lust for money and power.

This mystical chord in the American spirit, derived from Puritanism in the first instance, became a powerful element in the culture all Americans came to share, whether they were of British origin or not. As Tocqueville saw, the idea of equality was the key to the American outlook. The American spirit, as it developed, had a stronger influence on the practice of Catholicism and Judaism than did the cultures of any other countries where those religious bodies flourished. And, by its own alchemy, it remade the immigrants, European and non-European alike, in the American mold. Americans were always materialists, enthusiastic participants in the game of gain. But what makes America distinctive among the nations is that Americans have also partaken of another wafer. As a result, the American culture is a paradoxical combination of themes—worldly and otherworldly, practical and idealistic, pragmatic and quixotic. Americans love to become millionaires. But when they succeed, a surprisingly large number of them try to outdo the Rockefellers in philanthropy. America has been rich in the passion for social betterment—that is, for grace achieved by good works. It produced missionary societies without number; foundations, colleges and universities, hospitals, museums, and public libraries from one end of the country to the other. At the same time, American idealism acknowledged limits. It was never a recipe for martyrdom. The way in which it dealt with the American dilemma of slavery and then of race relations is only the supreme example of an almost Roman instinct for the compromises—and sometimes the hypocrisy—required to achieve the first goal of all societies: effective government.

II

In no realm is the American instinct for government more evident than in the theory and practice of foreign policy. The debate about what the goals of American foreign policy should be began before 1776, and it has continued unabated ever since in much the same terms. Both

---

5. Felix Gilbert, *The Beginnings of American Foreign Policy: To the Farewell Address* (Princeton, N.J.: Princeton University Press, 1961; reprint ed., New York: Harper and Row, 1965), 16.

before and since 1776, the American debate has been part of the debate on the same themes active in the public life of Great Britain, and to a lesser degree of France and Italy, since the Renaissance, and especially since the Reformation. In the English-speaking nations, the debate never seems to reach a conclusion, except in rare moments of visible crisis, when it is suspended rather than resolved. The reason for this extraordinary phenomenon, I suspect, is that the protagonists do not listen to each other. For them, the issues at stake are nearly religious in character, and in most instances the believers in each creed carefully shield themselves from the heresies of the others. They order these things better in France and Italy. Those Mediterranean peoples, and many others, have long since settled the matter in their minds. But we and the British, people of the northern mists, with our gifts for myth-making and self-deception, are still divided about whether the foreign policy of a democracy should be concerned primarily with the structure and dynamics of world politics, the balance of power, and the causes of war, or whether we should leave such cold and dangerous issues to less virtuous and more cynical peoples, and concentrate only on the vindication of liberty and democracy throughout the world. No members of the latter persuasion pause to note how many wars it would take to carry out a successful crusade for freedom throughout the world, and what intractable problems such a crusade would bring with it in trying to graft democracy onto cultures in which it is an alien creed.

A. J. P. Taylor once wrote a delightful book called *The Trouble Makers,* his favorite among all his books. It reviews the radical and dissenting tradition in British thought about foreign affairs with great sympathy. The heroes of that tradition are men like Fox, Tom Paine, and Cobbett, in one generation; in the next, Cobden, Bright, and Gladstone; and, in this century, Hobson, Norman Angell, Bertrand Russell, and Ramsay MacDonald. They are the ancestors of the contemporary foreign policy activists, the advocates of unilateral disarmament and of economic sanctions against South Africa and other pariahs, and those who protest only against injustice in South Africa or Chile but resolutely refuse to discuss the nature of the Soviet regime and the expansion of Soviet power. Taylor wrote that his book "deals with the Englishmen whom I most revere. I hope that, if I had been their contemporary, I should have shared their outlook. I should not have been ashamed to have made their mistakes."[6]

6. A. J. P. Taylor, *The Trouble Makers: Dissent over Foreign Policy, 1792–1939* (London: Hamish Hamilton, 1957; reprint ed., London: Panther Books, 1969), Preface, 9.

The spokesmen for the dissenting tradition have contributed immeasurably to policy over the years by goading their fellow citizens to confront moral issues which might otherwise have been ignored, or not confronted so soon. But, as Taylor sadly goes on to recognize, in foreign policy the mistakes of the dissenting tradition have been fundamental and extremely costly. These errors derive from a single source: the unwillingness of the dissenters to acknowledge the centrality of the problem of power in the functioning of human society. Their persistent battle cry has been the repudiation of the balance of power as a guiding idea. John Bright said, echoing Cobden, "The whole notion is a mischievous delusion which has come down to us from past times; we ought to drive it from our minds."[7] Both Wilson and Franklin Roosevelt, and many lesser American political leaders as well, have made equally foolish pronouncements.

As Taylor comments, Bright and most of his fellow "trouble makers" were usually content to denounce the doubtful morality of a given course of action and offer no alternative policy in its stead. Their work suffers, Taylor concludes, from a high-minded tendency to pass by on the other side, to abjure responsibility because responsibility almost invariably involves painful choices.[8]

Taylor's harsh judgment does not of course apply equally to all members of the band, nor even, always, to John Bright himself, whose antislavery agitation during the American Civil War helped to keep Britain from recognizing the Confederacy and thus destroying the Union. Bright had said that England cannot and should not be "the knight-errant of the human race,"[9] and that he was for nonintervention abroad as a consistent policy "except in so far as it affects the honour and interest of England."[10] But Taylor is correct in his general verdict: for all the appeal of its idealism, the dissenting tradition has contributed an element of irresponsibility to British and even more to American thought about foreign affairs.

There is another feature of English radicalism and dissent which from the beginning has been a conspicuous theme in the theory and practice of American foreign policy: a faith in economic motives as a substitute for military force. Tom Paine's *Common Sense* is one of the most influential pamphlets ever written. It brought into sharp

---

7. Ibid., 56.
8. Ibid.
9. Ibid., 57.
10. Ibid., 58, citing United Kingdom, Parliament, *Hansard's Parliamentary Debates* (Commons), 3d ser., vol. 157 (1860), 1260–61.

focus a theme in national opinion about foreign affairs which had been developing slowly for a century or more, and has remained alive ever since. From 1775 to this day, the American people and their governors turn automatically to boycotts, embargoes, and other economic sanctions as ways to solve international conflicts. Their enthusiasm for such measures is undiminished by the fact that during the entire history of the United States, from the Boston Tea Party and Jefferson's embargoes and measures of "non-intercourse" to recent economic sanctions against Rhodesia, the Soviet Union, South Africa, and Iran, such methods have never done any good and have often done a great deal of harm.

Sir Michael Howard dealt with the same issues in a somewhat different vocabulary in *War and the Liberal Conscience,* his 1977 Trevelyan Lectures at Cambridge.[11] Liberals, Howard says, are persons who "believe the world to be profoundly other than it should be, and who have faith in the power of human reason and human action so to change it that the inner potential of all human beings can be more fully realised."[12] He distinguishes thinkers of this persuasion from conservatives, on the one hand, who "accept the world as it unalterably is and adjust to it with more or less good grace", and, on the other, Marxists and other determinists "who see men as trapped in predicaments from which they can be rescued only by historical processes which they may understand but which they are powerless to control."[13]

Since the time of Erasmus, at least, certain writers in the liberal tradition have attacked war on a number of grounds. For some, including Erasmus himself, the objection is complete—war is barbaric and inhumane; for others, war is a violation of religious principle. But most liberal thinkers have accepted war as inescapable in the world of states, and concentrated their energies on confining its incidence and civilizing the way in which it is conducted. The goal of confining war required these writers to confront the causes of war and to consider what could be done to prevent it and, if and when it came, to make it less inhumane. For more than three centuries, an extensive literature, and the efforts of many statesmen, have been devoted to these two questions. Howard's lectures review the literature and examine, one by one, the circumstances which liberals of all schools and sects thought

11. Michael Howard, *War and the Liberal Conscience* (London: Maurice Temple Smith, 1978).
12. Ibid., 11.
13. Ibid.

caused and justified war, and the methods which might be employed to prevent it.

They all take for granted the moral right of states to use force in self-defense, and most of them concede that the concept of self-defense may well go beyond the use of force to repel invasions. Some thought wars were caused by monarchs and aristocracies, which always harbor a warrior class, and would cease to burden human history when popular movements topple the ancient tradition of monarchy, aristocracy, and empire. They persisted in their conviction even after the revolution of 1789 brought Republican government to France, and initiated a cycle of hatred and warfare unmatched in history. "That such a belief could survive not only the revolutionary and Napoleonic wars and the subsequent struggle for 'national liberation' which disturbed Europe during the nineteenth century, but also the gigantic holocausts of the twentieth—a period during which the power of the old aristocratic establishments was progressively constricted where it was not totally destroyed, and when popular pressure upon and participation within governments steadily increased, all without any noticeable reduction in the incidence of wars—this is in itself a legitimate subject for the historian's attention."[14]

Like Taylor's dissenters, some of Howard's liberals singled out economic forces as the cause of war and equally its cure. They pointed to international economic rivalry as a spur to war. On the other hand, many of the finest and most influential spirits among them found in free trade the promise of an influence which "would extirpate the system of war and produce a revolution in the uncivilised state of governments," as Tom Paine put it.[15]

The Socialists, when they appeared on the scene, concluded that war could be abolished not through free trade but through the abolition of capitalism. After the experience of the twentieth century with the Soviet Union and Communist China, that argument has lost its appeal even to the most devoutly liberal mind. Others found in nationalism and the national spirit the source of the evil, and concluded that war could not be eliminated until the state system was abolished and replaced by a world government. Howard concludes:

> At the root of this dilemma of liberal thinkers lies the habit, far older even than Erasmus, of seeing war as a distinct and abstract entity about which one can generalise at large. It was this habit

14. Ibid., 31–32.
15. Ibid., 29.

of thought that made possible the ludicrous confusion of the interwar years when liberals declared themselves passionately opposed to "war" but in favour of "military sanctions" to enforce collective security or, even more strongly, in favour of "resistance to Fascism." It has made it possible for enthusiasts in our own day to declare their opposition to war but their support for struggles for national liberation. But "war" is simply the generic term for the use of armed force by states or aspirants to statehood for the attainment of their political objectives. One may support the use of force to attain certain objectives but not others. One may support the use of force by some actors in the international system but not by others. One may support the use of certain kinds of force but not others. Only those absolute pacifists who, like Gandhi, totally renounce the use of force to defend themselves or their societies can claim to be opposed to war. And if they do so renounce the use of force while others do not, then not only their own survival but that of their value-system can be at a very high risk.

This does not mean that the liberal tradition in thinking about war and peace has been totally self-deluding and false. It has certainly been a tradition often marred by naivete, by intellectual arrogance, by ignorance, by confused thinking and sometimes, alas, by sheer hypocrisy. But how can one fail to share the aspirations of those who carried on this tradition, or deny credit to their achievements? It is thanks to the patient work, over nearly two centuries, of the men and women who have been inspired by the liberal conscience that so much progress has been made in the creation of a global community of nations; that values are today asserted as universal to which all states virtually without exception pay at least lip-service; that it is recognised even if only in principle that states have communal obligations and duties within a freely-accepted framework of international society. The danger lies in forgetting that each actor in this society of states, including those who have not yet achieved statehood, embodies distinct cultural perceptions and values; that it is ultimately concerned quite inevitably and properly with its own survival; and that it is unwilling, whatever declarations may be made to the contrary, totally to rely on the power and will of the international community as a whole to protect it.

We have thus not yet escaped from the world of power politics and *raison d'état*. Nor does an increasing multiplicity of national actors in itself guarantee a more peaceful and a better-ordered world. Kant was right when he said that a state of peace had to be "established." What perhaps even he did not discern was that this is a task which has to be tackled afresh every day of our lives; and that no formula, no organisation and no political or social revolution can ever free mankind from this inexorable duty.[16]

16. Ibid., 133–35.

5

Europe's Troubles, America's Opportunity, 1776–1801

The Era of Emancipation, the most dynamic half-century in the history of the modern world before our own times, was forged in the fires of three great revolutions. The Anglo-American Revolution, product of English political theory and the influence of the American frontier on colonial thought and action, established the independence of the United States in alliance with France. The North American Revolution served as a prelude to the French Revolution. This second revolution galvanized with the force of nationalism first the French people, then the other peoples of Europe, finally the whole world. It gave rise to two decades of wars which gripped the attention and energy of Great Britain and Spain and France in Europe and left the distant United States relatively uncudgeled on its continent to organize its nationality, to redeem its territorial integrity, then to follow its natural path of western expansion through an empty continent to the shores of the other ocean. Napoleon's invasion of Spain, a disruptive phase of those great wars in Europe, led to the third and final revolution of the era: the revolt of Spain's colonies in America and the independence of Latin America.—Samuel Flagg Bemis

Common Sense was written toward the end of 1775, during the first confused and uncertain period of the Revolution. Scattered fighting had begun. The Second Continental Congress was in session. George Washington had been appointed commander in chief, and an army was being formed and tested in battle, as it boldly moved on Quebec. But both Congressional and public opinion hesitated at the brink. Most Americans were still seeking autonomy and self-government within the British Empire. Independence seemed a dubious and strange idea, for which they were emotionally unprepared. Paine's pamphlet changed

The epigraph for this chapter is taken from Samuel Flagg Bemis, *The Latin American Policy of the United States: An Historical Interpretation* (1943; reprint ed., New York: W. W. Norton, 1967), 16.

the atmosphere. It precipitated and released the convictions which were the unacknowledged source and motivation for the course of action the colonies were in fact pursuing, articulated in terms people immediately recognized as their own.

Paine wrote that America's "plan is commerce, and that, well attended to, will ensure the peace and friendship of all Europe, because it is in the interest of all Europe to have America a free port." These benefits, he pointed out, could not be obtained without independence. Only an independent America could end the British monopoly of American trade. Paine's argument had political as well as economic themes. He excoriated the corruption and the class system of Britain, and wrote proudly of the free spirit and boundless future of America, the new Atlantis. But his economic argument was central to his thesis.

Both before and after the Declaration of Independence, American political leaders clung to a kind of Marxist belief that politics are economics in disguise, and that political policies are determined by economic advantage. Their first response to the punitive trade legislation in 1774 was a disastrous boycott of British trade. The boycott led only to even more restrictive British legislation. Later, as Congress approached the problem of obtaining military aid from France, Spain, and other European states hostile to Great Britain, most members firmly believed that by ending the British monopoly of trade with North America and thus offering the other European nations access to the American market, they were granting a gift of such economic value that no military or political commitments would be necessary to obtain military and political assistance.

As nearly its first official act after the Declaration of Independence, Congress sent a delegation of three men, led by Franklin, to negotiate for French help. Although the leaders of the new Republic were sustained by the exalted optimism natural to such occasions, they understood perfectly that without French aid the Revolutionary cause was all but hopeless. Most of them had already concluded that French help would have to include some military participation as well as provision of supplies, a point that became more vivid if not more palatable after the bad military news of the early grim months of fighting.

Congress wrangled bitterly over the instructions Franklin and his colleagues took with them. And in the end, those instructions were a monument to illusion. They contemplated French recognition and French assistance on a massive scale without any significant American political commitment in return—not even the normal commitment of allies not to make a separate peace. In fact, Franklin was sent off to negotiate a treaty of navigation and commerce, not a military alliance at all. The instructions avoided territorial issues and other difficult topics. Instead, they sketched a vision of idyllic commercial relations and neutral rights open not only to France but to all nations on equal terms: a vision of a new world of free trade designed to replace the restrictions of mercantilism. The American approach to commercial policy, navigation, and the law of neutrality, drawn from a careful study of the experience and literature of the eighteenth century, was to have considerable influence on the evolution of international trade and international law. But, as Franklin and his colleagues discovered quickly after their arrival in Paris, and Congress came to realize more slowly, their instructions had nothing to do with the negotiation of a military alliance.

For some years before 1776, France had been exploring and encouraging the possibility of an American revolution against British rule. In the aftermath of the French defeat in the Seven Years' War, France's interest in such a development was obvious and intense. And for a year before the Declaration of Independence, the French government had given sympathetic consideration to a plan for selling arms and other military supplies covertly to the rebellious colonies. The playwright and idealist Beaumarchais was the originator of the plan and its enthusiastic promoter. The experienced French foreign minister, Vergennes, became more and more convinced that Beaumarchais' plan was feasible. In May 1776, France and Spain approved the scheme and launched it on a considerable scale.

A few months earlier, in anticipation that Beaumarchais' project would be approved, the Congress had sent Silas Deane to Paris under a false name to purchase French arms as a "merchant," and to enquire about the possibility of political and other military assistance. Thus a flow of munitions and an ongoing political contact were organized before the Declaration of Independence. The arms proved to be an invaluable resource to the Americans in the early battles of the war, and especially in the crucial American victory at Saratoga in 1777.

Until Saratoga gave France some hope that the war could be won, the French preserved the facade of neutrality, and conducted relations with America on a covert and deniable basis so far as arms shipments were concerned. The arms cargoes were handled by Beaumarchais' company and sent to French and Dutch islands in the West Indies for transshipment to the United States. But Saratoga changed everything. The British government offered its former American colonies self-government within the British Empire, a plan Congress would have accepted gladly in 1775. And the French government became alarmed about the possibility that the Americans would take the British compromise, and thus scuttle France's plan for profoundly weakening Great Britain by helping the United States to secede.

In Paris, Franklin and Deane discussed the British compromise proposal secretly with a British secret agent, confident that Vergennes would be promptly and fully informed. Vergennes was indeed informed by his own spies, and reacted vigorously, promising French recognition of American independence and a treaty of alliance, on the condition that the talks with the British agent should be broken off. There was some delay while France sought to persuade Spain to join the alliance. But when Vergennes concluded that Spain was procrastinating, France and the United States signed two treaties on 6 February 1778, one a treaty of amity and commerce, based in considerable part on the ideas embodied in Franklin's instructions, and the other a treaty of perpetual alliance.

The alliance was described as "conditional and defensive"—a point that became critical in 1793, when France declared war against Great Britain. It provided that if war should break out between France and Great Britain as a result of France's recognition of and assistance to the United States, the two allies would carry on the war together and neither would make a peace or truce with their common enemy without the consent of the other. Furthermore, they agreed to carry on the war until the independence of the United States should be assured by a treaty or treaties of peace. British possessions on the continent of North America were reserved for conquest by the United States, and British islands in the West Indies—except for Bermuda—for France. The treaty provided that after the Revolution was sucessfully terminated, if war broke out between France and Great Britain, the United States would assist France by protecting French possessions in the West Indies and by allowing France to fit out privateers in American harbors and to hold prize courts on American soil where British vessels captured on the high seas, and their cargoes, would be condemned and sold.

A year later, France succeeded in making a separate alliance with Spain with regard to the war in America. Spain and France agreed to fight, if Britain refused Spanish mediation, until Spain recovered Gibraltar. Spain was also interested in other territories then held by Britain: Jamaica, Minorca, Florida, and Honduras among them. Spain was opposed to recognizing the independence of the United States, because of the impact such a step would have in South America. The Spanish role in the war itself was minimal from the American point of view, although it was of some political value. But the provision about Gibraltar in the Franco-Spanish treaty proved to be a difficulty when the time came to make peace with Great Britain in 1782. If the United States was bound to France not to make a separate peace with Great Britain, and France was bound not to make peace until Spain had recovered Gibraltar, where did that leave the United States? In the end, both France and the United States finessed the question of Gibraltar. France did not insist on the letter of the Franco-American alliance, and did not object formally when the United States and Great Britain made a separate peace.

The other countries of Europe remained aloof from the American war for a long time. The American representatives sent to Russia, Spain, Holland, and Tuscany were not received officially or even unofficially. The appeal of trade in the American market proved to be a weak lure compared with the risk of British reprisals or even war.

II

Many lessons have been drawn from the complex diplomacy of the American Revolution, which involved Russia and the Netherlands as well as France, Spain, and Great Britain. A gallery of American diplomats demonstrated genius, competence, incompetence, wisdom, knavery, and folly in almost equal parts. Luckily for the American cause, the share of genius and competence prevailed, significantly aided by the element of chance. The one conclusion that cannot be drawn from the colorful tale, however, is that it demonstrates the pertinence of the main propositions on which Americans thought their foreign policy should be based. The appeal of America as a free port turned out to be of no influence on the course of events. The United States could not conceivably have gained its independence by staying aloof from the wars and politics of Europe, and confining its role in world affairs to trade and setting a virtuous example. On the contrary, American victory in the Revolution, like the emergence of America as a political entity during and after the Seven Years' War, demonstrated that America was inextricably and inescapably part of the European state system. American independence was the product not only of war but of European politics at its most earthy. The Americans could not disdain the grubby rough-and-tumble of eighteenth-century diplomacy; they had to play the game, and did, like hardened veterans.

The United States was born out of the rivalry between France and Great Britain for primacy in European politics. Quite wrongly, France

believed that losing its American colonies would gravely weaken Great
Britain as a world power. Instead, freed of its American colonies, Great
Britain began a century of unparalleled power and effectiveness, the
high point of British political influence in the entire chronicle of its
history. In order to pursue its American policy, France refrained from
interfering in the war between Prussia and Austria over the control of
Bavaria in 1778. That abstention may well have cost France a chance
to seize Flanders and establish a relation with Prussia which might have
led to a different outcome at Waterloo, and much besides. And its
American adventure cost France so much money that the consequent
rise in taxation is generally thought to have contributed significantly to
the coming of the French Revolution.

These harsh and vivid experiences with the Revolutionary War had
no visible effect on the American articles of faith about the nature of
the United States and its role in world politics. The utopian vision of
the United States as a nation apart, insulated by the oceans from con-
tamination with the evil of a warring world, was if anything confirmed
and fortified by the struggles of the Revolution. The amoral idea of
balance of power politics became more odious than ever. And John
Adams' principle that "the business of America with Europe is commerce, not politics or war" survived the revolutionary years unscathed.

III

In one realm, however, the Revolutionary War did profoundly
change the intellectual climate of the United States. The war itself, and
the presence of British and Spanish military forces within nominally
American boundaries, or near them, made the new country acutely
conscious of the necessity for a strong central government which could
transform the loose league or confederation of the thirteen colonies
into a single nation. The Articles of Confederation had gone into effect
in 1781, replacing the government by the Continental Congress, which
had declared and carried on the Revolutionary War. The government
of the United States under the Articles was a process of experiment
and transition. It slowly changed the relation between the states and
the national government, began to develop executive departments, and
legislated for the new national territories acquired under the Treaty of
Peace. The most celebrated of those legislative acts was the Northwest
Ordinance of 1787, banning slavery in the new territories north of the
Ohio River and providing that they should have republican forms of
government and ultimately should become states.

But the new national government lacked the power of taxation. Its executive was rudimentary. It had no courts and it could not command the state governments. It was unable to prevent or resolve acute friction among the states on matters of trade, or deal effectively with foreign policy problems of steadily increasing gravity. Neither Spain nor Great Britain accepted the independence of the United States as permanent, and both made serious efforts to detach parts of the country from the union. Spain put pressure on the United States from New Orleans and Florida, Great Britain from the Great Lakes area and Canada. The British kept forts and active troops within territories ceded to the United States by the Treaty of Peace, on the ground that the United States had not carried out its obligations under the treaty to allow British claimants to recover their properties and collect their debts in America. Under the Articles of Confederation, the national government was unable to require the states to carry out these provisions of the treaty.

Clearly, fundamental reform was necessary if the nation was to survive. America became a huge debating society, examining the theory and practice of republics ancient and modern in pamphlets, meetings, and letters on a grand scale. Designing a new and ideal political order proved to be heady work. The tiny intellectual and political elite of the frontier community rose to the occasion brilliantly, goaded on by the confrontation of one inadequacy after another in the government established under the Articles.

IV

The new government for the United States created under the Constitution in 1789 was in every sense the successor of the old one. There were new institutions—the President, the federal courts, and a Congress elected directly by the people and endowed with the power to tax, among others. There were also adjustments to be made in the relationship between the states and what Washington always carefully called the "national" rather than the "federal" government. But the men and the ideas ruling our politics were the same. And, in the beginning at least, so were the problems. The experience of the Revolutionary War and the internal and external pressures of the postwar period had steadily strengthened the sense of America as a nation. As was noted earlier, that idea had emerged early in the colonial period and had been gaining ground rapidly since the French and Indian War. The Constitution and its hotly contested adoption manifested the power of the national principle. As Richard B. Morris has recently shown, the consciousness of the United States as an indissoluble union of people, and not a loose and suspicious alliance of sovereign states, was decisively forged during the decade of the 1780s.[1]

The end of the Revolutionary War seemed to release boundless energy among Americans. They flowed West at a new pace. And American ships, sailors, and traders pressed out to every corner of the world. These were national activities, carried out under the protection of the American flag, which became a familiar sight in the ports of the Far East and the Mediterranean as well as in those of Europe, the West Indies, and South America.

The flag was not welcomed everywhere with enthusiasm, however. The main powers of Europe, Britain and Spain in particular, were by no means convinced that the new republic could or should long endure. In the West, frontier settlements continued to be harassed, this time not by French but by British forces and the Indians they incited or in any event supported. Navigation on the Mississippi and the Great Lakes was a matter of endless controversy and anxiety. And England's vexing restrictions on American trade with British colonies in the West Indies and elsewhere remained a source of friction.

A few months after President Washington was inaugurated, however, the international environment was transformed forever by the outbreak of the French Revolution, which Bemis rightly called "one of the most consequential events in American history."[2] The European state system was convulsed by a succession of volcanic eruptions which lasted, with short intervals of truce, for more than twenty-five years. The climate of opinion in Europe and every part of the world affected by European thought was equally transformed. New intellectual fashions gained ascendancy: "the consent of the governed" began to supplant dynastic legitimacy as the accepted source of political power; the world experienced a season of romanticism after the cold and lucid classicism of the eighteenth century; and new and terrible myths and symbols came to obsess the Western imagination—Thermidor, the Terror, the Consulate, Marengo, Napoleon, the *levée en masse,* Waterloo, Elba, and St. Helena. The cataclysm which followed the storming of the Bastille on 14 July 1789 can be compared in its magnitude and

---

1. Richard B. Morris, *The Forging of the Union, 1781–1789* (New York: Harper and Row, 1987). See also Edmund S. Morgan, "Popular Fiction," *New Republic,* June 28, 1987, p. 25.
2. Samuel Flagg Bemis, "The Background of Washington's Foreign Policy," *Yale Review* 16 (January 1927): 326–27.

profundity of effect only to that which began in August 1914 and has not yet run its course.

For the United States, these titanic events were experienced first as a diminution or at least a potential diminution of threat. America's enemies were preoccupied by situations which menaced their security far more directly than the fate of a few small forts around the frontiers of the United States or the question of free navigation on the Mississippi. Once again, as in the decade after 1763, the intense rivalry of the Great Powers gave the American people and their government a precious opportunity. They took full advantage of it to consolidate their nationhood, enlarge their territories, and achieve the energy, optimism, and self-assurance which remain the hallmarks of the national temperament.

The Great European War between 1789 and 1815 did not provide the United States with an easy period of incubation. Great Britain and France each put violent pressure on the United States to induce it not to help its adversary, at a minimum. France pressed America for active help. America was drawn into the conflict twice, once on each side, and threatened by it in many ways throughout its spectacular course. An active American diplomacy perceived openings which the war made possible for favorable agreements with Great Britain, France, and Spain. The territorial provisions of the Treaty of Peace with Great Britain in 1783 were finally carried out; the Louisiana Territory was acquired; and in the end East and West Florida were added to the national domain. In addition, the United States acquired claims to Spanish territories reaching the Pacific.

For the United States, the initial crisis of the Great European War came in 1793. The three years immediately following the fall of the Bastille were a time of indecision in France. There was turbulence and conflict enough, and ominous portents, but the storm had not yet broken. In 1793, however, it came with the force of a hurricane. Under circumstances of terror and near-anarchy, the government of France was taken over by a succession of revolutionary factions within a legislative assembly, and the First Republic was proclaimed. Lurid and fantastic reports from France horrified and frightened the Western world. The guillotine claimed its thousands and the former monarch—a friend and ally during the American Revolution—was among them. The Revolutionary armies had been active and victorious along the borders of France. Now the fervor of the Revolution reached a new pitch. France declared war on Great Britain, which had received many aristocratic exiles and was visibly concerned about the specter of France on a crusade in the name of Revolution.

When the news of war between France and Great Britain reached President Washington in Mount Vernon, he rushed to Philadelphia, where he met with his cabinet in an atmosphere of the utmost gravity. The United States was allied to France under Franklin's treaty of 1778, which every American revered. The Treaty of Alliance seemed to apply to the new situation—an outbreak of war between France and Britain after the conclusion of peace between Great Britain and the United States. For practical purposes, our armed forces consisted almost entirely of state militias. There was no navy. British forces in Canada and on the seas could have snuffed out the United States without difficulty, and indeed with relish, had we given Britain an excuse by aiding France in the war.

Washington's procedure for dealing with the storm was a model of order and rationality. He asked each member of his cabinet to respond to thirteen written questions. Washington's questions and his colleagues' answers provided the basis for their subsequent discussions and the President's decisions.

The atmosphere was hardly propitious for calm decisionmaking. Public opinion was passionately pro-French and anti-British, although a substantial minority saw the situation soberly, and the second thoughts of many others came to support them later. But leaders as distinguished as Gouverneur Morris argued for faithful compliance with the French treaty, whatever the cost. "The honest nation," he said, "is that which, like the honest man,"

> Hath to its plighted faith and vow forever firmly stood,
> And tho' it promise to its loss, yet makes that promise good.[3]

Thomas Jefferson was secretary of state at the time. He had served as minister to France, and was deeply sympathetic to France, the French intellectual outlook, and the French Revolution. Temperamentally, he was the antithesis of everything the Federalists represented, and was already the natural leader of the strong popular movement which became what was then called the Republican Party, the ancestor of the modern Democratic Party. Within the Cabinet, the disagreements be-

3. Quoted in John W. Foster, *A Century of American Diplomacy: Being a Brief Review of the Foreign Relations of the United States, 1776–1876* (Boston and New York: Houghton Mifflin, 1900), 152.

tween Jefferson and Alexander Hamilton, the secretary of the treasury, had an animal ferocity. But, on the surface at least, Jefferson agreed with the President from the beginning that neutrality was the only possible policy for the United States. Privately, however, he wrote to his friends criticizing the President's policy bitterly.

The first question the President had to decide was whether, under the new Constitution, he could issue a proclamation of neutrality on his own authority or whether he required the approval of Congress. Many argued that the Constitutional power of Congress to "declare" war necessarily implied Congressional control over every possible use of the armed forces short of war, and over the status of neutrality as well. The President was reluctant to call Congress into special session. Given the feverish state of public opinion, Congress might easily be swept to the wrong conclusion by the memories and loyalties of the Revolutionary War.

Washington sought a ruling on the question from the Supreme Court. The Court refused to give an advisory opinion, pointing out that it was authorized by the Constitution only to decide cases in litigation before it. Thus President Washington, like many of his successors, had to confront one of the most important issues raised by the new Constitution—the extent of the President's Constitutional prerogative in the field of foreign affairs. He decided, as all our strongest Presidents have decided, that one of the overriding policy goals of the Constitutional Convention in recommending the Presidency was to enable the Chief Executive to take prompt and effective action in behalf of the nation when, in his judgment, such action is required by circumstance. The need for an "energetic" President was one of the most urgent themes of the Federalist Papers; that policy should govern the construction of the Constitution. Washington determined to issue the proclamation of neutrality on his own authority.

That decision, however, did not resolve the President's larger problem. How was he to deal with Franklin's treaties? Were they still in effect? Did they apply to the current situation, and if so, how? Did they require the United States to protect the French islands in the West Indies against the British fleet? To allow the French to hold prize courts on American territory, to recruit soldiers and sailors, and to outfit men-of-war and privateers in American ports?

Hamilton argued that the alliance of 1778 was a treaty of collective self-defense and could not apply to the present situation because France had declared war against Great Britain, and was therefore the aggressor. If this view was unpalatable politically, he offered a second argument: that since there had been a revolution within the revolution in France, and the prospects for the new government in Paris were uncertain, the President should refuse to receive the egregious Citizen Genet, the French minister who was then on his way to Philadelphia from Charleston, South Carolina, being greeted by enthusiastic crowds at every stagecoach stop. Under the Constitution the President alone had the power to recognize foreign governments and to receive their ambassadors. If recognition of the French government were suspended, Hamilton pointed out, the treaties would be suspended also, and the President could avoid a series of difficult and politically sensitive decisions.

Hamilton's argument was too much for Jefferson. Appealing to the pro-French sympathies of the American people, he argued that the treaties plainly survived the Revolution and that the representative of the French Republic should be received as warmly as the minister of the Bourbon King; but that the President could and should on his own authority interpret and apply the treaties to deny France the right to use American soil as a base for any hostile acts against Great Britain, including the holding of prize courts, the recruitment and organization of armed forces, or the outfitting of vessels of war. American protection for the French islands of the West Indies was out of the question. The United States could, however, carry on peaceful trade with France as a neutral, pursuant to the provisions of the Treaty of Amity and Commerce, that is, on the principle that "free ships make free goods"— except for contraband of war, a category which should never apply to foodstuffs, timber, or other naval supplies.

The astute President agreed in part with each of his key advisers. He received Citizen Genêt and declared the treaties to be still in effect. At the same time he issued a proclamation of neutrality based on his own interpretation of the treaties. Genêt ignored the proclamation and appealed to the American people in support of his program of commissioning privateers, holding French prize courts in American ports, and organizing an army of enthusiasts to liberate New Orleans from Spain. The stormy French diplomat was promptly declared persona non grata, but was allowed asylum in the United States, since he may well have faced the guillotine if he returned home. He married the daughter of a prominent New York family and lived out his life near Albany.

British doubts about American neutrality, inflamed by Genêt's activities, were somewhat allayed by Hamilton's highly irregular conversations with George Hammond, the British minister, in which the secretary of the treasury expounded a far more aloof policy of American neutrality than that of the secretary of state.

President Washington, having successfully established a critically important Constitutional precedent demonstrating that in carrying out treaties the President of the United States has certain independent powers of construction and action, now discovered that under our ingenious Constitution, most such independent powers collide sooner or later with equally "independent" powers vested in the other two branches of the government. In order to enforce his policy of neutrality, Washington needed a statute; juries would not convict for violations of a Presidential proclamation alone. In reporting the criminal trials of American sailors for violating the President's proclamation, the newspapers of the time explained that the chief issue in the jurors' minds was that the government should not be allowed to interfere with the God-given right of a free American citizen to go forth and fight in a foreign war if he wanted to. In any event, if we had to follow such a weak-kneed policy, it should be established by Congress, not the President. *Nulla poena sine lege* (No punishment without a law).

In the next year, Congress reluctantly passed our first Neutrality Act; large parts of it are still on the books. If America is neutral with respect to a foreign war, the statute prohibits the recruitment of men for military service by foreign belligerents on American soil. This is the reason why, during the early stages of both world wars, American volunteers went to Canada, Great Britain, or France to enlist. The statute also forbade the arming of belligerent vessels in American ports, but declared legal the equipment of merchant ships of belligerent flags and made a number of other statements which have become an integral part of the international law of neutrality.

There is not much dispute among the nations about the formed obligations of a neutral under international law. It is accepted that the neutral state is absolutely responsible for the use of force from its territory against the territorial integrity or political independence not only of a belligerent but of any other state. That responsibility is the same whether the neutral state uses its own forces, allows another state or an armed band to do so, or fails to prevent its territory from being used for the purpose when it knows, or should know, that such activities are afoot.

Applying these formal rules and enforcing the legal rights of a neutral and its citizens with respect to belligerent powers is another matter, however. Neutral states have for centuries complained about, and often fought as best they could against, what they regarded as unlawful searches and seizures on the high seas. Their principal protection, however, has been in the admiralty courts of the belligerent countries which are supposed to apply the rules of international law impartially, and often do. Despite some progress in the codification of the law on the subject, there are still wide differences among nations on a number of the key issues. And, under the pressures of war, belligerents often violate the agreed standards of international law and gamble on having to pay later for their transgressions.

Since international law is deemed to arise only from the general consent of the principal nations, such disagreements are crucial. In the late eighteenth and early nineteenth century, Great Britain, the leading maritime nation of the time, firmly rejected the conception of neutral rights advocated by the smaller states of Europe and the United States, and embodied in the Franco-American Treaty of Amity and Commerce and other American treaties of amity and commerce.

The Washington Administration had scarcely dared to breathe more easily after the first stage of the neutrality crisis had passed when it became embroiled with Great Britain over a series of seizures of American vessels and cargoes in West Indian waters. The controversy within the United States over the President's declaration of neutrality was still inflamed. The inflammation was made more acute by the news of British victories, insults, and provocations in the Northwest. The fever approached an intolerable level when, early in 1794, reports arrived that a British fleet in the West Indies had rounded up three hundred American vessels bound for French ports.

The drastic British action was fully consistent with the traditional laws of war. The weakness of our legal case did not, however, calm American opinion, which exploded into rage. Once again, Washington correctly saw grave danger of a war which could undo all that had been achieved since 1776.

Acting on Hamilton's advice, the President took a strong diplomatic initiative. Over vehement political objection at home, he sent John Jay to London to seek a general settlement of outstanding issues between the United States and Great Britain: the continued presence of British troops on American soil; the payment of each side's debts and claims for damages; boundary questions; and, of course, the perennial problem of neutral rights at sea. Jay was then Chief Justice of the United States. He earlier had been the first and only secretary of foreign affairs under the Articles of Confederation. With Hamilton and Madison, he was one of the authors of the Federalist Papers—a man of high specific gravity, judgment, ability, and diplomatic experience.

Jay found an ideal partner in William Pitt the younger, the far-sighted and conciliatory genius of British politics, who in 1794, at the age of thirty-five, had already been prime minister of Great Britain for eleven years and was to serve in that office with one short interruption until his death in 1806. Pitt's conception of British foreign policy was pacific, large-minded, and profound. In foreign affairs, he was the preceptor of Castlereagh, one of the chief architects of the conciliatory and creative peace achieved by the Congress of Vienna in 1815.

Pitt did not want to be diverted from Britain's life-and-death struggle with France by another American campaign. Indeed, he was deeply opposed to military action against America under any circumstances. As a sixteen-year-old boy in 1775, he had heard his father deliver his famous appeal for conciliation with the American colonies in the House of Commons, the first time the younger Pitt had heard his father in that hall. His father's view of what Britain's policy toward America should be always remained his own. On the other hand, neither he nor any other British minister could accept the radical American claims of neutral rights, which in their view would cripple British sea power, the pillar of the kingdom.

Despite the elaborate instructions given to Jay, he accepted an agreement which did not honor the principle that free ships make free goods nor the proposition that food and naval stores cannot be contraband of war. Jay's Treaty did, however, go far to meet the other American grievances. It called for the British evacuation of American territories in accordance with the peace treaty of 1783. The counterpart of that concession was an American agreement to pay Britain for bona fide private debts owed to Englishmen by Americans and contracted before the peace. Under the Constitution, the government of the United States had the power to make financial commitments which were beyond its capacity under the Articles of Confederation. The amounts owed were to be determined by a mixed commission, that is, a commission made up of representatives of both nations. Arbitration was also invoked to determine the amount to be paid by Great Britain for spoliations on American shipping made under color of orders-in-council offensive to the American government, although Britain did not thereby repudiate those hotly contested orders. Similarly, a third mixed commission was to settle certain boundary disputes which had arisen under the 1783 treaty. The navigation of the entire Mississippi was declared to be free to citizens of both countries. And commerce between the two nations was established on the basis of the principle of non-discrimination.

From the vantage point of the twentieth century, it is difficult to understand why Jay's Treaty was so violently unpopular in the United States. But its manifest advantages were nearly overborne by the passions and loyalties of the Revolution. Hamilton was stoned and led away bleeding from a meeting at which he defended the treaty. Jay was burned in effigy. After bitter and prolonged debates, the House of Representatives grudgingly consented by a close vote to appropriate the money required to pay the claims to be settled by arbitration under the treaty. In the political life of the nation as it was taking shape under the rival leadership of Hamilton and Jefferson, the rising populist party of Jeffersonian Republicans tended to be emotionally pro-French and anti-British, the Federalists—less emotional altogether—more detached, but somewhat oriented to the British.

Whatever the sources of the conflict may have been, there can be no doubt about its gravity. John Quincy Adams thought the controversy over the ratification of Jay's Treaty "brought on the severest trial which the character of Washington and the fortunes of our country have ever passed through. No period of the War of Independence, no other emergency of our history since its close, not even the ordeal of establishing the Constitution . . . has convulsed to its inmost fibers the political associations of the North American people with such excruciating agonies as the consummation and fulfillment of this great national composition of the conflicting rights, interests, and pretensions of this country and Great Britain."[4] In the end, however, the Senate consented to ratification by a bare two-thirds majority, and the treaty was ratified by the President, again under tumultuous circumstances.

Bemis is surely right in his judgments that only Washington's prestige carried Jay's Treaty to ratification and fulfillment during a riotous and irrational moment in American politics; that only the necessities of the war with France induced Great Britain to evacuate the Northwest territories and make other concessions to the United States; and that Jay's Treaty "saved American nationality in an hour of crisis."[5]

There was another thread in the cloth: the wisdom and character of the younger Pitt. That extraordinary figure, whose vision shaped

4. Foster, *Century of American Diplomacy*, 161.
5. Samuel Flagg Bemis, *A Diplomatic History of the United States* (New York: Henry Holt, 1936), 103.

British foreign policy for more than a century, worked always and only to transform the state system into a system of peace. Pitt was among the first in Britain to see Anglo-American cooperation as an important, perhaps in the long run a decisively important, instrument for achieving and maintaining the goal of peace. It was another of Pitt's protégés, George Canning, who said of his part in the development of the Monroe Doctrine as British minister of foreign affairs, "I called the New World into existence, to redress the balance of the Old."[6] Without Pitt, Washington's powerful diplomatic initiative could well have foundered.

Once Jay's Treaty was signed, Washington sent Pinckney to Madrid to negotiate the opening of navigation on the Mississippi to Americans. There were rumors afloat that Anglo-Spanish relations were deteriorating, and rumors as well that Jay's Treaty had secret clauses making America Britain's ally in the Great War. Moved perhaps by these reports, Spain tried to persuade Pinckney to agree to alliance with Spain, or with Spain and France together, for the preservation of their American colonies. Pinckney refused even to refer the question to Philadelphia. Spain then promptly accepted an agreement opening the Mississippi to American shipping, with entrepôt facilities in New Orleans for American use in transshipping cargoes, and agreed also to the pacification of its boundaries with the United States, each side undertaking to control Indian and other incursions.

The American agreements with Britain and Spain infuriated France, which had hardly been pleased by the neutrality proclamation the year before, the dismissal of Genêt, and the American Neutrality Act of 1794. Both Britain and France were actively attempting to stop American commerce with the other nation, in accordance with the customs of naval warfare. The American reconciliation with Britain struck France as a betrayal of Franklin's treaty, and an act of ingratitude to boot. France intensified its naval attacks on American shipping to British ports even if they were not blockaded. If Jay's Treaty diminished the risk of war with Great Britain for the United States, it led in due course to a limited maritime war with France.

Shortly after John Adams succeeded Washington as President in 1797, he sent a diplomatic mission to Paris to seek a settlement with France comparable in effect to that of Jay's Treaty with Great Britain. The government of France was in no mood to conciliate the Americans. The victories of its armies all over the Continent intoxicated French

6. United Kingdom, *Hansard's Parliamentary Debates* (Commons), 2d ser., vol. 16 (1827), col. 397.

spirits. Even the cold and detached Talleyrand, the foreign minister, expected England to capitulate very soon. The American commissioners were treated abominably. Talleyrand tried to extract outrageous bribes before addressing the substance of the issues. John Marshall's sober and powerful report on the talks led Adams to recommend preparations for war. Washington came out of retirement to lead the army. There was talk of naval cooperation with Britain if war came, and some thought of borrowing British warships. The British Admiralty was not keen to see a strong American navy develop. But Adams was. He brushed aside the idea of borrowing British ships, and proceeded with his preparations for war. His policy was politically popular at home. And for once Britain and the United States agreed on arrangements for neutral commerce. Americans prospered immoderately on wartime trade under the new British rules.

A limited maritime war between France and the United States ensued. It lasted between 1798 and 1801, and was confined by Congress to defensive actions. With much of the French fleet blockaded by the British, the American navy did reasonably well against French shipping and French warships. And the American naval victories stirred the nation. Most important, the process of building and making the navy began, an undertaking which made possible the spectacular American naval victories in the War of 1812. Taking advantage of this opportunity, Congress formally abrogated the Franco-American alliance of 1778, against which opinion had turned. The next treaty with military obligations ratified by the United States was the United Nations Charter, in 1945.

In France, the Directory was running its course, ending the most anarchic period of the French Revolution. Napoleon became First Consul in December 1799. Even before that decisive event, under thoughtful and insistent advice from a number of colleagues, Talleyrand was induced to reverse his policy. He came to realize the folly of alienating America and driving it into a tacit alliance with Great Britain. If the limited maritime war should develop into general war, the ambitious French plans for restoring the French empire in America could be utterly ruined. Those plans depended on a powerful French position in the Caribbean, notably in Santo Domingo, and the recovery of New Orleans and the Louisiana Territory from Spain. After the Spanish settlement with the United States in Pinckney's Treaty, Spain lost interest in Louisiana and was willing to exchange it for advantage in Europe. Such a development, Napoleon and Talleyrand believed, would not only be splendid in itself but would permit France to keep both Spain and the United States out of British hands and under strong French influence. Talleyrand invited a new American delegation to come to Paris, and assured it respectful treatment.

Adams opposed the rising war spirit of his own party, and accepted Talleyrand's invitation despite outspoken opposition from some members of his cabinet and supporters in Congress. He was firmly against allowing the conflict with France to degenerate into general war, and went to his grave convinced that his response to Talleyrand was the most prudent and successful act of his whole life.

One of Napoleon's first actions when he came to power was to repeal the maritime decrees which had been the focal point of American resentment. The French delayed the negotiations with the United States until France was assured the retrocession of Louisiana from Spain, but then quickly reached an agreement which ended the limited war between France and the United States, prevented general war, and established relations based on the principle of neutrality. France regarded the unilateral American abrogation of the 1778 Treaty of Alliance as a wrongful act under international law, and obtained compensation for it in the settlement of 1800. But France acknowledged that the Franco-American alliance was over.

On the commercial side, the new treaty echoed the terms of the 1778 Treaty of Amity and Commerce. It affirmed the view, as between France and the United States, that free ships make free goods, except for contraband of war. The contraband list did not include foodstuffs or naval stores, which was not, however, quite the same as stating flatly that foodstuffs and naval stores could not be considered contraband. And the treaty confirmed the right of neutral vessels to sail between ports of a belligerent.

In short, the dynamics of the immense struggle between France and Great Britain required both powers to appease the United States. France swallowed its pique and settled its skirmish with the United States. Reinforced by Jay's Treaty, America refused British overtures for an alliance and the loan of warships and proceeded briskly to enlarge its navy and to fight France for its legal rights on the high seas, not without success. The result was that the United States consolidated its independence, abrogated its alliance with France, and succeeded in placing its economic relations with both great maritime powers on a legal and political footing which promised to be peaceful and profitable. Spain, also caught between Britain and France, likewise sought agreement with the United States. The turn of the century saw the United

States in a greatly strengthened position as compared with that of 1793: larger, more populous, richer, and more confident.

Psychologically and politically, the attitude of the country toward foreign affairs changed in a fundamental way during the first decade under the Constitution. As the experience of the Revolution receded, it ceased to dominate America's sense of its place in world affairs. Rough treatment at the hands of both great powers after 1793 permitted the Americans to take their distance from France and to accept the necessity for less hostile relations with England. The new outlook found its classic expression in Washington's Farewell Address, published in September 1796. The timing of the address was significant. It was issued well before the Presidential elections in November of that year. Its purpose was to announce Washington's retirement, and to convey to his countrymen the "counsels of an old and affectionate friend," in the hope of helping "to moderate the fury of party spirit, to warn against the mischiefs of foreign Intriegue, to guard against the Impostures of pretended patriotism."[7]

On foreign affairs, Washington's argument was simple. "Our detached and distant situation," he wrote, enables us to stay out of "the ordinary vicissitudes of [Europe's] politics, or the ordinary combinations and collisions of her friendships, or enmities." If we succeed in remaining one people, under an efficient government, we shall soon be strong enough to "defy material injury from external annoyance," insist on respect for our neutrality, and "choose peace or war, as our interest guided by justice shall counsel." He continued, "Why forego the advantages of so peculiar a situation?—Why quit our own to stand on foreign ground? Why, by interweaving our destiny with that of any part of Europe, entangle our peace and prosperity in the toils of European ambition, Rivalship, Interest, Humour or Caprice?" Washington argued, "'Tis our true policy to steer clear of permanent alliances, with any portion of the foreign world," insofar as we are free to do so. At this point, he carefully excepted the French alliance, to which we were committed and should remain faithful, in its "genuine sense." But it would be unwise to extend that policy: "Taking care always to keep ourselves, by suitable establishments, on a respectable defensive pos-

---

7. These quotations and those which follow are taken from Washington's final manuscript of his Farewell Address, dated September 1796; reprinted in Felix Gilbert, *The Beginning of American Foreign Policy: To the Farewell Address* (1961; New York: Harper and Row, Harper Torchbooks, 1965), 144–47.

ture, we may safely trust to temporary alliances for extraordinary emergencies."

The moving and dramatic circumstances of the address, its intellectual power, and the awesome prestige of Washington helped to transform his message into a shibboleth. Washington was an austere and momentous man, who had led his people in war and peace for more than twenty years. There was always something majestic and remote about his person; no one dared clap him on the shoulder. When, on a bet, Gouverneur Morris did so, Washington coldly removed his hand.[8] After two Presidential terms which translated the Constitution into a dynamic reality, he was preparing to retire as a matter of Constitutional policy: his own decision, and one of critical weight in the life of the nation. It was treated reverently as a tradition for one hundred and fifty years, and enacted as a Constitutional amendment after the death of Franklin D. Roosevelt, who had been elected four times. The amendment has survived, and will survive indefinitely, because it embodies the first principle of American social and political life, the fear of excessive power.

As a statement of foreign policy objectives for the United States within the state system of the late eighteenth and early nineteenth centuries, Washington's Farewell Address was unanswerably sound. The great rule of conduct for the new nation in the world community, he said, was to extend our commercial relations everywhere, and to have as little political connection as possible with any one nation, except that specified in the French treaties of 1778. Europe had a set of primary interests which had little immediate bearing on the national interests of the United States. His readers understood Washington perfectly when he advised the American people not to become embroiled in the "ordinary vicissitudes, combinations, and collisions" of European politics. They were also fully aware that there could be extraordinary vicissitudes, combinations, and collisions from time to time which would involve the supreme interests of the nation. How could it be otherwise for a people which had directly experienced the force of the storm throughout Washington's second term? And he spoke directly to the issue when he said that in such periods of threat, temporary alliances would suffice.

Washington's advice was altogether prudent and realistic for a world in which the United States was first a small and then a medium-sized

8. Edmund S. Morgan, *The Genius of George Washington* (New York: W. W. Norton, 1980), 5–6.

power living within a state system dominated by the jostle and bustle of the European balance of power, a world before the steam engine, the ironclad vessel, the plane, the missile, the computer, and nuclear energy. Washington's counsel was not for a policy of hermetic isolation, like that of Japan before 1853, but for one of active (and armed) neutrality, a familiar idea practiced by most of the small states of Europe, and the only possible policy for the United States at the time, unless it wanted to become a protectorate of Great Britain or France.

6

Europe's Troubles, America's Opportunity, 1801–1830

Nowhere in the world had Toussaint a friend or a hope except in himself. Two continents looked on with folded arms, more and more interested in the result, as Bonaparte's ripening schemes began to show their character. As yet President Jefferson had no inkling of their meaning. The British government was somewhat better informed, and perhaps Godoy knew more than all the rest: but none of them grasped the whole truth, or felt their own dependence on Toussaint's courage. If he and his blacks should succumb easily to their fate, the wave of French empire would roll on to Louisiana and sweep far up the Mississippi; if St. Domingo should resist, and succeed in resistance, the recoil would spend its force on Europe, while America would be left to pursue her democratic destiny in peace.— Henry Adams

The agreement John Adams made with Napoleon and Talleyrand in 1800 led to the Louisiana Purchase three years later. The tides of European politics and the shifting fortunes of war persuaded Napoleon suddenly to abandon his grandiose plan for restoring the French colonial empire in America. Santo Domingo was to have been the center of his empire and the base of French naval power in the Caribbean and the Gulf of Mexico. The power radiating from the French West Indies would have been reinforced by the vast Louisiana territory which Napoleon had obtained from Spain through an exchange and a secret treaty in 1800.

But word of Napoleon's first moves toward a renewal of the French presence on the continent aroused the martial spirit of Thomas Jefferson, the staunchly Francophile new American President, who was, how-

The epigraph for this chapter is taken from Henry Adams, *History of the United States of America during the Administrations of Thomas Jefferson and James Madison,* vol. 1 (1889–91; reprint ed., New York Literary Classics of the United States, and Viking Press, 1986), 1:263–64.

ever, anti-militarist in spirit. While the weak Spanish presence in Florida, New Orleans, and the Louisiana Territory was a constant preoccupation and cause for concern, the prospect of France under Napoleon in those territories was a nightmare. In 1802, Jefferson had reached a state of high anxiety, which by then most of the country fully shared. Rumors and more than rumors persuaded America that France would suspend or even abrogate the important entrepôt privileges in New Orleans guaranteed by Pinckney's treaty with Spain. The American West was stirred to fury—a state of mind which had decidedly unpleasant political implications for Jefferson, still basking in the glow of his great electoral victory in 1800.

Jefferson responded to the threat by moving forcefully beyond established national policy with respect to the Mississippi. Before Jefferson, the goal of American policy had been to obtain treaties assuring the United States free navigation on the Mississippi and the use of an area near the mouth of the river where American exports could be unloaded from river boats, stored, and transshipped. In view of the vital importance of the Mississippi to the commerce and security of the nation and to its hopes for expansion, Jefferson decided that treaty rights were no longer enough to protect the national interest. He asked a French citizen living in America, Pierre S. Du Pont de Nemours, to carry a letter to the American minister in Paris, and to make sure the letter was seen by Napoleon and Talleyrand. The purpose of the abrupt message was to suggest the American purchase of New Orleans and perhaps of West Florida, the Florida Panhandle, as well. French ownership of New Orleans, Jefferson wrote, would force America "to marry" itself "to the British fleet and nation" and seal "the union of the two nations, who, in conjunction, can maintain exclusive possession of the ocean."[1] Jefferson's hints were not subtle, but Napoleon responded to them. In due course, Jefferson sent Monroe to Paris on a forlorn mission to persuade the greatest captain of the age, at the peak of his glory, to give up New Orleans and West Florida, critical weapons in his cherished plan to revive the French empire in America and checkmate both Britain and the United States in the process. Jefferson spoke often and semipublicly to the effect that Monroe might well go to London if he did not receive satisfaction in Paris.

Jefferson's reaction to the prospect of France taking over New

---

1. John W. Foster, *A Century of American Diplomacy: Being a Brief Review of the Foreign Relations of the United States, 1776–1876* (Boston and New York: Houghton Mifflin, 1900), 189.

Orleans was proof that America's instinct for self-preservation was healthy and alert. It was the first manifestation of a continuing policy later called No Transfer—the resolution to oppose the transfer of a European colony anywhere in the Western Hemisphere from a weak power like Spain to a strong one like France or Great Britain.[2] The policy was stated categorically for the first time in a secret law passed on 15 January 1811, declaring that the United States "cannot without serious inquietude see any part" of Spain's provinces adjoining the southern border of the United States pass into the hands of any foreign power, and "Enabling" the President to undertake the temporary occupation of such territory under certain contingencies.[3]

Jefferson's public and diplomatic approach was decidedly militant in tone. But whether he intended to do more than soothe the rage of his supporters in the American West is not clear. Like many other American politicians, he spoke loudly but reduced military appropriations. Luckily, the navy had flourished during the recent war with France, and soon had to be enlarged in order to deal with the Barbary pirates. In any event, Jefferson, an icy realist beneath the near-pacifism and idealism of his rhetoric, did not expect Napoleon to yield until one of the great powers broke the Anglo-French truce of Amiens, signed in 1801, and the European war flared up again.

In the event, the war was resumed much sooner than Jefferson had anticipated. Napoleon had suffered a costly setback in his effort to put down the rebellion started by Toussaint L'Ouverture in Santo Domingo. At that time Santo Domingo was one of the most prosperous and flourishing islands of the West Indies. It was also the indispensable keystone in Napoleon's plan for a new empire on the American continent. Toussaint, one of the most extraordinary figures in an age rich in supermen, exercised on the history of the United States "an influence as decisive as that of any European ruler," in Henry Adams' measured words.[4] Before Napoleon could move in Louisiana, Toussaint's spectacular assumption of power in Santo Domingo, encouraged by the United States, had to be crushed.

Napoleon's first attempt was led by his brother-in-law General Victor Emmanuel Leclerc, who arrived in Santo Domingo in 1802. At first

2. John A. Logan, Jr., *No Transfer: An American Security Principle* (New Haven, Conn.: Yale University Press, 1961).

3. Resolution relative to the occupation of the Floridas by the United States of America, 15 Jan. 1811, 11th Cong., 3d sess., an act to enable the President of the United States, under certain contingencies, to take possession of Florida (3 STAT. 471–72 [1861]).

4. Adams, *History,* 1:255.

Leclerc seemed to succeed. Despite bloody fighting, Toussaint was betrayed by Napoleon and by his own generals and sent off to France to die in prison. But Napoleon's effort to restore slavery, which had been abolished in the first flush of Toussaint's ascension, provoked violent resistance, and Napoleon's armies were destroyed both by an uprising and by yellow fever.

Napoleon prepared grimly to avenge the catastrophe which had consumed his troops in Santo Domingo, but the expeditionary force he assembled in Holland to pacify Santo Domingo and garrison Louisiana was delayed by freezing weather during the winter of 1802–03. Meanwhile, the peace of Amiens was collapsing. Testing British resolve, Napoleon contemptuously violated the agreement in Holland, Italy, and Switzerland. The British were showing increasing signs of restiveness not only because of these European events but because of the retrocession of Louisiana and West Florida from Spain to France, and the assertive French military presence in the Caribbean. Napoleon concluded that Britain had no intention of becoming a passive appendage of the French empire. And surely he had no intention of slowing down his spectacular drive to bring all Europe into his domain. With characteristic insight and dispatch, he decided therefore that another round of war with Britain was inevitable and made his dispositions accordingly. One of his first moves was to reverse course in America.

Even before Monroe arrived, Talleyrand offered the surprised American minister to Paris, Robert Livingston, not only New Orleans and perhaps West Florida but the Louisiana territory which France had just received from Spain. As Napoleon remarked later, "They ask of me a town . . . and I give them an empire."[5] Louisiana and New Orleans would be vulnerable to British attack in the event of war with Great Britain. Better transfer them to the Americans as an act of policy than allow Britain to take them, and thus envelop America from the West and South as well as the North. Some say that the brilliant Corsican also remarked that if he failed, world politics would necessarily be dominated a century later by the rivalry of Russia and the United States, and that it was in France's interest to strengthen America rather

    5. Foster, *Century of American Diplomacy,* 196. In part 5 of his excellent biography of Livingston, George Dangerfield reviews Livingston's persistent campaign to persuade Talleyrand, Joseph Bonaparte, and Napoleon himself that the territory would be costly and useless to France, and a political and military hazard as well, because of the danger of friction with the United States. Dangerfield concludes that "Bonaparte did not give up Louisiana because of the imminence of war with England;—the war with England was due to his losing interest in Louisiana." See George Dangerfield, *Chancellor Robert R. Livingston of New York, 1746–1813* (New York: Harcourt, Brace, 1960), 370.

than Russia. When he agreed to the treaty, Napoleon said, "I have given England a maritime rival which will sooner or later humble her pride."[6]

The American representatives, going far beyond their instructions, decided to sign before Napoleon changed his mind again. In fact they knew that under a provision of the Franco-Spanish agreement which had transferred the territory to France, if France wished to withdraw from Louisiana, the territory was to be returned to Spain. Thus France had no legal power to sell Louisiana to the United States. Nonetheless, our representatives signed.

Two weeks later, on 15 May, 1803, Great Britain declared war on France, and the second and final round of the wars of the French Revolution began. Jefferson had believed that under the Constitution, which he sometimes tended to view as a compact among the states, territory could be added to the nation only by Constitutional amendment. The opportunity of the Louisiana Purchase persuaded him, however, that the United States, like any other nation, could acquire territory by treaty or indeed by any other procedure known to international law. After a struggle with his conscience, Jefferson yielded to the imperatives of American politics and history, and the treaty Monroe and Livingston had signed in Paris was ratified. France duly conveyed to the United States what it had received from Spain: the area between the Mississippi and the Rocky Mountains surely, and perhaps a good deal more. The boundaries were hopelessly obscure. From time to time, for example, the United States claimed that they included Texas and both West and East Florida. We also claimed that under the agreement the Rio Grande was the southern boundary of Texas, a matter finally settled by the Mexican War. When Talleyrand was asked by the American envoys how France herself would define the boundaries, he replied, "I do not know. . . . You have made a noble bargain for yourselves, and I suppose you will make the most of it."[7]

Even under the most conservative reading of the documents, however, the Louisiana Purchase doubled the territory of the United States, and gave a decisive impetus to the American conviction that the Lord intended the United States to encompass at least the area bounded by Canada, Mexico, and the two oceans. And, by moving the Western boundary of the United States decisively beyond the Mississippi, it

6. Ibid., 195; quoting François de Barbé-Marbois, *Histoire de la Louisiane* (Paris, 1829), translated as *History of Louisiana* by an American Citizen [Lawrence] (Philadelphia, 1830), 312.

7. Adams, *History* 1:331.

began to moot the vexed question of treating the great river as an international waterway. With the acquisition of the Louisiana Territory and New Orleans, American rights of navigation on the Mississippi were no longer governed by Pinckney's treaty with Spain, although British rights on the Mississippi, assured by the Treaty of Peace in 1783, survived until the peace that ended the War of 1812.

II

The renewal and intensification of the European war in 1803 automatically revived the problems of neutral shipping and revealed the fragility on that issue of the settlements the United States had made with Britain in Jay's Treaty of 1794 and with France in the treaty of 1800. The international law of neutrality could not withstand the pressures of prolonged war without being bent, to put it mildly. The belligerents often preferred to seize the vessel and chance being required to pay damages for unlawful seizure later.

The military situation in 1803 was altogether different from that of 1793. In 1793, after a period of weak and uncertain government, France was in the grip of a revolutionary explosion radiating energy all over Europe in wild and unstable bursts. Ten years later, the Revolution had been taken over by a dictatorship which would soon become an empire; order had been restored in France; the government was strong and active; and the triumphant armies of France dominated the continent to the Russian border. Britain, however, remained the mistress of the seas. Napoleon's effort to challenge British sea power, even with the help of Spain and Holland, was to fail irrevocably at Trafalgar in 1805. Thereafter, his plans to invade England thwarted, Napoleon sought to defeat England by denying the ports of Europe and its overseas territories to British commerce. British trade, he believed, was the source of British wealth, which permitted England to subsidize its allies and thus pursue the fixed goal of British policy, the idea of a balance of power. Despite its naval supremacy, Britain could not blockade every port in Europe. France would take a liberal view of neutral rights and obtain what it needed from abroad. England would wither on the vine and die. Through his Continental System, Napoleon sought to blockade the blockader.

Thus the status of neutral shipping became a central factor—though never the crucial factor—in the titanic struggle between land power and sea power. The war was settled in Spain, in Russia, and at Waterloo and other famous battlefields. But much of the fighting took place at sea and in the admiralties and admiralty courts of the two belligerents. Britain could hardly allow the Continental System to strangle it. And it was determined to prevent the neutrals from either supplying Napoleon for war or taking over the British maritime trade. The neutrals, of course, were eagerly making money trading with the belligerents. As loopholes developed, belligerents and neutrals alike stretched and twisted the approved principles of international law and the practices which had developed during the previous round of the war. Foreign offices, politicians, journalists, and prize courts fired off decrees, legal arguments, orders in council, and ultimata in ferocious salvos. Meanwhile, the British and French navies did their work.

For the United States, the first consequences of the renewal of the European war were rapid growth, great prosperity, and clamorous resentment against French and British restrictions on American shipping. The total value of American exports doubled between 1803 and 1807. By 1805, most of the carrying trade to Europe was in American hands; the merchant flag of every belligerent except Great Britain almost disappeared from the Atlantic and the Caribbean.

Both France and Britain reacted strongly to the extraordinary development of American trade with Europe. Their decrees cut severely into the foundation of the American boom, and resulted in the capture of hundreds of American vessels. Especially, but not exclusively, in New England and the other maritime states, the public demanded protection. Jefferson's response was a series of economic measures intended first to prevent exports to the United States from Great Britain or its colonies and then, when the policy of "non-intercourse" proved futile or worse, to embargo American exports to Great Britain and France. Jefferson's reliance on economic reprisals manifested his passion for peace, and the national conviction, which has survived for more than two centuries, that economic sanctions are an effective form of coercion. Jefferson's embargoes transformed the wartime boom into a slump, but did nothing to mollify the rage and frustration of New England and the other seacoast communities.

America had two further grievances which became politically explosive: the insoluble issue of impressment and the maritime clauses of Jay's Treaty, due to expire in 1807. Jay's Treaty allowed British warships and privateers and their prizes the freedom of American ports. By patrolling just outside American harbors, the British ships could readily pounce on their prey without an arduous chase on the high seas.

Impressment was another matter altogether.

As a nation of immigrants, the United States has always taken the view that the right to change nationality at will is one of the most fundamental aspects of human liberty, a truly "unalienable" right. Correlatively, the United States has insisted that people born in the United States are citizens by virtue of that fact, "natural born citizens," in the language of the Constitution. In the early nineteenth century and for many years thereafter, however, Great Britain and most other European states based their law on an entirely different conception of nationality and citizenship. The term *citizen* was not used in English law until well into the twentieth century. Before then the people of Great Britain were called British *subjects,* and their relationship to the crown was thus visibly a feudal bond, involving the royal protection of the subject, on the one hand, and the subject's obligation of fealty and obedience, on the other. In English law at that time, the bond of nationality could only be dissolved by mutual consent, and not by the unilateral act of the subject.

Obviously, there can be no compromise between these two conceptions of citizenship. The feudal view has gradually faded out in Western Europe, although it survives still in a few countries which do not recognize the naturalization of their citizens by a foreign nation until the countries of origin have consented. Some, notably the Soviet Union, claimed and exercised the power to strip persons of their citizenship by their unilateral action.

The impressment problem, which was the main precipitant of America's decision to declare war against Great Britain in 1812, arose from a clash between these two legal theories. Britain had long "impressed" seamen into naval service, most often by having "press gangs" seize them in the public houses or on the streets of British seaports, and from British merchant vessels. Men were also pressed into the British service from American ships stopped and searched on the high seas. Many of the sailors thus forced into service were naturalized American citizens who had been born in England. Others were deserters from the Royal Navy, tempted by the high wages paid by the flourishing American merchant marine.

As a matter of national pride as well as international law, the United States was outraged by the practice, and demanded that it be stopped, that Americans impressed into the Royal Navy be released and that damages be paid for the wrongful acts of the British government. The British government was equally vehement in declaring its position. The practice, it said, was regarded by the British people as fundamental to British sea power, and no government could expect to stay in office if it wavered on the point. The irony of the controversy was brought out in a Parliamentary speech by Castlereagh, then the British foreign minister. The contest concerned the forcible retention of some 800 American seamen among the 145,000 men employed in the British service at the time.[8] To abstain from stopping and searching American merchant vessels on the high seas could hardly have affected the vitality of the Royal Navy or the course of the war against Napoleon, even if twice that many sailors were involved, as Castlereagh remarked. But the controversy had become too inflamed for the British to consider such a concession, and it was never made, even in the peace treaty which ended the war.

Fourth among the events which together precipitated the war was the British return to the practice of stirring up Indian tribes on the Northwest frontier. While Anglo-American relations were becoming more and more envenomed by controversies over neutral rights and impressment, Indian troubles in the interior of the country were growing acute. Americans were certain that the difficulties were caused by British policy and British agents. While Britain was probably not responsible for all the raids the frontier towns and settlements had to endure, there was some substance to the charges, especially in the major case of Tecumseh's War in 1811.

Nothing aroused America more profoundly than Indian attacks. Opinion in the states bordering Canada and the Mississippi approached the boiling point. The Western War Hawks strongly favored war against Great Britain, and hoped that a war would permit the United States not only to stamp out the threat of Indian uprisings forever but to conquer Canada as well. Similarly, the turbulence of the times encouraged the southern and southwestern states to urge the annexation of Florida from Britain's Spanish ally. Indeed, as was noted earlier, Congress passed a secret statute in 1811, encouraging the President to occupy Florida if he found a propitious opportunity to do so without too much risk from Great Britain.

President Madison was not eager for war; on the contrary, he opposed it. He also realized, however, that Britain did not want to wage a minor war in America when it needed every ounce of its strength to prevail in its terrible war with France. And he believed that France would probably succeed in its looming invasion of Russia, which had been in preparation for a year or more, and would perhaps drive Wellington and his armies out of Spain, despite Wellington's recent vic-

8. Adams, *History,* 2:633. Other estimates put the number of impressed seamen as high as 2,500 or 3,000 (See Foster, *Century of American Diplomacy,* 236.)

tories. Whatever the outcome of these campaigns, Madison believed, Britain would be strained by the war for years. The President concluded that he could insist on British compliance with his terms as the price of peace. To the end of his life, he maintained that his strategy in the crisis was "a fair calculation."[9]

Madison demanded that the British concede on four key points before negotiations began: the end of impressments, the release of impressed sailors, indemnity for the wrongful seizure of vessels and other illegal acts, and the abandonment of paper blockades, that is, blockades which were declared but not made generally effective by the presence of warships. Castlereagh, eager as he was to avoid war with America, told the American minister that such concessions would only lead to the fall of the government. The maritime instincts of the British people were too strong to tolerate an end of impressment. The British government did, however, withdraw the application to American trade of the orders in council governing blockades, searches, seizures, and contraband which had been the focus of American irritation in the endless conflict over neutral commerce.

Castlereagh's move came too late. The British announced on 16 June 1812 that they would withdraw all the offending orders in council, and did so on 23 June. But the United States declared war on 18 June. Would the United States have declared war if there had been a trans-atlantic cable through which the government might have been warned that the offending orders in council were about to be revoked? The vote for war was close, both in the House and the Senate, with the eastern seaboard states largely against war, and the western and southern states largely in favor. A joint resolution to declare war on France at the same time failed by only two votes.

Madison's calculation proved to be too optimistic, but it was not far off the mark. Napoleon declared war against Russia on June 22, and the invasion of Russia began on June 24. Wellington's victory in Spain was still two years away. It was surely a moment to exploit, from the point of view of an entirely unsentimental conception of American foreign policy. True, there was always the chance that Napoleon would prevail in the war, and France emerge as master of Europe from the Urals and beyond to the Atlantic Ocean. Madison knew as well as Jefferson that such an outcome would profoundly threaten the United States. But it was a risk he thought we had to take. There was little or nothing the United States could do to influence the course of the larger

9. Adams, *History,* 2:621.

war. Meanwhile, we should do what we could to protect our maritime rights and perhaps marginally improve our security. Madison was in no sense a War Hawk. For him the issue justifying war was national pride and national honor—the duty to protect American citizens from impressment, and a sturdy insistence on the maritime rights of the nation under international law. The declaration of war, in his mind, was no more than a diplomatic chess move, designed to extract British concessions he had been unable to obtain without such a threat.

Eight days after the American declaration of war, Madison therefore instructed his minister in London to propose an armistice looking to peace negotiations. This time the President laid down only two conditions for the talks: that Britain revoke the orders in council and abolish the impressment of American seamen. Since the orders in council had been withdrawn before the minister could carry out his instructions, the serious initiation of hostilities turned for the moment on the issue of impressment.

Madison's astonishing move throws light on how one of the most important theorists and draftsmen of the American Constitution viewed the relationship of the Presidency to Congress. Congress, exercising its exclusive power to "declare" war, had decreed general and unlimited war against Great Britain. The President had signed the joint resolution declaring war, which thus became part of "the supreme law of the land." The President was obliged by the Constitution faithfully to execute the laws. But the President was also the head of a constitutionally independent, or at least autonomous, branch of government, endowed with "the executive power of the United States." Clearly, Madison believed that he had the exclusive power to conduct the foreign relations of the United States, including the power to negotiate armistice agreements and treaties of peace. He therefore felt free to parley for peace almost before a shot was fired in the war.

The episode reveals something about Madison's psychological sophistication as well. He thought Castlereagh would be more impressed by a declaration of war than by the threat and risk of war. Faced with Madison's message, however, Castlereagh refused once again to yield on impressment. The war declaration did not affect the British position, which was based, he said, on the necessities of defense. Madison proceeded with the war. His powerful Western and Southern supporters, who constituted the Congressional majority in favor of war, looked forward to the acquisition of Florida and Canada. Madison could hardly make peace in 1812 by surrendering on what was emotionally and politically the chief cause of the war. Two years later, of course, circumstances had changed. Peace was cheered in America then, although impressment was not even mentioned in the treaty of peace.

The progress of the war soon chastened the War Hawks. The nation was utterly unprepared for the conflict. At first, the war was not conducted well, and the government reacted slowly and erratically to its necessities. For all his talent and virtues in other spheres, Madison was an incompetent leader of the nation at war. He lacked the energy, self-confidence, and drive to dominate the turbulence and confusion of war. The army was mismanaged and badly led. The civilian authorities were equally inadequate, and it took an unusually long time, even by American standards, for the political process to find and promote an effective fighting team. The American attack on Canada failed ignominiously. While British counterattacks from Canada were also repulsed, it soon became apparent that Britain could, if it wished, overrun the United States as soon as it could spare a serious force for such a campaign.

While the American navy had some success on the lakes and in the Atlantic, and American privateers did extremely well, American naval operations did not decisively influence the course of the war. The British navy blockaded the United States south of New England, seeking to achieve the secession of the New England states and northern New York, where the war was violently unpopular. Later, the Royal Navy landed troops easily near Baltimore, Washington, and New Orleans. Many governors and state legislatures were halfhearted or worse in mobilizing their militias for national service and often failed to cooperate in the war effort. The war and its exigencies did lead some many of the leading men in New England to consider secession—the first time the idea was put forward as a serious possibility.

After a time, of course, able civilian officials and officers emerged both in the army and the navy. The first graduates of West Point distinguished themselves, especially as engineers and artillerymen. Many of their fortifications proved their value in combat. Americans were superior to the British in marksmanship at sea and on land, both with rifles and with ordnance. The superiority of American ship design, ship construction, and ship handling was equally marked. By 1814, the American navy and American privateers were inflicting serious damage on the Royal Navy and on British commerce, conducting successful operations even in the English Channel and along the English coast.

While the United States was slowly organizing itself for effective war, the diplomats continued to probe for ways to make peace. About three months after Madison's first peace overture, Czar Alexander I offered his good offices as a mediator. The Czar's action was surprising, since he had just become Britain's ally. What was even more surprising was that it succeeded, although not in the form the Russian government had originally envisaged.

Following the lead of Peter the Great, Russia under Catherine had become a powerful and active force in the European state system, still on its flanks, as the United States was, but more and more a force to be reckoned with, especially in view of its expansion into Central and Eastern Europe, and its movement from Siberia into the Western Hemisphere.

Napoleon was caught in a trap. England was his major enemy, its great fleets nearly invisible over the horizon. He had been forced by the facts to abandon his effort to invade England from Boulogne. Aboukir and Trafalgar had been strategic defeats from which it would be nearly impossible for him to recover. As Ludwig Dehio wrote, the semialliance between Alexander and Napoleon,

> begun with so many hopes, had produced as little result as the earlier one with Paul. By her very nature, Russia could never sincerely support any power seeking supremacy in the West. Yet such support was indispensable to the Continental System, which was bound to be ineffective if there were any gaps in its net around the continent.
>
> Thus the Emperor was left with no alternative but the use of force against a recalcitrant Russia. He also had to consider that if he did not himself attack, his opponent might one day force war upon him at the most inopportune moment. Britain might join up with Russia, start a fire in the east as she had done in the south, in Spain, and roast the Empire at a slow flame. To forestall the enemy before the drain on Napoleon's own strength had gone any further was wiser than to wait—and that meant preventive war! "To rob Britain of every hope of forming a new coalition by undermining the power of the only great state that might still become her ally—that is a great, a sublime thought" (Napoleon to Coulaincourt). In truth, this was the bitter consequence of Boulogne and Trafalgar: Napoleon had to fight his maritime enemy indirectly by means of land wars of ever widening scope.[10]

10. Ludwig Dehio, *The Precarious Balance: Four Centuries of the European Power Struggle,* trans. Charles Fullman (1948; reprint ed., New York: Alfred A. Knopf, Vintage, 1962), 171.

Napoleon's invasion of Russia made the Czar Britain's ally, while the American declaration of war against Great Britain required him to consider the United States as France's ally-in-fact. Russian rivalry with Great Britain was deeply rooted, and its attitude towards the United States, which had initially been somewhat reserved, had developed positively during the years of the Great European War. Russia had been the leader of the movement of armed neutrality at an earlier stage of the war, and its views on neutrality and maritime rights were decidedly hostile to those of the British, and close to those strongly advocated by the United States. Moreover, America's entry into the war meant that American shipping could not reach the Baltic, a matter of considerable importance to Russia in its effort to escape from the irritations of Napoleon's Continental System. More generally, Russia's natural inclination for the longer run in the complex and shifting power configuration of Europe was to try to keep the rising new American power from gravitating into Napoleon's orbit while encouraging it to remain an independent regional counterweight to England. Alexander had no illusions about his alliance with England against Napoleon, indispensable as it was under the circumstances. The world would surely revert to its usual patterns once Napoleon was defeated.

Whatever Alexander's motives were, they were sufficiently strong to induce him to propose Russian mediation to end the war between Britain and the United States. The Russian proposal of 21 September 1812 could hardly have been made in a more dramatic setting. Three months after Napoleon's armies crossed the Nieman, the Russians were falling back after a series of stunning defeats, and the French had already occupied Moscow. John Quincy Adams, then our minister in St. Petersburg, received the Czar's offer politely, and promised to transmit it at once. He had no instructions on the question, he commented, but ventured to say that he thought the Russian proposal would be favorably received. In response to his inquiry, he was told that the Russian suggestion had already been given to the British.[11]

Castlereagh found the idea of mediation by a third power unattractive. His first impulse was to ignore the Russian initiative altogether. But he did not wish to offend his new ally, and therefore decided to reply noncommittally. The Americans, he said, would probably reject the Russian offer.

11. Samuel Flagg Bemis, *John Quincy Adams and the Foundations of American Foreign Policy* (New York: Alfred A. Knopf, 1949), 185–86.

When Adams' message reached Washington in March 1813, however, the American government grasped the straw eagerly. Napoleon's disasters in Russia would surely make England less likely to satisfy the United States on the key issue of impressment. The American government was violently divided by personal rivalries. The war was not going well, and public support for the war effort was spotty, at best. Madison, whose equivocal attitude toward the war did not change, welcomed the Russian move. If Britain rejected the Russian proposal, the President would benefit politically at home. If, on the other hand, Britain accepted, so much the better. The Russians might be more successful than the United States alone in helping to persuade the British to abandon impressment and accept more liberal rules of neutrality. They could hardly be less successful. At a minimum, time would be gained for military preparation. And, more fundamentally, diplomatic support from Russia could only be helpful to the United States in the long run. The Russian armies had survived Napoleon's onslaught, and were being renewed and hardened. Russia would surely be a major factor in the future world order. Poised between Britain, France, and Spain, America would need support from countries whose interests were congruent. Russia could be a strong and important friend.

Madison decided to send a mission to St. Petersburg before receiving the final British answer, a procedure calculated to maximize the chance to achieve a relationship of active cooperation with Russia. He named Albert Gallatin and Senator Bayard of Delaware to serve with John Quincy Adams as commissioners to negotiate peace.

Gallatin was one of the greatest, most modest, and most attractive men of his time. He had been a creative and successful secretary of the treasury for twelve years, and was now to begin an equally lustrous career in diplomacy. While Gallatin and Bayard were en route, word arrived of Britain's rejection of the Russian proposal on the ground that the issues between Britain and the United States involved the domestic affairs of Great Britain—a reference, obviously, to the vexed question of impressment. Undaunted, Alexander formally reiterated his proposal for mediation. Again the United States accepted, and again the British refused, but this time they offered to meet the American commissioners directly, either in Sweden or in London. The United States, more eager than ever to be liberated from the unfortunate war, quickly agreed. Ultimately, the meetings were held in Ghent. Meanwhile, Madison added Henry Clay and Jonathan Russell to the American delegation. Both in ability and sagacity, the delegation proved to be one of the finest in our diplomatic history, in large part because of Gallatin's insight, leadership, and good humor.

The course of the negotiations at Ghent was determined by the course of the European war, which in turn also governed the course of the war in America. After Napoleon's first surrender, large contingents of British veterans were sent both to Canada and to New Orleans. Britain, elated by victory in Europe, proposed harsh terms at Ghent, and delayed the negotiations in the expectation of military success in America. While the American delegation offered one compromise after another, the prospects for peace seemed nearly hopeless. Then the atmosphere changed. British troops were defeated at Baltimore, and their invasion from Canada failed as a result of an American naval victory on Lake Champlain. The Congress of Vienna was mired in endless disputes over insoluble problems, and in France there were ominous signs of the revolt which preceded Napoleon's return from Elba.

The wisest heads in England—Castlereagh, Wellington, and Bathurst—took control of the British side of the negotiations at Ghent. And Gallatins's realistic advice—to seek peace based on the status quo ante, and to forget impressment—began to influence American policy, which had been frozen until then in patterns of self-deception. Both sides were tired of the war. In Britain policy was dominated, as the prime minister, put it, by "the unsatisfactory state of the negotiations at Vienna, and by that of the alarming situation of the interior of France."[12] The British had to prepare for the campaign which ended at Waterloo. Wellington concluded that it would take great armies to achieve British war aims in America, and counseled a settlement on the basis of the territorial situation as it was before the war. The British government promptly followed his advice, and the United States concurred, with relief.

One issue after another was dropped from the draft treaty. The Americans agreed not to mention impressment or neutral rights, while the British withdrew from their favorite project of an Indian republic in the Northwest, a barrier state designed to contain American expansion. The intractable problem of American fishing rights in Nova Scotia was mercifully put off to a better day. Arbitral bodies were envisioned to settle boundary disputes. And at British insistence, the treaty an-

---

12. Samuel Flagg Bemis, *A Diplomatic History of the United States,* (New York: Henry Holt, 1936), 167.

nounced the agreement of both parties to use their best efforts to abolish the slave trade. This declaration became part of the Treaty of Vienna the next year, and led to joint British and American naval operations against the slave trade in the South Atlantic—an important step in the great rapprochement between Britain and the United States which was one of the first principles of Castlereagh's foreign policy.

Thus ended the War of 1812, a byproduct of the world war centered in Europe which had raged for more than twenty years. With the approaching end of the European war, the disputes over impressment and the maritime rights of neutrals receded in importance. Impressment was never heard of again. The press gang ceased to be a feature of British naval practice, and the problem was formally interred by a treaty in 1870 through which Great Britain recognized American naturalization. Neutral rights in wartime are still a contentious issue which has inflamed the relations of neutral states and belligerents in every war since 1815, despite progress in the codification of the international law on the subject. But with the end of the Great European War in 1815, both sides were happy to put the matter aside for a time. Most important of all politically, the Treaty of Ghent reflected the fact that Great Britain had finally accepted the permanence of the United States, and that the United States—perhaps not yet so decisively—has abandoned the notion of conquering Canada. Florida was another story, of course, but Florida was held by Spain, a much weaker power than Great Britain.

The war had another consequence in the United States: it strengthened the spirit of American nationality. Bemis writes, "The war had the effect on national self-respect that an individual experiences when he finally punches out at an inveterate bully. It galvanized American nationality. It swelled a new pride in the Union which was to triumph over the great threat of state rights in the middle of the century. In this sense, we may say that if it had not been for the War of 1812 the Union might not have triumphed in 1865."[13]

Pride in the success of American arms was a vital element in this resurgence of the national spirit. If the war was a stalemate strategically, there were many tactical victories for Americans to savor, and savor they did. Jackson's success at New Orleans, Macdonough's important triumph on Lake Champlain, Perry's on Lake Erie, and the exploits of naval vessels and privateers in many encounters at sea and on the Great Lakes became part of every American's memory. Henry Adams writes that its "mortifying and bloody experiences" with American privateers

---

13. Bemis, *Diplomatic History of the United States,* 171.

made even the British navy weary of the war. Valuable prizes were few, and the service, especially in winter, was severe. Undoubtedly the British cruisers caught privateers by dozens, and were as successful in the performance of their duties as ever they had been in any war in Europe. Their blockade of American ports was real and ruinous, and nothing pretended to resist them. Yet after catching scores of swift cruisers, they saw scores of faster and better vessels issue from the blockaded ports and harry British commerce in every sea. Scolded by the press, worried by the Admiralty, and mortified by their own want of success, the British navy was obliged to hear language altogether strange to its experience.

"The American cruisers daily enter in among our convoys," said the "Times" of February 11, 1815, "seize prizes in sight of those that should afford protection, and if pursued 'put on their sea-wings' and laugh at the clumsy English pursuers. To what is this owing? Cannot we build ships? . . . It must indeed be encouraging to Mr. Madison to read the logs of his cruisers. If they fight, they are sure to conquer; if they fly, they are sure to escape."[14]

The social and political consequences of the War of 1812 were at least as significant as the revival of national pride. In his suggestive recent study, Steven Watts argues that American "victory—or perhaps more realistically, survival—in 1815" had released energies which remade America as a liberal, middle-class, capitalist society. The influence of the war stimulated changes in industry and commerce, in ideology and outlook, which define a new stage in the American experience. Watts concludes that its consequences made the War of 1812 "the equal of the Revolution in shaping the nation."[15]

III

With peace in Europe, and the War of 1812 behind them, the new President and his secretary of state decided the time was ripe for an attempt to acquire Florida as part of a general settlement with Spain. France was weakened for the moment, and a new era of peaceful relations with Britain was fairly launched.

The American interest in Florida was hardly a surprise to the Spanish diplomats. It had been manifested many times since the Louisiana

14. Adams, *History of the United States,* 2:1057.
15. Steven Watts, *The Republic Reborn: War and the Making of Liberal America, 1790–1820* (Baltimore: Johns Hopkins University Press, 1987), 316.

Purchase episode, especially after the first revolutionary outbreaks in Spanish America in 1808. The future of Florida, however, was part of a larger and more difficult question: the future of Spain and of Europe.

From the vantage point of American foreign policy, the world state system for the century after the Napoleonic Wars was dominated by a series of related changes originating in Europe and directly affecting the environment within which the United States had to function. Those cycles of change took place gradually—a period of restoration first, followed by revolutions—some seeking mere changes of government, other demanding social and political reform, constitutionalism, democracy, and even more radical transformations. Italy and Germany were created as modern states; the idea of constitutionalism spread everywhere; and the claim of national self-determination began to erode the foundations of the Turkish, Russian, and Austro-Hungarian empires. The first Socialist parties appeared on the Continent, and the *Communist Manifesto* was published. The revolutions of 1848 occurred and were—for the moment—put down. The newly strengthened middle classes became steadily more important, and, as the franchise was broadened, working-class politicians and parties made their way into the parliaments of Europe.

When Monroe became President in 1817, with France defeated and Germany and Italy not yet born, Russia and Great Britain were the most important magnetic poles of world politics. On the surface, the European powers were engaged in a determined effort to cooperate peacefully in managing the diplomacy of the state system, and they did so, all things considered, remarkably well. But under the surface, old doubts, fears, and suspicions remained. No one supposed for a moment that the Congress of Vienna had introduced a utopian era of peace. Many were concerned, as both Britain and the United States were, that France restored might be seized again by Napoleonic fever as it sought to reassert its importance in world affairs. And the idea of Russia, huge and powerful, and the memory of Russian troops parading in Paris and fighting in Italy, never quite left the consciousness of European and therefore of American diplomacy. The latent rivalry between Britain and Russia remained the ultimate theme in nearly every diplomatic conflict of the nineteenth century, until the rise of Germany after 1871 forced Britain and Russia to suspend their efforts against each other, at least for the duration. The pattern of Anglo-Russian rivalry emerged early in the postwar period in the brief but significant and revealing episode of the Holy Alliance.

The architects of the new order after 1815 had relied on the Quadruple Alliance of Russia, Austria, Great Britain, and Prussia to keep the peace. The Czar soon sought to enlarge this grouping and to expand its mandate by forming the Holy Alliance, an association of the legitimate monarchs of Europe. Its task was to reestablish legitimate governments where they had been overturned since 1789, and to defend them when they might be threatened in the future by the insidious forces of Jacobinism. The protection of Spain's rights as the colonial proprietor of Florida was therefore inevitably an item on the agenda of the Holy Alliance.

Britain refused to join the Holy Alliance when it was formed, offering as an excuse the fact that the British monarchy had taken power through the Glorious Revolution of 1688. Its real reasons were much deeper.

Britain's relationship with the Holy Alliance was at first equivocal, then dubious, and finally hostile. By instinct, Britain preferred a more flexible policy, supporting the restoration and protection of the old legitimacy in one situation, and the acceptance of change, even revolutionary change, in another. The pragmatic British could not believe it was possible or desirable to exorcise the surging forces released by the long years of war and revolution. The supreme goal of British policy was not a perpetual crusade for legitimacy, but a long period of peace. While Britain was not yet willing to recognize the revolutionary governments in Latin America, it looked askance at the prospect of a war to overturn them. Britain also took an active interest in its growing economic position in Latin America, and would strongly oppose the return of imperial preferences and discriminations there as elsewhere. And the notion of military intervention to stop the American absorption of Florida so soon after the War of 1812 seemed out of the question. Britain had discovered that such enterprises could be costly and frustrating. Confident in the strength and vitality of its institutions, it did not share the fear which the French Revolution and its aftermath had aroused in the traditional ruling classes of the rest of Europe, especially in Russia and the Austrian Empire. The new spirit stirred by the banner of Liberty, Equality, and Fraternity, and the aspirations it released among the European peoples, were to coexist in uneasy tension with the political and social structures of the Old Regime for more than a century. Indeed, in many countries, that tension still continues.

The Czar invited the United States to join the Holy Alliance in 1820; the United States declined, citing as "a cardinal point of their policy under every administration of their government from the peace of 1783 to this day" to avoid "all entanglement in the European system."[16] The United States was, of course, entirely sympathetic to the Latin American revolutionaries. Some help and encouragement had been provided and consular "agents" were sent and received. The United States carefully refrained from recognizing the new governments, however. For the moment, its overriding interest was to reach a comprehensive settlement with Spain, and it would do nothing which might make that difficult negotiation more difficult. With the restoration of the Bourbons in Spain, the United States ceased to send consular agents to the revolted provinces of Spanish America, and replaced them with informal "agents for seamen and commerce."

While the United States government was officially neutral, highly visible shipments of arms to revolutionary forces occurred, and American neutrality laws were not vigorously enforced. Even when they were invoked, juries often refused to convict those involved in sending arms to the revolutionaries, or sailing as privateers against the Spanish. The Latin American revolutionaries bought military supplies in the United States, and then privateers picked them up at islands or other refuges near the United States. Turbulence along the Florida border and in Texas became commonplace, and on several occasions raids against American territory were mounted from Florida by Indians, runaway slaves, or adventurers. In turn, these guerrilla episodes led to American military intervention in order to suppress illegalities Spain was unable to prevent.

Adams pressed the Spanish to discuss a long list of American grievances, going back to violations of Pinckney's Treaty, and indicated that the United States would recognize the revolutionary governments and perhaps occupy the whole of Florida if Spain refused to come to a full settlement of all outstanding issues. The British refused repeated Spanish pleas for military and diplomatic assistance. Castlereagh did offer to mediate between Spain and the United States, if the United States joined Spain in requesting mediation, but advised Spain to yield on Florida and hope for compensation in other parts of the negotiation. Both Spain and the United States declined the British offer of mediation. Spain still hoped the Holy Alliance would send armies to help restore the Spanish domain in the name of the principle of legitimacy. But that, too, was not to be. Instead, Monroe sent General Andrew Jackson into Florida with orders to disperse armed bands of guerrillas operating against the United States from Spanish territory.[17] It became

16. Bemis, *John Quincy Adams*, 265.
17. Ibid., 313.

cruelly obvious that the United States could take Florida without difficulty if it decided to do so. In the course of Jackson's spectacular operation, two British subjects were convicted by an American court-martial of leading these guerrilla activities, and promptly executed. The United States prudently dispatched the evidence in the case to Castlereagh. Despite the inflamed state of public opinion in Britain, Castlereagh declined even to protest the American action. On the contrary, he signed an important agreement with the United States settling a number of outstanding controversies.

With the risks of British mediation and European intervention out of the way, Adams pressed the Spanish hard. They had no choice but to negotiate. The transcontinental treaty of 1819 which resulted from these negotiations was one of John Quincy Adams' greatest triumphs. East and West Florida were ceded to the United States. In return, the agreement finally settled some of the territorial ambiguities of the Louisiana Purchase, largely in favor of Spain. The United States ceded to Spain all its claims to land south and west of a boundary established by the treaty, which started with what is now the western boundary of Louisiana, and proceeded north and then west to the Pacific on the line of the northern boundaries of Utah, Nevada, and California; Spain correspondingly ceded to the United States all its claims to territory north of that line. Thus the United States abandoned its claims to Texas under the Louisiana Purchase agreement, but strengthened its claim to the vast northwestern Oregon Territory. The American concession on Texas was a significant compensation for the cession of Florida. Spain sought a pledge from the United States not to recognize the new republics of Latin America, but Adams refused. Spain gave in.

IV

The territorial settlements of 1818 and 1819 with England and Spain finally established the boundaries of the United States, except for the dispute with Great Britain over the northern boundary of the Oregon Territory, and a new boundary to the Pacific between the Spanish colonies and the United States. Thus they cleared the way for the final major achievement of the American policy of Manifest Destiny, the treaty ending the Mexican War.

Both the British and the American governments had come to understand that while they approached the problem of the Latin American revolutions from different premises, their interests were identical. Both were opposed to a return of French or Spanish power to the Western

Hemisphere, just as they also opposed the rapid enlargement of the Russian presence from Alaska along the western coast of Canada and the United States. Britain and the United States were learning they could live together in a state of rather irritated familiarity which was not too uncomfortable, whereas they both foresaw serious trouble if Western Hemisphere politics again became a game of several strong players.

The British realized that for the next generation or two the preoccupation of American foreign policy would be expansion to the Pacific, not building a large navy and becoming an active participant in European and world politics. American trade all over the world was extraordinarily active. American shipping was everywhere visible, but the thrust of American political concern was to fulfill and consolidate the continental republic, not to launch a new career as a middle-level European power. Its interest in Latin America was to prevent anything like a return to the situation of peril the United States had endured between 1783 and 1815, when one or another of the European powers could conduct or underwrite attacks against the United States at will. In short, the United States considered itself a regional power—an island, in effect, not a serious actor outside the Western Hemisphere.

For the longer run, Britain had a certain prudent anxiety about the possibility that the United States might become too big and too strong. It kept a watchful eye on American relations with Spain, with Mexico, and with other Caribbean and Central American areas. "Castlereagh pointed out to Washington that the British had as much territory as they could manage. 'Do you only observe the same moderation. If we should find you hereafter pursuing a system of encroachment . . . what we might do defensively is another consideration.'"[18]

The American attitude to the Anglo-American relationship was colored by the passionate feelings of the Revolutionary era, revived and intensified for a time by the War of 1812. Beneath the theatrical vehemence of this deep and abiding American Anglophobia, however, policy was in fact based on new realities. The United States was Great Britain's largest trading partner. Americans studied and traveled in Britain in considerable numbers and talked about England and the English much as the Scots and the Welsh did—not, however, as the Irish did. And they felt that Great Britain would and perhaps could no longer pursue an aggressive policy against the United States. The passage of time, the growth of the United States, and the War of 1812 had

18. C. J. Bartlett, Castlereagh (London: Macmillan, 1966), 243.

diminished, if it did not entirely eliminate, this specter. In the American mind, Canada was ceasing to be feared as the staging ground for invasions, but was seen instead as a hostage whose presence set limits to Anglo-American friction in all the controversies of international life.

Anxiety about the future of Spain and of Spain's former colonies in the Western Hemisphere was thus a tense and urgent issue of world politics. France, representing the Holy Alliance, put down a liberal insurrection in Spain in 1823, as Austria had done in Piedmont and Naples two years before. Britain was dubious about both the wisdom and the feasibility of such actions by the Holy Alliance, and increasingly suspicious that the alliance was no more than a device to permit Russia to lead a coalition capable of dominating Europe. After the interventions in Spain and Italy, the British were acutely concerned about the possibility that the alliance might actually undertake to restore Spain's former colonies in the New World to the Bourbon monarch. While Austria, Prussia, and Russia were not likely to commit their arms to such a venture, France might well do so, not only to strike a blow for the principle of legitimacy, but to take a step toward Napoleonic grandeur.

> Success would have given France a new foothold in America and allowed her to break through the barrier cutting her off from overseas territories, thus jeopardizing Britain's recently created maritime monopoly. A storm of indignation arose in Britain—characteristically, without regard to party. Then, with its sure instinct, private initiative—the mainspring of Britain's prestige since the freebooters' days—sided with the Spanish insurgents, thus espousing the cause of freedom while at the same time guarding its own interests. The Government followed public opinion. Canning, though a Conservative, emphatically dissociated himself from the Continental Restoration. While the European governments were fearfully suppressing every stirring of movement, a whole continent on the far side of the ocean changed ownership under the protection of Britain's navy. Where was there another naval power to challenge her?
>
> Through the secession of Europe's oldest colonies, the isolation of the old Continent from the overseas territories was carried an enormous step forward, a belated but logical effect of the Napoleonic Wars. And Britain retaliated, as it were, against Spain and France for the role they had played in the revolt of her own American colonies.

This event also demonstrated to the world at large what the Union's independence meant. For the developments in Latin America no longer brought benefit to England alone, but also—and with more important consequences—to her daughter country. The United States proclaimed the Monroe Doctrine. By doing so she ranged herself for the moment at Britain's side; but with her gigantic claim, which might someday clash with Britain's interests, the United States also reached out for a preferential position on both American continents—or, to put it more precisely, she was making a bid for insularity within this broadest of all frameworks.

We know how the character of the English people and the essence of their power grew from their insular background, and how the insular position was consolidated in Scotland and Ireland by great, even terrible, exertions. The Union, too, had striven for an insular position since its inception. The existence of neighbors of equal status on land would have compelled it to build up its military establishment and evolve into a power on Continental lines. In other words, the United States would have been robbed of her birthright, her Anglo-Saxon insular status. Her task therefore was to forestall this danger through expansion on a huge scale.

It was a paradoxical phenomenon: a people proud of their liberty and contemptuous of war as the tragic privilege of the old monarchies and oligarchies nevertheless developed in their foreign policy the same forcefulness that marked their economy and their way of life. In the New World, the expansive powers of civilization, freed from tradition and borne up by faith, surpassed all the experience of the Old World as thoroughly as those German long-range guns of 1918 exceeded all the earlier performances of artillery by hurling their shells into the rarefied layers of the atmosphere. The Peace of Paris in 1762 had doubled the territory of the Thirteen States; the Louisiana Purchase of 1803 redoubled it; and in the meantime the Union had been further augmented by the purchase of Florida. True, the attempt to seize Canada had failed; but then Britain was not an aggressive military power on the Continent. Could France, the old dominant military power on the Continent, which had been driven from North America in 1762 and 1803, now be allowed to establish herself in South America in the place of a moribund Spain? Was it to be tolerated into the bargain that Russia, the friend of France under the Restoration, should at the same time expand from Alaska to a point south of Vancouver? So the Union proclaimed the imperious principle that no European power might extend its sway into either of the Americas. In spite of the geographical and cultural disparities within this vast area, the United States henceforth considered it, in the last analysis, a single island in which the Union intended to secure for itself the privileges of insular existence, tolerating no rival of equal status. Some people in Europe were heard to say that America would see the emergence of a balance of power system on the European model; in reality the Latin-American states were overshadowed from the moment of their birth by their great northern neighbor. To establish a balance with her would have been possible only through the aid of powers outside America, an unthinkable development as long as the United States was able to implement the Monroe Doctrine.

By that doctrine the American continent became a closed preserve. As civilization progresses, the freedom of a system of states can be maintained only in an open area such as Europe was; otherwise, this freedom succumbs to a hegemony.

Still, we must bear in mind that the two Anglo-Saxon powers at that time had parallel interests in regard to French and Russian ambitions in America, and that the benefits of their Pan-American co-operation outweighed their lingering differences over Canada. Certainly, Canada's southern border was vulnerable; but the long straggling coasts of the continent would prove equally sensitive unless they were protected by a good relationship between the Union and Britain, with her command of the sea. For the first time, then, there emerged the outline of a solidarity between the two kindred insular nations against the Continentals such as had once bridged Anglo-Dutch antagonisms. The expansion of each was in itself great enough; now, in addition, the first signs of coalescence between the two became discernible.[19]

In August 1823 George Canning, Castlereagh's successor as British foreign minister, proposed that the United States and Great Britain jointly make a public announcement to the effect that they viewed the recovery of its former provinces by Spain as hopeless; that recognition of their independence was simply a question of time and circumstances; and that they did not aspire to possess "any portion of them," but could not see "any portion of them transferred to any other power with indifference." Richard Rush, the American minister of the day in London, would have accepted the proposal on the spot if Britain had agreed

19. Dehio, *Precarious Balance,* 191–94.

to immediate recognition of the revolutionary republics of South America.[20]

Canning was not ready for that step. It was not, he thought, the moment for Britain so grievously to offend its troubled Spanish ally. Rush sent a report of Canning's offer to Washington. In October 1823, before Canning received Monroe's answer, he took the precaution of warning France privately that England would recognize the independence of the former Spanish colonies if any attempt were made to restrict British trade with them, or if any foreign power interfered in the contest between the former colonies and Spain. Furthermore, he added, Britain would not enter into any joint deliberation with the European powers on the question unless the United States were invited to participate. This is what Canning meant by his famous quip, quoted earlier, that he called in the New World to redress the balance of the Old.

When Canning's proposal reached Washington, a significant discussion took place. Monroe consulted Jefferson and Madison as well as John Quincy Adams, his secretary of state. The two former Presidents advised Monroe to accept Canning's offer. Adams disagreed. He urged the President to reject the principle of joint action. We should not appear as a "cock-boat in the wake of the British man-of-war," but act on our own even when we were moving in parallel with the British. It remained important—for Europe as well as for the United States—to keep the European and American systems as separate and distinct as possible. Moreover, a blanket pledge might be inconvenient for us at some later time, in Cuba, for example.[21]

Monroe decided to state the American policy in his next annual message to Congress, scheduled for December 1823. In that document he would also allude to the dispute with Russia which raised the same issue in another form. The Russians had been extending their activities in North America since 1799, pausing only for the worst period of the Napoleonic Wars and reaching the area of San Francisco. In 1821 the Czar issued a ukase purporting to exclude all foreigners from fishing or trading within one hundred miles of the coast north of 51° north latitude, the approximate latitude, that is, of modern Vancouver. Brit-

20. Dexter Perkins, *A History of the Monroe Doctrine* (originally titled *Hands Off: A History of the Monroe Doctrine* [1941]; rev. ed, Boston: Little, Brown, 1963), 38; and Samuel Flagg Bemis, *The Latin American Policy of the United States: An Historical Interpretation* (1943; reprint ed. New York: W. W. Norton, 1967), 56–57.

21. John Quincy Adams, *Memoirs of John Quincy Adams;* quoted in Perkins, *History of the Monroe Doctrine,* 43.

ain and the United States protested. Adams was eager to contest Russian sovereignty not only along the coast but in Alaska as well. Monroe would not go so far. The Russian government proposed that the controversy be settled by negotiation and agreement. Both Britain and the United States agreed separately with Russia that the southern border of Alaska should be 54°40′ north latitude.

At this date it is difficult to distinguish fact from myth about the Monroe Doctrine. Monroe's words have been interpreted and applied many times for many purposes. Formally, the doctrine has evolved into a pan-American system of cooperation, rather than a principle on the basis of which the United States may act unilaterally in the exercise of certain aspects of its sovereignty. The presence of the Castro regime in Cuba poses a challenge to nearly every version of the Monroe Doctrine and its successor, the Rio Treaty of 1947, now supervised by the Organization of American States. That challenge, of course, has been sidestepped. The former Soviet Union was not nineteenth-century Spain.

For present purposes, one should begin with what Monroe said and the context within which the doctrine was announced, leaving for a later point the question of its role, if any, in American foreign policy today. Confronting the possibility that France and perhaps other members of the Holy Alliance might invade the former Spanish colonies of the Western Hemisphere in order to restore Spanish rule, Britain gave France a discreet but entirely credible and effective private ultimatum. This ended the risk for the moment, although it was to recur in another form when France sent troops to Mexico during the American Civil War. Britain and the United States were equally concerned about the Russian policy of expansion south from Alaska.

Monroe's annual message to Congress contained two widely separated passages dealing with these problems, but their substance overlaps. On the controversy with Russia, Monroe announced that Britain and the United States had accepted Russia's invitation to settle the controversy "by amicable negotiation," and announced "that the occasion has been judged proper for asserting as a principle in which the rights and interests of the United States are involved, that the American continents, by the free and independent condition which they have assumed and maintain, are henceforth not to be considered as subjects for future colonization by any European powers." Did "future colonization" here mean only the acquisition of uninhabited territory or Indian territory by original occupation or settlement, or did it include any acquisition of a colony—by conquest, by purchase, or by transfer in another form, for example, the kind of transfer represented by Napoleon's acquisition of Louisiana from Spain? It has been plausibly argued that in Monroe's time the statement about future colonization was understood to have only the first meaning, and did not assert an American security interest in the possible establishment of all possible future European colonies in the Western Hemisphere.[22]

The second and principal declaration in the President's message dealt directly with the threat that France and Spain, with the backing of the Holy Alliance, might use force to undo the revolutions in Latin America and return Spain's former colonies to Spanish or perhaps French dominion. The United States, he said, has never taken part

> in the wars of the European powers in matters relating to them-
> selves, ... nor does it comport with our policy to do so. It is only
> when our rights are invaded or seriously menaced that we resent
> injuries or make preparation for our defense. With the movements
> in this hemisphere, we are, of necessity, more immediately con-
> nected, and by causes which must be obvious to all enlightened and
> impartial observers. The political system of the allied powers is
> essentially different in this respect from that of America.... We
> owe it, therefore, to candor and to the amicable relations existing
> between the United States and those powers, to declare that we
> should consider any attempt on their part to extend their system
> to any portion of this hemisphere as dangerous to our peace and
> safety.[23]

The United States would not interfere with the existing colonies of European powers in the Western Hemisphere, the President continued, but it would regard any interposition by a European power in the affairs of the former Spanish colonies, which had established their independence and had been recognized by the United States, "as the manifestation of an unfriendly disposition towards the United States." He pledged that the United States would not interfere in the internal affairs of any European power, and could not witness any such intervention in the Western Hemisphere by a European power "in any form, with indifference."[24]

Following Britain's warning to France a few months earlier, President Monroe's statement effectively ended the danger of armed intervention by the Holy Alliance in Latin American affairs, and indeed

22. James Monroe, Message of 2 December 1823; quoted in John Bassett Moore, "The Monroe Doctrine," *Political Science Quarterly* 11 (March 1896): 1–2.
23. Ibid., 2.
24. Ibid., 3.

helped to contribute to its demise as a powerful force in world affairs. The conservative rulers of Russia, Austria, and Prussia, together with the weak but ambitious Bourbon regime in France, suddenly confronted the vision of an alliance between Great Britain and the United States, representing liberalism, parliamentary government, the new young social classes of the Industrial Revolution, a free press, and other ideas they regarded as anathema. Moreover, as they knew too well, that vision represented unmatchable sea power as well. They recoiled, and never recovered.

Many have seen in this sequence no more than the reiteration of the doctrine of Washington's Farewell Address, and the assertion of a supposed principle of "isolation" from the European and the world balance of power as the rightful governing principle of American foreign policy. Nothing could be further from reality. As Hans Morgenthau once said, "The isolationism of the Federalist period, as formulated in Washington's Farewell Address, saw in America's isolation from the conflicts of European powers, whose colonies surrounded the United States on three sides, a precondition for its survival as an independent nation. It sought to achieve this end by an active foreign policy, keeping the European powers away from the United States."[25] The foreign policy of the United States in the period between 1776 and 1830 was one not of passivity and abstention but of vigilant and even belligerent neutrality, except for the alliance with France, which the United States jettisoned at the first convenient opportunity. It was never conceived as a substitute for the balance of power as the key to American security; the policy simply was the most appropriate way to pursue that goal under the circumstances of the early republican period.

25. Hans J. Morgenthau, Foreword to *The Limits of American Isolation: The United States and the Crimean War,* by Alan Dowty (New York: New York University Press, 1971), vii.

7

The United States within the Concert of Europe, 1830–1865

Ease and prosperity have made us wish the whole world to be as happy and well to do as ourselves; and we have supposed that institutions and principles like our own were the simple prescription for making them so. And yet, when issues of our own interest arose, we have not been unselfish. We have shown ourselves kin to all the world, when it came to pushing an advantage. Our action against Spain in the Floridas, and against Mexico on the coasts of the Pacific; our attitude toward first the Spaniards, and then the French, with regard to the control of the Mississippi; the unpitying force with which we thrust the Indians to the wall wherever they stood in our way, have suited our professions of peacefulness and justice and liberality no better than the aggressions of other nations that were strong and not to be gainsaid. Even Mr. Jefferson, philanthropist and champion of peaceable and modest government though he was, exemplified this double temper of the people he ruled. "Peace is our passion," he had declared; but the passion abated when he saw the mouth of the Mississippi about to pass into the hands of France. Though he had loved France and hated England, he did not hesitate then what language to hold. "There is on the globe," he wrote to Mr. Livingston at Paris, "one single spot the possessor of which is our natural and habitual enemy. The day that France takes possession of New Orleans seals the union of two nations, who, in conjunction, can maintain exclusive possession of the sea. From that moment we must marry ourselves to the British fleet and nation." Our interests must march forward, altruists though we are; other nations must see to it that they stand off, and do not seek to stay us.—Woodrow Wilson

The international experience of the United States reviewed in Chapters 5 and 6 has been of decisive importance to the American people in two

The epigraph for this chapter is taken from Woodrow Wilson, "Democracy and Efficiency," *Atlantic Monthly,* March 1901, pp. 289, 293–94.

perspectives: it launched the United States as a state among the states with a policy, a style, and a diplomatic profile of its own; and it supplied the raw materials out of which the modern myth of American isolationism was built. The nature and history of the American culture made it all too easy for Americans to imagine that the great American continental republic was created by a process of immaculate conception, and that their Founding Fathers had commanded them forever to avoid entangling alliances, to abstain from participating in foreign politics, and to pursue a virtuous rural life at home on family farms and in small agricultural towns.

The American culture, deeply affected by the tradition of Low Church Protestantism, tends to endow the Founding Fathers with the authority of the Biblical prophets. Just as some interpreters of the American Constitution forget what they take for granted in dealing with every other branch of law—that "the original intent" of those who drafted a law is only one among many factors which govern its growth—some who study and practice American foreign policy seem to imagine that the positions developed by the United States during its first forty years under the Constitution of 1787 were not simply a wise and prudent response to the dangers the nation faced at a particular time and within a particular configuration of world power, but a rigid blueprint to which their successors must forever be faithful, or suffer damnation.

The American language and its rhetoric made this curious apotheosis of Washington's Farewell Address and the Monroe Doctrine nearly inevitable. For all its austere precision, the Farewell Address touches the chords of America's faith in its special destiny, while Monroe's message of 1823 is rich with the passion of republican self-righteousness.

The Monroe Doctrine was designed to deal with two tangible problems: Russian expansion southwards from Alaska along the Pacific Coast, and the threat of a military effort, largely by France and Spain, to return the new republics of Latin America to colonial status. Monroe's message was written and then expounded, however, in a vocabulary of ideological universals: the United States would always refrain from participating in the affairs of monarchical Europe, and the European states should similarly refrain from participating in the republican political "system" of the Western Hemisphere, whether by the acquisition of territory or through influence otherwise achieved. We told each other and the world endlessly that we were a chosen people who abominated imperialism, militarism, the balance of power, and war. In our international dealings, we proclaimed, we would pursue a foreign policy dominated by our humanitarian and pacific traditions;

practice trade, not politics; support democracy, liberty, and the rule of law; and be a scourge to oligarchy, despotism, and dictatorship. Furthermore, we would accomplish these noble aims without interfering in the domestic affairs of any nation. It is no wonder that even some Americans were confused by the language of their leaders and other representatives who tried to explain what in fact we did.

II

The Holy Alliance never recovered its élan after the bubble of its plan for Latin America was punctured in 1823. The allies lost confidence in their capacity to stamp out the democratic and nationalist movements stimulated by the French Revolution, the Industrial Revolution, and the war itself. Alexander I was frightened to discover that his great armies, returning from their triumphs in Western Europe, had been infected with revolutionary ideas. He himself disappeared into the snow, and Russia turned away from the temptation to seize large parts of Western Europe as it had partitioned Poland in the previous century. Instead, it devoted itself to repressing Jacobin impulses at home, and sent its armies on far less dangerous expeditions against the Turks and the Central Asian tribes and principalities. His troops would not contract dangerous political diseases there.

It was therefore a major policy concern of America after the Monroe Doctrine was announced to consolidate its relationship with Great Britain in order to minimize any risk that Britain might make common cause with the Holy Allies on Latin American or other questions of special concern to the United States. In transmitting the Monroe Doctrine and related documents to the American minister in London, Adams wrote, "The President is anxiously desirous that the opening to a cordial harmony, in the policy of the United States and of Britain offered on this occasion, may be extended to the general relations between the two Countries." About all aspects of the present emergency, he added, "you will, in the most conciliatory and friendly manner, lead the mind of Mr. Canning to the necessary inference, that to the end of concert and co-operation, the *intentions* of Great Britain, under all the contingent aspects, which the subject may assume, should be as unequivocally known to us."[1]

---

1. Adams' instructions to Richard Rush are taken from the Manuscript Diary of John Quincy Adams, printed for the first time at pp. 577–79 of Samuel Flagg Bemis, *John Quincy Adams and the Foundations of American Foreign Policy.*

The problem facing Adams was to be the principal item on the State Department's agenda throughout the nineteenth century. From every point of view—economic, human, territorial, and political—Britain was America's most important diplomatic partner. That was not the case, obviously, for Great Britain, the greatest power of the time, deeply engaged in diplomatic encounters all over the world. The management of Anglo-American relations was not a negligible matter for the British; for the United States, however, it was the key to American grand strategy.

In the forum of world politics, the United States was surely of the British camp, but not in it. The United States wanted the benefit of proximity to British power without the disadvantages of being a full-blown ally. Adams had persuaded Monroe that the Monroe Doctrine should not be announced as the joint policy of the United States and Great Britain. Instead, the United States and Great Britain would act in parallel to deter European military intervention in Spain's former Latin American colonies, while the United States kept a free hand for dealing independently with other problems as they emerged. Of these, the most important by far was ensuring that Great Britain continue to oppose the pretensions of the Holy Alliance. It was unlikely that Britain would reverse that policy, but it was prudent to take precautions.

The security interests of Britain and the United States were thus congruent but not identical. On the main issue, they were agreed: that is, both recoiled at the possibility a new Napoleon might gain control of the immense potential of Eurasia. Temperamentally, instinctively, and as a matter of political principle, both aspired to a state system governed by the balance of power, not by hegemony. But the United States also knew that if Europe were too perfectly balanced, too peaceful, Britain would have more time and energy to devote to American affairs. By the same token, Britain was more and more concerned about what might happen in time if a highly independent United States became too strong. The French were even more emphatic on the subject. The British and the French could hardly approve the transformation of the Western Hemisphere into an exclusively American sphere of influence. And if Britain and France should become too active in trying to contain American expansion in Mexico, the Caribbean, or Central America, the United States wanted to be free to improve its relations with Russia or other states which might rival Great Britain in the future.

In short, both Britain and the United States were conscious of the fact that they should not allow themselves to drift too far apart. The past had been traumatic and the future was uncertain. The British wanted as much influence as possible in American policy; the United States preferred to keep a certain distance. For both countries, the new relationship exerted a pervasive influence. How stubborn could they be in negotiations with each other, especially where emotionally sensitive issues were involved? If war was out of the question for many reasons, was compromise the inevitable outcome in all cases of conflict?

These considerations constitute the background of America's diplomatic history between the end of John Quincy Adams' Presidency and the end of Woodrow Wilson's. In this period, of course, both the absolute and the relative power of the United States in the theatre of world politics changed immeasurably; so did the cast of principal participants. The daily diplomatic business of the United States was not confined by any means to bilateral negotiations with Great Britain. But concerns about Britain's response to American actions, and about their effect on the larger matrix of great power relations, entered into every American analysis and calculation involving problems beyond the level of routine. The bilateral diplomacy between Britain and the United States was extraordinarily active, however. The two nations had to negotiate endlessly about boundary problems in the Northwest, with an eye always cocked for the presence of Russia; about conflict in the Caribbean and in Central America; and at various times about the isthmian canal project and American intentions towards Mexico, Cuba, and California; about fisheries, the Far East, and problems arising out of the Civil War; about the development of international law; and about many other matters.

III

Before 1917, the formidable energies of the American people were concentrated largely on expanding to the west and building the nation within boundaries which steadily became more ample. That task was the constant, almost the obsessive, preoccupation of American policy. The process of expansion generated international concern, international resistance, and some international conflict which helped to define the feasible limits of American growth already suggested by America's conception of its own destiny. What are now universally taken to be the "natural" boundaries of the continental United States were reached by 1867, with the purchase of Alaska from Russia, although public support for the acquisition of Alaska was decidedly lukewarm, as compared, say, with the support for the acquisition of California. During this period, the United States also perceived a number of external threats to its security which did not arise as a direct response to American expansion. Of these, the most serious occurred during and immediately after the American Civil War.

There were varying degrees of enthusiasm in domestic popular support for the westward expansion of the United States. After the War of 1812 the notion of conquering Canada lost much of its appeal; the sense of threat from Canada had disappeared. The idea of acquiring Cuba, Texas, and the smaller Caribbean islands ran into resistance on two grounds. Many Americans, starting with Jefferson, saw the acquisition of Cuba as inevitable and strategically important because of its location commanding the maritime approaches to the United States from the south. But when the issue arose before the Civil War, the normal American opposition to the idea of offshore and therefore "foreign" military adventure was intensified by the domestic politics of the slavery question. To annex Cuba (or Texas, for that matter) would add slave states to the Union, affecting the balance of American politics. There was also a profound if intangible resistance in popular opinion to acquiring territory inhabited by people of an alien culture, people who might not readily submit to the chemistry of the American melting pot. For a long time, the Americans considered themselves an Anglo-American people, or at least a people whose ancestors were Northern Europeans; perhaps they still do.

During the period before the Civil War, the United States entered into a series of treaties and other agreements with Great Britain, dealing with the settlement of disputed boundaries and related questions affecting Canada, the West Indies, Central America, and Texas. In many instances, the negotiations were affected by the course of other disputes involving one or another of the nations. Several dealt with issues of major importance—the project of an isthmian canal, for example, the possible annexation of Cuba by the United States, and the Mexican War.

The dispute over Texas and Mexico demonstrates better than any other the patterns of connection between the domestic and international dimensions of American diplomacy.

Shortly after Mexico became independent in 1821, it invited Americans to settle in its nearly empty northern territories, including Texas. The invitation was accepted on a large scale, and soon the Anglo-Americans constituted the largest and most active part of the population of Texas. When Mexico tried—too late—to reverse its policy of open immigration and land settlement, the Anglo-American population became turbulent, and a revolution broke out in 1835, leading to the proclamation of the Republic of Texas, "the Lone Star Republic." France recognized the new state in 1839; Britain, Holland, and Belgium did so in 1840.

Texas requested annexation by the United States immediately after its revolution, but the United States cautiously rejected its appeal and abstained from recognition, having just made a treaty of amity and commerce with Mexico. President Van Buren was against adding another slave state to the nation, or indeed the three, four, or even five slave states that might be carved out of Texas. Britain and France strongly supported the new republic, and offered their good offices to persuade Mexico to recognize Texas. Britain and France, having witnessed the astonishing growth of the United States in the west, began to take increasingly active measures to stop American expansion to the south.

As an independent country, Texas presented a puzzling challenge to the United States. The southern states were eager to acquire the territory not only on patriotic principles of expansion, but because Texas might add to the numbers of slave states, thus helping to keep the precarious Congressional balance between North and South, which was threatened by the steady expansion of the nation to the northwest. On the other hand, a second American republic, stretching from the Sabine River to the Pacific, would gravely weaken the United States. It would be a barrier to further expansion, and if it remained a slave area, it might lead some southern states to secede and join it. And if it became a free-soil republic, it would be a natural refuge for runaway slaves, far more accessible than Canada.

After a few years of discussion, the question of annexing Texas changed in character. The growing antislavery sector of opinion remained adamantly opposed to annexation, and the South and its sympathizers as adamantly in favor. Meanwhile, those who viewed the problem from the national point of view became more and more deeply concerned. If the situation were allowed to drag on for a few more years, the unitary continental republic of the American dream would become an impossibility, and the United States could well break up into a number of regional republics. Would America then become like Europe—quarrelsome, unstable, militarized, and prone to war?

President Tyler reopened the Texas question in 1843, and negotiations for annexation proceeded rapidly. At the same time, the British and French pressed Mexico to recognize Texas, on condition that Texas abolish slavery and agree never to be annexed to the United States. The inevitable furor over the affair was heightened by the fact that

1844 was an election year. The secretary of state, Abel P. Upshur, was killed by the accidental explosion of a gun on a naval vessel while he was visiting it. His successor, John C. Calhoun, the strongest voice of the South, defiantly made the protection of slavery the key argument for annexation. He twisted the British lion's tail unmercifully for its abolitionist policies and its "meddling" in the relationship between Mexico and the United States.

The treaty of annexation signed by the United States and Mexico failed in the Senate a month after the redoubtable James K. Polk was nominated by the Democrats. Polk, a dark horse who turned out to be a remarkably clearheaded and disciplined President, strongly supported the annexation both of Texas and of Oregon, while his Whig opponent, Henry Clay, was visibly equivocal. The argument over the two proposed annexations were a major issue in the electoral campaign. The election was close, but Polk and the Democrats prevailed. Texas was admitted to the Union as a single state three days before Tyler left office. Because of the slavery question, the annexation was accomplished not by treaty but by a joint resolution of Congress, which requires only a simple majority. Texas was offered a treaty of peace with Mexico, achieved by British and French diplomacy, at the same time. The Mexican treaty would have foreclosed the option of annexation "to any third power." The Texans overwhelmingly chose annexation and entered the Union as a single state.

The annexation of Texas and its admission to the Union was treated by Mexico as a hostile act, perhaps an act of war. Mexico broke diplomatic relations with the United States, and made threatening statements, but did not declare war or engage in overt hostilities. Polk, eager to make the Rio Grande the southern boundary of the United States, and to buy the Mexican provinces between Texas and the Pacific, immediately sent a special representative to reach a settlement of all outstanding issues between the two countries. The claim that the Rio Grande was the proper boundary of Texas went back to the ambiguities of the Louisiana Purchase. It had been settled contrary to the American claim in the Transcontinental Treaty of 1819, which recognized the Sabine River as the boundary, and in compensation ceded to the United States all Spanish claims to the vast Oregon Territory, then still jointly occupied by Great Britain and the United States. Polk offered Mexico fair exchange for the Rio Grande boundary in a waiver of Mexico's obligation to pay certain American claims, and what was then handsome payment for the rest of Mexico's northwestern inheritance from Spain.

After initially indicating that Polk's envoy would be received, the

Mexican government refused to see him. Apparently the Mexicans expected assistance from the British, who had opposed the annexation of Texas to the United States, frowned on American aspirations towards Cuba, and were engaged in a long and difficult negotiation with the United States about how to partition the Oregon Territory between the United States and Canada. The Mexican estimate turned out to be disastrously in error. The British had no intention of intervening. Polk prudently held his hand in Mexico until he had reached agreement with the British on the Oregon boundary, compromising the American position drastically in order to settle the Oregon question, at least for the time being.

With Mexico's refusal to negotiate, war was almost inevitable. Polk authorized General Taylor to advance to the Rio Grande from Corpus Christi on the eastern edge of the territory in dispute. His orders were to treat any considerable Mexican crossing of the river as "as an invasion of the United States and the commencement of hostilities." Polk had already taken naval and other precautions in California, because the British and French governments had been urged by their representatives both in Mexico and California to seize California before the United States could. The American consul in Monterey, for example, was instructed to watch developments closely with a view to preventing California from falling into the hands of a European power in case there should be a revolution there on the Texan model. He was told to assure Californians that if they wanted independence they would of course be welcomed into the United States. Colonel Fremont, who was engaged with a company of troops in a topographical reconnaissance of California, received orders presumably of similar import. Meanwhile, Polk gave the Monroe Doctrine a new gloss in his annual message of 2 December 1845. He announced that it was the "settled policy" of the United States that "no future European colony or dominion shall, with our consent, be planted or established on any part of the North American continent."[2]

The war broke out under circumstances still in dispute. Lincoln was not alone in opposing it, and in his memoirs General Grant said we had in effect forced Mexico to initiate war, and criticized America's actions severely as aggressive and immoral. "The Southern rebellion," he wrote, "was largely the outgrowth of the Mexican war. Nations, like

2. John Bassett Moore, "The Monroe Doctrine", *Political Science Quarterly* 11 (March 1896): 17.

individuals, are punished for their transgressions. We got our punishment in the most sanguinary and expensive war of modern times."[3]

Perhaps war could have been prevented if Polk had not sent Taylor to the Rio Grande. But the United States was not responsible for the mass immigration of Americans into Mexico; that movement was at the invitation of the Mexican Government. Nor did the United States encourage the Texan revolution against Mexico, save by not enforcing its own neutrality legislation effectively. The Lone Star Republic functioned for nine years, and even Mexico was ready to recognize its independence as a fait accompli before the United States decided to admit Texas into the Union.

Moreover, President Polk settled the war as quickly as he could on exactly the terms he had laid out in his instruction to Slidell, the envoy the Mexicans had refused to receive: recognition of the Rio Grande as the boundary of Texas, and the purchase of the rest of the Mexican territory in what is now New Mexico, Arizona, California, Nevada, Utah, and a corner of Wyoming and Colorado. Polk faced down the rising tide of opinion which demanded the annexation of all of Mexico; any such step, he knew, would change the character of the nation, and might well precipitate its dissolution by enlarging the slave-state fraction in Congress beyond endurance.

What is undeniable, however, is that the Mexican War and the huge accession of territory which resulted from it made the political tensions of the slavery question within the United States decidedly more acute, and therefore played an important role in the coming of the Civil War. Perhaps the Civil War was truly an "irrepressible conflict" which could not have been avoided in any event. Be that as it may, it would be difficult to find an American who regrets the outcome of the Mexican War, and would undo it.

The complex diplomacy of the dispute over Texas and Mexico illuminates the character and relative strength of the international forces at work: the power of the American drive for what is now the continental United States, on the one hand, and, on the other, the increasing concern of France and Great Britain about the possible growth of the United States to excessive power. The United States dealt with Spain and then with Mexico altogether differently than it dealt with Great Britain. Still, its dealings with moribund Spain and weak Mexico were

3. Ulysses S. Grant, *Personal Memoirs of U. S. Grant,* ed. E. B. Long (1917; reprint ed., New York: Da Capo, 1982), 24.

restrained always by its estimates of what Great Britain would do if it were provoked too far. Britain and the United States shared common interests, but their differences were important too, and sometimes irritating. Naturally enough, neither side wished to test the other's final boundary of toleration. Thus the many Anglo-American conflicts of the nineteenth century were settled as Castelreagh, Wellington, and Gallatin settled the war of 1812, by subordinating the lesser considerations to the greater.

The French position in the Mexican dispute marked a new stage in the steady return of France to the center stage of world politics thirty years after Waterloo. But France under Louis Philippe and then Napoleon III, while steadily gaining in strength, wealth, and political importance, could no longer aspire to the role of Louis XIV and Napoleon. France had been reborn as a moderate-sized power, important to world politics only when it was allied to Great Britain, and then only when its foreign policy was well conceived and well managed.

IV

Great Britain, France, and, from time to time, other European countries as well continued to offer vigorous diplomatic but not military objection to American projects for expansion even after the decisive conclusion of the Mexican War and the settlement of the Oregon boundary dispute.

The acquisition of California and what is now Oregon and Washington by the United States and the California Gold Rush made the idea of a canal across the Isthmus of Panama highly topical. Great Britain had been trying for years to gain control of a possible route for such a canal. With its new dimensions, the United States now actively joined in the effort, but the exclusive control of such a canal was not then an objective of American policy. Insofar as the United States had a policy, it was to assure that any canal which might be built would be an international waterway, open to all on equal terms.

In 1846, during the Mexican War, the government of New Granada (now Colombia) approached the United States for help because it was concerned about the active British effort to obtain the Isthmus of Panama for itself. Britain had just declared a protectorate over the lands where the Mosquito Indians lived. Most of those lands were in Nicaragua, but some were in New Granada. The British and the French had refused to give New Granada assurances guaranteeing the neutrality of the Isthmus. Alarmed about British and French intentions, the New

Granadans turned to the United States for protection. The United States wished to settle an old controversy with New Granada about tariff discrimination against American goods imported in foreign ships, so it entered into negotiations. Assurances about neutrality were put into a draft treaty between Granada and the United States at the instance of the Granadans. The American minister to Granada, without instructions on the point, accepted the treaty subject to ratification. It provided not only an American guaranty, but a right of way, or transit, upon all ways of communication across the isthmus "that now exist or may hereafter be constructed." Although somewhat troubled by the guaranty provisions of the treaty, the Senate consented to ratification, and President Polk ratified the treaty in 1848. The guaranty feature, along with the Monroe Doctrine, became the legal justification for several important later assertions of American policy.

After the Mexican War, an intense diplomatic conflict between Britain and the United States developed over control of a possible canal through Nicaragua, then considered more practicable then the Panamanian route. Each country was trying to prevent the other from dominating the hypothetical canal. Britain and the United States had been in a state of active rivalry in the area for a long time, and Polk's representative had signed a treaty with Nicaragua which went further than the Granadan treaty. It gave the United States the exclusive right to build, fortify, and control a canal, or railroad, or both between the oceans, and established an American protectorate over Nicaragua, guaranteeing its "sovereignty, dominion, peace, and neutrality." This treaty came back to Washington as a Whig administration took over from Polk in 1849.

The diplomatic contest began to have military overtones. A British naval officer seized an island thought to control one of the entrances to the possible canal, causing a furor in the United States. The new American President, General Taylor, had three treaties on his desk waiting ratification—two with Nicaragua, and one with Honduras. To ratify them would be to invite a severe dispute with Britain, which neither Taylor nor Lord Russell, the new British prime minister, wanted. They therefore reached the compromise of the Clayton-Bulwer Treaty of 1850, which declared that neither signatory would obtain or maintain exclusive control over any ship canal through any part of Central America or occupy, fortify, or colonize Nicaragua, Costa Rica, the Mosquito Coast, or any part of Central America.

The Clayton-Bulwer Treaty was extremely unpopular in the United States, and it came under scrutiny again when the Panama Canal problem arose fifty years later. At the time, however, it faithfully mirrored the facts that in both countries the idea of international or more probably joint Anglo-American control of an isthmian interoceanic canal was strongly favored, and that in the Western Hemisphere the United States and Great Britain were nearly equal in influence and authority. It demonstrated also that the shadow of their relative power, however vaguely perceived, was an inevitable component of every bargain affecting their interests.[4]

The interplay of these factors became quite dramatic—even melodramatic—before, during, and after the Crimean War of 1854–56. Franklin Pierce, the Democratic President who succeeded Fillmore in 1853, was an enthusiastic expansionist, but did not compare to Polk in ability, insight, or specific gravity. The nation and its politics were dominated by what Allan Nevins has called the Ordeal of the Union. During the 1850s, the ordeal was rapidly becoming a lowering storm. The Democratic Party, completely split by the conflict, included a large and energetic group of "Young America" Democrats, fervent activists who advocated a program of aid to European republicans, territorial and political expansion, and support for guerrilla groups in Latin America. These men had been much affected by the European revolutions of 1848. They were ultranationalistic, exuberant, and unrestrained by considerations of prudence, diplomacy, or international law. To them, the older and more experienced leaders of their party were "old fogies," to put it mildly. Grandchildren of the War Hawks of 1812, they were harbingers of the spirit of the Confederacy. As Alan Dowty writes, "the contrast between American republicanism and Old World despotism was intentionally underlined, and assertions of moral superiority, combined with boastful arrogance on the future growth of American power, set European nerves on edge during much of this period."[5] Pierce wanted to purchase Cuba, Alaska, and the Sandwich Islands during his Presidency, force Britain to withdraw altogether as a participant in Central American affairs, and move the international law of neutrality decisively in the direction of the goals American diplomacy had sought to achieve for more than sixty years.

As the Crimean War approached, the United States did everything in its power to exploit its friendly relations with Russia in order to advance its diplomatic agenda with England and France. Louis Na-

4. Samuel Flagg Bemis, *The Latin American Policy of the United States: An Historical Interpretation* (1943; reprint ed., New York: W. W. Norton, 1967), 102–08.

5. Alan Dowty, *The Limits of American Isolation: The United States and the Crimean War* (New York; New York University Press, 1971), 43.

poleon, having been elected President after the uprising of 1848,made himself dictator and Emperor of France as Napoleon III in 1852. Ludwig Dehio remarks, "The French Revolution had given birth to a great Caesar; the revolution of 1848, a revolution that had broken down inwardly, brought forth a small Caesar."[6] Napoleon III, full of aspiration, moved quickly after his inauguration toward a career of semi-Napoleonic glory, which began successfully in the Crimea and in Italy, but ended in folly and disaster in Mexico. The Franco-Prussian War finally cost him his throne.

Czar Nicholas had decided that the moment had come to realize Russia's ancient dream of conquering Constantinople, and started a war with Turkey. Although Russian troops had put down a Hungarian rebellion for the Emperor of Austria just a few years before, the Holy Alliance demonstrated that it was indeed dead: Prussia and the Austro-Hungarian Empire remained neutral, and Spain, restrained by American threats to Cuba, did not send troops to Crimea. The Czar had thought that a Napoleon on the throne of France would assure him British support. He was mistaken. The prospect of Russia controlling the Bosporus and becoming active in the Mediterranean appalled the British. Napoleon III persuaded them to enter into an alliance with France—an *entente cordiale,* as it was called—to resist the Russian move and sustain the decaying Ottoman Empire. British and French troops, joined by some Sardinians, proceeded to Crimea. The astute Cavour, the maker of modern Italy, was then prime minister of the Kingdom of Sardinia. He calculated correctly that by visibly joining the Anglo-French alliance in resisting Russian expansion, he would gain important support for the ultimate unification of Italy.

The Crimean War was fought for limited goals and confined to the Black Sea, the Baltic, and the conquest of a Russian port on the Pacific. The Russian government sued for peace shortly after the death of Czar Nicholas and the fall of Sebastopol. Peace was made in Paris early in 1856 by a congress representing six powers. The agreement of peace guaranteed the integrity of the Ottoman Empire, the neutrality of the Black Sea, and freedom of navigation on the Danube, and it made Moldavia and Wallachia autonomous. The Congress of Paris also proposed an important treaty on maritime law. It abolished privateering; declared that hostile merchandise, except for contraband of war, is neutral if carried under a neutral flag, and that neutral merchandise

6. Ludwig Dehio, *The Precarious Balance: Four Centuries of the European Power Struggle,* trans. Charles Fullman (1948; New York: Vintage, 1965), 203.

remains neutral if carried under a hostile flag; and acknowledged the principle that a blockade is not valid unless it is effective: that is, that "paper blockades" are nugatory. The United States welcomed the latter three pronouncements of the Congress of Paris, but as a nation which had depended heavily on privateers, it vehemently objected to the first, although in time it came to accept the idea. The most important consequence of the Crimean War, however, was in a different sphere. The Russians were kept out of the Mediterranean for a century.[7]

The American government had sought to take advantage of Anglo-French involvement in the Eastern crisis even before the Crimean War began. Our ambassadors advised Washington that the inflamed condition of European politics made it certain that Britain would not support Spain in the event of a war with the United States over Cuba, and that France, too, would be unlikely to intervene. American representatives were instructed to press Britain hard for a favorable resolution of the long list of sticky and contentious Central American problems. And our minister in Spain, Pierre Soulé, a singularly foolish and bombastic member of the Young America group, never stopped hectoring the Spanish about our interest in Cuba, our desire to purchase Cuba, and the dire consequences which would follow any attempt by Britain or France or both together to interfere in Cuban affairs to our disadvantage.[8]

Early in 1854, the British foreign minister, Lord Clarendon, made a statement in Parliament which thoroughly aroused the American government and American public opinion. "The happy and good understanding between France and England," he said, "have been extended beyond Eastern policy to the policy affecting all parts of the world, and I am heartily rejoiced to say that there is no portion of the two hemispheres with regard to which the policy of the two countries, however heretofore antagonistic, is not now in entire harmony."[9]

In response, the American minister in London, James Buchanan, reported that he had "playfully" observed to Lord Clarendon "that as Great Britain and France did not seem to be content to confine themselves to the regulations of the balance of power in Europe, but were willing to extend their care to our hemisphere, it might be necessary for us to ally ourselves with Russia for the purpose of counteracting

---

7. Andrew D. Lambert, *The Crimean War: British Grand Strategy, 1853–56* (Manchester and New York: Manchester University Press, 1990), 334.

8. Dowty, *Limits of American Isolation,* 51–52.

9. United Kingdom, *Hansard's Parliamentary Debates* (Lords), 3d ser., vol. 130 (1854), 43.

their designs."[10] The same thought was expressed less playfully in many Russian and American diplomatic conversations and in American political speeches.

The Russians, of course, had long considered good relations with the United States desirable as a counterweight to British influence, and had favored the development of a strong America which might help Russia in the event of war with England. Czar Alexander I had moved to mediate the war of 1812 between Great Britain and the United States even as Napoleon was invading Russia. In 1853 and 1854, what many then called the "traditional friendship" between Russia and America was much on display, and produced a few practical results. For example, we enforced our neutrality laws vigorously against the British, but winked at a number of Russian violations.

As war became imminent, the United States realized that it had another great diplomatic advantage—the threat that the Russians might employ some of the enormous American merchant marine of the time as privateers. Ten days before war broke out, therefore, the British and the French adopted a radically new policy toward neutral shipping, accepting the positions for which the United States and the other neutrals had contended in vain during the wars of the French Revolution and the Napoleonic period. The British concession on neutral commerce, Dowty concludes, prevented "an eruption" over the potentially dangerous issue of privateering.[11]

With the coming of war, Pierce instructed his diplomats to negotiate for the purchase of Cuba, the annexation of the Sandwich Islands, and the purchase of Santo Domingo, and also inquired of the Russians about the possibility of buying Alaska. Other American diplomats were involved in even more spectacular plans. The United States consul in London, George Sanders, was frequently host to a group of European exiles of the republican persuasion, who discussed a revival of revolutionary activity in Europe in the spirit of 1848. Kossuth, Garibaldi, Herzen, and other well-known figures were part of his circle. Such activities were extraordinarily indiscreet, of course, even by American diplomatic standards, which have often been outspoken and unconventional. They suffered a natural decline, however, when the European radicals confronted the implications of the American slavery question.

In the event, none of Pierce's grandiose schemes for expansion

10. Dowty, *Limits of American Isolation,* 58
11. Ibid., 62.

materialized. His attempt to provoke a crisis with Spain over Cuba came to nothing. The occasion for the crisis, the arrest of an American ship in Havana on customs charges, was defused by a Spanish retreat, strongly advised by Britain and France. And Pierce's enthusiasm for seizing Cuba was dissipated by the political reality of the slavery issue; under the circumstances, annexing Cuba would have been far more controversial than annexing Texas had been a few years before. Southern and Young American opinion was still favorable, but the rest of the country was even more vehemently opposed. Pierce therefore stopped at the water's edge so far as a quasi-military move was concerned, and Anglo-French diplomatic support for Spain was enough to postpone the issue for another generation. The Spanish refused to sell, and we did nothing—or at least nothing effective.

So far as the complex Central American negotiations are concerned, Dowty argues that what he calls "the tactical clumsiness" of American diplomacy was more responsible "than any other single factor" for the fact that Britain did not withdraw from active participation in Central American affairs until the next American administration.[12] The Russo-American rapprochement accomplished during the Crimean War played a part in the reorientation of British policy. But Pierce did not use his opportunities well. In all probability, however, not even a President of the first order could have acquired more territory in the 1850s. The United States was reaching the limits of expansion imposed by the approaching crisis over slavery, and, beyond that, by the built-in tensions of the state system itself.

V

The diplomacy of the Civil War was the diplomacy of Texas and the Mexican War writ large. It was dominated by the supreme and final effort of Great Britain and France to prevent the United States from becoming a superpower by encouraging its partition. Britain and France had failed to keep Texas from joining the Union, and Britain was unable to make a serious bid for California. But the Civil War was an irresistible temptation to try again. If Britain and France never quite dared to embrace that temptation with open gusto, they flirted with it in decidedly nonplatonic ways until Gettysburg and Vicksburg made it clear that the North would win, and the Emancipation Proclamation trans-

12. Ibid., 227–28.

formed the European perception of the moral and political significance
of the Civil War.

Russia was the only important country which supported the United
States in the early stages of the Civil War. It actively displayed its
opposition to the Franco-British effort, even sending a fleet to visit
American ports in 1862.

In October 1861, a few months after the war began, Great Britain,
France, and Spain agreed to send military forces to Mexico to protect
their citizens and enforce their claims for damage to property caused
by the breakdown of order in that country. They carefully disavowed
any territorial or political ambitions. Civil disturbances and indeed revolutionary divisions had developed in Mexico some years before, and
had persisted. The Liberals under Juarez had established a government
in Vera Cruz, contesting the position of the Clerical Party, which held
the seat of the recognized government in Mexico City. Foreigners were
suffering considerable injury from the disturbances. In the nineteenth-
century environment of diplomacy and international law, foreign intervention was nearly inevitable under the circumstances.

In the dying days of his administration, Buchanan had proposed
American military and political action to make Juarez President of
Mexico and thus forestall intervention by the European powers, but
Congress would not consider his program until the crucial election of
1860 had taken place. In the meantime, the British, French, and Spanish
carefully invited the United States to join in their enterprise. Just as
carefully, Secretary of State Seward acknowledged the right of limited
foreign intervention to protect citizens and their property in danger
abroad, but declined to join their expedition.

Within a few months, the British and the Spanish realized that
Napoleon III had entered Mexico to establish a French colony or protectorate, and withdrew their troops. They were not disposed to challenge the Monroe Doctrine directly or indirectly. France remained in
Mexico with a considerable force which ultimately came under the
competent command of Marshal Bazaine. A Hapsburg prince was installed on the throne of Mexico as Emperor Maximilian. Maximilian's
regime received considerable help from the Confederacy. Although
Bazaine did well in the field, using the tactics France had developed in
Algeria, he did not succeed in destroying Juarez and his forces before
the American Civil War ended. Juarez and the remnants of his army
and government moved north to the American border, and Maximilian's regime postured happily in Mexico City.

While scattered pockets of Confederate resistance were still being mopped up in 1865, the United States government moved with stunning speed to bring Napoleon III's imperial experiment in Mexico to an abrupt end. General Grant wanted to use force immediately to install Juarez and chase Maximilian away, but Seward prevailed with a policy of firm diplomacy backed by the movement of 50,000 battle-hardened cavalrymen to the Mexican border, under the command of General Philip Sheridan. Seward wished to permit the mercurial Napoleon to save face, and to avoid even a small war with France. Sheridan grumbled, as his memoirs attest, about the "slow and poky methods" of the State Department, but Seward's policy worked.[13] French troops were withdrawn—28,000 in number, largely Foreign Legionnaires; Juarez came to power; and Maximilian was put against a wall and shot. Eliminating the French presence in Mexico was a matter of such high priority to the American government that it refused to delay Sheridan's departure for even a few days so that he could march with his Union troops in the great Victory Parade in Washington.

Shortly after Lincoln was inaugurated, while the startling Mexican melodrama was gestating in the mind of Napoleon III, the French had attempted to form a coalition with Great Britain and Russia to recognize the Confederacy. Russia rejected the French proposal, and informed the United States what was afoot. Britain was not then ready to recognize the Confederacy, but did pledge that it would act jointly with France on the question of recognition. Britain informed the United States about the Anglo-French agreement as early as 2 May 1861. Thereafter Seward refused to see the British and French ambassadors together when they came for joint discussions, and instructed his ministers in other capitals to follow the same practice.

The French were more active than the British on the issue of recognition, and later even hinted at the possible use of force in support of mediation. They knew that their Mexican adventure could succeed only if the Confederacy won the Civil War. For their part, Lincoln and Seward also knew that France could not act without Britain. Britain came close to the brink of recognition and to attempting mediation on several occasions. Each time the crucial decision seemed imminent, however, a Union victory changed the political climate in Great Britain, and the British government drew back.

Palmerston was prime minister at the time, Lord John Russell foreign minister, and Gladstone chancellor of the exchequer—a formidable

---

13. Philip Sheridan, *Personal Memoirs of P. H. Sheridan, General, United States Army* (New York: Charles L. Webster, 1888), 2: 217.

team by any standard. At seventy-seven Palmerston was a man of immense ability, charm, color, and experience. He was given to caustic remarks about America and Americans, but then, he made caustic remarks about most subjects and all foreigners. His approach to foreign policy is summed up in his famous observation that great powers do not have permanent friends; they have permanent interests. Gorbachev quoted it with relish in his Geneva press conference in 1985. About the Civil War, Palmerston's stated attitude was that "they who in quarrels interpose, will often get a bloody nose,"[14] and his influence on most occasions during the war was cautious. On the other hand, he shared the general attitude of the British governing classes toward American democracy, and thoroughly understood what most people thought was the British interest in a Southern victory. In July 1861, when the war was a few months old and going badly, August Belmont, a New York banker, sought to present the Union point of view to Palmerston. The prime minister commented, "We do not like slavery, but we want cotton, and we dislike very much your Morrill tariff."[15] Gladstone, the great moralist in British politics and the future leader of the Liberal Party, strongly favored the South as well, despite the incubus of slavery. For him, as for Palmerston and Russell, a promising opportunity to weaken the emerging American giant was in the end too important to be ignored, provided the risks were not too great.

At that stage in the evolution of Anglo-American relations, the British position was in fact more ambiguous than it seemed. Britain pursued the policy of doing what it could to weaken the United States, so long as it could do so without being drawn into war. The qualification highlights the essentially equivocal character of Britain's American policy. The first impulse of British foreign policy was the familiar rule of the balance of power "Never allow a potential enemy to become too strong." A good rule, to be sure, but was America really a potential enemy of Great Britain, despite the two Anglo-American wars and America's icy diplomacy during the Crimean War? In British eyes, America was a rude, brash, bumptious, and not very civilized country, conceited, self-important, often arrogant, and above all, tiresome. But the ties of kinship were strong and the sense of a shared civilization pervasive. Furthermore, the reasoning of Pitt, Castlereagh, and Can-

14. Quoted in James M. McPherson, *The Battle Cry of Freedom: The Civil War Era* (New York: Oxford University Press, 1988), 384.
15. John W. Foster, *A Century of American Diplomacy: Being a Brief Review of the Foreign Relations of the United States, 1776–1876* (Boston and New York: Houghton Mifflin, 1900), 373.

ning never lost its influence. The United States could be an indispensable ally some day if the European balance of power threatened to become unfavorable to Great Britain.

Throughout the war, there was a strong current of British opinion favorable to the North. Its spokesmen included some intellectuals, like John Stuart Mill; the abolitionists; a considerable body of nonconformist radical opinion led by Cobden and Bright; and the newly articulate workingmen's movement, whose leaders spoke out for the North even when unemployment in the textile industry was at its worst. There was always Canada as a hostage and a restraint—more so than ever, now that the United States had become so big.

In the end, British policy depended on the answers to questions that could not be answered rationally: Was the United States reaching self-imposed limits on its growth? Was it likely to bid for international supremacy, as Spain and France had done in earlier centuries? Or was it, like Britain itself, a confirmed believer in a state system based on the balance of power? British uncertainty about the answers to this set of questions affected the clarity of its policy. Neither Palmerston nor his cabinet wanted to get into war with the United States, but they never stopped experimenting with circumstance in order to help break up the Union on the cheap through a Confederate victory.

Britain's cautious policy of official neutrality somewhat tilted against the North was nearly overwhelmed in the early months of the war by the wayward intervention of chance.

An American naval vessel, the sloop *San Jacinto,* fifteen guns, put into Havana. It was returning home after twenty months off the African coast, where it had been part of a squadron on duty in the war against the slave trade. While in Havana, the ship's captain, Charles Wilkes, read in a local newspaper that two senior Confederate diplomats, James Murray Mason and John Slidell, both former senators, were also in the city as passengers on a British mail packet, the *Trent,* which was preparing to sail shortly for England. The mission of Mason and Slidell was to replace a team of Confederate commissioners who had thus far failed to persuade the British and French governments to recognize the Confederacy and thus allow it to purchase arms. Captain Wilkes had no relevant orders, and indeed had only recently learned that the Civil War had begun. But he had a stout heart and patriotic instincts, and a couple of books on international law in his cabin. Over the vehement objections of his executive officer, Lieutenant MacNeill Fairfax, he decided to stalk the British merchantman when it left Havana, stop it on the high seas, and either take it to the United States as a prize or capture Mason and Slidell as "contraband."

On 8 November 1861, Lieutenant Fairfax, who commanded the boarding party, took Mason, Slidell, and their aides prisoner and sent the *Trent* on its way. Fairfax told his captain that they did not have enough sailors or marines to sail the *Trent* to New York as a prize. Later he explained that his real reason for the decision to release the vessel was his fear that if the *Trent* were hauled before an American prize court, the reaction in England might result in war.

Ironically, Lieutenant Fairfax might have caused less of an outcry if he had taken the vessel to an American port as a prize. The recent Declaration of Paris, adopted after the Crimean War, made it clear that contraband of war could be taken from neutral ships only after a prize court had determined that it was in fact contraband. The declaration included "dispatches" of a belligerent in the contraband list. Be that as it may, Captain Wilkes decided for himself that Mason and Slidell were contraband; the *Trent* was not brought to an American port as a prize; and the story reached the United States and England when the *San Jacinto* and the *Trent* arrived at their respective destinations.

The report was greeted with jubilation in the North, which was aching for good news in a season of misery and defeat. A few pointed out that the United States had since its birth protested very strongly—sometimes with force—against illegal British and French searches and seizures on the high seas; that Wilkes had not searched the cargo for dispatches; that civilians were never contraband of war; and that no prize court had passed on the legality of Wilkes' action. Their voices were lost in a clamor of enthusiasm. Wilkes became a hero. Congress, the press, and assorted experts on international law cheered what he had done. "As to the irresponsible out-pourings and journalistic utterances of those delirious three weeks," the younger Charles Francis Adams wrote, "it is no exaggeration to say that, read today, they are more suggestive of the incoherences of the inmates of an insane asylum than of any well-considered expression of the organs of a sober and policed community—a community which half a century only before had gone to war in defense of the great principles of immunity from ocean search, and seamen's rights."[16] In the South, meanwhile, the Confederate gov-

---

16. C. F. Adams, "The Trent Affair, November 1911," in *Proceedings of the Massachusetts Historical Society,* vol. 45, *October 1911–June 1912* (Boston: Massachusetts Historical

ernment was suddenly buoyed by the hope that anger about the *Trent* affair would lead the British government to recognize the Confederacy and thus transform the legal and political environment of the war.

In Britain the reaction to the episode was nearly as hysterical as that in the American North. The country was in a state of highly articulate rage over what was regarded as an insult to the flag and a typical piece of Yankee buccaneering. Palmerston sent 8,000 troops to Canada, including a detachment of a Guards regiment, and mobilized a considerable part of the fleet. While the law officers of the Crown had at first expressed doubt that the search was illegal in the light of the Declaration of Paris, they gave Palmerston the opinion he wanted when more details were known, and the prime minister denounced Wilkes' action as illegal, if not piratical.

The diplomatic exchanges, cooled somewhat by the inevitable slowness of communications before the transatlantic cable, were highly charged. American opinion and the United States government recovered some of their equilibrium as they contemplated the implications of war with Great Britain in the midst of what they were coming to realize would be a long, difficult, and costly civil war. And in Britain too, the rage for war began to abate.

The critical step toward finding a way out of the crisis was taken by Prince Albert and Queen Victoria, in what proved to be Prince Albert's final act before his death. The prime minister had sent the Queen the draft text of the instructions he proposed to send to Lord Lyons, the British minister in Washington. The draft was peremptory in tone. It declared Captain Wilkes' action to be illegal, demanded the liberation of the four men captured, and insisted on an apology for the insult offered to the British flag. Lyons was instructed to request his passports if Seward refused to accept the British terms within seven days.

Prince Albert was already a dying man. He had performed arduous ceremonial functions during the preceding two days, once in a pouring rain. Nonetheless, he and the Queen discussed the paper at length, and he stayed up most of the night drafting a memorandum which outlined an alternative approach. At eight in the morning, he gave it to his wife, remarking that he was so weak he could no longer hold his pen. The Queen adopted his suggestions with few changes, and the cabinet

---

Society, 1912), 35, 50; Adams adds, however, that by the time the affair had reached its diplomatic climax, forty days later, the popular effervescence had had a chance to subside. "An Anglo-Saxon community rarely goes daft permanently," he said (p. 67).

agreed, largely with relief. The instruction as sent to Lyons was designed to give the United States government a dignified opportunity to retreat, by stressing that the British government "was willing to believe" that Captain Wilkes did not act in compliance with his orders or, if he conceived himself to be so authorized, "greatly misunderstood the instructions which he had received." The British government, the document continued, "are unwilling to believe it could be the deliberate intention of the government of the United States unnecessarily to force into discussion between the two governments a question of so grave a character," about which the entire British nation would entertain "such unanimity of feeling." The British government therefore trusted that when the United States government considered the matter, it would "of its own accord" offer to release the prisoners to the protection of the British government and proffer a suitable apology for the aggression committed.[17]

Seward had some difficulty persuading all concerned in Washington to accept this solution, and wrote a long, tortuous, and rather dense reply. But what he said sufficed to clear the air. The prisoners were released to Lord Lyons' care. "The spectre of war," writes Wheeler-Bennett, was removed "from the field of Anglo-American relations, and it had been a very substantial spectre." He adds, "By this supreme and dying effort, therefore, the Prince Consort not only saved his own country from war, but preserved the present form of government on the other side of the Atlantic."[18]

The United States turned to its problems of war-making, and Britain sought to achieve its ends by exploiting the international law of neutrality, a fluid but also a tenacious and rapidly expanding body of ideas. Like all international law, it reflected not the immediate pressures of events, but the longer-range interests and aspirations of all the nations, and the necessities of their peaceful coexistence within a relatively unified state system.

Under the prevailing international law of the time, which is still considered to be at least the nominal international law, a state is entitled to help another state suppress a rebellion against its authority, even if hostilities rise to the level of belligerence or civil war, but may not assist a rebellion in any way.[19] No other rule is possible for a world political order which purports to be a system of sovereign states. Thus

17. Chap. 8, "The Trent Affair: How the Prince Consort Saved the United States," in John W. Wheeler-Bennett, *A Wreath to Clio* (New York: St. Martin's, 1967), 110, 118–27.
18. Ibid., 126–27.
19. See Chapter 3.

when France, for example, covertly allowed a nominally private company to sell arms to the American revolutionaries between 1775 and 1778, those arms sales constituted an act of war by France against Great Britain, as France clearly understood. By the same reasoning, it was universally accepted as legal for India to help Sri Lanka put down a rebellion in 1988, just as it was deemed proper for Nigeria during the 1960s to get help from Britain, Egypt, and the Soviet Union in ending the secession of Biafra. On the other hand, states are forbidden from selling arms or military equipment to a revolutionary movement within another state, or from assisting the revolutionary movement in prosecuting its rebellion. The rule applies not only to acts of the uninvolved state itself, but to acts by individuals within its jurisdiction, if the state knows or should have known that hostile activities of this kind are taking place. Such conduct is characterized as a violation of neutrality and, in addition, as an armed attack on the state in which the insurrection or revolution is taking place. That was the charge by the Austro-Hungarian Empire against Serbia after the murder at Sarajevo in 1914.

This rule, which has been invoked at least a dozen times a year since 1945, was the basis for the most serious dispute the United States had with Great Britain during and after the Civil War, the controversy over the failure of Great Britain to prevent the Confederate cruisers *Alabama, Florida,* and *Shenandoah* from escaping to sea. The ships were being built—but not armed—in British shipyards for the Confederate government under clandestine arrangements which were almost comically transparent.

The critical issue in the application of the rule, as the *Alabama* affair brings out, is how a political entity becomes a state. International law is deemed to arise from the will and the agreement of states, and to embody their customs and practices. Accordingly, if the principal states of the international system recognize a revolutionary group as a state, it is a state for the purposes of international law. There are supposed to be objective legal criteria for diplomatic recognition: the de facto control of definite territories, the conduct of ordinary governmental activities, and so on. But in the end recognition is a political act. The American revolutionaries understood the rule and its corollary perfectly in 1776, and dispatched envoys to Europe immediately after their declaration of independence to solicit recognition. The authorities of the Confederate government followed the same procedure. If the Confederacy had been widely recognized as a state, neutral states could have allowed it to purchase anything it wished, and could have used their navies to assure the Confederacy the advantages of the new rules

of maritime law codified in 1856. In order to stop the traffic in contraband of war, the United States would have had to mount an effective
blockade around 3,500 miles of the Confederate coast from Norfolk to
Galveston, or gone to war with half the world. The American diplomatic
effort to prevent great power recognition of the Confederacy was therefore crucial to the possibility of victory, and the secretary of state,
William H. Seward, and our ministers in London, Paris, St. Petersburg,
and Madrid were as important to the struggle as the fighting men
themselves.

Seward was a man of exceptional ability and force who had been
one of Lincoln's chief rivals for the Republican nomination for the
Presidency. He became one of our greatest secretaries of state. In the
beginning of the administration, however, he suffered from curious
delusions. Like most people at that point, he undervalued Lincoln.
Moreover, he thought that a popular foreign war would be the best
way to drown the Confederacy in a tidal wave of national fervor. In
April 1861, scarcely a month after the President took office, Seward
therefore proposed that Lincoln provoke war with France and Spain,
and transfer his executive functions to him, Seward, as dictator. Lincoln
wrote a thoughtful and reasoned reply, turning down Seward's pre-
posterous memorandum, which was not published for many years.[20]
Lincoln's decision to keep Seward on despite this bizarre beginning was
singular evidence of his serenity, self-confidence, and perception as a
judge of men.

Seward's initial handling of the diplomacy of the war reveals, however, that the notion that a foreign war could end the Civil War in an
outburst of national patriotism died hard, although Lincoln carefully
supervised Seward's most important dispatches. The secretary's early
diplomatic conversations and instructions often had a provocative quality calculated to make every contretemps a crisis. Luckily, our representatives abroad were of unusual quality. Charles Francis Adams in
London was altogether remarkable in handling his mission, one of the
most difficult and important any American ambassador has ever had,
and his colleagues in the other European capitals were not far behind
him. It was Henry Cabot Lodge's judgment that Adams "was given the
opportunity in the darkest hour of his country's trial to perform the
greatest service rendered by any civilian except Lincoln himself, with
whom none other can be compared."[21]

20. See McPherson, *Battle Cry of Freedom*, 270.
21. Henry Cabot Lodge, Memorial Address, reprinted as Preface to Charles Francis

The diplomatic situation as Lincoln found it could hardly have been more dismal. In his final annual message to Congress, on 4 December 1860, President Buchanan had said that while the right of secession did not exist, the federal government had no power to coerce a state. William Seward, then a senator, commented that according to Buchanan, "It is the duty of the President to execute the laws—unless somebody opposes him; and that no State has a right to go out of the Union—unless it wants to."[22] Until Lincoln assumed office, this was the official policy of the United States with regard to the Confederacy, then rapidly consolidating its government and organizing its armed forces. It is hardly remarkable that opinion abroad accepted the breakup of the Union as inevitable.

On the first of March 1861, four days before Lincoln was inaugurated, a circular dispatch was sent to our diplomatic posts abroad, instructing them to oppose all moves to recognize the Confederacy. When Seward took office, this instruction was vigorously repeated, and enlarged to include opposition to all forms of foreign intervention.

The Confederate government understood the centrality of the international dimension of the war as well as Lincoln, Seward, and Palmerston. Jefferson Davis sent emissaries abroad as quickly as he could, not only to seek recognition from foreign governments but also to arrange for the secret procurement of arms, ships, and other sinews of war. Like nearly all Americans, the Confederates had great faith in economics as a weapon of war, and thought King Cotton alone would force England in particular to recognize the Confederacy and support it as an independent state. The British textile industry depended on the American South for three-quarters of its cotton, and the weight of Lancashire, the textile producing area, in the British economy and political system was considerable.

When the Civil War began, Lincoln proclaimed the rebels to be in a state of insurrection. From the point of view of international law, Lincoln's words meant that Confederate prisoners could be treated not as prisoners of war but as common criminals, and that the Confederacy would be considered not a state, but an armed band, a conspiracy. It soon became obvious that this position was untenable. There were Union as well as Confederate prisoners. Obviously, they all had to be

---

Adams, *Charles Francis Adams, 1835–1915: An Autobiography* (Boston and New York: Houghton Mifflin, 1916), xv.

22. Quoted in Foster, *Century of American Diplomacy,* 359.

treated as prisoners of war; nor was it conceivable that the crews of Confederate naval vessels would be hanged as pirates. When the possibility materialized, Lincoln retreated.

The issue was sharpened by the proclamation of a blockade of Southern ports on 19 April 1861. In international law a blockade is an act of war by one belligerent against another: that is, it presupposes that a state of belligerency exists, and directly affects the rights of neutral states. Britain declared its neutrality on May 13, raising a sensitive question: Did the British declaration of neutrality constitute diplomatic recognition of the Confederacy as a state, or only recognition that a condition of belligerency existed as a military fact?

The United States reacted strongly to the British announcement. Before Adams arrived in London to take up his post, his predecessor, George M. Dallas, had talked to Lord John Russell about recognition and related problems, and the foreign minister had assured him that Britain would not decide the question of recognition and the implications of a possible blockade until the issues had been discussed with Adams. In their next conversation, however, the foreign minister told Dallas that it was his intention "unofficially" to receive the Confederate commissioners who had just arrived in London. And five days after his first conversation with Dallas, Russell announced in Parliament that it had been determined to concede belligerent rights to the Confederacy, and referred to the United States as "the late Union." The British proclamation of neutrality was announced the day Adams arrived.

Seward's draft of his instruction to Adams on these developments was a classic instance of the secretary of state's capacity for fury. It ordered Adams to resist British recognition of Confederate belligerency as "hasty and unfriendly" under the circumstances; to threaten war if Britain did recognize the Confederacy; and to break off diplomatic relations if even unofficial intercourse was established with the rebel commissioners. Furthermore, it required Adams to read the full text of his instruction to Russell. Lincoln sharply modified the text, and gave Adams discretion to use it simply as guidance for the conversation. Since the British position was that they were doing no more than Lincoln had done in acknowledging the Confederacy as a belligerent, and were following the practice the United States had used in dealing with the revolutionary regimes of Latin America, Adams in the end confined his objections to the speed of the British action, to the language used in Parliament, and to the fact that Russell had received the Confederate commissioners. Within a few weeks, Russell assured Adams that while he had met twice with the Confederate commissioners, "'he had no expectation of seeing them any more,'" and that Britain had no present intention of granting diplomatic recognition to the Confederacy.[23]

The next step in the drama could easily have been more damaging even than British recognition of Confederate belligerency, which was promptly imitated by France, Spain, and other governments, and greatly facilitated Confederate procurement in Europe. Our ministers to Great Britain and France were instructed to request that those governments agree to the adhesion of the United States to the Declaration of Paris of 1856, including its prohibition of privateering. Previously, the United States had objected to the provision against privateering in the first article of the declaration. Now, however, the United States realized that privateering could be a potent weapon in the hands of the Confederacy, which had few naval officers and almost no ship-building capacity. It therefore withdrew its earlier objection, and requested permission to sign the declaration. Britain and France, acting in concert, refused to agree unless American adherence was considered to be prospective only, and to have no "bearing, direct or indirect, on the internal difficulties prevailing in the United States." Simultaneously, through the British consul in Charleston, who functioned under documents issued by the United States, Britain and France secretly negotiated the acceptance of the Declaration of Paris by the Confederate government, except for the article against privateering.[24] Lincoln withdrew the consul's exequatur and a British warship called at Charleston to take him home. It is hard to imagine a more deliberately (and gratuitously) hostile act on the part of the British and French governments.

The Confederacy experimented with privateers, and initially had considerable success with them. But as the Union blockade slowly achieved effectiveness, it became more difficult to bring prizes into Southern ports, and neutral nations would not allow Confederate prize courts to be held on their territory. In any event, the Confederacy acted promptly to procure naval cruisers abroad, despite the difficulties of the law of neutrality. One James D. Bulloch arrived in London as early as June 1861 to obtain vessels for the Confederate navy. Bulloch was an able and experienced business man, a former naval officer, and an exceptionally skilful diplomat. He was also Theodore Roosevelt's uncle. He soon succeeded in contracting for the vessels which became the

---

23. Lord John Russell Statement from E. Adams, *Great Britain and the American Civil War* (1925), 1: 106; quoted in McPherson, *Battle Cry of Freedom*, 389.

24. Foster, *Century of American Diplomacy*, 367

Florida and the *Alabama,* the devastatingly destructive Confederate cruisers used to capture and often to sink United States merchant vessels, and bought a number of other ships as well.

Adams conducted an intensive diplomatic campaign with Lord Russell, based on ingenious investigation of the contractual arrangements by which Bulloch sought to evade the English neutrality laws, and the progress of the vessel in the yards. Despite his efforts the *Alabama* escaped, unarmed and flying the British flag, as the *Florida* had escaped earlier. The *Alabama* was armed in the Azores and became a major factor in the Confederate war effort. Indeed, some students believe that the American shipping industry has never recovered from the damages inflicted by the Confederate commerce raiders led by the *Alabama.*

In his battle to prevent the escape of the *Alabama,* Adams had obtained the written opinion of an eminent lawyer, Sir Robert Collier, who concluded on the basis of Adams' documents that it was "difficult to make out a stronger case of infringement of the Foreign Enlistment Act, which, if not enforced on this occasion, is little better than a dead letter." The documents and Sir Robert's opinion were sent to the chief law officer of the Crown, but he was ill at the time, and the Foreign Office was unacquainted with the problem. The papers shuffled about through an English weekend. Finally, the law officers gave their opinion that the vessel should be detained, but they were too late. The *Alabama* had slipped out of Liverpool, ostensibly for a trial run; it was picked up by a tug which put a crew on board and then it vanished into the mists. In later years, Russell, saying that he was deeply chagrined, claimed he had urged the cabinet to order the Royal Navy to capture the ship wherever she could be found, but the cabinet would not take so bold a step.[25]

A few months later the United States presented its claim for damages for the national and private injuries sustained as a result of the depredations of the *Alabama,* and to solicit more effective measures for the prevention "of such lawless and injurious proceedings in her Majesty's ports hereafter." The basis of the American claims, triumphantly vindicated by an international arbitration tribunal in Geneva in 1872, was the charge that Britain had violated the international law of neutrality by failing to prevent the ship from leaving the Liverpool harbor. The foundation for liability was the rule that it was Britain's duty as a neutral to prevent her territory from being used in any way

25. Spencer Walpole, *The Life of Lord John Russell* (London and New York: Longmans, Green, 1889), 2:335–67.

to support the Confederate war effort with instruments of war, and that in the case of the *Alabama* (and two other vessels, the *Florida* and the *Shenandoah*) Britain had been negligent in discharging that duty, and was therefore liable for the resulting damages.[26]

Bulloch contracted with the builders of the *Alabama* for the construction of two ironclad rams, with which he confidently expected that the Northern blockade could be swept away and Washington captured from the Potomac. In this judgment he was almost certainly correct. The ironclads were rapidly making the old naval fleets obsolete. Adams pressed the Foreign Office about the rams as diligently as he had urged the case against the *Alabama*. The debate in the House of Commons on the *Alabama* affair had been an easy victory for the government. Palmerston had dismissed the American charges with contempt, saying, "Whenever any political party, whether in or out of office in the United States, finds itself in difficulties, it raises a cry against England as a means of creating what in American language is called political capital. ... The solicitor-general has demonstrated, indisputably, that the Americans have no cause of complaint against us."[27]

In the aftermath of that debate, Russell at first flatly rejected Adams' new demarche about the rams. After a sleepless night, Adams wrote another note. As always, his tone was polite and cogent without being severe. This time, however, he concluded by saying that he could not help but regard the British decision not to detain the rams as opening to the Confederates free liberty to conduct war against the United States from British soil, by attacking all the seaboard cities of the North, and raising the blockade. "It would be superfluous in me to point out to your lordship that this is war."[28] At about the same time, the news of Gettysburg and Vicksburg reached England, changing the climate decisively. Russell replied at once to Adams' note that the matter was under "serious and anxious consideration" by her Majesty's government.[29] The decision was reversed the next day, and the rams were ultimately bought by the British government.

The classic account of these events appears in five coruscating chap-

26. See further discussion of the *Alabama* case in Chap. 8.

27. Quoted in Foster, *Century of American Diplomacy*, 389.

28. Foster, *Century of American Diplomacy*, 391; Henry Adams, *The Education of Henry Adams: An Autobiography* (Boston and New York: Houghton Mifflin, 1918), 172. No foreign government had ever addressed Palmerston in such terms. Three weeks later, with the rams safely in British custody, Palmerston complained to Russell about Adams' "somewhat insolent threats of war." He went on, "We ought to say to him in civil terms. 'You be damned.' " (See Jasper Ridley, *Lord Palmerston* [London: Constable, 1970], 561).

29. Adams, *Education of Henry Adams*, 178.

ters of Henry Adams' autobiography, *The Education of Henry Adams*. Adams went to London as his father's volunteer private secretary in 1861, aged twenty-three, and served throughout the war. His book was written in 1905 (in the third person), as a sequel to his *Mont-Saint-Michel and Chartres*. It was privately printed in 1907, but not published until after the author's death in 1918.

When Russell's reply was received at the American legation, announcing that "instructions have been issued which will prevent the departure of the two ironclad vessels from Liverpool," the members of the legation accepted it, Henry Adams wrote, "as Grant had accepted the capitulation of Vicksburg.

> The private secretary conceived that as Secretary Stanton had struck and crushed by superior weight the rebel left on the Mississippi, so Secretary Seward had struck and crushed the rebel right in England, and he never felt a doubt as to the nature of the battle. Though Minister Adams should stay in office till he were ninety, he would never fight another campaign of life and death like this; and though the private secretary should covet and attain every office in the gift of President or people, he would never again find education to compare with the life-and-death alternative of this two-year-and-a-half struggle in London, as it had racked and thumb-screwed him in its shifting phases. . . . As he understood it, Russell had followed [traditional British] policy steadily, ably, even vigorously, and had brought it to the moment of execution. Then he had met wills stronger than his own, and, after persevering to the last possible instant, had been beaten. Lord North and George Canning had a like experience. . . .
>
> This was no discredit to Russell or Palmerston or Gladstone. They [like Seward and Adams] had shown power, patience, and steadiness of purpose. They had persisted for two years and a half in their plan for breaking up the Union, and had yielded at last only in the jaws of war. After a long and desperate struggle, the American Minister had trumped their best card and won the game.[30]

The Emancipation Proclamation, issued on 1 January 1863, was having an immense effect on opinion throughout the world, and especially in Great Britain. In the blazing light of the military news, it suddenly became clear that the war was a struggle not only to preserve the American Union but to vindicate human liberty. The followers of

---

30. Ibid., 173–74.

Cobden and Bright took heart, the working-class leaders who had supported the cause of the Union in the darkest period of the war surged forward, and the Liberal government began to sense new pressure both from its own constituents and from its Tory opponents. After three long years, the lonely apostles of the Union cause were becoming the leaders of a new British majority.

8

Premonitions of Change, 1865–1914

After the Civil War, two alternative ways of expansion were open to the United States. She could resume and push to a conclusion the controversy with Britain over Canada and the other British possessions in the Western Hemisphere and so win complete insular status vis-à-vis the one power outside America that could be considered an opponent to reckon with in the hemisphere. Conversely, the United States could join forces with Britain and, following the parallel policies of Monroe and Canning, ward off any threat from the European Continent to their common insular existence. At first it seemed unlikely that the second course would be followed. Britain's equivocal attitude during the Civil War was still remembered with bitterness in the United States. The Alaska Purchase, which drove Russia from the American continent, could be looked at as a preparatory step for similar treatment of Britain; Canada was now clasped on two sides by American territory.

However, in the depths of public opinion a change began to take shape: confronted in Asia and in Europe with peoples and powers of an alien character, both nations gradually found their natural affinity to be of greater importance to them than their old antagonism. The diplomats of Washington and London translated these feelings into the realities of foreign policy.—Ludwig Dehio

One of the most important consequences of the Union victory in the Civil War was that the notion of opposing American expansion and even of trying to divide the United States finally disappeared from the agenda of British and French foreign policy. The Spanish had been the first to attempt such a venture through the plot of Aaron Burr and General Wilkinson during the Jefferson administration.[1] There was an

The epigraph for this chapter is taken from Ludwig Dehio, *The Precarious Balance: Four Centuries of the European Power Struggle*, trans. Charles Fullman (1948; New York: Vintage, 1965), 237–38.

1. See Thomas P. Abernathy, *The Burr Conspiracy* (New York: Oxford University

echo of it during the First World War, when Germany sought the cooperation of Mexico against the United States, offering Mexico Texas and the territories it lost after the Mexican War as compensation.[2] But for all practical purposes, the idea died, with many others, at Appomattox Courthouse. Ideas can always be revived, of course. Perhaps the Soviet Union's long and expensive campaign in South and Central America represented the flickering rebirth of an old ambition. But in the period between 1865 and the attack on Pearl Harbor, no serious threat was made directly against the territorial integrity of the United States itself.

The circumstances of European and world politics began to change radically during the second half of the nineteenth century. The mighty American armed forces created in four years of furious war taught their own simple lesson. And the Union forces, moreover, were forged without significant help from the immense territories Polk had added to the Union. After Appomattox, Britain and France could not rationally imagine that they could split the United States into separate countries. The states of the Union had been annealed into the provinces of a single nation. It was no longer accurate to refer to the United States as a "federation" or a "federal union." To recall the argument of Edmund Morgan's brilliant book,[3] the notion that the United States had been created by an act of the American people and not by the states had ceased to be a metaphysical whimsy; it was a political and military fact no country could challenge, at least through the military technology of the period.

Besides, Britain and France were rapidly losing interest in the idea. On the contrary, they soon came to rejoice that the United States had survived so many assaults on its growth. In the new configuration of world power which began to emerge about the time of our Civil War, the United States loomed up in British and French consciousness as an indispensable member of the combinations needed by the European coastal states, China, and Japan to prevent Germany or Russia from achieving dominion over the Eurasian land mass. Fifty years before, Castlereagh and Canning had reached the conclusion that the United States was potentially important to the British interest in the balance

---

Press, 1954); and Dumas Malone, *Jefferson and His Times,* vol. 5, *Jefferson the President: Second Term, 1805–1809* (1948; reprint ed., Boston: Little, Brown, 1974), chaps. 13–21.

2. See Barbara Tuchman, *The Zimmerman Telegram* (1959; reprint ed., New York: Ballantine, 1988).

3. Edmund S. Morgan, *Inventing the People: The Rise of Popular Sovereignty in England and America* (New York: W. W. Norton, 1988).

of power. Russia had sensed the significance of the United States to its own interests even earlier. And Napoleon had grasped the point first of all, when he decided to sell Louisiana to the Americans.

The principal catalyst for this transformation in consciousness was the creation of Germany under Prussian leadership by a gradual process which reached its climax in 1871. The formation of Italy was also an important milestone in the march of the national principle to victory in Europe, although Italy lacked both the power and the ambition to claim an imperial mission. And the nationalist movements which destroyed the unity of the Ottoman and Austro-Hungarian empires were important in themselves and important also as foci and catalysts for competitive Russian and Austrian expansion. Japan had been brought into the modern world by an American diplomatic and naval initiative in 1853, and within a generation became a significant participant in world politics. But these events were of minor consequence when compared to the thrust of German policy, especially after the fall of Bismarck in 1890. For nearly a century, world politics was to be dominated by Germany's bid for mastery, which required Russia, on the one hand, and Britain, France, and the United States, on the other, to join forces twice in order to put down the German thrust. In the process, the bipolar nineteenth-century system of world order organized around the rivalry of Russia and Great Britain evolved into a new state system, even more bipolar, in which the Soviet Union and the United States represented the opposing principles of hegemony and pluralism.

When Henry Adams traveled in Europe after he graduated from Harvard College in 1838, "Germany" was a literary and geographical, but not a political expression. People feared a Napoleonic revival of militarism and imperialism in France, but the word *Germany* evoked only the images of small duchies whose princes were patrons of the arts, of industriousness, culture, education, tranquillity, and peace. "The Holy Roman Empire of the German Nation" which Napoleon had conquered in 1806 consisted of more than three hundred principalities and free cities. In the German Confederation which the Congress of Vienna established to succeed it, under the leadership of the new Austrian Empire, there were some thirty states, combining many small German entities of the old regime into larger ones. The resulting polity was both artificial and unstable, and survived for only fifty years. Beneath its idyllic surface, the political and social caldron boiled. Significant socialist parties developed. And Prussia and Austria competed for political leadership: one Protestant, the other Catholic; one hard-driving, strongly militaristic, intensely German, and highly organized;

the other a loosely held combination of many ethnic groups whose principal concern was not conquest but survival. Prussia sought to unite all Northern Germany into a strong unitary state, leaving Vienna to rule as it could in its diverse and polyglot empire. Austria wanted only to preserve at least the facade of its primacy in a single state.

In Henry Adams' youth, Germany was a *cordon sanitaire,* in effect, a relatively quiet zone of military weakness between the world powers of the time, Russia on the one side, and France and Great Britain on the other. As a result, Anglo-Russian rivalry was confined to Asia, at least until Russia took advantage of the French defeat in 1871 to denounce the neutralization of the Black Sea imposed upon it after the Crimean War, and began once again to take an active interest in the Balkans and the Middle East.

The rise of Prussia, a poor country far to the Slavic East, began with the great elector Frederick William I, who built modern Prussia on the foundation of a fanatically efficient army. His son, Frederick the Great, made Prussia an active force in European politics, and prepared the way for Prussia's important part in the defeat of Napoleon. Prussia played a leading role in the political maneuvering of the post-Napoleonic period, during which German national feeling, nourished by the romanticism of the times, became a mighty popular force demanding a political as well as a linguistic, poetic, and musical outlet.

When Bismarck became chancellor of Prussia in 1862, he took over an ideal instrument for fulfilling those aspirations, a well-managed eighteenth-century monarchy with a strong military tradition, uncontaminated by traces of European parliamentarism. He used that instrument with genius, forging alliances with the new industrial and financial classes as well as with the landowners, the nobility, and the military—and later with the working class and its leaders as well—to shape a state of extraordinary potential.

Both Russia and France were greatly concerned by Bismarck's steady progress in creating a unified German state based on Prussian military power. The process included a series of short, brilliant, and successful wars against lesser countries, in an environment whose resistance to Prussian expansion had been weakened by the failure after 1856 to restore the alliance between Russia and Austria.[4] Bismarck bought off the Russians, not only as a sound tactical move but as a matter of principle as well. If Bismarck believed in anything, he believed

4. See C. J. Bartlett, *The Global Conflict: The International Rivalry of the Great Powers, 1880–1970* (London and New York: Longman, 1984), 4–6.

that Prussia should have good and peaceful relations with Russia. His aspirations for Germany were exceptionally sensitive to the risks of going beyond the limits of prudence.

France was a more immediate question. Keeping Germany divided had always been a fundamental principle of French policy. Now, with Bismarck's task two-thirds completed, France objected to the incorporation of the three principal South German states into the North German Confederation and their alliance with Prussia. Bismarck provoked the Franco-Prussian War, defeated France decisively, and announced the formation of the new German Empire at Versailles in 1871. The King of Prussia became Emperor, Kaiser of a realm which included four kingdoms, six duchies, six principalities, and three Free Cities. The imperial constitution established a Parliament with limited power, but some power nonetheless; basically, however, the Kaiser had more direct authority than any other ruler of his time except the Czar.

Under Bismarck, the new German state seemed relatively content with the role of a middle-sized power functioning cooperatively within the state system as it had developed since 1815. The annexation of Alsace and Lorraine in 1871, however, had made France an implacable enemy. In response to this and other developments, Bismarck made an alliance with the Austro-Hungarian empire which greatly increased the weight of the First Reich vis-à-vis Russia as well as France, and raised the specter of German dominance in Central Europe, a prospect calculated to ring alarm bells in every foreign ministry of the world. And the Germans began to manifest a brusque interest in Africa and in the Far East which caught the attention of observers and students in the maritime nations particularly. Germany had not yet launched its "Icarian flight," in Dehio's vivid phrase,[5] but people everywhere were becoming conscious of the possibility that it might.

II

A small but influential group of American intellectuals and political leaders shared this consciousness of change in the structure and dynamics of the state system. We had emerged from the Civil War in a state of rage with Great Britain as well as France. It was well understood, however, that the first task of American diplomacy was to settle those grievances as quickly and as quietly as possible, and thus to restore amicable relations with the two leading nations of the Atlantic basin.

5. Dehio, *Precarious Balance*, 212.

Britain was by far the more powerful of the two. Bonds of kinship apart, a long list of problems was always on the table, from fishing rights and boundary disputes regarding Canada to Caribbean issues; and latterly a new cycle of concerns about the Sandwich Islands, Samoa, and other Pacific problems.

The incorporation of Alaska and the new states of the West Coast into the United States intensified American interest in an isthmian canal and in Caribbean and mid-Pacific naval bases and other defensive strong points. As President, Grant pushed tenaciously for the annexation of Santo Domingo as a naval base, and in 1881, Secretary of State Blaine explained that just as an isthmian canal should be "a purely American waterway to be treated as part of our own coast line," so the position of the Hawaiian Islands, giving them strategic control of the North Pacific, "brings their possession within the range of questions of purely American policy, as much as that of the Isthmus itself." He compared the strategic importance of Hawaii in the Pacific to that of Cuba in the Caribbean, and concluded that "under no circumstances [could] the United States permit any change in the territorial control of either which would cut it adrift from the American system."[6]

It is easy to mistake the import of these developments. They did not bespeak the acceptance by the United States of a new mission as a "world power," necessarily concerned with the management of the state system as a whole. Psychologically, they were no more than the natural adjustment of old ideas about the defense of the realm to its new geographical position. While a small number of intellectuals and military officers were aware of deeper changes in the security position of the United States, public opinion as a whole continued to view the problem of security through the optics of the past. America still thought of itself as an island safely anchored in a distant sea, far from trouble.

The American perception of Canada changed dramatically in the post–Civil War period. In 1867, Canada became a self-governing Dominion of the British Empire, with a government of its own and considerable autonomy even in foreign affairs. In the American mind, the possibility of an attack on the United States from Canada virtually disappeared, and with it the occasional American impulse to conquer Canada or to annex it by other means. True, during the heated controversy over the *Alabama* claims, Senator Summer, then chairman of

---

6. From Secretary of State James G. Blaine's instructions to James H. Comly; quoted in Charles S. Campbell, *The Transformation of American Foreign Relations, 1865–1900* (New York: Harper and Row, 1976), 177.

the Senate Committee on Foreign Relations, suggested that Britain cede Canada to the United States as compensation for the direct damages and the prolongation of the war caused by the Confederate cruisers which had escaped from British harbors. But floating the issue in the course of a complex and heated controversy about another matter was altogether different from sending a military expedition to Montreal or Toronto.

The *Alabama* arbitration was the most important controversy of the time between Great Britain and the United States, and jingoes on both sides of the Atlantic exercised their lungs exuberantly on the subject. But sober opinion thoroughly understood the importance to both countries of a quick and amicable resolution of the dispute. Sober opinion prevailed, and public opinion welcomed the result. The affair took careful management, and there were moments of tension and doubt. In the end, however, able and prudent British and American teams of negotiators achieved a settlement which remains an important precedent both in diplomacy and in the development of international law.

Under an 1871 Anglo-American treaty designed to achieve the settlement by arbitration of all outstanding controversies—boundary questions and fishing rights as well as the *Alabama* claims—a special tribunal was established to deal with the Confederate cruisers. It had five members named by Great Britain, the United States, Italy, Brazil, and the Swiss Confederation, and it met in Geneva. In the treaty, Britain and the United States agreed that neutral states owe belligerents a duty to exercise "due diligence" to prevent any warship intended for a belligerent from leaving their ports, and Britain expressed its regret for the escape of the Confederate cruisers. In 1872, the tribunal found that Great Britain had failed to exercise "due diligence," and awarded $15,500,000 in damages, a considerable sum at that time. Taken with the formal British statement of regret, the award satisfied American opinion, and the matter receded as a political irritant.[7]

As Charles S. Campbell has pointed out, the quasi settlement of 1871 with Great Britain by no means made Anglo-American diplomacy an area of sweetness and light.[8] There were contentious issues galore.

---

7. See Adrian Cook, *The Alabama Claims: American Politics and Anglo-American Relations, 1865–1872* (Ithaca, N.Y.: Cornell University Press, 1975); *Papers Relating to the Treaty of Washington* (Washington, D.C.: G.P.O., 1872–74); Campbell, *Transformation of American Foreign Relations*, 25–49; and John C. Davis, *Mr. Fish and the Alabama Claims* (Boston: Houghton Mifflin, 1893).

8. Campbell, *Transformation of American Foreign Relations*.

Several were calculated to stir political passion nearly to the point of apoplexy. Disputes over fishing rights have been for centuries among the most volatile and least tractable problems of diplomacy, and the fishing controversies between Britain and the United States in the period between 1865 and 1900 were hardly exceptions to the rule. On the contrary, the emotional content of those disputes was exacerbated by the inflamed state of Anglo-American relations in general. The normal hostility to Great Britain characteristic of the first century of American history had been intensified by British foreign policy during the Civil War. It was to remain a political landmine for another generation at least, and is still a force to be reckoned with.

Despite this experience, and a number of others equally sensitive,[9] Britain and the United States achieved what Bradford Perkins rightly called "the great rapprochement" in the years before 1914. The diplomacy both of the Panama Canal Treaty and of the Spanish American War attest to the reality of the achievement.

It is difficult to imagine a more startling contrast than that between the conduct of Great Britain and the smaller European powers concerning the Spanish-American War and their conduct with respect to the Mexican War and the American Civil War. The European governments were sympathetic to Spain, and anxious for the Spanish monarchy to survive, but they had no intention of running any risks for the Spanish cause. The German foreign minister, Prince Bernhard von Bulow, told the Spanish ambassador in Berlin, "You are isolated . . . because everybody wants to be pleasant to the United States, or, at any rate, nobody wants to arouse America's anger."[10] The European powers made a precatory and toothless joint appeal for peace to the United States, but the Continental powers would not act without the British, and the British would not move until they were assured by the United States that such an appeal would be helpful and welcome. Even then the European draft statement was approved by the United States in advance. The President read a formal and responsive reply as soon as the

9. Of these, America's diplomatic intervention in the Anglo-Venezuelan boundary dispute of 1895 was the most spectacular because President Cleveland lost his temper in public, and Secretary of State Olney, an intemperate man at the best of times, claimed, "Today the United States is practically sovereign on this continent, and its fiat is law upon the subjects to which it confines its interposition" (quoted in Henry James, *Richard Olney and His Public Service* [Boston and New York: Houghton Mifflin, 1923], 109). Campbell's treatment of the episode in *The Transformation of American Foreign Relations,* chapter 11, and his bibliography, pages 365–68, are excellent.

10. Quoted in Bradford Perkins, *The Great Rapprochement: England and the United States, 1895–1914* (New York: Atheneum, 1968), 35.

dean of the diplomatic corps in Washington finished reading the European statement. The President's remarks had obviously been prepared in advance. And, as the crisis developed, the British and the other powers as well were at pains to reassure the United States privately that they had nothing to say in the matter, whatever course America might decide to pursue. After the war, there were enthusiastic demonstrations in England, and the American flag was much in evidence.

The ending of the long and rancorous Anglo-American dispute about the isthmian canal in 1903 was quite as dramatic. The Clayton-Bulwer Treaty of 1850, providing for joint British and American control of the canal, was given a decent burial. The new treaty did not prohibit the United States from fortifying the canal, nor did it require that the canal remain open to the vessels of all nations in time of war, as the Suez Canal Convention of 1888 did.

Other controversies of the time were resolved in the same pattern: an Anglo-German blockade of Venezuela to enforce the payment of debts, for example; an Alaskan boundary dispute; and others as well.

The British governing classes were acutely aware and the British public was dimly aware that the map of power in the world was changing rapidly, and that Britain's century of unchallenged preeminence after Trafalgar and Waterloo was coming to an end. The emergence of Germany, the growth of Russia, and the development of Japan made Englishmen and Americans alike uncomfortable. German policy was an irritant, both in substance and in tone. It dramatized a threat of hostility, which in turn produced antibodies. Almost without conscious articulation, friendship and more than friendship—alliance—between what was then the British Empire and the United States became popular themes on both sides of the Atlantic.

Both for Great Britain and for the United States, concern about German policy stimulated the process of rapprochement. As early as 1896, Britain became conscious of the fact that building to match the growth of the American navy was neither possible nor desirable, and that war between the two countries had become most unlikely. After 1898, and the great increase in German naval expenditure, both Britain and the United States responded in kind, and British and American naval cooperation became active. In 1904, the British Admiralty removed its West Indies fleet and China fleet to home waters in order to face the looming danger across the North Sea. Arthur Marder concluded that this withdrawal of British naval power "was made possible only by the good Anglo-American relations and the supposition that the protection of British interests in American waters could safely be left to the benevolent protection of American sea power."[11]

The vocabulary of the day has overtones which are strange and sometimes repellent today. The rapprochement of Britain, the United States, and the "white" Dominions—Canada, Australia, New Zealand, and South Africa—was usually explained and advocated in tribal terms, rarely in terms of interests and power. There was talk of the community of English-speaking peoples, of the Anglo-Saxon race, and of the white race threatened by the Yellow Peril and other racial perils. In the United States, a few boasted that it was America's turn to become not only a great power but an imperial power, at least in the Pacific and the Caribbean.

In each country, a few writers, speakers, politicians, and journalists analyzed the security problems of the nation in terms of interests rather than of sentiments and prejudices. They were always a minority. Both island peoples had a tenacious preference for insular policies. The "little Englanders" supported a maritime strategy for Great Britain: they believed the Khyber Pass was on the frontier of the British national interest, but could not be persuaded that at least the Rhine, if not the Elbe or the Vistula, was also important. Their battle continued well into the First World War. In the United States, military attention was focused on Indian fighting or, as an outer limit, on the Caribbean, although small naval squadrons were stationed in the Mediterranean and the Far East as well.

An extraordinary admiral, Stephen B. Luce, and his protégé, Captain Alfred T. Mahan, took the lead in generating the renaissance of the United States Navy after its post–Civil War slump, and in concentrating the naval mind on the higher branches of strategy.[12] Luce's campaign took years of struggle with the entrenched powers of the Old Guard, for whom thinking, to recall Lloyd George's phrase, was "a form of treason." After an Homeric political and bureaucratic battle, Luce and his allies in the navy, in Congress, and in the press, obtained the establishment—and then the survival—of the Naval War College in Newport, the first of the senior military colleges in the United States,

11. Arthur J. Marder, *The Anatomy of British Sea Power: A History of British Naval Policy in the Pre-Dreadnought Era, 1880–1905* (New York: Octagon, 1976), 450. See also p. 255.

12. See John A. Grenville and George B. Young, *Politics, Strategy, and American Diplomacy: Studies in Foreign Policy, 1873–1917* (New Haven, Conn.: Yale University Press, 1966), chap. 10, especially pp. 276–78; and W. D. Puleston, *Mahan: the Life and Work of Captain Alfred Thayer Mahan, U.S.N.* (London: J. Cape, 1939), chaps. 11–13.

and one of the first such institutions in the world, and set about reorg-anizing the navy and modernizing and enlarging the fleet.

The debates among Americans about the Spanish-American War demonstrate how tenaciously we resist the thesis that the war represents a significant change in the goals or methods of American foreign policy. It has often been described and attacked as marking America's emer-gence as a great power, its debut in world politics and in imperialism. It came about, we were told, because of the influence in our government of jingoes, colonialists, and dabblers in other strange, dangerous, and alien faiths. The annexation of the Philippines was an "aberration," a mistake which would entangle us in the Pacific far beyond our legitimate interest in defending the West Coast of the United States and an isth-mian canal.

In itself, the Spanish-American War was not a real departure from the pattern of nineteenth-century American foreign policy. It was no more than the last act in the prolonged disintegration of Spain's Amer-ican empire, which had begun nearly a century before—perhaps earlier, with the Armada. The Cuban insurrection against Spanish rule had been prolonged and bloody. American sentiment, always sympathetic to rebellious colonists seeking their independence, had been actively aroused for many years, and had teetered on the brink of intervention a number of times.

Americans who viewed the problem in the perspective of national security had long since concluded that we should take any convenient opportunity either to annex Cuba or at least to obtain a naval base there. While the Monroe Doctrine respected the legitimacy of the existing European colonies in Latin America, it did not require the United States to stand by and witness horrendous massacres and other massive violations of human rights; international law recognized the propriety of humanitarian intervention in extreme situations. We had offered our good offices as mediator and conciliator, but it was ap-parent that Spain would not recognize the independence of the island as a new nation, and that the rebels would not settle for less. The emotional fervor behind the idea of Manifest Destiny, it is true, did not seem to embrace territories beyond the continental limits of the United States. But Cuba was not Samoa or the Philippines, or even Hawaii. It was close to the United States; the question of annexation was a familiar one; had it not been for the slavery issue, Cuba would have been annexed many years earlier; and finally, the battleship *Maine* was blown up.

Thus on the surface of things, the American decision to declare war on Spain was a humanitarian intervention to terminate a long and increasingly cruel civil war in Cuba, and a response to a major attack on a United States naval vessel. The United States did not annex Cuba, but assured its independence, asking only the lease of a naval base in return. American action in Cuba fits into the tradition of the Monroe Doctrine without much difficulty, and into the tradition of international law as it stood at the time.

Viewed in the context of world politics, however, the Spanish-American War was also something quite different, the first act of America's visible adaptation to the emerging structure of world politics. The United States had confronted German ambition directly in Samoa, Hawaii, and the Caribbean. And the United States and especially its navy were already sensitive to the military potential of Japan. During the Spanish-American War, the German desire to take over the Philippines if the United States decided not to do so was asserted with considerable emphasis, and was widely remarked in the United States. It was remarked also in England, where the American action saved Britain the task of seeking the Philippines for itself, in order to prevent Germany from doing so. In the glow of Anglo-American rapprochement, American administration of the Philippines served the cause of stability in the Far East, and thus the British interest, whereas a German presence could only stimulate the rancorous rivalries of European politics in the region.

The American decision to carry the war against Spain to the Philippines has a colorful history. On 24 February 1898, a telegram to Commodore Dewey, commander of the Far Eastern Squadron of the navy, ordered him to assemble his ships in Hong Kong and prepare to carry out the war plan against Spain if and when war was declared. The "anti-imperialists" in American politics and historiography have claimed that Dewey's order was a sly trick of Theodore Roosevelt, whom they regard as an arch-jingo and imperialist, and who was then assistant secretary of the navy, executed behind the backs of the secretary of the navy and the President. The basis for the story is the fact that the operational telegram to Dewey from the Navy Department was signed by Roosevelt as acting secretary, his superior being absent at the time. Similar orders under the signature of the secretary of the navy had gone out to the commanders of other American naval squadrons throughout the world. Those orders were based on carefully considered plans for conducting a largely naval war against Cuba in order to help the rebels achieve its liberation. In developing the plans over a period of several years the new naval war college and the Navy

Department had assumed that the principal tasks of the navy in such a war would be to blockade Cuba and destroy any Spanish fleets which might seek to break the blockade and relieve the island. The orders to Dewey were in no way exceptional. The entire navy was on the alert, and its principal forces were concentrated near the Florida Straits ready to intercept and destroy any Spanish naval vessels which might approach the island. The outlying squadrons, like Dewey's in Hong Kong, were to deal with smaller Spanish concentrations where they could be found. Roosevelt was surely one of the activists in the navy who participated in the preparation of the war plan, and strongly approved it. But Dewey's momentous trip to Manila Bay was in no sense a secret private adventure of Theodore Roosevelt.

Roosevelt was given credit for the plan by contemporary writers, however, because the cautious bureau chiefs of the navy, for reasons any one with bureaucratic experience will readily understand, were reluctant to appear in public as preparing for war while the President was still pursuing an active diplomacy designed to preserve the peace. The landings in Manila and Luzon were necessary for the purpose of providing Dewey's squadron with coal and other supplies, and the decision for annexation arose later in the course of the war, out of the necessity for fortifying Manila against the risk that strong Spanish naval forces might appear to challenge what Dewey had accomplished. Thus Grenville and Young conclude, "In this way, no long term strategic plan but rather the exigencies of war and faulty appraisal of Spain's naval strength led the United States into deep involvement in the Philippines."[13]

Nonetheless, the United States' interest in China had well-established roots and a long history, and many in the United States were concerned that the rise of Japan and the possible partition of China might adversely affect American interests. The American presence in the Philippines was widely perceived as giving us a firm base for protecting those interests, and many others in the Far East. While only a few extremely dogmatic and often eccentric individuals ventured to anticipate the future, and none of them were eccentric enough to imagine the fantastic events which actually did occur in the Pacific Basin during the twentieth century, there was a substantial body of American opinion willing to ratify the treaty of peace with Spain, which included the annexation of the Philippines. Patriotic enthusiasm gave momentum

13. Grenville and Young, *Politics, Strategy, and American Diplomacy*, especially pp., 276–78; quote on p. 292.

to the movement for expansion. But there was sober if still inchoate thought behind the enthusiasm for glory and a place at the great power table.

Many Americans were skeptical and critical about the Spanish-American War, and the war itself had its dark side, both in the lamentable performance of the army, and in the prolonged and costly Philippine campaign to suppress the resistance led by Aguinaldo. But victory, gallantry, and excitement generated a mood of exhilaration. The succession of Theodore Roosevelt to the Presidency when McKinley was murdered intensified that mood.

Theodore Roosevelt was one of the most colorful, interesting, and effective men who ever occupied the White House. He was a person of contrasts and paradoxes—a sickly boy who made himself strong, healthy, and an exemplar of the strenuous life; an intellectual of quite extraordinary talents, who wrote the classic naval history of the War of 1812, which he began as a student at Harvard, and finished the year after he graduated. At the same time he was a populist progressive politician, loved by the people, and a hero as well to a generation of young college-trained idealists whom he led into public life. He was full of boyish and often jejune enthusiasms. The British ambassador of the day, Sir Cecil Spring-Rice, said of him, "You must always remember . . . that the President is about six,"[14] but he was also a shrewd, worldly, and wily diplomat, well informed, insightful, and capable of action. John M. Cooper concludes that because of Roosevelt's cosmopolitan background, his scholarship, and the intellectual quality of his milieu, "he was much better prepared in foreign affairs than any of his predecessors since John Quincy Adams. His social position supplied a network of connections in the leading world capitals, which proved invaluable in his diplomatic dealings. Reading and reflection instilled in him a keen appreciation of the balance of power in international affairs and of his country's vital stake in certain aspects of that balance."[15]

Roosevelt himself regarded his work in foreign affairs and his success in doubling the size of the navy as his greatest accomplishments. By secret warnings, he deterred Germany from intervening in Venezuela. He managed the spectacular and controversial diplomacy which gave the United States the right to build, manage, and defend the

---

14. Quoted in Richard Hofstadter, *The American Political Tradition and the Men Who Made It* (1948; reprint ed., New York: Alfred A. Knopf, 1973), 233.

15. John Milton Cooper, Jr., *The Warrior and the Priest: Woodrow Wilson and Theodore Roosevelt* (Cambridge, Mass.: Havard University, Belknap Press, 1983), 73.

Panama Canal. Most important of all, he conducted the long and complex negotiations which led to a balanced peace between Russia and Japan after the Russo-Japanese War, and played an active role in the Algeciras Conference of 1906, backing Britain and France against Germany's vigorous pressure in Morocco. In mediating the Russo-Japanese War and in the Moroccan crisis, which was one of the critical episodes leading to the First World War, Roosevelt showed a prescient understanding of the American interest in the management of the balance of power both in Europe and in Asia. In the Far East, he tilted somewhat toward Russia; in Europe, toward Britain and France. In both these efforts, Roosevelt was the initiator of sustained programs, not a spectator. In both, his conduct was secret, carefully modulated, and effective in achieving his ends. In Cooper's judgment,

> Roosevelt's lusty arrogance, at least on a verbal level, about his enjoyment of power has left lingering doubts about his ultimate stature as a leader. But the fact remains that in several situations of great potential danger for the United States and the world, he acted with restraint and self-effacement to preserve peace and order. That conduct, more than anything specific on his list of accomplishments, constituted his greatest achievement as president.[16]

These and other American actions, especially in the Far East—the proclamation of the Open Door policy for China and the American role in suppressing the Boxer Rebellion—accustomed both the American people and the European powers to the possibility of American participation in world politics outside the Western Hemisphere. But Roosevelt never used "the bully pulpit" of his Presidency to begin the process of leading the American people to understand why these developments were necessary. Roosevelt made speech after speech preaching the need for greater American participation in world affairs, but always in his own special vocabulary, which combined Darwinism, Hegelianism, and muscular Christianity in almost equal parts. Strife, struggle, and great efforts, he told his countrymen, brought out the best in men and nations alike. The Anglo-Saxon race had achieved greatness and was destined to achieve more greatness if only the American people applied their talents and energies to the challenge. But he never explained what the challenge was, and why the exertions he extolled were necessary. The immense weight of the isolationist tradition in American politics restrained even Theodore Roosevelt. "Roo-

16. Ibid., 75.

sevelt frankly battled apathy and implicitly challenged the isolationist tradition in his utterances and publicized actions," Cooper writes, "but, like any prudent politician, he recognized the limits of his situation. Besides concealing his own momentous breaks with the isolationist tradition, he never directly challenged it in public."[17]

There was, nonetheless, a growing consciousness in the United States that all was not well with the world, and that America was somehow involved or affected. A few voices of the period—Walter Lippmann, Herbert Croly, Lewis Einstein—said that the transformations of the world balance of power were transforming the nature of America's security problem—that the United States could no longer enjoy the luxury of dependence in a world political system where order was maintained by others, but that we had to become an actor. Instead of accepting this analysis, however, the vast bulk of American opinion either paid no attention to it or denounced and resisted a view which seemed to deny the most sacred tenets of the American creed.

This kind of conflict between ideas and events is by no means peculiar to the American mind. In every country, decisions emerge from the same mix of themes, but in each, the combination of the elements is different, reflecting differences in histories, educational systems, and cultures. In the end a country's policies derive from assumptions which its statesmen regard as so obvious and axiomatic as hardly to be worth stating. What is apparent in the American reaction to the Spanish-American War and its consequences has two facets: facts changed, but ideas did not change nearly as much, and not nearly enough. There were changes in the structure of American life. The atmosphere of American politics reflected a greater and more active concern with issues of foreign policy than before. Certain actions took place—the annexation of the Philippines and Hawaii, for example, which turned out to be constructive factors in the evolution of American foreign and security policy. But while one could detect slight movement in the intellectual content of the American foreign policy tradition, Washington's Farewell Address and the Monroe Doctrine still had so much prestige as icons, and so much inertia, that they easily resisted the forces for change. When the First World War began in 1914, only a tiny group of Americans perceived any national interest in its outcome.

What did emerge as a result of the experience reflected in the

17. Ibid., 76.

Spanish-American War was characteristic of the American culture: an intensification of interest in arbitration and other peaceful ways to resolve international conflicts. Peace societies proliferated, and involved citizens and citizen leaders of consequence. They preached the virtues of the rule of law, the desirability of a world court to adjudicate disputes which might lead to war, and the need for a League to Keep the Peace. They were ridiculed by many as naive and unworldly, and many of their spokesmen deserved the criticism. But the essence of their message had something positive to contribute to the formation of American policy, and it played a vital part in one of the most important events in recent American and world history: Woodrow Wilson's decision to lead the United States into the First World War in 1917.

9

The Death of the Vienna System, July 1914

The British Government and the Parliaments out of which it sprang, did not believe in the approach of a great war, and were determined to prevent it; but at the same time the sinister hypothesis was continually present in their thoughts, and was repeatedly brought to the attention of Ministers by disquieting incidents and tendencies.

During the whole of those ten years this duality and discordance were the keynote of British politics; and those whose duty it was to watch over the safety of the country lived simultaneously in two different worlds of thought. There was the actual visible world with its peaceful activities and cosmopolitan aims; and there was a hypothetical world, a world "beneath the threshold," as it were, a world at one moment utterly fantastic, at the next seeming about to leap into reality—a world of monstrous shadows moving in convulsive combinations through vistas of fathomless catastrophe.—Winston S. Churchill

Just as the memory, the symbols, and the language of the French Revolution produced a sharp and abiding change in every aspect of French and European life—and in the life of countries far beyond Europe as well—so the First World War has dominated our minds and imaginations ever since. It was the tragedy from which the other political tragedies of the twentieth century all flowed. The twentieth century has known triumph as well as tragedy; its triumphs, too, have their roots in what used to be called the Great War.

While the state system was rebuilt after the war under the banner of the League of Nations as a reformed and improved version of the Concert of Europe, its vitality and the self-confidence of those who governed it were wounded beyond recognition. For the twenty years of the interwar period, both the peoples and the leaders of the western

The epigraph for this chapter is taken from Winston S. Churchill, *The World Crisis,* vol. 1, *1911–1914* (London: T. Butterworth, and New York: Charles Scribner's Sons, 1923), 18.

countries were paralyzed by the fear that a diplomacy of defending their interest in the peaceful management of the world order would lead to another world war. Moreover, the First World War weakened the restraints which civilization necessarily imposes on the aggressive instinct, and allowed Fascism, Communism, and other forms of modern tyranny to overwhelm nations which had been making steady progress for a century toward social improvement and the rule of law.

At the same time, the horror and devastation of the First World War encouraged men and women to seek bold and idealistic solutions both for the problem of war and for the political and social diseases of modern societies. Many of those programs immeasurably improved the quality of life in the Western countries; some, alas, turned out to be millenary recipes for self-deception and disaster. But one—Wilson's great idea—was planted and began to grow. It has had good seasons and bad, but it cannot be killed and must in the end prevail. It is the realization that international war cannot be made tolerable by humanitarian palliatives, however worthy, but must be outlawed altogether, and the peace enforced.

The First War also led within a generation to the end of the European empires, save only the Russian, and the emergence of ancient societies as new nations, determined to master the secrets of twentieth-century science and technology. And, above all, it destroyed the idea of progress, the Darwinian faith of the nineteenth century that if men worked hard and intelligently, their lives would improve, and their descendants would enjoy the blessings of abundance, peace, political liberty, and high culture. After 1918, everyone knew what Sophocles knew: that always and everywhere, civilization hangs by a single thread.

The bare bones of the story are clear and familiar. After a century of what now looms up as a nearly miraculous degree of restraint and cooperation among the great powers in accordance with the habits of the Vienna state system, that system collapsed in 1914. It was not a system of rigid stability like that advocated by the Holy Alliance, but one of flexible and pragmatic governance in the style of Pitt, Castlereagh, Talleyrand, Bismarck, Salisbury, and Disraeli. It had permitted the adaptation of the political order to great changes in the structure and dynamics of world politics without general war. The crisis which precipitated the war in 1914 was not nearly so serious in itself as many which had been successfully surmounted by diplomacy during the preceding fifty years. But this time war came, and raged for four years, spreading throughout the world.

The United States entered the war on the side of Britain, France, and Russia in April 1917. It fought in France and on the seas; at the end of the war, it landed troops in Murmansk in order to support Russian forces opposed to the Bolshevik Revolution, and in Siberia to protect Russia against what was perceived as a Japanese threat. From every vantage point, the American entry into the war was a decisive factor in the Allied victory. For a time, we participated in the occupation of Germany. Then the United States, in the grip of the conviction that its entry into the war had been a mistake, retreated into what it imagined was the safe orthodoxy of Washington's Farewell Address. Less than twenty years later, America discovered that the tides of war were engulfing the new state system and drawing the United States inexorably into their vortex for reasons which are still the subject of active and often virulent American debate.

Looking back at these events for the purposes of the present inquiry, two questions present themselves: First, why did the state system collapse in 1914 into general war—the catastrophe it was designed and developed to prevent? And second, why did the United States become a belligerent? Was that decision required by the national interest of the United States, or was it the result of folly, sentimentality, and a nefarious conspiracy of bankers, arms merchants, and British agents?

II

The vast literature of the First World War suggests three categories of causes which might explain the coming of the war: (1) economic rivalries, including colonial rivalries; (2) domestic pressures of various kinds, and especially the lust for power, or even for war itself, as a deliberate preference; or (3) the malfunctioning of the state system because of the stupidity or blindness of the democratic statesmen and of the public opinion which had chosen them and kept them in office; because of accident or miscalculation; or, finally, because the structure of the state system was simply not strong enough, institutionally and intellectually, to withstand the pressures to which it was exposed by a number of factors in combination, and particularly by Germany's drive for excessive power.

One can dismiss the economic explanations of the war out of hand. In all their forms, Marxist and non-Marxist alike, they explain nothing. They are immensely persistent, and strongly rooted in the American and indeed in the Western outlook. The rational Western mind finds it reassuring to think that men fight for something as tangible as profits rather than in response to unmeasurable emotions like patriotism, fear, the love of adventure and excitement, and even, in pathological cases like those of Napoleon and Hitler, the love of war itself.

Some writers contend that trade among nations is a factor for peace, others that economic rivalry among nations leads to war. Americans espouse both hypotheses with equal warmth, often at the same time. Neither has any substance. No countries could have traded with each other on a larger scale than Great Britain, France, and Germany. They went to war nonetheless. Equally, the active competition between British and American firms on the world market did not prevent Great Britain and the United States from making common cause against Germany.

The attempt to find an economic cause for the First World War has a special variant—the theory that colonial rivalries, and especially the German challenge to French and British power in Africa, the Middle East, and Asia, was an important cause of the war. There is no doubt that colonial rivalries were significant factors in convincing Britain, France, and Russia that German policies of expansion were becoming a threat to the peace. Germany's colonial policies were far less important in this respect than the scale of German armaments and its policies within Europe, but they were surely of importance. The attempt to go beyond the political and military implications of Germany's colonial efforts, however, and to ascribe economic motivations to them, are without weight.

In the period between 1880 and 1914, people generally believed that colonial empires were an important source of power and wealth. Lenin, following John A. Hobson, even constructed a theory of imperialism on the basis of that hypothesis. But there was nothing in it. From the time of Bentham, economist after economist has patiently demonstrated that empires were costly. Empire didn't make the imperial powers rich; they could afford empires because they were rich. The imperial powers had to invest vast resources in the armed forces needed to pacify and protect their colonies, and in the railroads, roads, schools, hospitals, harbors, and other govenmental services required to make them function. These costs, even for rich colonies like the Belgian Congo, were always greater than the taxes colonies could pay to their imperial masters and the profits citizens of the imperial power could bring home to enlarge the national income. Norman Angell wrote a book on the subject in 1910 called *The Great Illusion*. It was a best seller all over the world. Angell was knighted and honored for his services. Except for a few finance ministers, nobody really believed him.

In the years before 1914, Germany, France, Russia, the Austro-Hungarian Empire, the United States, Italy, and Great Britain lived in a rich, growing, and interdependent economy. The British pound was the stable basis for international trade and finance; passports were not required for travel in Europe, except in Russia; and tariffs were low. Workers, money, goods, and tourists moved freely among the countries. The old mercantilist anxieties about closed colonial markets and imperial preferences had long since diminished even as an irritant. They were of no consequence as a possible cause of war. Of course countries were increasing their prosperity at different rates; Germany, the United States, Russia, and Sweden were growing more rapidly than Great Britain, but they were all prosperous, and becoming more prosperous. A very large fraction of their trade was with each other, not with their colonies. There were disputes among the nations about economic policies, but they were the small beer of diplomacy, not the basis for blood feuds. The war simply cannot be explained on economic grounds. As Sir Michael Howard has said, "The origins of the tension which developed between Great Britain and Germany at the end of the Nineteenth Century have been exhaustively described and analysed, and one thing at least can be said of them with little fear of contradiction. They cannot be attributed to simple political or commercial rivalries."[1]

It is equally impossible to find a clue to the cause or causes of the war in domestic political pressures, either in the governing classes or the broader publics of any of the key countries. Although the war was welcomed in a burst of patriotic fervor in Germany, France, and Great Britain, there was neither a clamor for war nor a popular war party in any of those countries, and certainly not in Russia or in the Austro-Hungarian Empire, the two major powers most directly involved in the crisis that took shape after the assassination at Sarajevo. Russia was still licking its wounds after its defeat in the Russo-Japanese War of 1905 and the revolutionary events which had followed it. Its economy was booming, social conflict was diminishing, and Russian intellectual and artistic life was in a period of creative brilliance. And Vienna in 1914 was the last city on earth to nurture a generation of hawks. The people of the Dual Monarchy, like their government, understood the weakness of the multinational empire, and its vulnerability to the pressures of nationalism. There were concern and anxiety about war, as

---

1. Michael Howard, *The Continental Commitment: The Dilemma of British Defence Policy in the Era of the Two World Wars* (London: Maurice Temple Smith, 1972), 31.

well as a prudent emphasis on avoiding policies which might endanger stability, but no bloodthirsty demonstrations for war.

In Britain, political life was dominated by two issues: Home Rule for Ireland and Votes for Women. The Irish question led to mutiny or near-mutiny at the British military base at Curragh in Ireland. Many of the officers there, especially the Irish Protestants among them, were unwilling to use force against the Protestants in Ulster who feared domination by the Catholic South in the event home rule was adopted. The suffragettes and their movement touched an equally strong nerve in British life, and their efforts aroused intense feelings. The nation was also preoccupied with the radical welfare-state programs adopted by Parliament in 1910 under the pressure of the Liberal government's threat to pack the House of Lords if need be. The Labour Party, antimilitarist in principle, was beginning its Parliamentary career, and growing in strength with each election. While public opinion was keenly conscious of the German naval building program, and supported the policy of maintaining British naval supremacy, it was unwilling to enlarge the army, to adopt conscription, or to undertake military alliances. Certainly there was no jingoism in the British outlook, no thought, for example, of preventative war or any policy approaching it. And the Liberal Party, the party of the government, was deeply divided. A considerable part of its leadership and membership was nearly pacifist in outlook, and absorbed in one or another phase of the worldwide peace movement. Another sizeable fraction were Liberal imperialists of the Blue Water School. They supported the empire and the big navy it required, but were violently opposed to any involvement on the European continent.[2]

The position of public opinion in France and Germany was different, but certainly did not constitute a pressure for war, even in Germany. The French, more realistic about the true nature of the political situation than any of the other peoples about to be consumed in the holocaust, thought war was likely sooner or later, but did not anticipate a general war in 1914, and obviously did not favor one. They expected any new crisis to be managed and settled as the Moroccan crisis and

2. See George Dangerfield, *The Strange Death of Liberal England, 1910–1914* (New York: H. Smith and R. Haas, 1935). "It was ironic," Michael Howard wrote, that the Liberal Party "which traditionally regarded the whole concept of 'the balance of power' with such profound suspicion, should assume office almost at the exact moment when, for the first time for nearly a century, that concept was assuming so inescapable a relevance to the security of their country" (Howard, *Continental Commitment,* 33–34).

two Balkan wars of the recent past had been localized and resolved. The notion that France might start a war for Alsace and Lorraine was ridiculous. The political and social divisions of France were sharp, and they had been exacerbated shortly before 1914 by the intense and prolonged controversy over the Dreyfus case. But they were the divisions France had known since the Revolution, a normal and familiar part of French life. As a wise Frenchman once remarked, "You Americans think France has many political parties, but in fact it has only two: the party of the Revolution, and the party of the counter-Revolution." The two greatest French leaders of the war, Clemenceau and Marshal Foch, represented these two parties in extreme form: Clemenceau Republican, radical, anticlerical, and a Dreyfusard; Foch, a traditionalist, a Catholic, and a monarchist. They had no unusual difficulties in working together.

France was increasingly concerned by the growing military power of Germany and by the tone and direction of its foreign policy. It had an interest in containing and curbing that force, and building alliances that might cause it to mellow in time. But France's concern was an inducement to diplomatic, not to military action. No party and no faction in France favored preemptive war.

While the German policy of expansion as a military power had strong popular support, it was the policy of the government not of an aroused people. The Socialist Party had just become the largest party in the Reichstag. Before August 1914, it was definitely antiwar, although not pacifist. No one could say that the German government was pushed towards war by a bellicose nation, or that it turned to war as a way of unifying a fatally divided nation. German society had social divisions and divisions of interest like all the others, and it was undergoing large-scale processes of change, but its internal social and political tensions were in many ways less acute than those of France and Great Britain; its economic progress was rapid, and widely shared; and its systems of state-supported education and welfare were among the most advanced in the world.

While Germany in 1914 was economically and socially a leader, even a pioneer among the Western states, it was a political anomaly in Western Europe, an eighteenth-century autocracy with a thin and fragile overlay of democratic institutions. In theory and in practice, power was centralized in the Crown. The monarchy depended heavily on the support of the Prussian landowning aristocracy, from which most of the officers of the army were drawn. The constitution was limited, and the Kaiser's government often flirted with the idea of undoing even that restricted degree of constitutionalism and ruling by decree. Again, however, it would be difficult to contend that the political frustrations of the German people constituted in any sense a pressure for war.

There were interests and groups in Germany which might gain through German expansion to the West if Germany were to win a war against France—steel companies and other heavy industries interested in Lorraine and parts of northern France, and the military and naval leaders who favored the annexation of Belgium as "a pistol aimed at the head of England," for example. Such views did not surface until after the war began. As Hans Gatzke demonstrated, before war broke out, "both government and people had no aim beyond that of defending the Fatherland."[3]

One is left, then, with the proposition that the war came in 1914 because of the structural inadequacy or the defective management of the European state system—or both—in the face of a conjuncture of pressures which in combination proved to be too much for its built-in stabilizers.

Between 1871 and 1914, the European state system consisted of five major powers—Russia, Germany, the Austro-Hungarian Empire, Great Britain, and France; a considerable number of smaller powers; and the tradition of the Concert of Europe. The great powers adjusted their relations regularly in the ancient pattern of the balance of power minuet, as they perceived changes in their relative strength and in their ambitions. When frictions became acute, the great powers had developed the habit of consulting with each other, and sometimes meeting in congress at a high level, in order to find peaceful solutions for conflicts which threatened the peace. During the crisis which began at Sarajevo in June 1914, one of the major powers—Germany, and Germany alone—preferred war to the procedures of conciliation and compromise which had defused so many such disturbances since 1815. What Germany favored was a limited war, designed "to teach Serbia a lesson" and to protect Austria, its only reliable ally, against the risk of erosion. But the network of alliances which had been developing for a generation to contain the rising strength of Germany converted the Balkan quarrel into general war.

On the surface, the crisis of 1914 was dominated by two cycles of change, independent in their origins, but by then closely interrelated. The first was the formation of Germany in 1871 and the character of

---

3. Hans W. Gatzke, *Germany's Drive to the West: A Study of Germany's Western War Aims during the First World War* (Baltimore: Johns Hopkins University Press, 1950), 62.

its foreign policy, especially after the dismissal of Bismarck in 1890; the second was the final defeat of the Ottoman Empire in Europe, and its withdrawal by 1913 from all its European territory except for Constantinople itself and a thin strip of land on the European shores of the Bosporus and the Dardanelles. The emergence of Wilhelmine Germany was the engine that drove the old system over the cliff. The rivalry of Russia and Austria over their respective influence in the former European territories of the Ottoman Empire was simply the episode which demonstrated that the Concert of Europe was no longer able to find diplomatic compromises for conflicts which threatened the stability of the state system as a whole. That the explosion came in the Balkans was a coincidence; it could have happened at any one of a half-dozen neuralgic points affecting what had been for nearly half a century the relatively balanced relationship among the five great powers of the time.

The principal reason why the relationship among the five powers had become so fragile was that in 1871 Prussia suddenly became the German Empire, which had a vastly greater territory than Prussia, a much larger population, and a rapidly growing industrial base. From the moment Germany was established, it was the strongest military power on the continent, and, somewhat later, a pushing, probing, restless bidder for world power as well. Its birth immediately activated the conditioned reflexes of the state system. The nations were realigned, and the strength and style of Germany generated an atmosphere of tension and concern in the other countries.

Against Bismarck's instincts and counsel, Germany had annexed Alsace and Lorraine after the Franco-Prussian War, an act the French could neither forgive nor forget. Germany therefore built a system of alliances designed to make a French war of revenge unthinkable. A military alliance with Austria was signed in 1879 primarily as a defensive alliance against Russia. France could not contemplate war against Germany without Russia as an ally. But Bismarck's policy was to have good relations with Russia as well as with Austria, and his League of the Three Emperors—signed in 1872, renewed in 1884, and terminated in 1887—required the three monarchs to consult with each other about threatening problems and to remain neutral if one of the signatories was attacked by a fourth party. The League of the Three Emperors was the keystone of Bismarck's policy in this period. It was designed to keep Russia at arm's length from France and England, and somewhat to restrain Russian and Austrian rivalry in Eastern Europe.

In 1875, Germany seriously considered a second war with France as a way to make French revenge impossible. However, Great Britain, which had done nothing during the Franco-Prussian War, warned Germany against such folly, and Germany abstained. Instead, it entered into the Triple Alliance with Austro-Hungary and Italy. After the Bulgarian crisis of 1885–86, Bismarck reinforced the Triple Alliance by negotiating a "reinsurance" treaty with Russia, designed to keep always an open line between Berlin and St. Petersburg. Accepting Germany's strong interest in protecting the integrity of the Austro-Hungarian Empire, Russia was assured of German support for its ambitions in Bulgaria and other eastern parts of Southern Europe, and Germany was promised Russian neutrality in the event of a French attack.[4]

Germany's assertion of interests in Africa, the Far East, the Near East, and Turkey stirred Britain slowly and reluctantly to take an interest in Continental affairs. But the acceleration of the German naval building program after 1890 aroused Britain as nothing else could. France became more and more alarmed. It was no longer separated from the huge mass of Russia by a relatively harmless collection of small German states. On the contrary, the small German states had become a great and bellicose military power.

The Russian reaction was the same as that of France. After the new German state was formed in 1871, Bismarck's policy became one of European stabilization, not indefinite German expansion. When Bismarck was dismissed, however, that policy changed. Russia was willing to renew the Reinsurance Treaty of 1877, but the Kaiser was not. In the context of other disturbing developments, the end of the treaty increased Russian worries about the security of its most important frontier, that with Prussia, and encouraged Russia's interest in closer relations with France. France and Russia began to come together in a relationship of cooperation which became an alliance.

For the same reasons, Britain and France resolved their differences over Egypt and Morocco and revived the *entente cordiale* of the Crimean War period. Given the strength of the British tradition of "splendid isolation," Britain was politically incapable of making a firm military alliance with France—and a fortiori with Russia—or of facing the menace of a Continental war in advance. It had only a tiny professional army and hated the thought of conscription. And pacifism, near-pacifism, and illusion were powerfully represented in its politics and public opinion, especially in the Liberal Party, the governing party at

---

4. If not always convincing, George F. Kennan's *The Decline of Bismarck's European Order: Franco-Russian Relations, 1875–1890* (Princeton, N.J.: Princeton University Press, 1975), is a witty and insightful analysis of these tangled events.

the time. Yet, starting in 1905, France and Britain began serious (and secret) military talks among senior officers, and set about contingency planning for a war against Germany in northern France. The chief of the British general staff, Sir Henry Wilson, spent his holidays bicycling over the future battlefields of the First World War. Furthermore, Britain and Russia improved their relations with each other, divided Persia into spheres of influence, and abated or at least suspended a number of other areas of Anglo-Russian friction in Asia. They also engaged in naval talks.[5]

Bismarck had once sardonically remarked that in a world of five great powers, he always wanted to be in an alliance of three. Suddenly Germany found that its brusque push for imperial expansion had left it with only one ally, the Austro-Hungarian Empire. Italy was a nominal ally, but not if Great Britain were to be a belligerent. The alliance with Turkey came later. Russia had rebuffed Germany's efforts to prevent its alliance with France and its rapprochement with Britain. And Britain was equally reserved in responding to German bids for an "understanding" with regard to colonies and neutrality in the event of a war between Germany and France.

The British understood perfectly that the goal of Germany's ambitious naval policy was not to fight the Royal Navy, but to build a fleet so formidable that Britain would have to be neutral in the event of war on the Continent. That point was made not only in the speeches and memoranda of Admiral von Tirpitz but in the official explanations and indeed even in the text of the Second German Fleet Law of 1900. That astonishing document says:

> In order to protect German trade and commerce under existing conditions, only one thing will suffice, namely, Germany must possess a battle fleet of such a strength that, even for the most powerful naval adversary, a war would involve such risks as to make that Power's own supremacy doubtful.[6]

Four hundred years of history had taught the British what that statement meant.

All the powers settled down to expand their armed forces. Except

---

5. For pre–1914 diplomatic developments, see A.J.P. Taylor, *The Struggle for Mastery in Europe, 1848–1918,* Oxford: Clarendon Press, 1954; Howard, *Continental Commitment;* L.C.B. Seaman, *From Vienna to Versailles* (London: Methuen, 1955); and C.J. Bartlett, *The Global Conflict, 1880–1970* (London: Longman 1984).

6. Quoted in L. C. F. Turner, *Origins of the First World War* (New York: W. W. Norton, 1970), 2.

perhaps in Britain, the inner circles of most of the governments gradually came to believe that war was likely, perhaps inevitable. And the German general staff, facing this estimate of the future, decided that in the event of general war, with Italy an uncertainty, it would have to destroy the military power of France before dealing decisively with the more diffuse problems of the eastern front.

Meanwhile, in Eastern Europe, the concerted influence of the major powers had facilitated the settlement in 1913 of two Balkan Wars, and there was cautious optimism that the worst of Europe's Balkan troubles were over. The efforts of Russia and the Hapsburg Empire to drive Turkey out of Europe had lasted for more than a century, and had made the Eastern Question a perennial preoccupation of the European diplomats. Russia, an empire ruled by Slavs, pushed forward in the Balkans as the Ottoman Empire weakened. Austria-Hungary, far more threatened by Russia than by Turkey, began to feel that its survival was at stake. Britain and France moved from time to time to prevent Russia from capturing Constantinople, but abstained from the complex maneuvers, plots, assassinations, and wars of Balkan politics.

The explosive instability of the Balkans was no means cured in 1913, however. The Dual Monarchy was afraid that the Pan-Slav movement, with intermittent Russian backing, was leading Serbia to cast eyes on certain Austrian provinces populated by Slavs; the Hungarians wanted no more Slavs to be added to the Dual Empire; and the government in Vienna, encouraged by an earlier success in a similar situation, felt that if a crisis with Serbia should develop, it would have to be dealt with firmly in order to arrest the growing threat of nationalism to its continued existence. The Russian government knew that the Serbs and other Slavs in the Balkans were disappointed by Russia's failure to support all their claims in the negotiations which had settled the Second Balkan War. Although Serbia had gained a considerable territory in the settlement, the Russian ministers thought Russia would have to back Serbia firmly and visibly in the event of another Balkan crisis in order to maintain its position as a force in the region.

A key element in the final stages of the drama was the absence of the League of the Three Emperors—the cooperative relationship between Austria, Prussia, and Russia which had been an influence for stability if not always for justice after 1877 whenever trouble exploded in Eastern Europe. Now Russia and Austria were active rivals in the Balkans, and their relationship was such that Vienna did not consult St. Petersburg as the new crisis developed, perhaps because its ultimate goal was to absorb the Kingdom of Serbia into the empire or make it an Austrian satellite. Neither the Dual Monarchy nor the Russian government was the critical factor, however, in the next phases of the crisis. The German government was.

The archduke was murdered on 28 June by Gavrilo Princip, aided by a group of fellow Pan-Slav conspirators from the Austro-Hungarian province of Bosnia, a formerly Turkish territory which had been administered by the Dual Monarchy since 1878, and annexed in 1908. The assassin belonged to a circle of Pan-Slav nationalists living, meeting, and planning on Serbian soil. The government in Vienna immediately charged the Serbian government with responsibility for the outrage, either because Serbian officers were involved, or because the Serbs had failed to prevent their territory from being used as a launching pad for terrorist attacks against Austro-Hungary: precisely the legal argument, it should be noted, on which the United States had successfully relied in the *Alabama* affair during and after the Civil War. The Serbian government had been taken over in 1903 with the support of intensely nationalist officers who talked of annexing to Serbia parts of the Dual Monarchy inhabited by Southern Slavs: Serbs, and Croats as well.

The Dual Monarchy felt that military action was needed to force Serbia to suppress the terrorists and to stop all nationalist propaganda and subversive programs in Austro-Hungary emanating from Serbian territory. It was acutely conscious of the possibility that Russia might intervene to support Serbia if Austro-Hungary mobilized and demanded that Serbia accept its terms. But Austria could not make such a move without German backing. The authorities in Vienna therefore consulted at once with the German government, asking for German support of their proposed action against Serbia.

The assurance of German support had deterred Russian intervention when Austro-Hungary annexed Bosnia in 1908. Both Austria and Germany hoped the same procedure would produce the same result again. The Germans therefore quickly gave the Austrian delegates a promise of their full backing. The German reasoning seems to have been that since eventual war with Russia was nearly inevitable in any event, it was better to move while the Austro-Hungarian Empire was still a viable ally, even at the risk of Russian intervention, and Russian preparations for war were two or three years from completion. Other themes are sounded in the German documents of the period: the desire to see Serbia sharply punished for its sins; the strongly held policy of propping up the Hapsburg Empire as long as possible; and the belief that Germany could localize the resulting war by persuading Great

Britain and perhaps Russia and France to remain neutral. The German ambassador in London, Prince Karl Max Lichnowsky, warned Berlin with increasing anguish that it could not count on British neutrality; the chancellor, Theobald von Bethmann-Hollmeg, alternately frivolous or fatalistic, chose to be unconvinced. If Russia and France did enter the war, however, Germany was breezily confident it could cope, weakening both Russia and France for at least a generation. For these reasons, it made its fatal gamble.

The German blank check to Austria was given on 5 July, and reaffirmed with increasing urgency as the Austrians spent more than two weeks secretly debating the issues and drafting an ultimatum to be presented to Serbia. The tenor of German advice to its ally during this period was not caution and restraint but the desirability of rapid Austrian action against Serbia. The Germans did not approach the other powers in order to defuse the Serbian crisis. Quite the contrary. At this stage a compromise would have been easy to negotiate, since all the powers agreed that Serbia's action (or failure to act) was outrageous, and should be punished, but not too severely. On 23 July, the Austrian ultimatum was delivered to the Serbians, demanding an end of terrorism from Serbia, the suppression of anti-Austrian propaganda in Serbia, the arrest and punishment of any Serbian officers who had helped the conspirators in the murder, the tightening of border controls, and Austro-Hungarian participation in the Serbian investigation of possible Serbian involvement in the assassination plot. The Serbian response was to be submitted within forty-eight hours.

During this period, the Austrians took no steps to inform Russia or to consult with the Russian authorities, or, indeed, to consult with any power except Germany. While German diplomacy was busy trying to keep other powers out of a possible war, it did not consult either with Austria or with the other powers about the possibility of a peaceful solution of the Serbian issue. Despite their intelligence services, the Austrian ultimatum to Serbia was a bombshell to the other major powers, which began to react immediately and with foreboding when the news reached them. They knew how easily the network of alliances could convert the quarrel between Austria and Serbia into full-scale and general war.

The Serbs were stunned by the terms and the brutality of the ultimatum, but they were in no position to resist the Austrians. On the day after they received it, 24 July, a Serbian delegation visited Sergei Dimitrievich Sazonov, the Russian foreign minister, to ask for Russian support. "We confidently hope," the Serbian document said, "that this appeal will find an echo in your generous Slav heart." Sazonov saw the Austrian ultimatum as a deliberate act of war. "You have set fire to Europe," he said. The day after receiving the Serbians, the Czar authorized preparations for partial mobilization and word was telegraphed to Belgrade at once. The order for mobilization dealt with the southern part of Russia, facing Austria, but it was not issued immediately; the Czar hesitated. On the same day, just before the forty-eight-hour time limit expired, the Serbs accepted the Austro-Hungarian ultimatum except for the demand that Austria be permitted to participate in the Serbian inquiry into the assassination plot. Because Serbia had not accepted the ultimatum completely, the Austrian ambassador rejected the reply, pursuant to his instructions; called for his passports; and returned to Vienna.

Also on 25 July, the day the ultimatum expired, the Germans pressed the Austrians to start military action at once. Delay was dangerous, the Germans urged, because of the risk that the other powers might interfere. And, on the same day, Sir Edward Grey, the British foreign minister, sent invitations to Germany, France, and Italy, as powers "who had no direct interests in Serbia," to consult with the British in the interest of devising procedures of mediation and conciliation. The French and the Italians readily agreed to Grey's proposal, but the Germans refused on the ground that the matter concerned only Austria and Serbia, and should be settled by direct negotiations between them. Sazanov and the Austrian ambassador in St. Petersburg had a long and businesslike talk on 26 July. But Grey began to fear that his first round of efforts could not prevail. Throughout this crucial period, Germany found reason after reason for rejecting all the proposals for mediation and conciliation Sir Edward Grey put forward.

While under their mobilization plans the Austrians would not be ready to attack Serbia before 12 August, armed forces were assembling all across Europe. In Britain, the cabinet had been shocked on 27 July, when Grey raised the possibility of British participation in the war, if it came. Nonetheless, Britain was beginning to react to the danger. The British fleet, which had been on maneuvers, did not disperse to its normal stations after the maneuvers, and leaves were cancelled.

Hostilities had not broken out, however, and Grey turned to the Germans again. Grey had obtained some German cooperation in restraining Austria during the two recent Balkan crises, and hoped to persuade Germany to do so once more without imperiling the new understanding between Britain and Russia. Several of the best civil servants in the British Foreign Office thought the foreign minister was naive, and did not realize that Admiral Alfred von Tirpitz, Germany's veteran naval minister, and Count Helmuth von Moltke, German chief of staff, with the full backing of the German Foreign Office, were urging the Austrians to attack Serbia immediately.

Grey had urged moderation on the Russians, he said, and asked the Germans to do the same in Vienna. Britain was convinced that the Serbian reply to the Austrian ultimatum was an excellent basis for negotiations, far better than could have been expected. That fact, he thought, must reflect Russian advice to the Serbians. "The entire future of Anglo-German relations," Grey added, depended upon Germany's willingness to join Britain in trying to prevent war.

On reading the British message, the Kaiser advised the German foreign minister that the Austrians should occupy Belgrade even if general war were averted. Such a move was essential as a guaranty that Serbia would fulfill its promises, because the Serbs were "Orientals and so mendacious, false, and masters of obstruction." While the Germans passed Grey's message on to the Austro-Hungarian government, they did so without adding any message of their own. On the contrary. When the German ambassador in Vienna, acting without instructions, cautioned Austria "to exercise restraint," he was reprimanded for his indiscretion. And on 27 July, the Austrian ambassador to Berlin informed his foreign minister in Vienna that he would shortly receive the text of the British proposals for mediation from the German government. He wrote:

> The German government assures [us] in the most decided way that it does not identify itself with these propositions, that on the contrary it advises [us] to disregard them, but that it must pass them on, to satisfy the English government. The German government holds the belief that it is just now of the very highest importance that England should not side with Russia and France. Therefore everything must be done to prevent the wire still working between Germany and England from being broken.[7]

7. Imanuel Geiss, ed., *July 1914, The Outbreak of the First World War: Selected Documents* (1967; reprint ed., New York: W. W. Norton, Norton Library, 1974), 236. There are several reports of conversations having the same tenor (see Geiss, 218–26). At the same time, the Kaiser returned to Berlin from a visit to Sweden. When he read, for the first time, the Serbian reply to the Austrian ultimatum, he concluded that the Serbians had removed "every reason for war." The Kaiser instructed his chancellor "to advise Vienna to be conciliatory." Bethmann-Hollweg sent a watered-down and misleading version of the Kaiser's message to

The German military continued to push the Austrians to start bombarding Belgrade immediately. Austria declared war on Serbia on 28 July and shelled Belgrade on 29 July. At that point it was impossible for the German civilian government to move effectively for a diplomatic solution to the crisis, even if one assumes that some civilians would have preferred such a course. The Austrian government, confronting the German position, rejected the British proposal as "too late."

The focus of the crisis shifted. France, directly threatened by Germany, had decided to honor its treaty with Russia, and France and Russia both urged Britain to declare itself as the only way to prevent war. They were convinced that the German attitude would change if it confronted a firm British position, and that Austria would back down if the Germans did. The German evaluation of the British mind was quite different. As the Kaiser remarked, the British had only "a contemptible little army," and were not therefore a serious factor in the situation. On 28 July, Germany promised Britain that if it remained neutral, Germany would not annex French territory, although it would expect to take over French colonies. The British cabinet remained profoundly—and almost evenly—divided, so all Grey could tell the French and the Russians in those crucial days was that Britain had not yet made up its mind, and was continuing to preserve its freedom of action. Until the end, Grey kept trying one formula after another for a compromise solution, the last one being that Austria should occupy Belgrade until it was clear that Serbia would fulfill the terms laid down by the Austrian ultimatum.

As mobilizations proceeded, the whirlwind took over. The German battle plan against France required a violation of Belgian neutrality. That dimension of the war became manifest on 2 August, when the Germans invaded Belgium. That thunderclap helped to clarify many British minds, although in the end four members of the cabinet resigned. (Two later returned to the fold.) While the violation of Belgian neutrality outraged British public and official opinion, what the British decision for war represented in the end was the half-conscious realization that Britain would not be safe at home or abroad in the event of German victory. It could not be in Britain's interest to face a militant Germany which dominated Europe from the Channel to the Urals, and

Vienna, but not until the Austrians had finally declared war. The Kaiser's initiative disappeared in the avalanche of events (Geiss, *July 1914,* 222–23, 256–57). Grey's comment about the future of Anglo-German relations appears in Geiss, *July 1914,* 240.

Asia to Vladivostok. While few of the participants or writers of the time explained their conclusions in such language, James Joll concludes that this rather cloudy mood of rising anxiety was the force which overcame Britain's doubts and hesitations.[8] His judgment recalls Thucydides' observation that the most important cause of the Peloponnesian War was the rising power of Athens, and the fear it caused in Sparta.

For a decade or more, the Royal Navy, some of the leading Foreign Office officials, and a number of writers and political figures had been warning the government and the public about the threat of German power and German ambitions to the European balance of power, and thus to Britain's most vital security interest. Events were now perceived as confirming the analysis behind those early warnings. As Michael Howard has said:

> It was indeed precisely the failure of German power to find an outlet and its consequent concentration in Europe, its lack of any significant possessions overseas, that made it so peculiarly menacing to the sprawling British Empire in two World Wars. . . . But the German interests pressing for the development of world power were not concerned with expanding within what they saw as a British dominated world-system. It was precisely that system which they found intolerable, and which they were determined to challenge on a basis of equality.[9]

---

8. James Joll, *The Origins of the First World War,* Origins of Modern Wars Series (London and New York: Longman, 1984), 16–28, 206. See also V. R. Berghahn, *Germany and the Approach of War in 1914* (New York: St. Martin's Press, 1973); Zara S. Steiner, *Britain and the Origins of the First World War* (London: Macmillan, and New York: St. Martin's Press, 1977); Michael G. Ekstein and Zara Steiner, chap. 23, in *British Foreign Policy under Sir Edward Grey,* ed. F. H. Hinsley; Fritz Fischer, *Germany's Aims in the First World War* (New York: W. W. Norton, 1967); and idem, *War of Illusions: German Policies from 1911 to 1914* (New York: W. W. Norton, 1975). In 1912 Grey had said to the Committee on Imperial Defense that there was no appreciable danger of Britain's becoming involved in any considerable trouble unless "there is some Power, or group of Powers, in Europe which has the ambition of achieving what I would call the Napoleonic policy" (in Hinsley, *British Foreign Policy,* 403). In the same testimony, Grey continued "If a European conflict, not of our making, arose, in which it was quite clear that the struggle was one for supremacy in Europe, in fact, that you got back to a situation something like that in the old Napoleonic days, then . . . our concern in seeing that there did not arise a supremacy in Europe which entailed a combination that would deprive us of the command of the sea would be such that we might have to take part in that European war. That is why the naval position underlies our European policy" (quoted in Arthur J. Marder, *From the Dreadnought to Scapa Flow: The Royal Navy in the Fisher Era, 1904–1914,* vol. 1, *The Road to War, 1904–1914* [New York and London: Oxford University Press, 1961], 429).

9. Howard, *Continental Commitment,* 32

Sir Eyre Crowe, one of the ablest civil servants in the British Foreign Office, who had been a powerful influence for a realistic policy for at least a decade, raised a second point. In the final days before the war began, he warned his colleagues that it was already too late to persuade France to restrain Russia. If war came, and Britain attempted to remain neutral, she would find herself isolated and friendless whichever side won, and would therefore face threats to her interests all over the world.

The role of public opinion in the various governments' moves toward war was greater than in any previous war, especially but not only in the democracies. Germany carefully manipulated the timing of its visible decisions in order to make it appear that Russia took the first steps which made war inevitable. Thus Russia had announced partial mobilization in the south—that is, only against Austria—on 29 July, after long and anguished hesitation on the part of the Czar, while Germany deliberately waited. On 30 July, after the Austrian declaration of war against Serbia and the shelling of Belgrade, Russia decided on general mobilization to begin on 31 July. Germany issued a twelve-hour ultimatum to Russia to cancel its mobilization orders or face German mobilization; Russia rejected the ultimatum and Germany thereupon mobilized. The Austrian order of mobilization was also announced on 31 July; Germany declared war on Russia on 1 August and against France on 2 August, when the German ultimatum to Belgium was presented. The British decision went into effect at midnight on 4 August, and Britain resolved to send an expeditionary force to France on 6 August.

The literature on the causes of the First World War seems to have reached something like a consensus along the lines of the analysis summarized in the preceding pages. Few now embrace theories of economic causation or those which look to domestic political or social conditions in the various countries for the "underlying" causes of the war. Attention is directed mainly to the functioning of the state system as the fundamental matrix of the war. There were mistakes, miscalculations, and misperceptions galore among those who directed the governments. And many writers would put the emphasis differently. They ask whether Germany's responsibility for the war was really greater than that of Russia in deciding to support Serbia, or Britain's in failing to decide early enough to oppose Germany if it went to war with France and Russia.

There is, however, a profound difference between those who affirmatively will to initiate war or gamble irresponsibly on the long odds that they can keep others neutral, and those who dither about whether they have interests worth defending in the outcome of a war. The First World War was not caused by miscalculation or by the machinery of war, by the time tables of mobilization, or by sheer momentum. Germany's conduct in relation to the war was different from that of all the other principal actors. The Austro-Hungarian Empire could not have used force against Serbia without German support. Germany provided that support, either because it considered the viability of Austria indispensable to its security or because it had decided on war with Russia before Russian military power was fully restored. Germany never advised the Dual Monarchy to pursue a restrained and moderate policy; it never pointed out to Austria that Serbia had in fact accepted 98 percent of the Austrian ultimatum; over and over again, it refused to cooperate with the British, French, the Italians, or the Russians in putting the fire out. Instead, it repeatedly urged the Dual Monarchy to use force against Serbia and to do so promptly, before Britain and the other powers could "interfere." Germany concealed her true course in relation to the conflict between Austria and Serbia both before and after Grey finally discovered what was happening and tried to organize the kind of mediation which had worked so often before.

In short, Germany violated the first principles of the Concert of Europe. German foreign policy was pursuing goals of expansion which were incompatible with the major premise of the Concert—that general peace was the supreme national interest of the major powers, and keeping the peace, their greatest responsibility. The fear of German expansion had provoked Britain, France, and Russia to come together in a defensive posture. Germany claimed it feared "encirclement." But it was not "encircled" by hostile and aggressive powers capable of waging preventative or preemptive war against it. The Franco-Russian-British entente was not an alliance to destroy Germany. It was an association intended to deter and contain Germany's expansionist impulses. Germany definitely, repeatedly, and forcefully chose to go to war rather than give up its policy of indefinite and aggressive expansion.

From the point of view of the present enquiry, however, the question of German war guilt is secondary if not irrelevant. The key point for our purposes is that the state system lacked the power and the information to deal effectively with the threat to the peace which became manifest after Sarajevo.

10

The Vienna System Reborn, April 1917

As the story unwinds, while the others in it play according to their natures the roles that events assign to them, Wilson reveals himself as more than the leading character. His character becomes a part of the story itself. Events no longer matter only objectively. It becomes relevant to see how they appeared to Wilson, how they mixed with the sort of man he was, and how in the chemistry of his thoughts the future was precipitated. As Winston Churchill wrote in The World Crisis:

> *It seems no exaggeration to pronounce that the action of the United States with its repercussions on the history of the world depended, during the awful period of Armageddon, upon the workings of this man's mind and spirit to the exclusion of almost every other factor; and that he played a part in the fate of nations incomparably more direct and personal than any other man.*

The United States was not in April 1917 swept into war. She was not dragged into it by treaties she had to honour. She was not directly threatened. She made no calculation of probable gains and losses. Why then did she go to war? In this book I reach the conclusion that it was because Wilson so decided. This is a simple conclusion which depends for its validity on the weight of evidence. But when it is reached it raises inescapably a question far more complex. Why did Wilson go to war: what made the man who was "too proud to fight" descend into the arena?—Patrick Devlin

When the First World War began in 1914, there was a nearly universal belief among Americans that the war was none of their country's business. Opinion about the war was largely sentimental. Americans favored one side or the other as they favored one baseball team or another. The Anglophiles and the Francophiles sympathized with Eng-

The epigraph for this chapter is taken from Patrick Devlin, *Too Proud to Fight: Woodrow Wilson's Neutrality* (New York and London: Oxford University Press, 1974), vii–viii.

land and France. There was a good deal of anti-British feeling among people of German or Irish descent. There was also a general distaste for the autocratic character of the Czarist regime in Russia, and for Russian anti-Semitism and the violent pogroms against which the United States had been protesting for fifty years or more. The German violation of Belgian neutrality caused a moral shock in the United States as well as in England. The French were concerned but not shocked; they expected little. Most Americans would have preferred the democracies to win, simply because they were democracies. But most of them felt, and in 1914 and 1915 some said, that a German victory would be a matter of indifference to the United States from the point of view of its national security.

The American decision for neutrality in 1914 was not even a decision; it was taken as a matter of course. When the President issued a proclamation of neutrality, there was no protest in Congress or in the country. Of course we were neutral. The thought that we should send an expeditionary force to fight in Europe was a blasphemous and fantastic nightmare. True, the armed forces of the United States had already fought in the Philippines and in China. In China, however, they were part of an international police force instructed to restore order during the Boxer Rebellion, and one of America's motives was to prevent the disintegration of China into European spheres of influence. And by 1914 American opinion was inclined to view the Spanish-American War, at least in its Philippine phase, as a transient attack of the imperial virus from which the country had happily recovered.

Yet less than three years later, the United States declared war against Germany and sent a significant army and navy to share in the final year and a half of the fighting. The decision and its consequences turned out to be one of the most important events of the twentieth century.

How and why did it come about, and what did it mean? The United States had been created, enlarged, and sustained at every point of its history not only by its own exertions but by the workings of the European state system. Did the decision to go to war in April 1917 mean that the United States had come to realize that fundamental changes in the world balance of power now required direct and sustained American participation in the functioning of a reformed system of world public order? Or was America's entry into the war an aberration, the result of a clever plot on the part of the British, the international bankers, and the "merchants of death," or a folly caused by the dangerous dreams of Utopian idealists led by Woodrow Wilson?

Wilson, who took office in 1913, was an able Progressive Democrat without experience in foreign affairs. He had taken an interest in the subject during his years as a professor at Bryn Mawr, Wesleyan, and Princeton, but he was by no means a specialist. Nonetheless, he had read widely in the field, and handled his first diplomatic problems with assurance and energy. He was a man of exceptional ability and eloquence, endowed with remarkable will, self-discipline, and an ambition for greatness. Politics had always been his first choice among careers. His father was an intellectual Presbyterian minister, and his mother a clergyman's daughter. As president of Princeton University, Wilson had introduced many educational and social reforms, and was ultimately defeated by the resistance of the university's tradition-minded faculty and alumni. Rebuffed at Princeton, Wilson became governor of New Jersey for one spectacularly successful term before being chosen as the Democratic candidate for President at an exciting and divided convention in 1912. A decisive factor in his nomination was the support which William Jennings Bryan switched to Wilson after it became clear that the party would not nominate the Great Commoner from Nebraska to lose the national election for a fourth time.

Bryan was a pacifist, a populist, a simple man with little education and strong religious feelings who had electrified the country during the depression of the nineties with his great Cross of Gold speech at the Democratic Convention of 1896. Later he was to become a figure of fun at the Scopes trial, where a schoolteacher was tried under a statute which made it a crime to teach the theory of evolution. Richard Hofstadter characterized Bryan as "a circuit-riding evangelist in politics," a revivalist who appealed to the tradition of rural, lower-class, evangelical Protestantism, and a man who knew "little literature but the Bible."[1] Oswald Garrison Villard said of him, "Of all the men I have seen at close range in thirty-one years of newspaper service, Mr. Bryan seemed to me the most ignorant."[2] And Bernard De Voto wrote of "the sonorous, fraudulent voice of an eater of wild honey in the hills," which "had quieted a Chicago convention hall" with the electrifying words, "You shall not crucify mankind upon a cross of gold."[3] Nevertheless, Bryan was viewed by a considerable fraction of the Democratic party as a beloved prophet, and he was a political force Wilson had to

---

1. Richard Hofstadter, *The American Political Tradition and the Men Who Made It* (1948; reprint ed., New York: Alfred A. Knopf, 1973), 183.
2. Oswald Garrison Villard, *Prophets True and False* (New York: Alfred A. Knopf, 1928), 210.
3. Bernard De Voto, *The Easy Chair* (Boston: Houghton Mifflin, 1955), 21.

propitiate in selecting his cabinet. It was thus altogether natural, given the nature of American politics, that Wilson made Bryan his secretary of state. No other post would do for a man who had been the party's Presidential choice three times. It is hard to imagine a less plausible combination, however, than the austere Presbyterian Princetonian and the revivalist country preacher, or a man less likely to be even an adequate secretary of state than William Jennings Bryan.

Except for Cleveland, Wilson was the first Democrat to be elected since the Civil War. He owed his election largely to the coincidence that Theodore Roosevelt had split the Republican Party by running against William Howard Taft on a third-party Progressive ticket. That fact, as well as Bryan's presence in the government, reinforced Wilson's own rather cautious but fully considered impulses as a Progressive reformer of domestic policy, the principal focus of Wilson's interest during his first term. Those years were marked by a dramatic series of victories for the President in Congress, which established the Federal Reserve System; reformed the antitrust law and created the Federal Trade Commission; protected the legality of trade unions; provided an ongoing administrative procedure for reducing tariffs; and gave special assistance to agriculture. Virtually the whole of Theodore Roosevelt's Progressive platform of 1912 became law. Wilson's triumph stimulated the gradual shift of Progressives from the Republican to the Democratic Party, a trend which prepared the way twenty years later for Franklin D. Roosevelt, whose policies and popularity greatly accelerated the momentum of the movement.

But the war inevitably began to absorb more and more of the government's attention, and that of the country at large. The war news was vivid, continuous, and nearly all bad for the Allied cause. Strong voices, both within the government and in the press, began to contend for more and more active American measures to help Britain and France. Theodore Roosevelt was their leader. Deeply unhappy because he was not President, Roosevelt became shrill and intemperate. He was consumed with hatred for Wilson, the interloper who dared to occupy his rightful place. He flayed Wilson as a "coward," a "hypocrite," and a "poltroon." But even Roosevelt did not quite advocate a declaration of war. Nonetheless, the former President commanded the attention of the American public and was strongly supported in his views on the war by a considerable and influential segment of opinion.

In making and carrying out his policy toward the war, Wilson relied not on Bryan—or later on Lansing, Bryan's successor—but on his confidant and friend, Colonel Edward M. House. Wilson and House had met in 1912, before Wilson was nominated. They became friends at once at a level of intimacy rare for Wilson, especially in his relations with men. House was an idealist, devoted to good causes. In temperament, he was a man who preferred a role behind the scenes, working through a leader he admired. Extremely sensitive to the problems faced by a private citizen conducting such a relationship with a Prince, House managed for some six years to avoid arousing the President's suspicions, anxieties, or resentments about a servant who didn't know his place. While Wilson's letters to House seem to be written in the spontaneous personal voice of a public figure enjoying the relaxation of private and sometimes indiscreet talk with a trusted friend, House's letters to Wilson are works of art, blending respectful flattery and reportage with almost invisible recommendations for action. Those recommendations are always tempered by House's acute sensitivity both to the boundaries of his role and to his sense of what Wilson wanted to hear. While it lasted, it was an extraordinary relationship, comparable more to those of Elizabeth I and Catherine the Great with some of their favorites than to any precedent in American history.

Starting in 1912, Wilson used House as a sounding board and counsellor, and as a confidential agent in getting the nomination and organizing his administration. Later, House's role was almost exclusively to help Wilson develop his ideas about the ends and means of foreign policy, which was his adviser's special interest. House's claim to a place in history is that he served Wilson as his ambassador at large in exploring possible approaches to peace with the chief European governments on both sides of the war. The two men shared the same passionate conviction that the methods of international politics would have to be radically reformed in order to rid the world of war. From the first days of their momentous association, Wilson and House canvassed the implications of this thesis, which in the end became Wilson's proposal for the League of Nations, and the dominant reason why he recommended to Congress that the United States declare war against Germany.

As soon as the war at sea started, however, the international law of neutrality became the daily bread of American diplomacy and of the American newspapers. The diplomats, the pundits of the press, and the men in the corner saloon began to argue about the right of search and seizure, the list of contraband items, and the doctrine that "free flags make free goods." They also began to argue about whether we should be entirely even-handed in applying the law of neutrality to Germany and to Great Britain. American banks organized huge lines of credit for Britain and France, and the United States quickly became a major source of supplies for the allies.

In the 1914–18 war, the law of neutrality had to take account of a new technology, that of the submarine. While a number of German cruisers and small squadrons roamed the seas, looking for merchantmen or convoys, the larger part of the German high seas fleet spent the war in harbor, save for the foray which led to the Battle of Jutland. The submarine was therefore Germany's main naval weapon against both the allied blockade of Germany and the flow of supplies headed for Britain and France. New to naval warfare, the submarine proved to be an extremely powerful, effective, and elusive weapon system.

The submarine immediately challenged the traditional law of neutrality. It was supposed to surface before searching and seizing enemy or neutral merchant vessels. But submarines are vulnerable when on the surface. As a result, Germany was led to experiment with unrestricted submarine warfare, and opinion in Great Britain and the United States was scandalized by a series of disturbing episodes in which submerged German submarines torpedoed merchant vessels and liners without warning, killing many civilian passengers and crew members.

The United States protested vehemently and often both to Great Britain and to Germany about their treatment of American vessels and cargoes, but Germany soon noticed that the United States was not equally offended by the illegal behavior of the two belligerents. The Germans tended to dismiss the American complaints, the British to treat them more gently, although Britain too could not and did not fully accept the American view of the privileges of neutrals in time of war. British policy was dominated always by the fact that the United States was an important supplier, and by the hope that somehow, sometime, it would enter the war on the Allied side. Germany, on the other hand, could entertain no such hopes. With increasing asperity, Germany complained that the United States was unneutral in its sympathies and behavior, and was becoming an ally of Britain and France in everything but name. While the German Foreign Office repeatedly advised the Kaiser to treat American protests with more delicacy, and to refrain from adopting a policy of unrestricted submarine warfare, the bitter pressures of the war at sea, and the increasing German feeling that American policy toward Germany could hardly be more hostile, finally led the German government, after a public warning, to abandon all pretense of conducting submarine warfare in accordance with international law.

The result was that American opinion was bombarded not only with graphic reports of German atrocities in Belgium and France, but with an endless flow of news about German atrocities at sea—atrocities in which, as we believed, the Germans were violating international law and brushing aside the claims of American dignity and American honor.

The impact of the maritime war on American opinion was sharp and direct. It only served, however, to dramatize and reinforce the more complex influence which the course of the war on land was having on American attitudes. Month after month for nearly three years, Americans were forced to contemplate a prospect which became more and more troublesome. Germany and its allies were not quite winning the war, but they were gaining slowly and inexorably. Even before Russia withdrew from the war and made a separate peace with Germany and Austria at Brest-Litovsk in 1917, the Central Powers were visibly moving toward a position which would make a German victory nearly inevitable.

The American public and the American government began to view the war in an altogether different way. It was no longer a remote adventure story, but a monstrous event whose shadows darkened the horizon even for America. More and more Americans began to question the commonplace of 1914, that the United States had no stake in the outcome of the war, and could comfortably pursue its destiny whether Germany or the Allies won. While American opinion about the war became more sober and anxious by the day, the restraining weight of Washington's Farewell Address and the reluctance of a democratic and pacific people to make war in cold blood were too strong to be overcome by anything short of a perceived attack, or the leadership of an eloquent President. There was no Pearl Harbor, no sinking of the *Maine,* to produce the decision automatically.

The election of 1916 seemed to precipitate the issue, but ultimately did not. Charles Evans Hughes was the Republican candidate. No other election in American history matched two candidates who approached Hughes and Wilson in intellectual and personal quality. Hughes was a brilliant and courageous man, also a professor, who had been an out-standing reform governor of New York, a leader of Progressive forces in the decade before 1914, and a justice of the Supreme Court of the United States who had quickly become a force on the Court. Later, of course, he was to be one of our finest chief justices. Hughes resigned from the Supreme Court in order to accept the Republican nomination in 1916. The Progressive Party had been splintered by the war issue. Many of its strongest leaders, like Senator Hiram Johnson, were convinced isolationists. Theodore Roosevelt, saddened by these divisions among his followers, and infuriated because the Republican Party showed no sign of wanting to draft him, decided simply to support the Republican candidate. Wilson ran as the President "who kept us out of war." The campaign, however, did not fulfill Wilson's slogan. The debate about the war was moderate, and did not lock either candidate into an intransigent position.

While Wilson still spoke for "peace without victory," and continued to probe both the Western Allies and Germany about the possibility of a compromise peace, the focus of his concern, and the country's, changed month by month. The war was concentrating the American mind. The possibility of a German victory had ceased to be "a matter of indifference" to the United States. In a number of speeches, starting as early as January 1916, Wilson said that "what America has to fear, if it has anything to fear, are indirect, roundabout flank movements upon the Western Hemisphere," not a direct invasion. Such language, however guarded, was a long way from the language of confident neutrality used in 1914 and 1915. As Edward Buehrig has pointed out, it had become clear that a German victory would require the United States, and the New World as a whole, "to make a hazardous adjustment to the new dispensation across the Atlantic. Since the New World, and notably the United States as its dominant member, had happily achieved accommodation with British power, the prospect of facing a new adjustment, with an ill-disposed Power, was doubly unattractive."[4]

From the beginning of the War, Wilson talked continuously with House, and had House conduct sustained conversations and other exchanges with his European interlocutors about the possibility of a negotiated peace. In retrospect, Sir Edward Grey stands out as the most patient, farsighted, and sagacious of the European participants in this extraordinary dialogue which forced Wilson to think deeply about the interests at stake for each belligerent, and to define American foreign policy precisely and in detail. Grey understood that in his exchanges with Wilson, as in his relationship earlier with Theodore Roosevelt, he was dealing with a first-class intellect and an altogether serious and dedicated man—a man capable of being convinced by reason and by an appeal to values which Grey fully shared as an English Liberal and

4. Edward H. Buehrig, "Woodrow Wilson and Collective Security," in *Wilson's Foreign Policy in Perspective,* ed. Edward H. Buehrig (Bloomington: Indiana University Press, 1957), 34, 38. See also Professor Buehrig's *Woodrow Wilson and the Balance of Power* (Bloomington: Indiana University Press, 1955), and Arthur S. Link, *Wilson the Diplomatist: A Look at His Major Foreign Policies* (Baltimore: Johns Hopkins University Press, 1957), 88.

Whig. As early as the autumn of 1914, Grey responded to the first American questions about British war aims by asking whether the United States was prepared to become an active participant in a European peace settlement, and if so, what it was willing to do. Grey was seeking nothing short of an American guaranty for such a settlement and an assurance that the United States would remain continuously engaged in European and world diplomacy as a major power. As Buehrig writes,

> One cannot help admiring Grey's insight into the new requirements of world politics; and what he proposed was a veritable diplomatic revolution. It is reminiscent of Canning's calling in the New World to redress the balance of the old, but whereas Canning wished actually to seal off the New World to prevent its disturbing the balance of the old, Grey would summon the United States to an active role in Old World affairs. Such is the measure of the change wrought in international politics within a century's time.[5]

As House, Lansing, and Wilson addressed the questions Grey posed, the United States inevitably began to transform its foreign policy. The ultimate stage in that process, after Wilson had been briefed, and talk had yielded its impressions, was of Wilson alone at his typewriter, drafting his speeches and dispatches. At his typewriter, Wilson struggled to reconcile the old American foreign policy shibboleths to what the new conditions of the world required. The memory of a foreign policy seeming to consist only of Washington's Farewell Address and the Monroe Doctrine is still deeply and tenaciously rooted in the American mind and demonstrates its vitality every day. When House and Wilson began their exchanges with Grey, the power of Washington's legacy seemed unassailable and insuperable.

For several years, step by step, the colloquy between Grey, House, and Wilson continued. Wilson sought to adapt the Monroe Doctrine and the traditional American support for neutral rights to a policy of collective protection for "freedom of the seas." Grey replied that collective action to assure freedom of the seas was meaningless as long as Germany (or anyone else) was free to practice aggression on land. Since Wilson's mind, like Grey's, was filled with reports of the apparently endless fighting on both the eastern and western fronts, the Americans could not dispute Grey's point. Wilson began to draft sketches for a League of States to Keep the Peace, borrowing phrases as he could

5. Buehrig, "Woodrow Wilson and Collective Security," 44.

from Monroe's message and other sacred texts in the hope of making the idea of collective security palatable in American politics.

Thus Wilson's efforts to make peace during the war—a "peace without victory"—led to the articulation of a plan to institutionalize peace after an Allied victory. The concept of a League of Nations as it crystallized through the combined efforts of Grey, House, and Wilson was decidedly an Anglo-American achievement. Germany had rebuffed House's questions and suggestions over and over again, and clearly would not be interested in such a league if it won the war. The idea of the League of Nations came to fill Wilson's mind and spirit. To create it was the only possible war aim worthy of the United States, the only outcome of the war which could in part justify the suffering and inhumanity it had spawned.

Did the evolution of this conviction in Wilson's mind after nearly three years of struggling with the travails of neutrality and the disappointments of peacemaking have anything to do with his decision to lead his doubting, troubled, reluctant, and divided people into the war?

The most convincing answer to this question in the literature is offered by Patrick Devlin's luminous book, *Too Proud to Fight: Woodrow Wilson's Neutrality*. Lord Devlin is a retired English judge and man of affairs who worked on his book for more than twenty years in the interstices of an active and brilliantly successful public career. The driving force behind Devlin's effort, as the dedication of the book makes clear, is that he was too young for the First World War and got his chance for "early attainment through the gaps it blasted out of the classes above me. The chance was bought for me by the dead: my gain is what they lost." "All through the writing I have been pricked," he writes, by "the insistent drumming of the fight, of wounds and death. The death of the unripe. . . . and the Unfulfilled."

Devlin defines his task as that of explaining "the emergence of the United States into the international world" in April 1917. He brought to that effort the scrupulous discipline of a first-rate judge in marshalling and weighing the evidence; the wit and style of a master of English prose; and the psychological insight of a sensitive man who has spent a lifetime evaluating human motivations. His book stands out in a literature which has a considerable number of excellent books, and a large number of superior and useful ones.

Many serious students of the American decision to go to war conclude that the decision was determined by what America regarded as massive German violations of American neutrality and above all by its use of the submarine. Devlin comments that these legal perplexities

> do not explain why America went to war. As a matter of law she considered Germany to be hopelessly in the wrong but she did not go to war simply because of that. She considered with almost as much justification that Britain was hopelessly in the wrong too. Nations do not go to war because they have a good cause of action. The ultimatums and diplomatic exchanges reveal only the tip of a complex of calculations and emotions. Theoretically the American Civil War was fought about the doctrine of state sovereignty, but as Wilson wrote in the notes for a lecture he prepared in 1886: "Wars are seldom fought about abstract theories. . . . The North and South fought because their differences and antagonisms had become intolerable and state sovereignty was made the formal basis of the war."[6]

It is true, Devlin went on, that America

> had put herself forward as the custodian of neutral rights and that Wilson had spoken of "the whole fine fabric of international law" and America's "proud position as a spokesman even amidst the turmoil of war, for the law and the right." This would be a noble but dry reason for going to war and Wilson had never allowed it to appear cut off from the wells of sacred rights and the redolences of honour and dignity. He himself had no devotion to the law as such. His attitude was the common one that when it is on one's side it ought to be upheld and when it is not it is legalism. When America went to war her disregard of neutral nations was as great as that of the Allies and Wilson made no effort to ameliorate their lot.
>
> Something quite considerable must be allowed for the fact that what was at stake was not just legal principle but America's loud and insistent proclamation of it. National dignity was embroiled. For the fiery in the East this might be enough but for the lukewarm in the West not; and the wisest men in the East could see that outraged dignity, while it makes a good aperitif for war, will not sustain a long struggle. For that there must be some greater unitive force. It could be found in the conviction that an order of things

6. Devlin, *Too Proud to Fight*, 673.

erected on a German victory would not be safe for America or for the world.[7]

Devlin asks, "For the world or for America?" It is hard to imagine how Wilson would have answered the question, he remarks, or what he would have meant by his answer. Taking advantage of hindsight, however, it is clear enough that the American people as a whole would have said that Wilson's decision was based on the national security interests of the United States, and not on those of the world at large.

This explanation of the great event of 1917 smoothes the course of history. Self-interest as a motive is easier to handle than self-sacrifice which can lead to awkward historical developments like Christianity. Enlightened self-interest as the source of all progress was still the catchword of the time: its gentle horse-power pulled events quietly along. The explanation that this is what was really at work in America beneath the oratory is strongly confirmed by the great event of 1941 when, the previous exorcism having failed, American had to intervene again, this time without any great flourish of ideals, to help put down Hitler.[8]

For Wilson, however, it was not enough to conclude that the United States must fight in order to preserve a balance of power threatened by a Germany victory. Such a victory would have brought all Europe and a good deal of Asia under German control, and that much power would surely have been too much for America's comfort and safety. As Professor Buehrig has shown, Wilson finally accepted that line of reasoning, which House and Lansing had been pressing on him for several years. But he didn't care for it. It was not the whole nor even the decisive part of his position.

Wilson's view, deepened by his experience of the war, was different. It was simply wrong, he had concluded, to believe that the instinctive adjustment of states to changes in the balance of power would automatically preserve the peace. The fate of the Vienna system in 1914 showed how inadequate that assumption was. Nor was it enough for the leading powers to concert their influence during crises in the interest of averting war. Sometimes concerted crisis management by the great powers was not available. Sometimes one of the powers broke the rules, and broke them by stealth. What was required to keep the peace was

7. Ibid., 673–74.
8. Ibid., 675.

a system of cooperation more sustained than that of the Concert of Europe, better organized, equipped with a permanent international staff, capable of taking the initiative, and governed by a charter that would state its purposes and principles more firmly. Above all, what was needed was a system which could intervene effectively whether all the great powers wanted intervention or not, not only to deal with crises but also to help resolve situations which might otherwise lead to crises.

Wilson was by now convinced that the achievement of such a reform in the structure and governance of the state system would be impossible without American participation in the peace conference following the war. Even if Britain, France, and Russia won the war, they would be exhausted, angry, and cynical. They could make peace in such an event, but not a just and lasting peace. A just and lasting peace could be made only if the peace conference were inspired by the force of American idealism. But Wilson also concluded that America would not have a seat at the peace conference if she did not join the Allies in fighting the war. In his mind, his goal of reforming and strengthening the state system was of transcendent importance; it could not be achieved without strong American leadership. American would have no chance of offering such leadership from the sidelines; it followed, therefore, that America had to join the Allies in prosecuting the war.

Thus for Wilson, the vision of the League of Nations had become the heart of the matter. For America, or for the world? For Wilson, what the war demonstrated was that an effective League of Nations was the supreme security interest of every nation, including the United States. Because general war seemed to involve every major power, and small wars could easily become big ones, peace was indivisible. The Vienna system had failed not because of accidents or ordinary human stupidity, but because of systemic weakness. If that weakness was not cured, there would be more wars, even more terrible than the war of 1914–18. The war and the process of peacemaking after the war offered the nations a unique and transitory opportunity to take such a step. The hope of that opportunity could not be fulfilled unless the United States played its full part at the stage of peacemaking. The skeptical unkindly charged that Wilson's reasoning was dominated by what they called his messianic egoism. He took the nation into war, his enemies said, so that he could play a glorious role at the peace conference.

Surely Wilson was proud and ambitious, and well endowed with ego. But ego or no ego, it was a great contribution to see and to say that America's supreme national interest was not only a balance of power, but a system of order based on that balance of power, and managed by the nations in accordance with the rules necessary to their peaceful cooperation. Wilson always contrasted the idea of the balance of power, about which he was dubious, with that of a concert of power, which he warmly favored.

Devlin's thesis—that Wilson's conception of the League was central to his decision to recommend war in April 1917—goes beyond that of any other student of Wilson and his motivation, although it is altogether consistent with the less explicit conclusions which Arthur Link and the other leaders of Wilson scholarship draw from the evidence. His dissection of Wilson's personality and life history led Devlin to suggest that Wilson's apparent reversal of course on the issue of the war parallels a number of other key decisions in his life in which he subordinated one of his goals to another he regarded as more important.

> It was almost, but not quite, as if he were trying to bring Christianity into public life. The attempt fell short of that because there were flaws in Wilson's Christianity. The chief of them became significant only in 1919. The one that was already apparent was that his charity, that is, his sense of the duty of service to others which is part of charity and which with Wilson was very real, was marred by condescension. It was Lady Bountiful with her basket of spiritual goodies who was going to cross the Atlantic. Probably the image of Lady Bountiful with its appeal to vanity and self-importance was more saleable than that of St. Francis of Assisi. If Wilson's tone sounds pharisaical, it is to be remembered that the Pharisees came before the Christians and that only a society in which widows are ready to give their mites can afford to despise them. Wilson perceived the need for charity among nations and preached and practised it. The perception, the preaching, and the practice are all necessary to the spreading of a creed and this was the triple task he undertook. It is a creed whose acceptance is now rapidly becoming necessary to the survival of mankind. Wilson failed, of course, as all the world knows. He is and will always be historically great because he was the first to try.[9]

Devlin continues,

> All Wilson's acts had to be justified by a moral purpose. The supreme act of ordering blood to be shed needed more than justification; it had to be sanctified. So he had to convince himself that

---

9. Ibid., 679.

he was the leader of a crusade. It was, it must be assumed, a crusade that began in 1917. Although he referred to Germany's master plan, there is nothing in his war speeches to suggest that America was at last made free to join an existing crusade. He spoke as if Germany had shown her true colours only when she challenged American rights. Indeed he never lost his distrust of Allied motives. So it was only when Germany challenged America, whose motives he knew to be pure and disinterested, that she revealed herself to him as truly wicked. The Allies did not, he believed, genuinely care about democracy and the right to self-government. He did: and he could proclaim his faith as they had not truly and sincerely done. In his mind it was then, and not before, that the war to rid the world of tyranny and injustice really began. What America touched she made holy.[10]

The psychological strain of Wilson's decision was revealed in another way, Devlin found.

Speaking of Lincoln's Gettysburg Address, Wilson once said he had noticed that great orations, when spoken under deep emotion, were simple in language. His own style was often festooned in a manner that doubtless pleased an age accustomed to adornment and ashamed of bareness. But when he wrote his Message of 2 April to Congress, he was coming to the end of the time of agony in which his certitudes had been for a while dissolved. He had found for the first and perhaps the only time that acts could not always be determined by choice between good and evil or even between greater and lesser good. He had been given a sudden revelation of the tragedy at the fount of all human endeavour—which is that it is bad to fight but that only by fighting can the good be reached—and it caught at him for a moment as for all time it captured Lincoln, drained his words, and fined them to a great simplicity.

The hour was bigger even than he knew. It was not just the hour of committal of a great nation to a great task. It was the hour when America came of age. For a century and a half the new continent had nursed the thoughts of those who came from every country of the old world and brought with them, whether they knew and cared for it or not, bread ground in the mills of many hundred years. America had eaten of that bread. And now this child of Europe, heir to all the vast estates of Christendom, had stepped

10. Ibid., 686.

into his title and assumed his obligations. The burden was not to
be put down after a year or a decade. The human mind was heaving
itself, as it had done four hundred years before, into a new epoch.
Men like children waking in a fright were running back to the
notions that had mothered them or away to kiss new loyalties. They
were turning to face each other in new arrays. The turmoil of the
twentieth century had begun.

In language whose magnificence was for a generation une-
qualled and then was not surpassed, Wilson unfurled a creed for
his time and for thereafter; and each sentence was a pennant and
every word a blazoning and all of it a banner flown in a rushing
mighty pentecostal wind.

> But the right is more precious than peace, and we shall fight for
> the things which we have carried nearest our hearts—for de-
> mocracy, for the right of those who submit to authority to have
> a voice in their own governments, for the rights and liberties of
> small nations, for a universal dominion of right by such a concert
> of free peoples as shall bring peace and safety to all nations and
> make the world itself at last free. To such a task we can dedicate
> our lives and our fortunes, everything that we are and everything
> that we have, with the pride of those who know that the day has
> come when America is privileged to spend her blood and her
> might for the principles that gave her birth and happiness and
> the peace which she has treasured. God helping her, she can do
> no other.[11]

Others had glimpsed the lesson of August 1914 before Wilson—
Taft, Theodore Roosevelt, and Elihu Root, among others—and Wilson's formulation of his plan for the League of Nations had its roots
deep in the Anglo-American tradition of radical idealism, led by
the "trouble makers" and people of liberal conscience about
whom A. J. P. Taylor and Michael Howard have written with such
rueful affection.[12] But Wilson's contribution was immense. His proposals were not grounded in naive error about the causes of war, as so
many of the peace plans of the trouble makers were. He knew that the
strength of nationalism made plans for world government absurd; that

11. Ibid., 687–88.
12. See A. J. P. Taylor, *The Trouble Makers: Dissent over Foreign Policy, 1792–1939*
(London: Hamish Hamilton, 1957; reprint ed., London: Panther Books, 1969), and Michael
Howard, *War and the Liberal Conscience* (London: Maurice Temple Smith, 1978), discussed
in chapter 4.

the achievement of peace did not require the abolition of capitalism, or aristocracy, or monarchy, or the universal triumph of democracy; and that disarmament treaties, international courts of arbitration, and covenants seeking to humanize war, desirable as they are in themselves, are not magical devices for achieving peace without tears. The program hammered out in Wilson's extended exchanges with Sir Edward Grey and Colonel House grew out of the implacable realities of the First World War, and could not help addressing them. The central reality, whether one put the primary blame for the war on Germany, Russia, Great Britain, or Austro-Hungary, was that in the atmosphere of tension and instability prevailing in 1914, the great powers did not cooperate actively to resolve the flare-up after Sarejevo. Rather, Germany chose the path of aggression and expansion, and the others failed to smother the fire before it flared out of control. How the society of nations should respond to aggression or the threat of aggression was the issue on which Wilson focused; it is the very essence of peace, and Wilson's principle, embodied now in the Charter of the United Nations, has been the leitmotiv of world politics ever since his day.

Wilson did not answer many of the questions his thesis raised: how to reconcile the concept of peace among the states with the principle of the self-determination of peoples, for example; and whether keeping the peace requires the powers to cooperate in snuffing out all wars or only some. But he had raised the Concert of Europe from the dead and infused it with new promise. That was much—much more than all but a few statesmen, intellectuals, or prophets have accomplished in their lifetimes.

11

The Interwar Years: The Precarious Birth of the Modern World, 1919–1920

I find the great object of my life thus accomplished in the building up of the great community of Atlantic Powers which I hope will at least make a precedent that can never be forgotten. . . . Strange it is that we should have done it by means of inducing those blockheads of Germans to kick us into it. . . . It is really a joy to feel that we have established one great idea even though we have pulled all the stars out of their courses in order to do it.—Henry Adams

Henry Adams' uncharacteristic outburst of optimism was not to be fulfilled for another thirty years, and even now it is by no means certain that the precedent of America's declaration of war in April 1917 "can never be forgotten." The United States rejected both the League of Nations and an alliance with Britain and France at the end of the First World War and participated with conviction in the diplomatic follies of the interwar period. The North Atlantic Alliance was not created until 1949. While the idea of the Western security system which developed from the formation of NATO has now flourished for more than forty years, it is hardly without enemies in American politics.

The Second World War climaxed two decades of aggravated irrationality in the conduct of their foreign relations by all the Western democracies, and particularly by the United States and Great Britain. In fairness, it should be noted that France's instincts were usually sensible, but that France could not act effectively without Britain, which was in a trance. France was not blind, but, after the occupation of the Ruhr in 1923, it was paralyzed by its dependence on Great Britain— and for ultimate crises, on the United States. The behavior of the Western nations during the twenties and thirties has been characterized

The epigraph for this chapter is taken from a letter of Henry Adams to Charles M. Gaskell, 8 June 1917, in *Letters of Henry Adams, 1892–1918,* ed. Worthington Chauncey Ford (Boston and New York: Houghton Mifflin, 1938), 642.

in the literature by a number of metaphors—sleepwalking, grave dig-
ging, disorientation, and stupidity are among the kindest words that
have been used; cowardice, flight from reality, and putting profit before
patriotism are others. No one has ever defended or attempted to justify
the Allied record as a whole, although a few have tried to explain the
policy of appeasing Germany toward the end of the thirties on the
erroneous ground that Britain and France had no choice, in view of
the state of the military balance between them and Germany at the
time.[1]

Psychologically, the extraordinary pattern of Western behavior in
this period must be explained—in part, at least—as a phase of the
general reaction of the Western peoples to the trauma of the First World
War and to the specter of the Soviet revolution to which it led in Russia;
in the case of Germany, particularly, there was also the special trauma
of defeat.

One of the most suggestive studies of the interwar period in this
perspective is Modris Eksteins' recent book, *Rites of Spring*. Eksteins
calls the mood which prevailed in the West at that time one of deep
psychic depression, broken only by hysterical events: plague, revolution, inflation, dislocation . . . "The Great War was the psychological
turning point for modernism as a whole. The urge to create and the
urge to destroy had changed places." In the imagination of Europe,
Eksteins writes, the First World War had been part of a generalized
rebellion against bourgeois civilization which had begun some twenty-
five years earlier, and had revealed itself first in the arts. For Germany,
a new, innovative, and energetic country, "the very embodiment of
vitalism and technical brilliance," and the natural leader of the mod-
ernist revolution, the war was to be "a war of liberation . . . from the
hyprocrisy of bourgeois form and convenience, and Britain was to her
the principal representative of the order against which she was
rebelling."[2]

In short, the war was viewed not as a war for territory or power in
the ordinary sense, but as an act of destruction for its own sake. Thus
Britain came to sense and to fear Germany's thrusting energy as a
threat to its most fundamental values: progress, parliament, and law.

1. Williamson Murray, *The Change in the European Balance of Power, 1938–1939: The
Path to Ruin* (Princeton, N.J.: Princeton University Press, 1984); and idem, *Strategy for
Defeat; The Luftwaffe, 1933–1945* (Maxwell Air Force Base, Ala.: Air University Press,
1983).

2. Modris Eksteins, *Rites of Spring: The Great War of the Twentieth Century* (Boston:
Houghton Mifflin, 1989), xv–xvi. See also p. 169 and chap. 3.

When the war failed to satisfy the romantic hopes invested in it, there was general disillusion with old values, but no effort to replace them with new ones. Cynicism, despair, and flight from reality dominated the cultural atmosphere, accompanied by a frenetic hedonism which brought no joy. Modernism, the great goal of the avant garde in painting, sculpture, architecture, music, and literature, turned out to be nihilism, Bazarov's creed, and in politics produced the nightmare regimes of Fascism and Communism.

After a century of peaceful progress, the British and the Americans, at least, had come to believe that perpetual progress was now the rule of history. The experience of 1914–18 challenged that idea, and offered in its place visions of tragedy, terror, and mindless barbarism, which became steadily more tangible as the interwar period witnessed the rise of Communism, Fascism, and other systems of appalling thuggery. Those who conducted the business of government in the West during the twenties and thirties were not notably more stupid than their predecessors, nor less wise. But they were in something approximating a state of shock, overcome by the fear that what they did might bring back another round of war, or allow Fascists or Communists to seize power, or both. And those among them who understood what was happening—Churchill and Franklin D. Roosevelt, notably—were helpless before a public opinion which insisted on clinging to illusion.

Psychosocial theories of this kind surely explain part of the behavior of the Western peoples during the interwar years. But they are by no means satisfactory as explanations of their patterns of behavior as a whole. Cultures have their own momentum and continuity, and the countries involved reacted differently to their shared experience of the First World War. If the abiding stench of trench warfare on the Western front was the force which led Great Britain and the United States to pursue irrational foreign policies, how can we account for the fact that France never ceased to perceive and accept the dynamics of world politics for what it was, and to propose one realistic policy after another for dealing with it? France, after all, had suffered more than Great Britain during the First World War, and a great deal more than the United States. Its foreign policy, however, was different from theirs. And at the last possible moment, Britain and United States both rallied to defend not nihilism but their own liberal creed.

Others suggest that the weakness and disorientation of British and American policy in this period was caused by too much democracy. Theorists of this persuasion tell us that the democratic governments were dominated by an ignorant and stubborn public opinion, and the ignorant and stubborn men and women elected to carry out its wishes. Here again, the theories explain nothing. French public opinion has at least as much influence on French foreign policy as public opinion in Great Britain and the United States. With the advantages of hindsight, however, French policy in this period must be judged generally right, and British and American policy generally wrong. Eksteins' hypothesis is more suggestive in explaining German behavior, but the problem remains that when the Second World War ended, a strong majority of Germans returned to democratic values and procedures, apparently with conviction.

No, the bizarre quality of British and American foreign policy during the interwar years was not the product of a Dance of Death or an excess of democracy, but of ideas about the perfectability of man—and more specifically about the management of the state system—which are deeply embedded in the British and American cultures but not in that of France. The French fully shared the hopes of their British and American colleagues that a policy of magnanimity toward Germany and Russia might induce those angry nations to settle down as responsible members of the world community. All the French said to their Allies was that the West should not assume that such irreversible transformations had already taken place, and that precautions to deter recidivism could not yet be dispensed with.

Chance too, played its usual part in the drama. What would the story have been if Wilson had not suffered from arteriosclerosis, and if the United States had ratified the Treaty of Versailles? What would the perception of the peace have been in the West if Keynes had not conducted his dazzling, erroneous, and meretricious campaign against what he called the "Carthaginian" peace of Versailles?

While it is tempting to pass over the story of the interwar years quickly, because it is so depressing, it must be confronted because it is so important. There is little chance that the West can muster the will to pursue a foreign policy adequate to the challenges of the next fifty years unless it keeps firmly before its mind's eye the fact that between 1919 and 1939 Western civilization nearly allowed itself to be destroyed, and is quite capable of doing so again.

The theme of Churchill's final volume on the Second World War is "how the great democracies triumphed, and so were able to resume the follies which had so nearly cost them their life."[3] If by that scathing

3. Winston S. Churchill, *The Second World War,* vol. 6, *Triumph and Tragedy* (1953; Boston: Houghton Mifflin, 1983), v.

judgment, Churchill meant no more than the obvious fact that the victorious Allies did not translate their victory into a general peace, he is surely right. If, however, we judge Western policy by a more modest standard, Churchill's moral is more emphatically applicable to the pattern of Allied action and inaction for the twenty years after 1918 than to what they did and failed to do after 1945. While the Western Allies made many mistakes after 1945—one of them of critical importance—the programs they adopted then were well conceived and in the main reasonably well executed, certainly far better conceived and executed than the postwar reconstruction they sought to achieve after 1918.

II

On the side of the Western Allies, two forces combined to make their diplomacy during the interwar years such a disaster. The first, of course, was revulsion against the agony of the war. "Never again" was the nearly universal watchword. The second factor determining the surreal character of Western diplomacy in the twenties and thirties was the prevalence and intensity of mistrust and mutual distaste between France, Britain, and the United States. It burst into the open after the passage of time had weakened the restraints which required at least a facade of Allied unity during the war itself and the period of making peace.

Resentments and jealousies among allies is a normal incident of war. During the First World War such friction was unusually sharp and indeed virulent. Relations between the British and the French are complicated in the best of times by differences in temperament and education, and by the weight of history. The 1914–18 war made such differences more acute.

It was commonplace for Allied leaders to proclaim as a truism that the peace could not survive unless the Allies remained united. But the rule was honored more often in the breach than in the observance.

In the first place, who were "the Allies" in 1919 and the next two decades?

Russia had become the Soviet Union after defeat in a savage war with the Germans and Austrians, a separate peace at Brest-Litovsk, two revolutions, a civil war, and a war with the Finns. Even before the civil war was over, Trotsky had created formidable new armed forces out of the shards of the Czar's army, and the Soviet Union was actively trying to expand Soviet power in China and Central Asia; to ignite revolution in Hungary and Bavaria; and to invade Poland, which the

Western Allies had decreed should be restored as a state for the first time since the "final" partition of Poland in the eighteenth century. Backed by the new Red Army, which was built around fifty thousand officers of the Czar's army, the Soviet Union was organizing a network of revolutionary parties throughout the world in the name of the Third International.

The Soviets also established a program of secret military collaboration with the new Weimar Republic in Germany. Pursuant to that understanding, Germany built an armaments industry and trained a generation of German officers in Russia. This ominous arrangement was of course a blatant and most important violation of the Versailles Treaty. It began almost immediately after the war and continued well into the the thirties.[4] In short, through a fantastic burst of energy, and a sharp zig or zag in the long history of the fatal relation between Slav and Teuton, Russia ceased to be an ally and became an active enemy of the Western powers. The slogan "Socialism in one country" had not yet been invented by Stalin. And when it did appear, it turned out to be a deception.

During the war, Japan, an ally of Great Britain, had confined its military activities to the Far East. Its participation in the peacemaking process in 1919 was minimal and largely nominal. The only general policy question on which Japan took an active interest was a proposal that racial equality should be one of the principles upon which the new world order should be based. The Japanese resolution was premature. Britain and the United States were opposed, and it died. The rejection of Japan's initiative did not make even a ripple in the West, but it was not forgotten in Asia.

The Italian role in the peace conference was also peripheral. Italy was counted, with Japan, as one of the Big Five who constituted in effect the directorate of the peace conference. Her main concern, as she made clear in the preliminary meetings which prepared the conference, was to obtain the support of the larger Allies for the territorial gains secretly promised to Italy in 1915 in order to persuade her to enter the war. For a period of time, Italy even absented herself from the meetings as a protest when the major Allies showed signs of abandoning their secret commitments to Italy.

In fact, therefore, the conference was dominated by the represen-

4. Hans W. Gatzke, *Stresemann and the Rearmament of Germany* (Baltimore: Johns Hopkins University Press, 1954); and idem, "Russo-German Military Collaboration during the Weimar Republic" in *European Diplomacy between two Wars, 1919–1939*, ed. Hans W. Gatzke (Chicago: Quadrangle, 1972), 40.

tatives of France, Great Britain, and the United States. The leaders who represented the Big Three at the peace conference were altogether remarkable men. Wilson, Lloyd George, and Clemenceau were strong-minded, experienced, and adroit; accustomed to leadership; and skilled in the craft of democratic politics and government. All three decidedly belonged to what Americans would call the "liberal" or "progressive" wing of public and political opinion. They supported social and economic reform, were generally against military spending, and were without a trace of jingoism. For somewhat different reasons, they genuinely believed in the gospel of Allied unity, and sought to understand each other and accommodate to each other's views in rebuilding the state system after the war.

Clemenceau, then prime minister of France, had been a leader of French radicalism for fifty stormy years, minister many times, a doctor, a novelist, a man of principle and cultivation, a fierce patriot. Clemenceau directed that he be buried like a Visigoth, standing up, his face to the east. A splendid statue of Clemenceau, standing up and facing east, invigorates one of the park areas near the Grand Palais in Paris. His wit and quickness of mind were legendary, and his spirit remarkable. At the end of the war, his close friend Claude Monet called on him. They had not seen each other for four years. As the great painter was leaving, he said to Clemenceau, "My friend, you have saved France." "No," Clemenceau replied, "not I. It was the infantry." His war aims were simple, and he never wavered. Germany, which had become far more powerful than France between 1870 and 1914, should lose not only Alsace and Lorraine, and its colonies, but the area west of the Rhine, the Rhineland, as well. There was no reason for France to annex the Rhineland if the Allies retained military control of the Rhine bridges and kept forces in the area.

Lloyd George, the British prime minister, was a Welsh radical, leader of the Liberal Party, and a man of titanic energy who became prime minister when Asquith faltered under the burden of the war. He was a tribune of the people who established the modern welfare state in Great Britain, and led Britain to victory in the war.

For Wilson, the lesson of the war was twofold: that civilization could be preserved only if the burden of war were lifted from the backs of mankind; and that history—or perhaps a Higher Force— had chosen America to lead in the quest for a peace which would make it possible to achieve that goal. Against the advice of some of his most trusted advisers, Wilson decided to go to Paris himself as the head of the American delegation to the peace conference. The other heads of government would have to join him there. Under these circumstances, he concluded, the United States would have its best chance to fulfill the conception of peace he had worked out, step by step, in his prolonged search for "peace without victory." Without his presence, the United States could hardly expect to persuade its reluctant allies to accept his vision of the peace and of the league to enforce it.

Wilson took a typically provincial American view of his Western Allies—a view which became more negative and suspicious as his illness progressed. Wilson's decision to go to Paris was wise, however, because it permitted four vital and very different men to come to know each other extremely well. Without Wilson's prolonged private talks with Clemenceau, Lloyd George, and Orlando, the Italian prime minister, the outcome of the peace conference would almost surely have been different.

Stephen Bonsal's valuable memoir, *Unfinished Business,* contains his account of a private conversation with Clemenceau. Bonsal, an able and experienced journalist, and at that time a Colonel in the A.E.F., served Wilson as translator during the private meetings of the Big Four and was House's trusted aide throughout the period of peacemaking. One of Clemenceau's eccentricities, Bonsal writes,

> was to sleep from nine in the evening until midnight; then, bright as a button, he was ready for business, and, despite the protests of the doctors, his sickroom was thronged.
>
> "I must make a peace," said M. Clemenceau to me in one of these midnight sessions, "based upon my belief and upon my own experience of the world in which we have to live. My responsibility is personal and non-transferable. When called to the bar of history, I cannot say, 'Well, I made these arrangements to conform to Mr. Wilson's viewpoint.' Mr. Wilson has lived in a world that has been fairly safe for Democracy; I have lived in a world where it was good form to shoot a Democrat. After a few weeks of sparring I became convinced that your President wanted the same things that I did, although we were very far apart as to the ways and the means by which we could reach the desired end.
>
> "When he first developed his program, it seemed to me perfectly Utopian. I said to him, 'Mr. Wilson, if I accepted what you propose as ample for the security of France, after the millions who have died and the millions who have suffered, I believe, and indeed I hope, that my successor in office would take me by the nape of

the neck and have me shot at daylight before the donjon of Vincennes.' After that we began to get together.

"Once I said to him, 'Mr. Wilson, have you ever seen an elephant cross a swinging bamboo bridge?' Mr. Wilson said he had not. 'Well, I'll tell you how he goes about it. First, he trots down into the stream to see if the foundations are all right; then he comes back and puts one foot on the bridge. If the result is reassuring, he ventures its mate. Then he gives the bridge a sharp jolt. If it stands that, he gives it his trust and advances. Now that's my idea about your bridge leading to the New Jerusalem. I may be, as they say I am, a springing tiger where my personal fortunes are concerned, but where the safety of France is at stake—well, there never was an elephant more careful or more cautious than I am going to be.'"[5]

At a later point, Bonsal reports, Clemenceau told him,

"I never said, as widely reported (the Paris papers were filled with suggestions to this effect at the time),... that Wilson was pro-German, but I did think and I probably said, as I generally say what I think, that many of his plans and proposals were unduly and most unwisely helpful to the Germans in their present unregenerate state. I confess that from my first cable contact with it Wilsonism alarmed me, and that is why on the eve of the Conference I announced in the Chamber, 'It will be more difficult to make peace than it was to make war.' Now who can deny that in peacemaking France is meeting with great opposition from all her allies who were so noble and considerate while the battle was on? During the long war years we sustained the heaviest losses, we suffered the most, and now what is our fate at the Conference?

"We are blocked in our plea for security; only our undoubted claim to Alsace goes uncontested. For the little else we may obtain we shall have to fight and fight hard. I mean to do that very thing and Wilson knows it. There is one bright spot in the dark prospect. Wilson is as frank with me as I am with him. We have both placed our cards on the Peace table."[6]

Bonsal continues,

5. Stephen Bonsal, *Unfinished Business* (Garden City, N.Y.: Doubleday, Doran, 1944), 68–69.
6. Ibid., 71

There is, it is true, one criticism of Mr. Wilson to which M. Clemenceau often returns, as indeed he did today, which seems to me not without foundation. "I told your President that, in my judgment, the grave fault of his attitude is that he eliminated sentiment and endeavored to efface all memory of the past. A grave, a very grave fault it seems to me. It was then I would say, 'I am the last, the only survivor of the Protest of Bordeaux—against the infamy of the Treaty that the Prussians imposed at the point of the bayonet. M. le President, I speak for our glorious dead who fell in the two wars. For myself I can hold my tongue, but not for them.'"[7]

III

Wilson's conception of the peace had two elements: the Fourteen Points and the League of Nations.

The Fourteen Points were first stated in an address to Congress Wilson gave on 8 January 1918. They brought together in considered form the ideas about the peace he had been expounding in his speeches and his diplomacy during the previous three years. They were received as a powerful statement of American war aims, and compared in importance and nobility to Lincoln's Emancipation Proclamation, at least by American and some liberal European newspapers. Certain of the points were statements of principle, others were applications of principle. All required interpretation before they could become a useful instruction to negotiators. Two well-known journalists, Frank Cobb and Walter Lippmann, were the original draftsmen of an agreed "commentary" on the Fourteen Points which reflected the substance of Col. House's negotiations with the Allies and with Wilson. The commentary proved helpful in facilitating agreement among the Allies. In approving the document, Wilson said "that the details of application mentioned should be regarded as merely illustrative suggestions" and reserved for the peace conference.[8]

The general principles announced in the Fourteen Points included six famous ideas: (1) open covenants of peace, openly arrived at; (2) "absolute" freedom of navigation on the seas—a phrase, as interpreted, which did not exclude blockades and other naval limitations on the freedom of the seas approved by the law of nations; (3) the removal

7. Ibid.
8. Charles Seymour, *The Intimate Papers of Colonel House: The Ending of the War,* vol. 4, *The Ending of the War, June 1918–August 1919* (Boston and New York: Houghton Mifflin, 1928), 153. The text of the commentary appears on pp. 192–200.

of economic barriers; (4) arms reductions "to the lowest point consistent with domestic safety"; (5) the impartial adjustment of colonial claims—at least for German colonies and parts of the Turkish Empire—giving equal weight to the interests of the populations concerned and to the governments whose title was to be determined.

There was no separate general statement of the principle that states should be based on nationality, or, conversely, that all "peoples," should have the right to become states. The state system inherited from history, shaped as it is by conquest and the legitimacy of states and monarchs, is too complex to permit such a universal rule. But the idea of national liberation runs through the remaining nine points of Wilson's program. Two would require German and Austrian evacuation of all Russian territory and call on Russia's neighbors to show Russia sympathy, good will, and a comprehension of her needs. They specifically endorse the creation of a Polish state, and tentatively endorse the independence of Finland, Estonia, Lithuania, Latvia, and perhaps the Ukraine. Another says the readjustment of the frontiers of Italy "should be effected along clearly recognizable lines of nationality." A fourth declares that the peoples of Austria-Hungary should be afforded "the freest opportunity of autonomous development." On this point, the commentary of October 1918 says that the statement in the original speech, given in January, "no longer holds," because of the rapid changes which took place during the final period of the war. This guarded language refers to a Serbian uprising which hastened the end of the war on that front. This point also noted eight specific ethnic disputes which had already emerged, indicated American positions on some, and otherwise supported programs of "national unity and independence," tempered somewhat by the need of the new countries for access to the sea, economic viability, and security; and it encouraged the formation of a confederation of southeastern Europe. Comparable statements of policy were made with respect to Alsace and Lorraine, Rumania, Serbia, Montenegro, and the Ottoman Empire. Finally, in Point 14, Wilson declared that "a general association of nations must be formed under specific covenants for the purpose of affording mutual guarantees of political independence and territorial integrity to great and small states alike."

When the Germans approached Wilson for an armistice in October 1918, exhausted and in despair after the failure of their tremendous offensives on the Western front and the victories of the Allied armies during the spring and summer of that fateful year, they suggested that the peace negotiations be conducted on the basis of the Fourteen Points.

Wilson went a step further, and insisted that Germany accept the Fourteen Points as the basis of the peace settlement.

Wilson did not regard the Fourteen Points as commandments but
as general principles to be applied to the intricately reticulated problems
of the peace. When his preliminary exchanges with the Germans were
discussed with the Allies before the armistice was accepted, Wilson
readily agreed to a number of clarifications and revisions of his program.
In order to obtain British and French acceptance of Wilson's statement
on the freedom of the seas, however, Wilson and House had to threaten
to go home and make a separate peace with Germany and Austria.

The Germans immediately sought to treat the Fourteen Points tex-
tually as a contractual part of the armistice agreement, except for the
reservations of which they were notified at the time: a British caveat
on the subject of freedom of the seas, and a French reservation on the
thorny issue of reparations. A great deal of the controversy during and
after the peace conference arose from conflicts between a literal reading
of the Points and the compromises which the expert committees and
the Big Three found necessary in order to achieve workable solutions.
Point 13, for example, which called for the revival of the Polish state,
also required that Poland have free and secure access to the sea. The
Allies were faced with a dilemma: there had to be a corridor to the sea
from the new Poland; should that corridor be German or Polish territory? A German corridor solution would make Polish access to the
sea uncertain and vulnerable; a Polish corridor would separate East
Germany from the rest of the German nation. In either case, some
pockets of Poles and Germans would become citizens of the wrong
fatherland, under an absolutist interpretation of the nationality principle. The issue was discussed at length, and remitted by the Big Three
to the expert committee for reconsideration. In the end, the Polish
corridor solution was adopted as the lesser of two evils, allowing security
and economic considerations to prevail over those of nationality. Germany and its supporters never tired of denouncing the Polish corridor
and the internationalization of Danzig as a betrayal of the Allied promises embodied in the armistice agreement.[9]

The League of Nations was to be a permanent institution, staffed
by an international secretariat, and directed by a senior diplomat as
secretary general. It incorporated the Hague Court of International
Arbitration, and was governed by a council of ambassadors from the

9. See, for example Etienne Mantoux, *The Carthaginian Peace, or, The Economic
Consequences of Mr. Keynes* (New York: Charles Scribner's Sons, 1952), 56–58.

member states. The League was built on the practices developed after the Congress of Vienna to manage the crises of the state system. The new organization was intended to improve and institutionalize those practices in the interests of peace, international cooperation, and social progress. It had a broader mandate than the Concert of Europe. It was intended to anticipate crises, not simply to find peaceful solutions for them after they had come close to the boiling point.

The peace treaty had a number of other important features. The disintegration of the Ottoman and Austro-Hungarian empires and the partial disintegration of Russia made it possible to establish a number of new states based on the principle of nationality. Since it was impossible, however, to establish boundaries which perfectly fulfilled the principle of nationality, the new states (like nearly all the old ones) contained ethnic minorities. In the case of the Ottoman Empire, the British protectorate for Egypt was not disturbed, but League mandates were established for other non-Turkish parts of the Ottoman Empire as well as for the former German colonies.

The mandate system was an innovation introduced by the League Covenant as an alternative to the annexation of a defeated enemy's territory. Mandates were trusteeships under League supervision which would provide responsible government for underdeveloped colonies until the indigenous population was ready for self-government, or, in the case of Palestine, until its basic purpose, the establishment of a Jewish national home in Palestine, was satisfied.[10] The German overseas colonies also became League mandates.

In the most important territorial problem facing the conference, the Big Three were unanimous in resisting the temptation to partition Germany, although it would have been easy to do so in the final weeks before the treaty was signed, when Bavaria and several other of the larger component parts of Germany were on the verge of secession. The French had originally proposed an independent Rhenish republic in the area of Germany west of the Rhine. Britain and the United States were opposed and ultimately Clemenceau was convinced by the prolonged discussion of the subject among the Big Three. Clemenceau continued to want at least the demilitarization of the Rhineland, however, and Allied control of the Rhine bridges, but he settled finally for a fifteen-year occupation of the Rhineland, and its permanent demilitarization, backed by British and American security treaties protecting

10. H. Duncan Hall, *Mandates, Dependencies, and Trusteeship* (Washington, D.C.: Carnegie Endowment for International Peace, 1948).

France against German aggression in order to supplement what the Americans at least then expected to be a vibrant and effective League.

Under the peace treaty as it was finally adopted, Germany, without Alsace and Lorraine, was permitted to survive as the unitary state created by Bismarck, in considerable part as a counterweight to the unpredictable future of the Soviet Union. Germany lost only some 13 percent of her territory and about 10 percent of her population, including Alsace and Lorraine and the various boundary adjustments required by the creation of Poland and Czechoslovakia. If Alsace and Lorraine are left out of the calculation, Germany lost only about 4 percent of its prewar population and territory, including the Saar. The Saar Basin was transferred to France for a time, subject to final disposition by plebiscite after fifteen years. When the plebiscite was held, the Saar was duly returned. Schleswig was returned to Denmark immediately.[11]

The most contentious feature of the peace treaty was its requirement that Germany pay reparations for the "loss and damage" suffered by the Allied and associated governments and their nationals "as a consequence of the war imposed upon them by the aggression of Germany and her Allies." The treaty, however, recognized that full reparation for the damages caused by the war was beyond Germany's capacity to pay, and therefore limited reparations to compensation for damage done to the civilian populations and their property, and created a reparations commission to determine the amount to be paid. The "war guilt" clause in the reparations article of the treaty caused an emotional storm, not only in Germany but throughout the Western world, and colored the subsequent debate about the economic side of the reparations question, and indeed about the fairness of the treaty as a whole. As noted in Chapter 9, the prevailing view among historians supports the judgment expressed in the treaty about Germany's responsibility for the outbreak of war in 1914. It does not follow, however, that it was politic to include such a clause in the treaty of peace. On the contrary, the war guilt issue has remained a futile bone of extremely emotional contention ever since, and served no useful purpose.

In retrospect, it is difficult to see why the reparations question caused so much fuss. France had paid a substantial indemnity to Germany after the Franco-Prussian War—as tribute, in fact, since the war was fought on French soil, and most historians have concluded that Germany was largely responsible for causing the war. On that occasion,

11. Ibid., 69–75.

the problem of international transfers had not proved to be an economic strain. Since 1871, and again since 1945, international transfers have occurred on a much larger scale, and have all been managed more or less effectively, whether as loans, grants in kind, or monetary grants. Moreover, as a result of the political uproar about the Treaty of Versailles, Germany paid only 21 to 23 billion marks, some 5 billion dollars, in reparations, which were more than balanced by 35 to 38 billion marks in foreign loans she received during the period which ended with the Hoover Moratorium of 1932.[12]

It is hard to resist the conclusion that the endless squabble over reparations and the Allied war debts to the United States was not an economic issue at all, but a political one of the utmost importance. When the Second World War loomed up, the bitter recollection of those quarrels led Roosevelt to invent the idea of the Lend-Lease program, so that the postwar period after 1945 would not be poisoned by interallied disputes about such issues. If a neighbor is having a fire, Roosevelt pointed out in 1941, one naturally lends him a hose to help put it out. When the fire is over, the neighbor returns the hose if it survives, and not otherwise. Roosevelt's simple metaphor was the basis of interallied mutual assistance in munitions, shipping, food, industrial materials, the repair of ships, and many other war needs for more than four years.

By post–World War II standards, the interwar European economy was very badly managed. There was something of a boom until 1921, followed by a short depression, appalling inflation in France and Germany, some stabilization and improvement in the late twenties, and then a worldwide depression, caused by the collapse of the international banking system, which started in 1929 and continued more or less until 1939. Despite these immense handicaps, the standard of living in Germany regained 1913 levels by all measures in 1919; dropped slightly in 1923, the year of the Ruhr crisis; and recovered again by 1927 or so, matching the pattern of French experience.[13]

12. Bruce Kent, *The Spoils of War: The Politics, Economics, and Diplomacy of Reparations, 1918–1932* (Oxford: Clarendon Press, and New York: Oxford University Press, 1989), 11; and Mantoux, *Carthaginian Peace,* 155. Keynes' estimate of Germany's maximum capacity to pay from all sources was $10 billion, or $500 million a year (John Maynard Keynes, *The Economic Consequences of the Peace* [(London: Macmillan, and New York: Harcourt, Brace Howe, 1920], 200, 207). Keynes calculated that a total indemnity from Germany of $2.5 billion would be equivalent to the indemnity of $11 billion paid to Germany by France in 1871 (p. 201).

13. W. W. Rostow, *Why the Poor Get Richer and the Rich Slow Down: Essays in the Marshallian Long Period* (Austin: University of Texas Press, 1980), chap. 8; and James W.

Viewed as a whole, the peace treaty Wilson, Clemenceau, and Lloyd George produced was a constructive achievement (apart from its war guilt provision), a document in the liberal spirit which could well have provided a framework for a harmonious European recovery and a more stable world political order. Wilson did not succumb to the wiles of Clemenceau and Lloyd George in making the treaty. On the contrary, Wilson's view prevailed, for better or worse, on every major question. Like the work of the Congress of Vienna, however, the treaty was cursed not only by the defeated Germans, but by the liberal leaders of Western opinion as well, and became a symbol of shameful failure even before it was born. The bitter tragedies of the interwar years were not caused by flaws in the treaty, however, nor even by German resentment of its war guilt clause, but by the failure of the Western Allies to carry out its peacekeeping policies, especially when Germany, Italy, and Japan challenged some of its most important provisions later on. The mood of Western defeatism and passivity which led to this result is as hard to explain as the rebirth of Western self-confidence, creativity, and energy during and after the Second World War. However mysterious, the inadequacy of the foreign policies of the United States, Great Britain, and France during the interwar period is a palpable fact. For this reason, the familiar judgment that the Second World War was a continuation of the first, and that the interwar years were no more than a twenty-year armistice, is altogether realistic.

The Germans saw the treaty as an act of "blind hatred" and of a thirst for revenge. "What deeply embittered the Germans . . . was the victors' determination to so weaken Germany in every possible way that the much heralded 'freedom' in which they believed betokened nothing more than the freedom to be destitute."[14] This language comes from a highly praised recent one-volume history of Germany by an eminent German historian, by no means a chauvinist. Unfortunately, Professor Raff's judgment, with minor variations in tone, is a familiar cliché not only in Germany but in the world literature on the subject. A key point Raff adduces to support his argument is that Alsace and Lorraine were returned to France, thus for a short time diminishing Germany's production of coal, iron ore, and steel.

This German reaction to the treaty, supported in turn by sophisticated Western opinion, convinced the British and the Americans, at

Angell, *The Recovery of Germany*, rev. ed. (New Haven, Conn.: Yale University Press, 1932), 2–3 and chap. 8, especially 269–71.
    14. Diether Raff, *A History of Germany: From the Medieval Empire to the Present*, trans. Bruce Little (1985; Oxford, Hamburg, and New York: Berg, 1988), 239.

least, that the Treaty of Versailles was a brutal, reactionary, Carthaginian peace and therefore guaranteed mankind a future world war. The leading figure in the process which produced this reversal of opinion was a most unlikely nominee for such a role, the British economist John Maynard Keynes. Keynes was a formidable, overbearing man, with a flair for the dramatic. His literary style was an elegant combination of sardonic wit and prophetic majesty. He spoke ex cathedra and in his day, it required unusual courage to point out that like most people he sometimes talked nonsense. He was thirty-six years old at the time he fired the first shot in his battle against the treaty in 1919, and he kept up the campaign for many years thereafter.

Keynes came of a distinguished Cambridge family, rooted in the university, and part of a network of charming, worthy, extremely intelligent and responsible people of the Whig persuasion in British academic and public life. He had planned to be a mathematician, but switched to economics. As a result, Keynes' understanding of world politics was not the product of extended study, but simply reflected the attitudes and assumptions of his circle both at Cambridge and in London.

He was part of the Bloomsbury Group, which included Lytton Strachey, Virginia and Leonard Woolf, Roger Fry, Clive Bell, and a number of other rather precious literary and artistic people. They were decidedly "the happy few," and tended to speak and write about everybody else in a patronizing tone which lesser breeds found particularly irritating. Keynes was the only member of the group active in the wider world of finance and public affairs. Most of his close friends were opposed to the war; some were conscientious objectors; Keynes himself had a considerable moral struggle before accepting even a post in the Treasury during the war. His Bloomsbury friends criticized him for going so far in "collaboration."

Keynes was a member of the British delegation to the peace conference in Paris as an adviser on economic and financial matters. He resigned in protest over the treaty on 5 June 1919, and immediately published a short article called "The Council of Four, Paris, 1919," in a weekly. The article was reprinted in his famous tract *The Economic Consequences of the Peace,* also published in 1919, as well as in his *Essays in Biography,* published in 1933.

Keynes' acid article and the book were written in the white heat of rage at what he regarded as betrayal at Paris. His work as one of the chief critics of the peace was widely admired and caused a furor. It was vivid and extremely well written, although marred by prejudice and an intimidating tone of condescension; it was marred also by pervasive factual and analytical error, and by something even worse: vivid eyewitness testimony about meetings he could not have attended.

The political assumptions of Keynes' writing about the peace were shallow and jejune, and their economic analysis no better. But they made a major contribution to the mood of disillusion which set in soon after the war and characterized the attitudes of a considerable part of the literate Western public, especially in Britain and the United States, throughout the period and since. Keynes' views were also a significant factor in the American elections of 1920, and the first step in Keynes' career as one of the idols of the angry young men and women of two generations—those who protested against the First World War and the peace settlement, and those who fought the senselessness and waste of the Great Depression of the thirties.

The essence of Keynes' argument was that the peace treaty was too hard on Germany and not sufficiently sympathetic to its grievances. Although Keynes did not oppose the principle of reparations, he thought that the reparations imposed on Germany, although they were never in fact quantified, were too big, and therefore could not be paid. Trying to pay them, he argued, would wreck what was left of the prewar monetary system. Despite Keynes' admiration for Clemenceau as a man, he had nothing but scorn for Clemenceau's preoccupation with France's security. The French prime minister, in his views, was trying to turn the clock back to 1870. Clemenceau sought security from the old system of the balance of power reinforced by alliances, instead of relying on the new, idealistic, and "liberal" approach of the League of Nations. This was a particularly unfair argument, since Clemenceau had insisted on *not* returning Germany to its condition before 1870. For his pains, the great man was defeated in 1920 when he ran for President of France. The sad history of the thirties is a sufficient comment on the naiveté of Keynes' assumption that the League of Nations could control major threats to the peace.

Keynes' picture of Wilson is devastating. As prophet of a magnanimous peace, a peace without victory, Wilson of the Fourteen Points and the League of Nations had thrilled the democratic world and given it hope. But, Keynes tells us, the prophet turned out in Paris to be a stupid Presbyterian minister, "slow-minded and bewildered," and no match in council for the "Welsh witch," as he called Lloyd George, and the formidable prime minister of France. Wilson was a "blind and deaf Don Quixote entering a cavern where the swift and glittering blade was in the hands of the adversary." Those were not the judgments of asute and experienced senior observers like Balfour and Clemenceau, who saw Wilson at first-hand. And they bear no relation to the facts. For better or worse, Wilson dominated the peace process and almost invariably had his way. But Keynes put forth the plausible and poisonous charge that Clemenceau and Lloyd George led Wilson into compromising his Fourteen Points, and therefore ruined the peace. Moreover, by wasting their time on frontiers and nationality problems, the peacemakers of 1919 neglected the only important questions, Keynes said, those of economics.

Why Keynes took a strongly emotional pro-German attitude on nearly every question before the conference has remained unexplained. Whatever the cause may have been, Keynes' intensity and partisanship were undeniable.

Keynes' principal economic argument focused on the reparations problem. A country can make transfers to another only in goods, in gold, or in an international currency—pounds in those days, or dollars, deutschmarks, or yen today. A country can obtain gold or foreign exchange only by earning more abroad than it owes for imports or foreign services; by buying some of its citizens' foreign investments for its own currency and then selling them abroad; or by using its monetary reserves. France, for example, sold French foreign investments and drew down her reserves on a large scale in order to buy supplies in the United States during both world wars. Keynes' thesis was in essence that Germany did not have the reserves and could not hope to earn a large enough surplus on current account to pay reparations on the scale the Reparations Commission would probably impose. The subsequent success of Germany in international economic life is a sufficient comment on the economic element of Keynes' polemic.

But Keynes' economic calculations were not the heart of his case. Despite his disclaimers, he objected to any and all reparations on moral grounds: "The policy of reducing Germany to servitude for a generation, of degrading the lives of millions of human beings, and of depriving a whole nation of happiness should be abhorrent and detestable, even if it were possible, even if it enriched ourselves, even if it did not sow the decay of the whole civilized life of Europe."[15]

Keynes' analytic argument and the factual assumptions on which it was based were destroyed, piece by piece, in a long series of memoirs by statesmen and in academic articles and monographs, but most of them came out many years later, and none reached the general public.

15. Keynes, *Economic Consequences of the Peace,* 225.

For years, Keynes debated with his critics cleverly, almost never conceding error. While Keynes' crusade against the economic consequences of the Versailles Treaty is discredited in the economic literature, the general public still believes that the treaty was a cruel disaster, clearing the path for Hitler, and making the Second World War inevitable.

Nor does the rest of Keynes' thesis survive scrutiny any better. The picture of the innocent Yankee being fleeced by a pair of wily European rascals is ridiculous. Lloyd George and Clemenceau were not rascals, nor was Wilson an unworldly innocent; all three were experienced practicing politicians. Wilson stood alone against Lloyd George and Clemenceau on few issues, and on those, most notably on the Fourteen Points and the League of Nations, he prevailed.

The finest systematic treatment of Keynes' argument is a remarkable book called *The Carthaginian Peace: The Economic Consequences of Mr. Keynes,* by Etienne Mantoux.[16] Mantoux was thirty-two years old when he was killed fighting with his Free French unit in France, a few weeks before the end of the Second World War in Europe. He had finished his book during a fellowship at Princeton, and was obviously one of the ablest and most promising scholars of his generation in France. He too came of a distinguished intellectual family. Mantoux' book—unlike Keynes' writing on the subject—is calm, lucid, sophisticated, and polite. He shows great respect for Keynes' later work, and scores no cheap points. But his critique of Keynes' work on the peace of 1919 is overpowering. It can, however, make no difference to the legend. What Keynes wrote in 1919 and the next few years was of burning relevance to the principal political problems of the day. When Mantoux' book appeared in 1952, it was treated as a work of historical interest, perhaps, but of immediate concern only to a few specialists. Thus on 26 January 1990, a typical review of a recent book on the German reparations experience starts by saying:

> The attempt by the victorious Allies to make Germany pay for the First World War has long been condemned for its consequences, which included the poisoning of international relations, the destabilization of the world's financial system and the weakening of the Weimar Republic. These direct consequences in turn facilitated the rise to power of the Nazis within fourteen years of the signature of the Peace Treaty. In the English-speaking world, at least, the folly of imposing vast reparation obligations on Germany was es-

16. See Mantoux, *Carthaginian Peace,* 87, 90.

tablished by John Maynard Keynes in his polemic *The Economic Consequences of the Peace* (1920), but it is only now that we have a comprehensive account by a historian of both how this folly came about and why it was persisted in down to the early 1930s.[17]

The irony is that the book being reviewed, although rather Keynesian in tone, rejects Keynes' thesis root and branch.

Lord Boothby, who fully appreciated Keynes as an economist, said that "where politics are concerned, in contradistinction to economics, Keynes allowed himself to be governed by personal likes and dislikes, and even more by emotion. Where Germany was concerned, he was an irrational evangelist."[18] Smuts had advised Keynes to write his book. Some years later, Smuts expressed his disappointment at the outcome. He never expected Keynes' treatment of the personalities which made the book a bestseller. Within a few pages, Smuts says, Keynes turned Wilson "into a figure of fun. Those few pages about Wilson in Keynes' book made an Aunt Sally of the noblest figure—perhaps the only noble figure—in the history of the war. . . . Wilson was already going down in America. In their hearts, the Americans wanted him to go down; they wanted to evade the duties he imposed upon them. The book was absolutely to their purpose. It helped to finish Wilson, and it strengthened the Americans against the League." Boothby added, "Since Swift, no piece of sustained invective" compares with Keynes' writing about the peace.

Keynes' writings had another effect, Boothby pointed out. By his outrageous charge that "those who sign this Treaty will sign the death sentence of millions of German men, women, and children," Keynes helped to create the mood of self-reproach and "meaculpism" which did so much to paralyze the will of Great Britain and the United States for two fatal decades, and led them to "the pathetic series of surrenders which culminated in the catastrophes of 1939–1940." Boothby concluded, "The Treaty of Versailles was, in fact, a generous Treaty." It left Germany intact. "And, if you add up the figure of reparations paid, and loans from Britain and the United States subsequently repudiated, you find that she made no reparation at all." He noted, "The only trouble about the Treaty of Versailles was that the vital clauses affecting

---

17. George Peden, review of *The Spoils of War* by Bruce Kent, in *Times Literary Supplement* (London), 26 January–1 February, 1990, p. 98.
18. This and the following quotations from Robert John Graham Boothby's essay on Keynes appear in Boothby's memoir, *My Yesterday, Your Tomorrow* (London: Hutchinson, 1962), 112–15.

disarmament and the demilitarization of the Rhineland were never enforced."

With the benefit of hindsight, the peace treaty with Germany can readily be criticized on a number of grounds. The war guilt issue should have been left to the historians. As a practical matter, the treaty suffered from an excess of the nationality principle, not from too little, as Keynes and his followers charged. In his Fourteen Points speech, Wilson had recommended a confederation of states for south-eastern Europe, but his proposal was not followed up. Many students and practitioners of diplomacy have concluded that breaking up the Austro-Hungarian Empire without finding a politically acceptable way to carry on its economic functions, at least, was the worst mistake of the peacemaking process. Similarly, the reasonable treaty arrangements for the Rhineland failed when they were tested by Hitler in 1936. Here again, however, the fault was not a supposed compromise between the French position, on the one hand, and that of Britain and the United States, on the other, but the failure of Britain and the United States to carry out the pledges they had given Clemenceau in persuading him to recede. If Britain, France, and the United States—or Britain and France alone—had marched into the Rhineland in 1936, the Second World War could not have taken place.

From the political point of view, the most serious mistake of the peacemakers in 1919 occurred in their dealings with the Soviet Union. Winston Churchill had urged a policy of strangling Bolshevism at its birth and bringing Russia into the general democratic system by one means or another. This goal could easily have been accomplished, but it was not achieved because of "a complete absence of any definite or decided policy among the victorious Allies. Some were in favor of peace and some were in favor of war. In the result they made neither peace nor war."[19] The Allies half-heartedly experimented with supporting the White forces in the Russian civil war, but soon gave it up, and did little or nothing to bring Russia into the state system beyond sending relief supplies immediately after the war and economic aid during the period of Lenin's New Economic Policy after 1921. No Western government recognized the Soviet government until 1924.

It is difficult not to sympathize with the hard-pressed Allied statesmen of 1917. They faced the tremendous German offensive in France

---

19. Winston S. Churchill, *The Aftermath: The World Crisis, 1918–1928* (New York: Charles Scribner's Sons, 1929), 267.

being planned for the spring of 1918, reinforced by troops and artillery from the Eastern Front. Their armies and people were bone-tired after three years of trench warfare. There had been a French mutiny; the Americans were only beginning to confront the realities of world politics; and a large fraction of their people believed that Lenin's coup d'etat ushered in a glorious future for mankind. Nonetheless, with the advantages of hindsight, it is clear that the failure of the Western Allies to follow Churchill's advice was one of the worst diplomatic catastrophes of a century rich in catastrophe. Lenin's methods were consciously adopted by Mussolini and Hitler, and the struggle for the survival of Western civilization began.

IV

By one of the paradoxes of fate, the widespread acceptance of the Keynesian attack on the peace helped to reinforce its antithesis, the American isolationist creed, in a newly absolute form. Keynes was assuring the Western world that Wilson, Lloyd George, Clemenceau, and the other men who governed them were boobies and had betrayed the supremely important international idealism Wilson had been preaching for four years; the influence of isolationism in American life was somehow strengthened as a result. Why the Keynesian argument should fortify the case for American isolationism is puzzling, since the American isolationists reviled Wilson as unfairly as Keynes did. But Keynes was widely read and quoted, and his ideas played a part in the 1920 American election. Perhaps the isolationists found that Keynes and his supporters had demonstrated what the isolationists have always firmly believed, that foreigners were up to no good and were not worth saving. Since simple, honorable Americans could always be bamboozled by wily and unscrupulous Europeans, it was better for us to stay far away, and follow the course they thought Washington had ordained in his Farewell Address. We had strayed in April 1917, and should return to the true faith. In any event, a combination of factors, almost surely including Wilson's deteriorating health, led to radical change in the direction of American policy when the Treaty of Versailles failed in the Senate.

It is generally said that "a small band of wilful men" led the Senate to reject the Versailles treaty when it finally came to a vote. The facts are more complex. In September 1919 Wilson, exhausted by his campaign for the ratification of the treaty, suffered a massive stroke from which he never fully recovered. The treaty came before the Senate twice—once in November 1919, and again in March 1920. On both occasions, a majority but not a two-thirds majority of the senators present voted to advise the President to ratify the treaty, and consented to its ratification. But twenty Democratic senators voted "Nay": they were following Wilson's urgent request that they vote *against* ratification because the Senate Resolution of Advice and Consent was encumbered by reservations. Wilson believed that one of those reservations, that to Article 10 of the League Covenant, would gravely weaken the League of Nations as a peacekeeping institution. If in the final vote seven of the twenty Democratic senators who voted "Nay" had, like their fellows, ignored their stricken leader's advice and accepted the reservations, the President would have been free to ratify the treaty. Instead, world politics was dominated for the next twenty-three years by the fact that the United States had rejected the treaty, refused to join the League of Nations, abandoned the security treaty project for France, cut its military forces to the bone, and kept the weight of America outside the balance of power and the day-to-day conduct of foreign relations, except on a few issues, mainly economic.

Many have concluded that Wilson was being needlessly stubborn, because he could have found a way to compromise the division if he had been as adroit as he was during his first term. And they have argued that the League could have functioned under Lodge's reservations even in the rare cases when collective security was in issue.

The key question in the controversy over Senate reservations concerned Article X of the League Covenant, dealing with aggression. The reservation would have specified that in responding to a finding of aggression by the League Council, the United States could act only if Congress and the President had agreed in advance about what should be done. Since the League Council, unlike the United Nations Security Council, had only the power to advise the members what action it thought they should take, many contended that Lodge's reservation could not have made any difference. Wilson, however, and others as well, saw the Constitutional ambiguity about how the nation's war power is divided between Congress and the Presidency as a matter of crucial importance. Wilson therefore issued his appeal to the Democrats to insist on the text as submitted, without reservations, in order to preserve the President's authority to conduct multilateral diplomacy, and to instruct ambassadors about how to vote in international meetings.

Colonel Stephen Bonsal, House's assistant, worked out with Senator Henry Cabot Lodge, the powerful chairman of the Senate Foreign

Relations Committee, possible language the President might accept in a reservation to Article X of the League Covenant. House agreed, and sent the language on to the President during the worst period of Wilson's stroke. No answer came from the White House. To this day, no one knows whether Mrs. Wilson and the President's doctor showed House's report to the President, and whether at the time the President was capable of doing business at all. The United States had not then developed a Constitutional method to assure continuity in government in the event of serious Presidential illness. A possible solution to the crisis over the League in Wilson's day flickered out in frustration and mystery. And so the tragedy happened, the result of a bizarre combination of circumstances.[20]

Wilson was right to perceive the importance of the Constitutional issue, and to insist on not sacrificing the President's share of the nation's war powers. He perceived the battle for the principle of the League as a long struggle, which would indeed require the United States to pull the stars out of their old, familiar courses.

When the United Nations Charter was ratified in 1945, the Constitutional issues were better understood than in 1919, and handled differently. Franklin D. Roosevelt and Harry Truman after him, seeking to avoid Wilson's mistake, had senatorial advisers of both parties working closely with the task force on the United Nations Charter from its beginnings during the Second World War to the San Francisco Conference which drafted the Charter, and then during the ratification process. The solutions chosen were not without their ambiguities, and American politics has been grappling with them ever since. But despite those ambiguities, the Senate had comparatively little trouble passing the ratification resolution for the United Nations Charter, and Congress readily approved the United Nations Participation Act in 1945. Although the Constitutional debate about the war powers continues, the argument that the President cannot vote for sanctions in the United Nations or the North Atlantic Council without first getting a statute passed has disappeared from the political agenda.

A few days before Christmas in 1922, Wilson received Clemenceau, who was escorted by Bonsal. Wilson was broken in body, Bonsal observed, but his mental powers seemed unimpaired. Wilson complimented Bonsal on some of his articles, but asked, "Why have you not said that you were there, an eye and ear witness to all that took place while the Covenant was being drafted?" Bonsal explained his views on

20. Bonsal, *Unfinished Business,* 271–80.

confidentiality and discretion. "At this," Bonsal reports, "Mr. Wilson laughed heartily, but went on to say: 'You can't be too indiscreet to please me now. I give you full absolution in advance. We at least have nothing to conceal. I glory in the ideas that we defended in France and they will triumph. Perhaps the world charter which we fashioned in Paris will be redrawn in a happier form, but as to its ultimate acceptance I have not the shadow of a doubt. The world will not commit suicide.'"[21]

21. Ibid., 283.

12

The Interwar Years: Pretense and Self-Deception, 1920–1929

Ever since 1923, French governments had ultimately deferred to British wishes in any diplomatic problem that involved the Anglo-French relationship so that they should never again find themselves isolated in dealing with Germany.... Similarly, reluctance to accept unlimited responsibility for Europe's future continued to shape the British approach to international affairs. As a result of these twin preoccupations and policies, the ability to control events slipped away from Britain and France. With it vanished the power to protect their destinies.—Nicholas Rostow

The primary cause of the failure of Western diplomacy in the interwar period, and therefore the ultimate cause of the Second World War, was the attempt of the United States to escape down the rabbit-hole of history to the foreign policy of President James Monroe and Secretary of State John Quincy Adams. Instead of treating the defeat of the Versailles treaty in the Senate as a temporary setback to be overcome as quickly as possible, the leadership of both American political parties made it the first step in consolidating a new foreign policy—a policy of isolation, not mere neutrality.

The result was not foreordained. After all, a simple majority of the Senate had voted twice in favor of ratifying the Versailles treaty, and twenty Democrats were among those who voted "nay" at Wilson's request. But the verdict of American politics became clear almost immediately thereafter. The notion that the United States could insulate itself from significant changes in the structure and dynamics of world politics was popular, and few politicians, journalists, academics, clergymen, or trade union leaders challenged it. They chose instead to keep silent or to tell the people what they wanted to hear, that America would never again be involved in "foreign" wars. And both Presidents

The epigraph for this chapter is taken from Nicholas Rostow, *Anglo-French Relations, 1934–36,* (London: Macmillan, 1984), 248.

and public opinion accepted what was said as a guide for action: the American armed forces, created so quickly in 1917 and 1918, were reduced almost to oblivion.

The attempt of Britain and the United States to detach themselves from the troubles of the world was doomed to fail. It violated John Quincy Adams' most fundamental insight—that the principles of a nation's foreign policy do not change, but that circumstances do. The security both of Britain and of the United States in the broken world of 1919 required policies far different from those which had worked so well in Monroe's time.

The fate of the project for an Anglo-American guaranty of France against future German aggression revealed the strength of the isolationist impulse in American and British politics after the First World War. A few notable leaders of American opinion, with Theodore Roosevelt and Senator Henry Cabot Lodge at their head, supported the ratification of the Franco-American treaty which, together with its British counterpart, would have provided such a guaranty to France. The two treaties of guaranty were signed at the same time the Treaty of Versailles was signed, and in the same magnificent ceremony. They embodied the promises which had made it possible for Clemenceau to accept the Rhineland compromise of the Treaty of Versailles: that the Rhineland be permanently demilitarized and occupied by Allied troops for fifteen years, so that the Rhine would be the military frontier of France.

In 1919, a military alliance between France, Great Britain, and the United States, however denominated, might have become, like NATO later, the nucleus of an effective European security system to which Germany, Italy, the Soviet Union, and the smaller European states could ultimately have rallied. But the proposal put forward by Theodore Roosevelt and Senator Lodge attracted no following, and the treaty died of inanition, without even the courtesy of a Senate vote.

British public opinion, nearly as blind as our own, followed the American lead. Although Parliament had already voted to support the parallel Anglo-French Treaty, the government of the day decided not to put it into effect. The British took the position that the twin treaties were meant to have been a joint venture by the two English-speaking nations. The United States having refused to ratify, Britain was under no legal obligation to move alone. Few voices in either country protested that the issue was not one of legal obligation but of the national interest. No one was unkind enough to mention the words "national honor."

From the point of view of the national interests of all three countries, the question of ratifying a new triple alliance presented no difficulties. Whether one's goal was to achieve a new concert of Europe or to make the League of Nations an effective worldwide peacekeeping agency, or both, a firm alliance of the three leading powers of the West was indispensable.

The strategic position of the United States and of the Western Allies as a group was transformed by these events. Without the United States and Russia, and with the new German republic more and more firmly committed to the revision of the peace settlement, Britain and France were simply too weak to cope with the cascade of problems which beset them as the nominal leaders of Western Europe and of world politics. If Britain and France had been able to pursue a realistic and concerted policy, they could probably have contained German expansion in Europe and coped as well with the sideshows in Ethiopia and Spain. Without the weight of the United States in the scales, however, it was beyond their capacity to manage the Japanese drive for dominion in the Pacific Basin coupled with the German threat in Europe. In any event, alliance solidarity between Britain and France even in Europe proved to be beyond the reach of the British imagination and of British politics. France and Britain were too deeply divided by temperament, by history, and by education to confront the tortured aftermath of the First World War as determined allies, without the presence of the United States as a military partner and a conciliatory political influence.

The relationship between Britain and France is one of the most complex on earth, a palimpsest of memories, most of them troublesome to one or the other, or, quite often, to both. Joan of Arc, Napoleon, and Marlborough are not equally beloved in both countries, and Mrs. Thatcher was openly dubious about the French Revolution in the anniversary year of 1989. The experience of fighting a war as allies is invariably trying, and the First World War was particularly trying. The war had lasted for four years, and was brutal, frustrating, and exhausting. The Russians lost on the Eastern Front, and the Western Allies came close to losing in the West. The necessities of the war and the peacemaking process were a restraint on public expressions of mutual irritation among the Allies, but by 1919 pent-up anger began to break through. Civility was frayed. Although there are British Francophiles and French Anglophiles, and both peoples are reasonably comfortable with each other, there is nonetheless a puzzling difference in temperament between the British and the French. Perhaps it is traceable to differences in education and formation. Perhaps it is simply a residue of history or, like the frictions within a family, the consequence of inescapable intimacy over a long period of time. Whatever the cause or causes may be, it is a fact of life; it was manifest during the war and the peacemaking period; and it became much worse after the American withdrawal from world politics in 1919.

It is a commonplace that the French are "logical" and the British "pragmatic." As with most such generalizations, there is something in it, but not much. The British are quite as logical as the French, but on the subject of Germany during the interwar period they started with different premises and therefore reached different conclusions with equal logic. In instance after instance between 1919 and 1939, beginning with the Treaty of Versailles and ending with the Munich crisis of 1938, the British assumed that sympathetic concessions to Germany would eliminate its "legitimate grievances" and induce it to become a co-operative member of the family of nations At that time, moreover, Britain still viewed itself as the center of a worldwide empire and therefore primarily a naval power, whose interest in Europe was limited. The British found it hard to imagine, therefore, how British security could be affected by what happened in Poland or the other East European states. The French, on the other hand, knew in their bones that if Germany gained control of Eastern Europe she would become too strong to be restrained. Therefore the Treaty of Versailles was of crucial importance and should not be tampered with. It was all that stood between Britain and France and the abyss. Over and over again, the French tried to get Britain to declare itself the ally of France. But Britain refused to answer their pleas. The vision of England on its island, keeping the peace by moving from partner to partner in the slow quadrille of the balance of power, was too deeply ingrained in British memory.

The differences between the Western European Allies and the United States, in turn, were almost equally serious. The French and the British, happy as they were to welcome the Americans in the last year and a half of the war, often found their new allies brash, naive— even a bit simple—and not properly apologetic because they had taken so long to get into the war. And the frequent, innocent American boast that they had "won the war" was nearly unendurable to their allies, who had lived through the Marne, the Somme, and Verdun while the Americans were making a great deal of money as neutrals.

The collapse of American policy after 1919 concerned and troubled the British; for the French, the shock was much greater. They felt they had been deceived. They had reluctantly settled for a demilitarized

Rhineland plus British and American security guaranties. Would the League of Nations be an effective substitute for a triple alliance? Without Russia and the United States, could the League keep the peace effectively? The French were skeptical. And they were dismayed by what they thought were the absurd arguments of the British and others that the council of the League could enforce the treaty by votes, by resolutions, by persuasion, by sanctions, without military force, using only the force of public opinion.

To the French mind, the council could not be more than the sum of its parts—the League members assembled in congress, like the Concert of Europe in the previous century. The Concert of Europe had been persuasive many times because in the final analysis it believed in the principle of keeping the peace and was backed by force. With America on the sidelines, and Russia under the Bolsheviks secretly working with the Germans, how could a resolution of the League Council prevent the Germans from remilitarizing the Rhineland, if the Germans decided that the time had come? In such an event, would the British at least cooperate with France, even if the Americans shut their eyes to the implications of a German move into the Rhineland? Czechoslovakia and Poland had been organized into the nucleus of the Little Entente through security treaties with France. Surely they could not hold Germany back without leadership from France and Britain, especially if Germany and the Soviet Union were cooperating behind the scenes. Yet so long as the Rhineland was demilitarized, Germany could not go to war in the East.

The French were of course right in their analysis of the Rhineland problem, but their reasoning and their persistence only annoyed the British and the Americans. Who could imagine defeated Germany, republican Germany, beset by troubles of every kind, as a potential aggressor? In response, the French pointed out that countries often recover after defeats, as France did after 1870. And they repeated their arguments often and with emphasis. The British and the Americans found France's preoccupation with its security "tiresome" and old-fashioned. Keynes' sympathy for the Germans gained ground both in Britain and the United States. The war was over; "let bygones be bygones," and "fair play for the Germans" were the new slogans of policy in both countries.

In Germany, however, politics was powerfully influenced by an entirely different slogan: "the stab in the back," the myth that the German armed forces were not really beaten in 1918, but had been betrayed by a conspiracy of Socialist civilians who had captured the

German government, signed the armistice and the Treaty of Versailles, exiled the Kaiser, and formed a republic. Slowly at first, but steadily and then at an accelerating pace, this grim conviction came to dominate German opinion even when it was tacit rather than explicit. The fact that the legend was without substance had no effect on its plausibility: as early as September 1918, the German High Command had urgently pressed the head of the new government, Prince Max von Baden, to sue for peace. After knocking Russia out of the war and reinforcing its army in the West with one million men and thirty thousand artillery pieces from the eastern front, the Germans had mounted tremendous offensives in France. They had failed. The Allied forces, well led, and employing tanks effectively for the first time, launched powerful counteroffensives, which succeeded. In a panic, the German High Command told the government the army was beaten and demoralized. It was breaking up, and unless an armistice were signed quickly, Germany would repeat the tragedy of Russia, and perhaps undo the union of 1870. Furthermore, the spectacle of fresh American troops pouring into France made continuance of the war unthinkable.

II

The story of the interwar period begins with a comparatively narrow set of issues: German compliance with the Versailles treaty. The Allies pressed for compliance. Defeated Germany in the first years under the treaty was too weak for military resistance, but through diplomacy it countered the Allies at first with delay and then with increasingly active initiatives intended not to revise but to destroy the Versailles settlement.

It was clear almost before the ink was dry on the signatures of the treaty that Germany would do everything possible to escape from its restrictions. The secret arrangements for military cooperation between Germany and the Soviet Union were made in 1919 and accelerated in 1922 by the understandings reflected in the Treaty of Rapallo, which called for general economic and political cooperation between the two pariah nations. In Western Europe, it became apparent almost at once that Germany was going as far as she dared in resisting both the payment of reparations and disarmament. The various commissions established to monitor compliance with the treaty were faced with endless postponements, obfuscations, and plain lies in their attempts to collect information and negotiate compromises. Politics and public order in the new reich were constantly disrupted by the threats and violent acts of those who advocated revolution both from the left and the right. As the Allies were well aware, the new German government had a precarious grip on authority. Its diplomats often pointed out that if they were pushed too far the result could well be the collapse of the regime.

In the beginning, Britain and France acted together in seeking to enforce the treaty. But after a short time, they differed more and more openly on how far it was wise to insist on strict enforcement. Disagreement between Britain and France had revealed itself in a number of the relatively minor crises of the immediate postwar period—those involving war or the threat of war between Greece and Turkey in Anatolia, for example; and the conflicts over Fiume, Silesia, and other places where the new boundaries were challenged. The principal Allied powers allowed themselves to carry over their habit of quarreling with each other into their handling of the far more fundamental German issues. Such self-indulgence is always a mistake for those who must lead a group. In this case, the mistake was of major significance. Germany exploited the Franco-British disagreements steadily, and ultimately prevailed.

The differences between France and Britain on the German question were nominally differences of style, not of principle. As always, however, such distinctions are hard to preserve. In the end, many, perhaps all differences turn out to be differences of degree. In this case, the differences of style became disastrous differences of principle.

At the level of reason, Britain had learned—or rather relearned—the main strategic lesson of the First World War, that she could no longer safely confine herself to a blue-water security policy and a foreign policy of "splendid isolation" as arbiter of the European balance of power. She had to make a Continental commitment as well. Britain's safety required her to be sure that no Continental power became too big. But how big was too big? Surely Britain could not tolerate a Germany big enough to dominate all of Europe. But was republican Germany, Germany struggling to be accepted in European and world politics, likely to be infected by the "Napoleonic disease," to recall Grey's observation before 1914?[1] Surely, to entertain such concerns was fantastic, obsessive, neurotic, and unfair, most British leaders thought. Britain recognized her vital security interest in the independence of France, and France was entitled to recover her lost provinces of Alsace and Lorraine. But did the principle of the Anglo-French entente require Britain to fight in order to keep the French military

1. See Chapter 9, n. 8.

frontier on the Rhine? To insist on the Versailles solution for the insoluble problem of Silesia? To back France on the Saar question and her new treaties with Poland and Czechoslovakia? On reparations? In other words, could Britain be a faithful ally to France and still support a measure of diplomatic flexibility in order to eliminate some of Germany's grievances and thus, most British people thought, eliminate the causes of Germany's determination to revise the Treaty of Versailles? After all, both Britain and France had an interest in a prosperous and above all a satisfied Germany, a supporter of the status quo.

In one form or another, the principle of the *entente cordiale* was firmly in the British mind. In real life, however, the entente was anything but cordial, and the mind is not always the strongest force controlling the relations of people or states. No matter how often the British man of politics was convinced by reason that Britain and France simply had to be allied, and to behave accordingly, he turned skittish and withdrew when asked to admit it in public and in writing.

In France, the problem was perceived quite differently. France agreed, of course, that the Franco-British military alliance was indispensable to the security of both countries. But in 1919 she saw Germany as an angry and unreconstructed enemy, unwilling to accept the fact or the consequences of her defeat. Her population was larger than that of France, and her birthrate higher. And her industrial plant had not been damaged or allowed to deteriorate during the war. Nothing could prevent Germany from becoming again the leading industrial power of Europe. And policy should not assume that Germany had truly embraced either the Weimar constitution or the peaceful bourgeois role in Europe the British and Americans assured themselves was already Germany's destiny. Of course France favored plans for conciliating Germany and removing her legitimate grievances, if there were any. The French foreign minister, Aristide Briand, became the symbol of an active French policy of reconciliation and cooperation with Germany. It was France who proposed German membership in the League of Nations, and the formation of a United States of Europe, which the British and the Germans turned down.

But France also regarded the Treaty of Versailles as the absolutely minimal bulwark of its security, and never could understand why the British and Americans could not understand why this was so. France had been deprived of the tangible support of an open military alliance with Great Britain and the United States by Anglo-Saxon fuzzy-mindedness in 1919–20. She knew that Germany's so-called grievances against the treaty were trivial in themselves. Germany's real grievance was that victory in the war had been so unfairly snatched from her hands in 1918. There was no conciliatory formula which could cure that wound.

Germany wanted to be freed from the shackles of Versailles, the French thought, so that she could annex Austria—a step expressly forbidden in the treaty—, achieve unspecified expansion in Eastern Europe and the Middle East, build a navy, and conquer a colonial empire again. Once Britain and France consented to the revision of one important article of the treaty, another request for revision would surely come along. Where would the process end? The camel's nose would be under the tent with a vengeance. In the French view, the key question for Allied policy was whether Weimar Germany would in the long run follow the policy of Bismarck or that of the Kaiser—whether, that is, it would have a prudent sense of limits or indulge in Wagnerian excess. In the first few years after the war, no one could be sure how that question would be answered. Meanwhile, the French said, let us stick to the treaty. It is all we have.

III

The first opportunity Germany had to gain ground in its public campaign against the treaty was the conflict over the occupation of the Rhineland, which was linked in turn to the problem of reparations. And the first battle in that campaign was the Ruhr crisis of 1923.

The issue which precipitated the disastrous French occupation of the Ruhr was Germany's failure to pay reparations in kind (coal and timber) to France and Belgium on 1 January 1923. The German reparations problem had become a farcical merry-go-round. First the Germans would default, and then they would ask for a moratorium. There would be meetings and consultations; negotiations and further meetings, followed by the setting of new schedules; an occasional small payment on account; and then new defaults. When the Allies were united, Germany avoided default. When they were divided over this or other issues, or distracted by troubles elsewhere—and such troubles were numerous—the Germans would default again, proposing solutions which almost invariably required modifications of the treaty arrangement.

The quotas which were not fulfilled on 1 January 1923 had been established by this tortuous and inflammatory process some months before. Germany had been temporarily relieved of cash payments and her obligation to make payments in kind had been reduced. But, unless some new agreement intervened, a schedule established at an earlier meeting in London would go into effect. In July 1922, Germany asked for a moratorium on the payments. The British were sympathetic, and favored an even more extended moratorium than Germany had requested, because while the German economy was recovering rapidly, the mark was wobbling on the exchange markets and inflationary forces were attracting notice and concern.

Both British and French experts agreed that Germany was deliberately debauching the mark in order to avoid paying reparations. The British concluded that since Germany's monetary problems were so serious, a longer moratorium was needed in order to allow a steadily more properous Germany to put her finances in order. The French thought Germany should not be rewarded through yet another reparations moratorium for extraordinarily destructive monetary behavior, and opposed any relief for Germany unless the Allies took direct control of some income-bearing assets—the coal mines, the customs offices, the state forests, or the revenue services. France felt that the ridiculous game of cat-and-mouse had reached the point where vigorous Allied action was required. Unless the Allies, or some of them, moved decisively, no further reparations payments could be expected. Sally Marks comments:

> The only thing that could be done was an occupation of the Ruhr Valley, and Britain was by definition against that. So Britain insisted on a four-year moratorium without guarantees, while France, feeling that the Versailles Treaty was at stake, demanded both Entente unity and substantial guarantees.
>
> Through Entente conferences and Reparations Commission wrangles, the crisis deepened. At the end of the year Germany was in massive default on timber deliveries, and the default was formally declared over strenuous British opposition, although the Reparations Commission took no further action. Germany was defaulting regularly on her monthly coal quotas, and that question would loom in January for perhaps the last time as France decided that enough was enough. Also in January there must be a new reparations plan— and there was none.[2]

After a rancorous and inconclusive conference of Allied representatives and Germany in Paris early in January, the Reparations Com-

---

2. Sally Marks, *The Illusion of Peace: International Relations in Europe, 1918–1933* (New York: St Martin's Press, 1976), 48–49.

mission agreed by a vote of three to one that there was a default in Germany's required coal deliveries and that the Allies should occupy the Ruhr, moving in experts protected by Allied troops to take control of the mines, the railroads, and other facilities. While the occupation was accomplished by French, Belgian, and Italian troops, it was in fact a French and Belgian operation. The British abstained. In public, they criticized the action. In private diplomatic channels, they produced scathing full-dress attacks on the policy of France. Meanwhile, the German government ordered a policy of passive resistance to the occupation, and financed it by producing a runaway inflation which proved to be one of the most traumatic events in German social history. As the French government under Poincaré prolonged the occupation, Belgium and Italy weakened in the face of the extraordinary occurrences.

The Ruhr crisis of 1923–25 marked the end of the postwar period, and the beginning of the prewar period. It opened the door wide to further gradual revisions of the Versailles settlement. France concluded that it could never again use force without British support. Costly as the crisis was to Germany both economically and socially, it demonstrated the effectiveness and the potential of a policy of exploiting the power of weakness. And it brought Gustav Stresemann forward as chancellor and foreign minister.

Stresemann was one of the outstanding politicians of the Weimar Republic. He became a hero in Western Europe, where he was welcomed with relief and enthusiasm as the symbol of Franco-German reconciliation, a German nationalist who had become a good European. Photographs of Stresemann with his French colleague, Aristide Briand, were for years an icon of hope that a just and generous peace in Europe might still be achieved by goodwill and intelligence. Stresemann himself was an ambiguous and elusive figure. His carefully nurtured public image emphasized his benign intentions; his private papers, however, reveal a politician of great skill whose program was systematically to destroy the Treaty of Versailles, "trench by trench," as he once remarked. Under the circumstances of the twenties, with the German armed forces weakened and Germany, like nearly every other European country, riven by deep divisions, Stresemann had no choice but to proceed by wary diplomacy, pretending all the while to be an advocate of fulfilling the treaty and of European reconciliation, cooperation, and unity.

When Stresemann took office as chancellor, he stopped the German policy of passive resistance in the Ruhr. Gordon Craig wrote that this was "probably the bravest and certainly the most painful decision of his life, the decision to capitulate to the French by terminating the policy of passive resistance that was contributing so heavily to the dis-integration of the social fabric."[3]

Stresemann was violently critized in Germany for this decision, but he stood his ground and gained sympathy and support in Great Britain and the United States. This development in turn helped lead the way to the negotiation of the Dawes Plan, which was the first public man-ifestation since 1919 that the United States was a latent factor in Eu-ropean politics. Urged into action by the British, the United States convened an informal committee of international experts who came up with the plan in 1924.

Under considerable British pressure, all the governments involved accepted the Dawes Plan. It called for a substantial international loan to Germany in exchange for a reform and reorganization of German taxation and finances. The reforms in Germany would be surpervised by international experts, and German reparations payments would re-sume after a two-year moratorium through American Agent-General for Reparations S. Parker Gilbert. The French were to withdraw from the Ruhr. Moreover, the Reparations Commission established by the Versailles treaty was to be reorganized, and the French influence in the commission reduced. In the future, it would be procedurally almost impossible for the commission to order sanctions in the event of a default in reparations payments.

The Dawes Plan was castigated in Germany at first as another government capitulation. Stresemann dismissed these criticisms, Craig writes, "with contempt. The goal of all Germany's efforts, [Stresemann] felt, should be the regaining of her political and economic freedom; and the Dawes Plan was an essential step in that direction." It would bring Germany the loans she needed to pay her new reparations com-mitment. Unless that was done, the occupation of the Ruhr would not end. In addition, Stresemann saw, his strategy would attract foreign loans to Germany. He said in 1925, "One must simply have . . . so many debts that the creditor sees his own existence jeopardized if the debtor collapses. . . . These economic matters create bridges of political un-derstanding and future political support."[4]

In 1921, in an effort to head off the Ruhr crisis, Stresemann had

3. Gordon A. Craig, *From Bismarck to Adenauer: Aspects of German Statecraft* (1958; rev. ed., Harper and Row, Harper Torchbooks, 1965), 56.
4. Annelise Thimme, *Gustave Stresemann: Eine politische Biographie zur Geschichte der Weimarer Republik* (Hanover and Frankfurt-am-Main, 1957), 69; idem, "Gustave Stre-semann, Legende und Wirklichkeit," *Historische Zeitschrift* 181 (1956):314.

put forward the possibility of a general security treaty for the Rhineland through which the Western Allies would guarantee both France and Germany against direct aggression by the other. If France were protected by a clear-cut and categorical British, Belgian, and Italian guaranty, why continue with the occupation of the Rhineland? Under such circumstances, was it necessary to demilitarize the Rhineland, and to worry about each rifle issued to the German police in the area?

Two developments in Germany's relation to Europe led to the revival of Stresemann's idea some two years later: the first was the looming question whether the Allies would carry out their obligation under the Treaty of Versailles to evacuate the first zone of Rhineland occupation on 1 January 1925; the second, the anxious German reaction to a busy series of futile attempts to develop machinery for peacekeeping, largely in Europe, both through the League of Nations and through more familiar diplomatic procedures. The Germans were opposed to any restrictions on their freedom of action.

Under the Versailles treaty, the Rhineland was to be evacuated in stages from three zones in 1925, 1930, and 1935, but the Allies could prolong the occupation indefinitely if they found that Germany had not carried out her fundamental treaty obligations. The Dawes Plan had effectively put off the reparations issue, at least for the moment. The chief remaining question which could legally justify continuing the occupation was therefore the disarmament of Germany to the levels set in the treaty.

The Interallied Military Control Commission, a body of some strength and independence, was responsible for certifying German compliance with the arms control provisions of the treaty. Since the demilitarization of the Rhineland was one of the principal features of the Treaty, it was one of the commission's most sensitive concerns. During the latter part of 1924, the commission had warned the Allied governments and the Germans in general terms that it was by no means satisfied with the evidence on the scale and disposition of German armaments available to it.

Stresemann, of course, knew that Germany had not disarmed to the treaty limits. He also knew that Great Britain and France were hardly eager for another wrangle like that over the occupation of the Ruhr. Germany's first response to the commission's warnings therefore was to ridicule Allied anxiety about the easier aspects of the problem, and to make no comment at all on the issues of greater importance, about which he knew that Germany was in the wrong. The commission had had to leave the Rhineland during the worst period of the Ruhr crisis, and was therefore unable to complete a final report before 1 January 1925. It did, however, issue a lengthy interim report in December 1924. That document was devastating to the Germans. Although it did not mention the military aspects of German-Soviet cooperation, which were presumably unknown to the Allies, it found that Germany was not in compliance with the treaty on many other grounds. This time, Britain and France were agreed, however reluctantly, and the evacuation of the first zone of occupation was postponed. The final report of the commission was even more categorical.

During the preceding two years, a number of abortive diplomatic initiatives, largely by Great Britain, had begun to define possible approaches to the task of carrying out the peacekeeping and disarmament objectives of the Versailles treaty. The Washington Naval Conference in 1922 had produced a nine-power naval arms limitation treaty which at the time was widely considered a great success. Many wished to develop a multilateral arms control treaty to deal with the more difficult problem of limiting ground forces and their armaments. Other initiatives stressed compulsory arbitration as a remedy for disputes which threatened the peace; others still fell back on the principle of defensive security treaties which would assure each of the nations involved concerted protection against aggression. The latter approach raised for Germany the disturbing possibility of having to confront collective resistance to future German expansion in Eastern Europe.

Facing both the prospect of extended occupation of the Rhineland and the less tangible risks of a general collective security treaty in Europe, Stresemann again raised the idea of a treaty through which Great Britain, Belgium, and perhaps Italy would guarantee both France and Germany against "flagrant military aggression" by the other, but would say nothing about acts of aggression elsewhere. This time Stresemann's idea took off, and duly became the Treaty of Locarno in 1925. During the negotiations, Stresemann skillfully finessed a number of attempts to make the treaty a general security pact to guarantee all the boundaries established by the Treaty of Versailles, or at least the boundaries of Austria, Poland, and Czechoslovakia. As it emerged, the treaty applied only to Western Europe. The Germans often referred to it as the Rhineland Treaty.

Europe and the world hailed the Locarno treaty extravagantly as the basis for a new era of peace. Stresemann and his British and French colleagues, Aristide Briand and Sir Austen Chamberlain, were given the Nobel Peace Prize. The issue of German compliance with the disarmament requirements of the Versailles treaty was swept aside in the general excitement. The report of the military commission was never answered, and the first Allied withdrawals from the Rhineland started on the day the Locarno treaty was signed. In the next year, France supported Germany's application for membership in the League of Nations.

In itself, Locarno was a calamity, and its political effect was worse, because it encouraged the British and Americans to make policy on the basis of illusion. The treaty was a disaster for many reasons. The most dramatic was that it strengthened the persistent British (and American) tendency to believe that what happened in Eastern Europe was not a matter of concern to British security. Very few accepted the view put forward by Sir James Headlam-Morley, the Historical Adviser of the British Foreign Office, in his prescient memorandum of February 1925 to the foreign secretary. The danger point in Europe, Headlam-Morley argued, was not the Rhine but the Vistula, not Alsace-Lorraine, but the Polish corridor and Upper Silesia.

> Has anyone attempted to realize what would happen if there were to be a new partition of Poland, or if the Czechoslovak state were to be so curtailed and dismembered that in fact it disappeared from the map of Europe? The whole of Europe would at once be in chaos. There would no longer be any principle, meaning, or sense in the territorial arrangements of the continent. Imagine, for instance, that under some improbable condition, Austria rejoined Germany; that Germany, using the discontented minority in Bohemia, demanded a new frontier far over the mountains, including Carlsbad and Pilsen, and that at the same time, in alliance with Germany, the Hungarians recovered the southern slope of the Carpathians. This would be catastrophic, and, even if we neglected to interfere in time to prevent it, we should afterwards be driven to interfere, probably too late.[5]

The supreme achievement of the Concert of Europe after 1815, Headlam-Morley pointed out, was that it brought France "back to the councils of the great European powers without [her] being allowed to upset the order of Europe established by the Congress of Vienna." He advised a comparable approach to the German problem. Germany should join the councils of Europe as a major power, particularly for the purpose of discussing reparations, but not be given a "chance to

5. James Headlam-Morley, *Studies in Diplomatic History* (London: Methuen, 1930), 182, 184.

wreck the basic arrangements of the Paris settlement. Such sabotage would be possible," he correctly predicted, "if the new eastern European states were left without protection and if Germany were permitted to co-operate with Russia against them."[6] Marks noted,

> In negotiating the Rhineland pact, Germany made much of the fact that she was now offering voluntarily to affirm what had been imposed upon her by *force majeure* in the Versailles Treaty. Stresemann emphasised that the voluntary affirmation was considerably more binding than the Versailles *diktat*. [Austen] Chamberlain so badly wanted peace, while France and Belgium so deeply craved security that the argument was accepted. However, reaffirmation of some treaty clauses not only implied a need for such action but also cast doubt on the validity and binding force of others. Stresemann intended this effect regarding the Polish frontier which he flatly refused to mention in the treaties. Locarno was widely interpreted as a green light for Germany in the east. Well before the treaties were completed, a German diplomatist remarked, "I am a poor German but I would not wish to be Polish, for then there would not pass a night when I would sleep tranquilly."[7]

The Locarno treaty was thought to symbolize the end of the war and the acceptance of Germany as an equal. On the basis of the treaty, Germany was to be admitted to the League Council. Few noticed that Germany had obtained a most revealing provision, which in effect exempted her from any obligation, however nebulous, to apply sanctions against a state found by the Council to be an aggressor. The point of the exemption was to take account of Germany's relationship with the Soviet Union. Stresemann went to great lengths to protect Germany's secret connection with that country. Once the occupation of the Rhineland was ended, would it be possible under the Locarno treaty for the Allies to send their troops back into the Rhineland, even if Germany defaulted on reparations or deployed its own troops in the demilitarized area? Or would such a step constitute an aggression within the intendment of the treaty? All France received in compensation for these ambiguities was the equivocal British guaranty of its frontiers against "unprovoked and flagrant military violations"—the written guaranty France had sought so persistently before 1914 and after 1918.

---

6. Ibid., 179–81. See also Hajo Holborn, *The Political Collapse of Europe* (New York: Alfred A. Knopf, 1951), 129.

7. Marks, *Illusion of Peace*, 71.

Unfortunately, however, the Locarno treaty created a new obstacle to an effective military alliance between Britain and France. As Nicholas Rostow has pointed out,

> Locarno meant that Britain could not plan with France, or with Germany, to defend the Versailles settlement in the west by military means. Because of Locarno, the French needed British approval to fulfil the terms of their alliances with Poland and Czechoslovakia. If France were to act alone, and, for example, attack Germany in order to preserve the territorial settlement of Eastern Europe, the French had to be willing to put British goodwill at risk. After the occupation of the Ruhr in 1923, no French government would do it and, as a result, France's alliance system was now explicitly one-sided. The negative implications that seemed to flow from Locarno made it impracticable, indeed nearly impossible, to arrange Anglo-French military actions or demonstrations in support of diplomacy, short of general war.[8]

The five years after 1925 gave Europe a last Indian summer before the blizzard of the world economic crisis struck in 1931. Despite the economic turmoil of the early twenties, Europe was prosperous again, and growing. Holborn observes:

> By hindsight, it is easy to say that . . . Europe could have been reconstituted [during that period], not as an entirely self-contained political system, but as a strong powerblock in world politics if the beginnings of co-operation between Britain, France, and Germany had been carried to a full understanding on all the major issues of Europe. Such a firm understanding among the three powers could also have led to a common program for the strengthening of the eastern European states. Britain, however, was not willing to consider additional commitments in Europe. Perhaps Germany and France could have acted alone, disregarding the British sensitiveness to separate Franco-German co-operation; but Germany felt that France would never voluntarily make those concessions that Germany considered her due and that France was aiming exclusively at bolstering the *status quo*. Briand's proposal for the formation of a European Federal Union, first broached in 1929, was too vague and did not contain special concessions that might have won over Germany. Britain poured cold water on the plan, while Germany

---

8. Nicholas Rostow, *Anglo-French Relations*, 14.

at first took a reserved attitude. Later, in March, 1931, the German Government used the idea of a European federation as a cloak for the Austro-German customs union, judged by France to be a unilateral revision of the Paris settlement rather than a step in the direction of a European federation. By then the chance for real understanding was gone.[9]

9. Holborn, *Political Collapse of Europe,* 134–35.

13

The Interwar Years: Hitler's Icarian Flight, 1929–1939

The Versailles Treaty was not the real object of Hitler's criticism, though a large part of his propaganda dwelt on its alleged injustices. As a passionate champion of the revision of the treaty, he found a following not only among the lower German middle classes and farmers but also among the bourgeoisie *at large, whose strong nationalism was, however, tempered by the recognition of some moral obligations. Only the German working class and substantial Roman Catholic groups proved entirely impervious to Hitler's promises. Foreign statesmen made the same mistake as did many Germans in appraising him as the vindicator of Germany's claims for the revision of Versailles. Adolf Hitler thought of himself as a modern Genghis Kahn, capable of setting the course of history for the next thousand years by the application of his absolutely amoral and ruthless willpower. To use a phrase with which Ranke once described Napoleon, he was a "beast of conquest."—Hajo Holborn*

No new political ideas or movements emerged during the 1930s. The pages turned, but they were simply a more lurid chapter of the same book. The currents of behavior which had developed during the first stormy decade of the interwar period became stronger and more overt as world politics lurched toward general war. Year by year, the United States committed itself more deeply to the policy of isolationism which had evolved after the defeat of the Treaty of Versailles in the Senate. The British and the French could not resolve their quarrels. Italy agreed with the British and the French about Austria, but began to shift to the German side as Germany under Hitler openly succeeded in carrying Stresemann's campaign against the treaty to its conclusion. The bad dreams of the twenties were realized and then exceeded in Hitler's early years of maniacal power. Finally, starting in 1940, the American instinct

The epigraph for this chapter is taken from Hajo Holborn, *The Political Collapse of Europe* (New York: Alfred A. Knopf, 1951), 147.

of self-preservation began to stir as it had in 1917, and the world was given a second chance.

Like a bird mesmerized by a snake, the United States continued to withdraw from world politics as the threat of war grew worse. Even on economic questions, the United States remained aloof. The American intervention which helped to resolve the Ruhr crisis of 1923 had only one sequel: the similar "unofficial" initiative which produced the Young Plan for reparations. The United States never even cancelled the Allied debts arising out of the First World War. Formally, they are still on the Treasury's books. It simply accepted the moratorium on war debts and reparations negotiated in 1932 at the low point of the world depression of that period. During the twenties and early thirties, American tariffs rose both on principle and as a remedy against the depression—the remedy of beggar thy neighbor, which naturally made the problems of the world economy worse. And President Franklin D. Roosevelt withdrew the American delegation from the London Economic Conference of 1933 at the beginning of his first term, as a meeting which might tie America's hands in trying to achieve economic recovery by devaluing the dollar and other unilateral efforts.

Politically, the picture was even more dismal. The Americans were remote, inaccessible, and seemingly indifferent to international problems. As the pressures generated by German and Japanese policy became more intense, the United States sought to insulate itself against them by passing neutrality legislation in regards to Europe and adopting economic sanctions against Japan. Britain continued to sympathize with Germany's complaints, and to complain in turn about France's "senseless" preoccupation with security problems. France, despairing of Britain and the United States, waited for reason to prevail, and meanwhile sought whatever comfort she could find in her pacts with Poland and Czechoslovakia, and the possibility of an alliance with the Soviet Union.

II

The Great Depression which began after the New York stock market crashed in October 1929 was the worst the capitalist world had experienced for more than thirty years. The crash was worldwide in character, and the intervention of governments, practicing the economic orthodoxies of the time, prolonged and intensified the depression. The literature of economics offered little or no guidance about how to achieve economic recovery. A small number of economists around the world had written pioneering studies on the art of managing the trade cycle, but they were regarded by most of their fellows as eccentrics or worse, and their work was unknown to politicians, bankers, and business leaders. Building on the earlier work of Fisher, Wicksell, and D. H. Robertson, Keynes entered the fray with a widely read pamphlet and then with a series of articles and books urging active government policies of deficit financing to stimulate recovery, but he made no converts among the governments until after Roosevelt's first recovery program, the NRA, had failed.

The pre–1914 monetary system, rotating around the sun of the British pound, had lost its vitality, and the new one, based on organized great-power monetary cooperation, had not yet been born. Benjamin Strong, the creative head of the Federal Reserve System, had died the year before the crash. Milton Friedman once remarked that Strong's death was the main cause of the Great Depression. That comment was more than clever insight. Strong's replacement was weak; and the chief monetary officials of the United States, Great Britain, France, and Germany were incapable either of conceiving or of carrying out a program of monetary reconstruction which might have provided the world economy with a stabilizing monetary foundation. As the effects of the early bank failures and the stock market crash spread, more banks wavered and failed. Expectations for trade turned pessimistic, and business investment dropped. Employment and therefore consumption fell. Facing declining tax receipts and deficits, governments raised taxes in order to "restore confidence," thus driving the economy down further. Unemployment rose to unprecedented levels, and all the Western societies experienced the despair of economic suffering unmitigated by hope. Quacks and necromancers flourished, as respectable leaders suggested remedies which were more and more obviously calamitous.

In the countries where society had been most greviously wounded by the war and its aftermath—Germany and France—social divisions became so acute and so inflamed as to raise the specter of civil war—such war as had overwhelmed Russia a few years before and had been put down immediately after the war in Hungary, and in Bavaria and other parts of Germany. There were considerable Communist parties in both countries, and even stronger Social Democratic parties. On the other side of the political spectrum, beyond the orthodox Conservative parties, a variety of nationalist or Fascist movements flourished, some regularly employing both violence and the symbols of the Fascists as well. Riots became frequent, political assassinations were not uncommon. The social atmosphere was envenomed. Italy, Spain, and Portugal, inherently more vulnerable than the other Western nations, lived in a state of visible instability. Even in the most cohesive and self-confident societies, those of Great Britain and the United States, there were symptoms of the fevers which raged on the Continent.

People were forced to wonder whether the comfortable and familiar institutions of bourgeois civilization were capable of dealing with the problems of the modern world. Were the prophecies of Marx, Spengler, and Ortega y Gasset being fulfilled before their eyes? Was the West really in decline? Were the masses revolting against the tradition of Western civilization, seeking strange new gods? The specter of Communism in Russia and the presence of Communist trade unions and of Communist and Fascist political parties in the countries of Western Europe translated these anxieties into palpable threats.

Italy had the first openly Fascist regime. Mussolini took power in 1922 and established a dictatorship which promised the nation prosperity, pride, and a whiff of the glory of its Roman past. Mussolini was a former Socialist who built his movement on the claim that he would prevent the Socialists from coming to power. One of the best books of the period about Mussolini was called *Sawdust Caesar,* an apt title. Full of bombast, Mussolini strutted across the European stage like a buffoon. But he was not a buffoon, alas. As Phillipe Berthelot, the secretary general of the French Foreign Office, remarked during the early thirties, "The thugs are taking over."

Mussolini's cohorts, like those of Hitler later on, were mainly members of the working class—not skilled craftsmen and other trade union members, at least in the early years, but the next lower class of less firmly rooted workers who constitute the margin of the work force in all countries. Mussolini was finally accepted and tolerated by the older Establishment as preferable to the alternatives. In any event, the former governing class had no choice once Mussolini had consolidated his power in 1925. Italy became a one-party state, and Mussolini's violent methods of governing made opposition unthinkable. He consciously borrowed those methods from the Bolsheviks in the Soviet Union, adding a few touches which were Roman or Italian in origin. Garibaldi's militia had worn red shirts. Since the Communists had taken possession of the color red, Mussolini's private army wore black shirts. And the logo of his movement was not the hammer and sickle but the Roman fasces—a bundle of sticks tied together, symbolizing the strength of unity and authority. Otherwise, Mussolini relied on the methods of mass mobilization pioneered by the Bolsheviks—films, posters, and propaganda, backed by extralegal violence and the espionage of a secret police.

Hitler's brown-shirted storm troopers and their elite component, the S.S., in black uniforms and caps decorated with the skull and cross-bones, became familiar in Germany early in the twenties as one of a number of nationalist and militarist organizations which gave a sinister cast to German public life. They promised to redeem Germany from the stigma of defeat and the disgrace of the Diktat of Versailles and to prevent the Communists from seizing power in Germany. During the last days of the Weimar Republic, Hitler and his posturing Fascists were dismissed as ridiculous, especially after the Beer-Hall Putsch of 1923, an abortive coup d'etat which brought Hitler first to prison and then to power. After Hitler's release from a short term in prison, during which he wrote *Mein Kampf,* he reorganized his movement and intensified his political efforts.

Most observers of the scene in Germany continued to treat Hitlerism as a peripheral phenomenon. In 1928, a young American foreign service officer, Robert Murphy, was consul-general in Munich. His colleague there as papal nuncio was a Monsignor Pacelli, later to become Pope Pius XII. The priest and the young American became friends, and Pacelli discussed with Murphy several drafts of a long report he was writing for the Vatican about the significance of Hitler and Hitlerism. The two men agreed that Hitler was a transitory threat and that he never could amount to anything. Years later the Pope welcomed the British and American commanders of the Allied armies on the Capitoline Hill as they marched into Rome after their long and bitter campaign from North Africa and Sicily. Murphy was present as the political adviser to General Mark Clark, Field Marshal Alexander's American deputy. After Murphy and the Pope greeted each other, Murphy asked the Pope if he recalled the memorandum on Hitler he had written in Munich sixteen years before. "Of course, my son," the Pope replied, "but that was before I became infallible."

Whether Hitler could have come to power in Germany without the agony of the world depression is a question which can never be answered. Hitler's party gained one hundred seats in the Reichstag in the 1930 elections, before the stock market crash of late 1929 had begun seriously to affect employment and finances in Germany, and after the adoption of the Young Plan had "finally" settled the German reparations question. In that prosperous and diplomatically propitious year, the last of the Allied troops were withdrawn from the Rhineland, a successful conference on naval armaments was held in London, and the French proposed to form a United States of Europe. Hitler skyrocketed toward power nonetheless.

Be that as it may, Hitler did become chancellor of Germany in 1933, after an election held under the constitution of the Weimar Republic and in accordance with its forms. The history of the next twelve years was dominated by his personality and his mind, as he addressed the issues about which France and Great Britain had differed so dramatically during the first decade after Versailles. With more and more desperate anxiety, Britain pursued the policy of seeking a conciliatory accommodation with Germany, until the war came in 1939; indeed, Britain continued to flirt with those ideas until Churchill became prime minister in 1940. Despite all the social and political turmoil in France, the French government continued to press the British to adopt the policies of diplomatic vigor Churchill was recommending in vain on the other side of the channel—a firm public alliance between Britain and France, Allied rearmament in response to Hitler's secret rearmament in Germany, and joint resistance under the Versailles Treaty to the former reoccupation of the Rhineland in 1936.

The French urged the Churchillian policy on every possible occasion, and with energy, but also with a kind of resignation, as if they knew their efforts were doomed to fail. Forces beyond the reach of reason kept Britain from acting in time to protect its security without war, just as forces beyond the reach of reason paralysed the United States. The French acted throughout the 1930s like characters in a play by Sophocles, destined for a certain fate, and unable, as mortals, to alter the judgment of the gods. They had tried to persuade the Anglo-Saxons for more than thirty years. It would take events, not words, to fulfill their efforts, and they were weary.

III

In 1919, the state system had been reestablished on a nominally Wilsonian basis. The League of Nations was organized to play the stabilizing role of the Concert of Europe, and the new institutions of the League were set up in an atmosphere of idealism and hope. Unusually able and dedicated men led an international civil service pledged to a loyalty transcending national allegiances. The Concert of Europe had been an affair of largely secret diplomacy conducted by the great powers; the League gave the smaller powers and the public a stronger voice in foreign policy, although it remained true that the effectiveness of the League in major crises depended in the end on the willingness of the greater powers to use force if necessary to keep the peace. At the time, most people regarded the League's methods for achieving and maintaining peace as the antithesis of the older habits of the balance of power. Few realized that the two sets of ideas were not alternatives: the multilateral diplomacy of the League and its code of norms could and did complement the autonomous adjustments of the balance of power and the influence of the Concert of Europe. Since mankind could not rely on those adjustments alone to keep the peace, the League could offer what the Concert of Europe had failed to provide—an effective mechanism for stimulating and managing the process of adjustment.

In its first decade, the League of Nations had proved itself to be a useful influence in resolving a number of neuralgic disputes—those over Danzig, Upper Silesia, Corfu, and the Saar, for example. The debates in the Assembly and the Council of the League helped to crystallize public opinion in many parts of the world, and the corridors and lounges of the League became a useful forum for diplomacy. Plebiscites were held under the League's auspices, and international cities were managed. It was an active influence in the struggle to deal with refugee and minority problems, and sponsored international initiatives of importance on slavery, narcotics, labor relations, and other pressing social issues. The Permanent Court of Arbitration in the Hague and the Food and Agriculture Organization, both established earlier, became part of its network. For a new and novel institution, the League in its first years seemed promising.

Until 1931, the League did not have to confront a large-scale challenge to its peacekeeping capacity. There were a series of small wars as the First World War sputtered out; their diplomacy was conducted largely outside the League. During the twenties, Mussolini had begun to disturb the peace by his provocative policies toward Greece, Yugoslavia, Albania, and Austria, but at that time his actions were still on a small scale. While his grandiloquent advocacy of dynamic changes in the status quo helped to intensify the atmosphere of anxiety in Europe, he was still consolidating his political power in Italy and building his armed forces. And he remained, like any Italian, primarily concerned about the future of German policy and therefore sought to avoid any break with Britain and France. Until nearly the end, Italy opposed Germany's acquisition of Austria. Above all, Italy was not a major power. As subsequent events were to demonstrate again, Italy could be an important secondary actor either in making mischief or in keeping the peace, but she could never be a prime mover, as Germany or Japan could.

The first event which revealed and exploited the inherent weakness of the League in peacekeeping was the Japanese attack on Manchuria in 1931. The Japanese fully understood that the only military forces available to uphold the Covenant of the League were those of Britain and France, with the possible assistance of the Netherlands and other small countries of Europe and Asia. The United States, in her judgment, was decisively pacifist for the time being, and the Soviet Union, despite its inherent strength, was in no position to fight. While Britain, France, and the Netherlands had a military presence in the Far East, European countries would necessarily be preoccupied with the German question for a long time to come, and could not be expected to counter Japanese ambition in China and Southeast Asia without American help. From the Japanese point of view, the early thirties were therefore a promising time to use military force in order to achieve a great empire in China and Southeast Asia. The correlation of forces in the world was far more propitious for Japan than it might well be later. So Japan struck in Manchuria as the first step in a program of expansion which the Japanese thought would end their dependence on the West, force the Western nations to treat them with respect, and achieve both prosperity and what they viewed as the glamor of great-power status.

The Manchurian affair and the Japanese war against southern China which followed revealed a feature of the postwar system of public order which the statesmen of the day had not anticipated and did not yet understand: namely, the power of the Wilsonian idea in Western public opinion. The governments had reacted to the news of Japan's aggression with tepid and meaningless protest. Neither France nor Great Britain had as yet confronted the crucial difference between the old regime and the world organized under the League Covenant. Both France and England were powers whose foreign policy was a conscious policy of peace. They exerted their influence against changes achieved by force where such changes would adversely affect what they regarded as their national interests. They also believed in the wisdom of Disraeli's comment when he stepped down as prime minister in 1879: "So long as the power and advice of England are felt in the councils of Europe, peace, I believe, will be maintained, and maintained for a long period." The same comment could have been made as well about French policy. It never occurred to either country, however, that the League commitment to the principle of collective security required them to oppose all aggression, whether they thought their national interests were directly involved or not. The League Covenant asserted, in effect, that each major power's supreme national interest and special responsibility were to preserve the peace of the state system as a whole, by the force of arms if necessary.

As Chapter 5 notes, Britain had refused to join the Holy Alliance after the Congress of Vienna because the Holy Alliance would have attempted to impose too stiff an ideological rule—that of legitimacy—on the ebb and flow of world politics. Throughout the nineteenth and twentieth centuries Great Britain had sought peace through pragmatic flexibility in the face of pressure for change, in order to disarm would-be revisionists by offering them a quarter of a loaf, or even half a loaf where necessary, in order to obtain a peaceful compromise. In 1931, Britain thought its traditional approach to international conflict was still available, and that approach dominated its response to the Japanese attack on China. Britain's first thought was to explore the possibility of a compromise. Although Japan was no longer an ally, she was a traditional friend of England, and Britain had no desire to alienate her. Quite the contrary. The abrogation of the Anglo-Japanese treaty of alliance after the First World War had been the result of American pressure on Great Britain.

The French reached the same conclusion by a somewhat different intellectual path. France was becoming desperate about the direction and momentum of German policy and about her inability to persuade the British to take Germany seriously enough. The focus of France's concern in Europe was therefore the preservation and enforcement of the Versailles treaty. France recognized the inconsistency of its position in fighting for the strict enforcement of the treaty against Germany, but hesitating about its application to Japanese aggression against China. In French eyes, the Versailles treaty was a bulwark of French security in Europe, and it was being washed away. While the Japanese war against China was deplorable—inexcusable—it was far away and hardly so immediate a threat to France's interests as Germany. It would take a major war to throw Japan out of Manchuria. To divert significant British and French military resources from Europe to the Far East, however, would remove the last restraint against Germany in Europe. Such a step was unthinkable.

Meanwhile, the United States solemnly reiterated the terms of earlier treaties and other commitments through which many nations had promised to respect China's territorial integrity and political independence and to support the Open Door policy in China, that is, to refrain from seeking spheres of influence or special economic advantages in that unhappy country. To help achieve these ends, the United States announced that it would not recognize Japanese conquests in China. If the United States were not, potentially at least, so important a member of the state system, President Hoover's position would have been greeted with raucous laughter throughout the world. The response of other countries was hardly more heroic, however. Weak as the League position was, it had one important consequence: Japan left the League, weakening the institution further.

In large, though not yet decisive numbers, the people of the West criticized their governments for their failure to prevent or defeat Japanese aggression in China. It is immaterial that so many of those who most vigorously urged strong League action against Japan opposed military budgets in their own parliaments, and thought of League action against aggressors as precatory resolutions or economic sanctions, not the use of military force. To them, the League of Nations was an independent third force, a body to which the nations could refer difficult problems for peaceful settlement without cost to themselves.

The significance of the revulsion of popular opinion in the West against Japanese aggression in China was that it happened at all, and that it was repeated even more vehemently a few years later when Italy invaded Ethiopia. At that time a so-called Peace Ballot was circulated in England to which 11.5 million people responded—more than half the people who had voted in the previous general election. More than 90 percent of the respondents favored continued British membership in the League, and more than half supported collective military measures if necessary to stop aggression. Both cabinet members and senior civil servants in England began to realize that "fidelity to the League Covenant" would be an important issue in future electoral campaigns.

The Sino-Japanese War continued intermittently throughout the 1930s, ultimately becoming at Pearl Harbor the detonator of full American participation in the Second World War. German policy, however, was the force which made the war in the Pacific so important.

IV

With Hitler's coming to power, the pace of German policy accelerated, and its scale became grandiose. The scenario outlined in Headlam-Morley's 1925 memorandum turned out to be a good working approximation of Hitler's battle plan. A few secondary features of the campaign were different—the role of Mussolini's adventure in Abyssinia, for example, and the Spanish Civil War. In 1925, even the most prescient expert could not have imagined the macabre horrors of Hitler's policy toward the Jews and the Gypsies, toward Russian prisoners, and toward occupied countries. But the main elements of the story are not disputed, except in detail. There is no serious quarrel among historians about German responsibility for the Second World War.

The governments of the Weimar Republic had cleared the decks for the coming of a more active and outward-thrusting German foreign policy. They had actively exploited the differences between France and Great Britain. At the social cost of great inflation, they had destroyed the reparations programs of the Versailles treaty; they had achieved the Treaty of Locarno; and they had obtained the end of the Allied occupation of the Rhineland five years before the treaty schedule required it. Most important, they had developed a secret military and political relation with the Soviet Union which not only permitted Germany to prepare for rapid mobilization at a later point but satisfied one of Bismarck's most important maxims for German foreign policy: take precautions, always, to reinsure with Russia.

Hilter carefully preserved the forms of constitutionalism in assuming office. He was not yet sure his own forces could stage a successful putsch in the face of the small but disciplined Reichswehr, reinforced by the highly militarized police. But his purposes were soon manifest.

When Hitler came to power, his party was still a minority in the Reichstag, although it was already the largest single party. One of Hitler's first acts was to dissolve the Reichstag and call for new elections. During the campaign period, the Reichstag building was burned down, allegedly by Communists, and the episode became an enormous propaganda event. The government was transformed into an open dictatorship. The brown shirts largely supplanted the police, except for ordinary crime. Concentration camps made their first appearance. And all political parties except the Nazis were dissolved. The Reichstag ceased to be a normal parliament. And, when Hindenburg died in 1934, Hitler became President as well as chancellor.

These events shocked both public opinion and the attitude of governments throughout the world. There was an outcry in the Western countries about the violence and brutality of the regime and the ominous manifestations of anti-Semitism as a governmental policy. And there were signs of concern among all governments, Western and non-Western alike, about the significance of these obviously portentous events. Hitler moved carefully to reassure the governments and public opinion that his intentions were peaceful, and one of his first acts was to enter into a ten-year nonaggression treaty with Poland. It was also notable that Hitler's first rearmament programs neglected the German navy. He did not wish to make the Kaiser's mistake before 1914 of arousing British concern about an ambitious German naval program. Meanwhile, however, the pace of German rearmament quickened. Before Hitler, it had been cautious, secret, and comparatively modest; now it went forward with a rush, although still without conscription. Clearly, Hitler was preparing for war.

It was soon obvious that the annexation of Austria was Hitler's first objective. Two years earlier, a German proposal for a customs union with Austria had been turned down by the Allies in the name of the Versailles treaty. A German propaganda blitz was mounted, and Germany supplied funds and arms to Austrian Nazis. Britain, France, and especially Italy reacted with alarm. Democratic government in Austria disintegrated, and an Italian-oriented Fascist dictatorship seized power. A Nazi putsch was attempted in July, but failed. The Italians marched troops to the Austrian frontier. The failure of Hitler's initial move against Austria did not change his policy, but it persuaded him that his bid for power would not result in spontaneous revolutions even in areas as naturally sympathetic to his cause as Austria. His planning became more methodical.

On the political front, Germany withdrew from the elaborate disarmament conference which had begun in 1932. The mission of the conference was to make good the promise of the Versailles treaty that the treaty limitations on German arms would be matched by corresponding reductions in Allied armaments. After nearly fifteen years of disillusioning experience with the postwar world, and with Hitler in the wings and later in power, governments had abandoned hope for general disarmament. Britain had disarmed unilaterally. In the face of Hitler's rearmament campaign, there was no chance for obtaining any French disarmament unless Britain gave France an open guaranty, going well beyond the ambiguity of the Locarno treaty. Britain was in no mood to take that step. The disarmament conference ended in failure, and Germany withdrew from the League of Nations to boot.

Hitler's initial moves drew the Soviet Union and Italy closer to France. France and the Soviet Union eventually signed a treaty of mutual assistance, while France and Italy made agreements dealing with Austria, Eastern Europe, and some of Italy's ambitions in Africa. What France did in effect—and certainly what Mussolini thought France did—was to acquiesce in Italy's conquest of Ethiopia in exchange for Mussolini's assurance of Italian cooperation with French efforts to deter and contain German expansion in Europe.

Britain's first reaction to Hitler's assumption of power was even murkier than the course of British policy before 1914. In that period, Britain shifted instinctively to form tentative associations with France and Russia against Germany. While British policy before 1914 was slow, reluctant, and ultimately too equivocal to be effective as a deterrent against Germany, there was a reorientation. In the years immediately before 1939, however, Britain clung more and more desperately to the policy it had pursued during the twenties—much more preoccupied with its efforts to reach an understanding with Germany than with building a deterrent security system on the assumption that Hitler actually meant what he said.

In December 1934, the Italians launched their campaign against Ethiopia, a sideshow to the principal story, but an important secondary factor in determining the course of Hitler's road to war. Mussolini's aggression against Ethiopia was an absurd exercise in nineteenth-century imperialism, an adventure undertaken only for the purpose of indulging his vanity and hardening his armed forces. In its context of European and world politics, however, it became the most spectacular event of 1935. Even more intensely than in the Manchurian affair of 1931, it revealed the depth and passion of Western public attachment to the Wilsonian creed of collective security against aggression. When it became clear that Britain and France, backed remotely by the United States, were more concerned about the possibility of keeping Italy as a potential ally against Germany than in punishing Italian aggression, there was a prolonged demonstration of unprecedented outrage in Western Europe and the United States. The French and British foreign ministers responsible for making the deal, Sir Samuel Hoare and Pierre Laval, had to be dismissed. Like many politicians then and later, Laval had regarded the League and every other manifestation of Wilsonian idealism as myth and fluff. However practical the Anglo-French policy toward the Ethiopian war was in the cynical light of power politics, Laval's life and career were embittered and ultimately destroyed by the force of the public protest these events aroused. In later years, he became a collaborator with Hitler during the Vichy period and was condemned as a traitor after the war.

Behind the screen of Mussolini's war and its outcome, Germany continued steadily to move ahead both in its rearmament program and in its diplomacy. The Saar plebiscite was held, and the territory was returned to Germany by a majority of more than 90 percent. Part 5 of the treaty was formally abrogated when conscription was introduced. Offended by the equivocal way France and Britain had treated him during the Ethiopian war, and more and more convinced that Hitler would prevail, Mussolini began his fateful move toward Germany. And most important of all, the British made a bilateral naval treaty with Germany. The British regarded the treaty as a technical matter. It established a quota for Germany of 35 percent of Britain's naval tonnage in surface ships, and of 45 percent, or, in periods of tension, 100 percent in submarines. The French were furious at what they regarded as a breach of Allied solidarity on a most important subject, and a further violation of the Versailles treaty. The British replied that the Franco-Soviet security treaty was equally unilateral. The British regarded that treaty with special misgivings because it recalled the approach of 1914, and the thesis that the Franco-Russian alliance of the period precipitated the war by giving Germany the sense of being encircled. Besides, they said, their agreement with Germany put a cap on German rearmament in one area, which was preferable to leaving the terms obscure, and therefore unrestrained.

"The agreement poisoned Anglo-French relations," Nicholas Rostow wrote.

> Months, even years and seemingly unrelated crises later, it still affected French perceptions of British character and reliability. Often it was not mentioned. It simply festered and generated bile. The British discounted French feelings, which they thought previous French behavior and the terms themselves of the Agreement did not justify. Yet London had cast doubt on the ultimate outcome of the present drama and sowed anxiety about separate deals. The Anglo-German Naval Agreement was the predicate to Bordeaux. . . .
>
> [Europe] was a culture, a society, and a polity waiting to be born even when Hitler and Mussolini held power. Would it fall under the control of tyrants or, in developing, fulfill the promise of the balanced, open system of the nineteenth century? The Anglo-French relationship would be central to the answer. Just as Anglo-French unity had proved essential to the European military balance in the years of the *Entente Cordiale* and the Great War, so that same unity had already assured the dominance of democratic forces in European culture. Now it struggled to maintain that dominance. The British government failed to perceive this aspect of the problem when they concluded the Naval Agreement. To the French and to other observers of British behaviour, that failure of vision made the Agreement a more fundamental betrayal of British responsi-

bility to the European Community than any other British action of the interwar period.[1]

If 1935 was the year of the gathering storm, 1936 was the year the storm broke. In March, Hitler marched troops into the Rhineland and denounced the Treaty of Locarno; his apologists, especially in Britain, explained it was his answer to the Franco-Soviet pact of the year before. The Italians annexed Ethiopia. The Spanish Civil War began soon afterwards—the successful attempt by a large part of the Spanish Army to destroy the republic and install a Fascist regime led by General Franco. In a frightening demonstration of impotence, Britain, France, and the United States stood on the sidelines and allowed Hitler and Mussolini to outflank France and threaten Gibraltar. Italy and Germany intervened in Spain to fight on the side of Franco, despite a nonintervention agreement which both countries had accepted, along with British, France, the United States, the Soviet Union, and a number of smaller countries as well. The nonintervention agreement of 1937 abandoned one of the most fundamental principles of international law— that a nation can give military aid to a friendly nation in putting down an insurrection, but can never give aid to the insurrection. This was of course the principle on which American diplomacy had relied heavily and successfully during our Civil war.

Despite the agreement, the Soviet government helped Spain, although she also intervened brutally in an attempt to make sure that the Spanish army and government came under Communist control. Several thousand individual volunteers from many of the Western countries came to fight with the Spanish Republican Army against Fascism. Italy finally chose sides decisively: it adhered to the Rome-Berlin axis, having concluded that Germany was riding the wave of history. In the following year, Mussolini withdrew from the League as well. Japan and Germany entered into a treaty against the Comintern, and Belgium announced its neutrality. Clearly, the democracies were retreating in confusion and disarray, while the Fascist states and their foreign sympathizers celebrated their victories in a cacophony of martial noise.

The French and British excuse for their behavior in Spain was that they had not yet rearmed enough to be ready for war against Germany and that they did not want to be drawn into sideshows or secondary wars. The irony is that their evaluations of the intelligence turned out

1. Nicholas Rostow, *Anglo-French Relations,* 1934–36 (London: Macmillan, 1984), 171, 178–79.

to be wrong. The German armed forces did not match those of Britain and France until well after Munich in 1938.[2]

Hitler had renewed the German-Soviet treaty of 1926 when he came to power in 1933, but the "Rapallo" relationship had not long to run, although it was revived with critical consequences for three crucial years between 1939—before Hitler invaded Poland—and 1941, when he invaded the Soviet Union. In the early thirties, the Soviet Union understood as well as the French what Hitler's coming to power meant. While the Communists in Germany were ordered to cooperate with Hitler, on the ground that a Fascist Revolution in Germany would surely produce a Communist counterrevolution in due course, the leaders of the Soviet Union tentatively and equivocally hedged their bets. Moscow supplemented its alliance with France by giving Czechoslovakia a treaty of guaranty, conditioned on French compliance with its own treaty with the Czechs.

V

Of this dismal list of political and military disasters, the Franco-British decision not to resist the remilitarization of the Rhineland was by far the most serious militarily, and the abject behavior of the Western Allies during the Spanish Civil War and the Munich crisis of 1938 the most important politically.

On the military side, there can be no disputing J. T. Emmerson's conclusion that "with the disappearance of the demilitarized Rhineland, Europe had lost her last guarantee against German aggression."[3] Even in the age of air power and missiles, it is difficult to imagine circumstances that would have allowed Hitler to strike in Eastern or in Southern Europe if the Western Allies could have marched unopposed into the Rhineland, and therefore into the Saar and the Ruhr as well.

2. Williamson Murray, *The Change in the European Balance of Power, 1938–1939: The Path to Ruin* (Princeton, N.J.: Princeton University Press, 1984).

3. J. T. Emmerson, *The Rhineland Crisis, 7 March 1936: A Study in Multilateral Diplomacy* (London: Maurice Temple Smith, in association with the London School of Economics and Political Science, 1977), 248. In his introduction to Emmerson's book, D. C. Watt claims Emmerson has destroyed what Watt calls "the 'myth' that the Rhineland crisis was the last great unexploited opportunity to overthrow or 'stop' Hitler without a Second World War." Neither Watt's introduction nor Emmerson's thorough monograph justifies this conclusion. On the contrary, they confirm the essential correctness of the so-called myth—that Britain and France had sufficient military power in 1936 to defeat Hitler's bid, but lacked the political will to do so. They agree also that the ratio of Allied to German military strength was far more favorable to the Allies in 1936 than in 1939.

Hitler's open breach of the most important surviving security provision of the Versailles settlement, specially reinforced by the Locarno
treaty, precipitated another in the long cycle of disagreements between
Britain and France about how to treat Germany. Even in 1936, after
Britain had officially begun to rearm, the British government still clung
to its view that "appeasing" Germany could induce Hitler to give up
his policy of expansion. The British had not yet abandoned their conviction that Germany had not been treated fairly after 1918, and mused,
"How can we go to war to keep them from moving troops around in
their own country?"

Besides, an isolationist view of British security was then, as it is
still, a strong element in British opinion. The vision of England
protected by the moat of the English Channel and the North Sea is
nearly as hard to eradicate as the myth that the United States is
unassailable because it is flanked by the Atlantic and the Pacific
oceans. The isolationist impulse has never proved decisive in British
policy, but its strength has always been sufficient to make British
decision making a prolonged agony. In the mid-thirties, it was as
difficult for the British as it had been in 1914 to suppose that anything
that happened in Eastern Europe could threaten their own security.
For Englishmen of that view, the decision not to fight for the Rhineland was a relief.

The French took a less insular position. To be sure, there were
French isolationists who thought that France's security problems were
entirely European, and almost entirely confined to Germany. If France
could be assured against a German invasion, they thought, it would
have no security problems of consequence. Only such a view of French
security can explain France's preoccupation before 1939 with the Ma-
ginot Line. A country of forty million people that relies for its security
on a line of fortresses cannot seriously promise to protect Poland against
Germany or Russia. The French people as a whole had a more realistic
grasp of the situation, and therefore regarded the Rhineland crisis of
1936 as a catastrophic defeat.

The course of the Rhineland affair was simple. France proposed
to the British government of the day that Britain and France should
submit the German action to the League Council; lay down a series
of economic sanctions, and, if those remedies failed, France, or pref-
erably Britain and France together, should undertake a punitive expedition against Germany to restore the situation in the Rhineland.
The British reacted with horror. They rejected both war and economic
sanctions, but did agree to call a meeting of the League Council to

consider whether Germany had violated the treaties of Versailles and Locarno. First, the British and the French convened the other parties to the Locarno treaty, but Germany refused to attend, on the ground it had denounced the treaty. The British then met with France and the other Locarno guarantors, Italy and Belgium, and the French proposal was lost in an interminable and inconclusive search for a compromise formula.

Pierre Flandin, the French prime minister, convinced by Britain's prime minister, Stanley Baldwin, that Britain was utterly unprepared for war either morally or militarily, contented himself in the end with a strengthening of the British security guarantee. Britain also agreed to begin staff talks with France and Belgium. On 19 March 1936, the League Council found that Germany had indeed violated Articles 42 and 43 of the Treaty of Versailles and the Locarno treaty, but did nothing in response. Neither did the Allies.

The next three acts of the melodrama were the war in Spain, which began in July 1936; the annexation of Austria in March 1938; and the German seizure of Czechoslovakia, which started with the Munich agreement of September 1938 and was completed in March 1939. During that month, the Germans also seized Memel and proposed to Poland that Danzig be transferred to Germany, along with a strip of land across the Polish corridor.

The annexation of the Czech provinces of Bohemia and Moravia, in violation of Hitler's promises to France and Britain at Munich, finally persuaded the British government that its two costly decades of effort to satisfy Germany's "legitimate grievances" in Eastern Europe had been futile. Two days after Poland rejected Germany's proposals about Danzig, Britain and Poland announced their alliance. France followed suit, and together Britain and France also guaranteed Greece and Romania. The interwar period had come to an end. France and Britain, who had quarreled so long about the relevance of Eastern Europe to their security, were finally agreed in fact if not in theory. Not fully agreed, perhaps, for there were hints of positive British reactions to possible German peace feelers even after the war began. But the two countries, allied against Germany by geopolitical necessity, and exhausted by their futile argument over whether their military frontier was the Rhine or the Vistula, discovered that the Vistula was important after all, and sadly took up the burdens of 1914–19. As they marched off to war, the soldiers showed little of the exuberance of 1914, but their mood was determined nonetheless. The word in France was "Il faut en finir": We have to finish the job.

VI

The pattern of rivalries during the period 1933–39 recalls the decade before 1914. Germany, fueled by the conviction that it had been stabbed in the back by traitors and unjustly shackled at Versailles, had struggled skillfully for twenty years to revise the treaty, article by article, both under the Weimar Republic and then under Hitler. First, reparations were thrown off. Then in the Locarno treaty, Germany promised not to commit aggression against France or Belgium in exchange for a free hand in the East. After each German step was taken and accepted, the Western nations proclaimed that a peace of conciliation had finally been achieved. But there was no tranquillity in this succession of pathetic festivities. The news from Manchuria, Germany, Italy, Spain, Ethiopia, China, Austria, Czechoslovakia, and Poland was an ominous litany, with the choruses coming at shorter and shorter intervals, and at a louder and more hysterical pitch. Each act of aggression was followed by a more and more grandiloquent offer of a general peace settlement. Above all, the insidious, obsessively absorbing atmosphere of Hitlerism, presented by the Führer with "dazzling dramaturgical talent," pervaded the West. The Western peoples reacted with fear and loathing, although there were some who, like so many Germans, were sorely tempted to embrace the thrilling certitudes of the irrational and the antirational.[4]

Assaulted as they were by the shattering and apparently endless din of this ordeal; confronted by what became a terrifying array of German military power; and, in many cases, enduring depression, inflation, and sometimes severe domestic disorder as well, it is a psychosocial miracle that the Western democratic peoples and their governments withstood the attack as well as they did. No democratic country succumbed without being defeated militarily. Wounded and sometimes weakened, they revived after the war to resume their lives as civilized democracies. Their cultures proved to be stronger than many had believed would be the case.

Alliances shifted. Italy, abandoning its hope for Austrian independence, joined forces with Hitler. Germany formed an alliance with Japan that proved to be a fatal miscalculation for them both. In 1939, the Soviet Union allied itself with Germany in order, as it thought, to seize the Baltic States, partition Poland, and divert the war to the West.

4. See Fritz Stern, *Dreams and Delusions: The Drama of German History* (New York: Alfred A. Knopf, Borzoi Book, 1987), 119–21, 166.

With his rear secure, Hitler promptly attacked France, the Low Countries, and Great Britain. When he thought they were sufficiently subdued, he invaded the Soviet Union, despite his defeat in the air war over Britain. In the light of Hitler's smashing success during the first few months of his war against the Soviet Union, Japan attacked Pearl Harbor, thus bringing America into the war, and assuring the victory of the Allies.

VII

For the United States, the experience of the interwar years was altogether different from that of France or Great Britain. The pains of postwar reconstruction were far away. The twenties were a period of booming prosperity in America, and the early thirties were dominated first by the Great Depression and then by the New Deal. Jazz, the flapper, bootleg gin, and F. Scott Fitzgerald became symbols of the twenties and FDR the chief figure of the thirties. Few concerned themselves with foreign affairs until the Japanese invasion of Manchuria and Hitler's accession to power. Still, the sound of cannon in the distance was heard, and gradually attracted the attention and concern of a growing segment of public opinion.

Every visible manifestation of American public opinion about foreign affairs in the 1920s mirrored that of opinion in Great Britain: isolationist, rather pro-German, anti-French, happy to be free of world politics. Being further away from the vortex of world affairs, American attitudes were less tinged with anxiety than those of Britain. There were occasional exceptions, of course. A few older people spoke well of Woodrow Wilson, although no politicians, even in the Democratic Party, dared to carry his banner. The members of veterans' organizations remained loyal to the great adventure of their lives, but their political efforts were confined to testifying for military appropriations and making patriotic speeches. The two major diplomatic actions of the United States during the twenties, the Kellogg-Briand Treaty and the Washington Naval Arms Control Treaty of 1922, were formally regarded by the prevailing orthodoxy as diplomatic feathers in the American cap, despite their vacuity.

There was no American Churchill to proclaim the weakness and folly of American policy as Churchill had attacked the policies of Britain and France during the thirties. Nevertheless, the American people somehow understood that President Franklin D. Roosevelt was at heart an "internationalist" in the Wilson tradition, despite the fact that he

kept the League of Nations in Coventry and supported neutrality legislation designed to prevent American aid to Britain and France. No
one knew it at the time, but few would have been surprised to learn
that Roosevelt had initiated a private correspondence with Churchill
in the first months of his Presidency, and pursued it until his death.
The naval nerve, always sensitive in America, was touched both by the
Japanese aggression in China and by the later growth of the German
Navy. And Roosevelt, assistant secretary of the navy in Wilson's time,
was always deeply interested in the naval dimension of American security. The United States adopted a naval building program early in
Roosevelt's first term, ostensibly as a pump-priming measure.

    As Hitler's program took shape, the American people began to
repeat the intellectual and emotional experience of the years after 1915.
Active citizens' committees were formed to stimulate reflection about
the consequence for the United States of a German and Japanese victory, on the one hand, and of an Allied victory on the other. One of
those committees, the leader of interventionist opinion, was the William
Allen White Committee to Defend America by Aiding the Allies; the
other, the strongest of the isolationist groups, was simply called the
America First Committee. President Roosevelt contributed strongly to
this development in American public opinion. After the incident at the
Marco Polo Bridge—the opening signal for the second phase of the
Sino-Japanese War in 1937—he made his famous "quarantine" speech
in Chicago. The President warned that no country could expect to
escape from the spreading ravages of war, and called on the peace-
loving nations of the world to make a concerted effort to assure the
triumph of peace. There must be an end, he said to "acts of international
aggression." He went on, "It seems to be unfortunately true that the
epidemic of world lawlessness is spreading. When an epidemic of physical disease starts to spread, the community approves and joins in a
quarantine of the patients in order to protect the health of the community against the spread of the disease."

    There was an outcry in the United States against Roosevelt's quar-
antine speech; many recognized it as the portent of radical change in
American policy, and protested. The President, always politically prudent, retreated for the moment. But his speech was important evidence
of the transformation going on under the surface of American politics,
and an act of Presidential leadership in guiding that process. For Americans, there was no ambiguity in the President's thesis that "there can
be no stability or peace . . . except under laws and moral standards
adhered to by all." Under the spreading impact of war, "a state of

international anarchy" is being created, the President said, "from which there is no escape through mere isolation or neutrality."[5] Roosevelt, they saw, was beginning to echo his mentor, Wilson. The statement had a profound impact, even if that impact was delayed by the weight of the isolationist tradition in America's collective unconscious. People were impressed and troubled, though they protested still.

After the fall of France and the Battle of Britain in 1940, the tone and substance of American foreign policy changed radically. Roosevelt was elected for an unprecedented third term. As in 1916, the Republican Party nominated a candidate who agreed with the Democratic President's policies towards the war, and would probably have gone further and faster than the Democrat if he had been elected. While the United States remained officially committed to offering Britain all aid short of war, the relation of the United States to the war shifted. Conscription began. Roosevelt made his "destroyers for bases" deal with the British, transferring to Britain some World War I destroyers for bases in Bermuda, Newfoundland, and other British possessions in the Western hemisphere. Early in 1941, America occupied Greenland as a protectorate in behalf of occupied Denmark, took over the bases in Iceland from Britain, and established a base in the Azores. The Lend-Lease Act was adopted in the spring of 1941, and active American naval participation in Atlantic convoys began.

In the summer of 1941, Churchill and Roosevelt met on an American cruiser at sea off Newfoundland to review the state of the war and to proclaim in the Atlantic Charter their principles for a postwar settlement. It was a Wilsonian gesture for Roosevelt to make pronouncements about war aims while still president of a neutral country, and a super-Wilsonian gesture to do so on a warship, as almost an ally of the British prime minister. The document they produced was also Wilsonian in substance, though less detailed than Wilson's Fourteen Points. It reflected the power of Wilson's vision in the Western mind. For the first time, the leading statesmen of the West declared in effect that the war had come because the interwar generation had failed to fulfill the promise of the League of Nations, and that with victory that struggle should be resumed on a worldwide scale as the first of their war aims.

During the fall of 1941, polls recorded that for the first time a majority of Americans believed that the defeat of Hitler was more

5. Franklin D. Roosevelt, "Address at Chicago, October 5, 1937," in Franklin D. Roosevelt, *The Public Papers and Addresses of Franklin D. Roosevelt,* (New York: Macmillan, 1941), 406–11; and United States Department of State, *Peace and War: United States Foreign Policy, 1931–41* (Washington, D.C.: G.P.O., 1943).

important to the United States than the avoidance of war in all circumstances. Slowly and grudingly, opinion in Congress began to change as well. The Selective Service Act, which had been passed in 1940, was extended by a narrow vote, and the neutrality act was relaxed, also by a small majority. Roosevelt did not wish to enter the war with the nation still deeply divided, although he was determined, as it is reported he once remarked, to "wage war, but not declare it, and [to] become more and more provocative."[6] Roosevelt knew how deeply rooted isolationism was in the American mind, and he did not want to confront in head-on, as Wilson finally did in his great speech of 2 April 1917. Roosevelt's limited war continued, but America's energies did not transform the United States into a fighting nation and the arsenal of democracy until Pearl Harbor.

Like everyone else of his generation, the author remembers his reaction to the radio bulletin which interrupted a New York Philharmonic concert and announced the Japanese attack on Pearl Harbor. It was one of relief that the long wait was over, and that we had been drawn into the war before it was too late to achieve victory.

6. Elizabeth Barker, *Churchill and Eden at War* (London: Macmillan, 1978), 147.

PART III

The Age of Truman and Acheson, 1945 to the Present

Introduction

To do these jobs and conduct our own affairs with passable restraint and judgment—the type of judgment, as Justice Brandeis used to say, which leads a man not to stand in front of a locomotive—will be an achievement. Moreover, it will be an achievement which will profoundly modify many situations which now concern us, including—and I am now guessing—our relations with the Soviet Union. Problems which are difficult against a background of confusion, hesitation, and disintegration may well become quite possible of solution as national and international institutions and activities become healthy and confident and vigorous in a large part of the world. Certainly our troubles would not increase.

But it is a long and tough job and one for which we as a people are not particularly suited. We believe that any problem can be solved with a little ingenuity and without inconvenience to the folks at large. We have trouble shooters to do this. And our name for problems is significant. We call them headaches. You take a powder and they are gone. These pains about which we have been talking are not like that. They are like the pain of earning a living. They will stay with us until death. We have got to understand that all our lives the danger, the uncertainty, the need for alertness, for effort, for discipline will be upon us. This is new to us. It will be hard for us. But we are in for it and the only real question is whether we shall know it soon enough.—Dean Acheson

After the surrender of Germany and Japan in 1945, it seemed reasonable to hope that this time American national security policy would come of age. The experience of the two world wars and the period of armistice between them should surely have been enough to teach the American people and their government the wisdom of Samuel Bemis' observation, quoted as the epigraph to Chapter 1, that governments

---

The epigraph for Part III is taken from Dean Acheson, *Fragments of My Fleece* (New York: W. W. Norton, 1971), 25–26.

must adapt to the changes in the world balance of power "or sink amid the strife of nations." The Monroe Doctrine, backed by a tacit alliance with Great Britain, was a reasonable adaptation of American security policy to the world balance of power after the Napoleonic Wars; as a guiding principle of American foreign policy, however, it was irrelevant to the world that emerged from the furnace of war in the years after 1945.

An emotionally potent symbol helped Truman and his two great lieutenants, Dean G. Acheson and George Catlett Marshall, to propel the American people along the path toward a rational foreign policy: the generally shared conviction that Wilson had been right after all in 1919, and his opponents disastrously wrong. The revolutionary changes in American foreign and security policy accomplished by President Truman and followed by all his successors owe much to the compelling legend of Wilson, stricken like Lincoln and Roosevelt in the moment of victory. Thus the first diplomatic initiative of the United States, prepared by British and American experts during the war, and launched even before the Japanese surrender in 1945, was the establishment of the United Nations as the successor to Wilson's League of Nations.

Roosevelt's careful preparations in Congress and the cooperation between Truman and the bipartisan leadership of the Senate obtained Senate consent to the ratification of the Charter of the United Nations by a vote of 89 to 2; Congress as a whole passed the United Nations Participation Act in 1945 by an overwhelming majority. In neither case did Congress stumble over the issue which had killed the Treaty of Versailles in the Senate some twenty-five years before, the Constitutional division of the war power between Congress and the President.

Churchill was dubious about the United Nations, and Roosevelt really wanted the postwar world to be governed by "the Four Policemen"; Roosevelt's idea was the source of the great-power veto in the Security Council. But Wilson's vision of a universal league was too strong in the West to be challenged, and the Russians went along at Yalta in part because they could trade concessions on the United Nations for Western concessions on subjects they regarded as more serious, like Poland.

Chance, too, helped Truman and his colleagues accomplish so much so quickly in the first few years after 1945. In 1944, a few key leaders of the Democratic Party, sensing how ill Roosevelt was, persuaded the President to jettison Vice-President Henry Wallace and to substitute Harry Truman as his running-mate in the 1944 elections. Wallace was a visionary radical much under left-wing influence at the time. Truman was not known to the country at large, but he was highly respected within the Congress, and turned out to be the finest and most successful American President of the postwar period. Quick, intelligent, and above all decisive, Truman had the singular capacity to see almost at a glance the key issues in any problem put before him. A secure man, he liked to have able people around him. The combination of circumstances which made Truman President and his own qualities of heart and mind had extraordinary consequences. Acheson and Marshall, his two chief aides on foreign affairs, were themselves men of lustrous ability and character. Both picked and led outstanding staffs. The American foreign policy establishment was never stronger.

Chance made another contribution to the achievements of the Truman-Acheson era. All the leaders and many of the lesser officials and parliamentarians of the key countries of the West were also unusually able, large-minded, and self-confident. With their American colleagues, they cooperated in creating NATO, the U.N., the European and the Atlantic communities, and the key institutions which together created and managed the new international economy (that is, the Marshall Plan, the European Payments Union, the World Bank, the International Monetary Fund, and GATT). In Great Britain, Churchill and Eden were succeeded by Attlee, Bevin, Gaitskell, and Macmillan, all substantial statesmen. Churchill himself was a statesman of genius. Men of comparable quality led the transition in Germany and Japan and in the countries which had been overrun by Hitler. In most cases, these men had been tempered by adversity. They had passed the war years in jail, in exile, or in retreat; none was compromised by collaboration with the Fascist regimes. Several—de Gaulle, Schumann, and Jean Monnet in France; Einaudi, De Gasperi, and Sforza in Italy; Adenauer, Schumacher, and Schmidt in Germany; and Yoshida in Japan—were of towering stature. The affairs of the Western coalition were conducted for a long time at an unusually high level, until the new order of things was institutionalized and could be run by more commonplace people.

The American vocabulary for talking and thinking about national security has changed little since the pamphlets of Tom Paine and the eloquent but equivocal preachings of Thomas Jefferson.[1] As this book has tried to demonstrate, what we say about foreign affairs does not

---

1. The contradictions in Jefferson's thought about foreign policy are well brought out in Robert W. Tucker and David C. Hendrickson, *Empire of Liberty: The Statecraft of Thomas Jefferson* (New York: Oxford University Press, 1990).

always correspond to what we do. The American people and their political leaders still insist on talking about foreign policy in moral or ideological terms. Throughout the nineteenth century, however, we practiced power politics tempered by idealism. We took advantage of every increase in our own power and of the opportunities offered by the conflicts of larger states to advance our national goal of achieving and consolidating a continental republic. And in the twentieth century, almost by instinct, we entered both the First and Second World Wars when we began to fear that a hostile Germany was becoming uncomfortably strong. Exactly the same perception of the power and policy of the Soviet Union led us to help organize NATO and our other security arrangements during the first decade after 1945. We usually explained these decisions, however, as motivated by a desire to promote the spread of human rights and of democracy rather than by the necessity to protect the balance of power. For Wilson, of course, the goal was something more—to transform the conditioned reflexes of the balance of power into an organized world order, managed ultimately by the great powers in accordance with the accepted principles of international law.

This dissonance in the American attitude toward foreign affairs was greatly strengthened by the mismanagement of the war in Vietnam between 1965 and 1974. Clearly, as President Bush brilliantly demonstrated during the Persian Gulf crisis of 1990–91, "the Vietnam syndrome" is not so formidable an obstacle to a rational American foreign policy as some people believe it is. The American people have amply proven their good sense and tenacity. But the Vietnam experience is surely a significant political restraint on the conduct of foreign affairs, and has given renewed vitality to the isolationist theme in American public opinion and politics.

Despite the persistence and importance of this unresolved conflict about the goals of American foreign policy, however, what the United States has accomplished abroad since 1945 constitutes the most creative and successful achievement in the history of American diplomacy and of American arms. The word *arms* may startle some readers. It is often forgotten that since World War II collective security against aggression has cost the United States 600,000 casualties. And even if the changes in Soviet foreign policy and in the structure of the state system which have occurred since Gorbachev took power in 1985 have brought about the end of the Cold War, the future course of the state system is hardly likely to be one of perfect peace. To maintain peace in the state system of the looming future will require at least as much vigilance and management as was needed during the half century since the Second World War. That burden, like the "pain of earning a living," will be with us until the lions lie down with the lambs.

The policy of collective security since 1945 has required a far more complex and sustained effort than that needed in the earlier great periods of American diplomatic history—the age dominated by the ideas and leadership of John Quincy Adams between 1815 and 1830, and the age of William H. Seward during and after the Civil War. There have been mistakes, of course, as well as achievements during the generation since 1945, and some of the mistakes have been costly. Presidents and Congresses have varied greatly in skill, insight, decisiveness, and luck. The policy has been the same, however, with only minor variations, for more than forty years. The chief architect of that policy was Dean Acheson, Truman's great secretary of state, and the post–1945 period in the history of American foreign policy should be known by his name as well as that of the great President he served. Viewed in long perspective, it is fair to conclude that the foreign policy of the United States has pursued since the Second World War has successfully adapted this nation to the shifts which have occurred in the world balance of power, and is altogether capable of continuing to do so indefinitely. We have prudently protected our interests in ways which reflect our nature as a people.

In 1989 and 1990, a new, and—to the West—a most welcome, crisis became manifest in nearly all the Communist states of the world. That crisis had been developing for a long time. Suddenly there were outbreaks of nationalist protest and of protests against tyranny, poverty, and dictatorship from Eastern Europe to China. In Eastern Europe, the protesters discovered that Gorbachev would not attempt to maintain the rule of the Communist Party by force, and intensified their demonstrations. As a result, the states of Eastern Europe seceded from the Soviet empire, and the future of the former Soviet Union itself is in flux.

In part, the volcanic changes in the former Soviet empire are a protest against the dismal failure of the Communist economic model, which, like other schemes of monopoly, has proved incapable of dynamism. In part, they reflect the deep-seated longing of its people for governments which allow a much greater degree of personal freedom and which protect the individual through an enforceable rule of law. In larger part, in Russia and in Eastern Europe, the revolutions which began in 1989 embody the demand for government rooted in the inherited value systems of each society.

As this manuscript is being finished, it is not clear what the outcome of the changes in the former Warsaw Pact Countries will be. Many hail the end of the Cold War as the inauguration of an era of peace. Their euphoria is premature. One thing is clear. Russia and its erstwhile European satellites will depend urgently on the West for assistance in reconstructing their economies. It is not the time for them to indulge in mischief-making. As the attack by Iraq against Kuwait in 1990 demonstrated, however, the order of the state system can be threatened by conflicts which did not originate in the Cold War.

In any event, the foreign policy of the United States since 1945 has not been dominated by ideology but by the quest for peace; it was addressed to Soviet expansion, not to Soviet Communism. The Cold War was an episode which had to be dealt with, but the United States never lost sight of the fact that victory in the Cold War was not an end in itself, but an indispensable step toward the possibility of peace. For nearly half a century, the Soviet bid for supremacy has been the most dangerous issue on the foreign policy agenda. Even if the former members of the Soviet Union become as peaceful as Holland, it is certain that new problems, large and small, will continue to keep Foreign Offices busy. Russia was a powerful factor in world politics for more than two centuries before the Soviet Union came into being. And one lesson no Foreign Office can ever forget is that small fires can become big ones if they are not put out.

The period since 1945 is comparatively familiar to the contemporary reader and is voluminously documented. The three chapters of Part III will therefore contain less expository detail than those of Part II, and instead concentrate on the analysis of the key policy issues from the vantage point of the future.

14

The Soviet Union Reaches for Hegemony: The Stalin Years

The Soviet leadership, though haunted by many fears, still have the appetite, ferocity, smugness, and sense of mission which are the essential components of the imperial mood, and which in the West have given way to satiety, guilt, and doubt. . . . [Soviet imperialism is] very different from the so-called "Liberal imperialism" of Great Britain, which unnerved its servants, encouraged its opponents, and organized its own decline and fall.—Bernard Lewis

No aspect of modern politics has been so difficult for the Western mind to encompass and accept as the nature of Soviet policy. Churchill said Soviet policy was a mystery—"a riddle wrapped in an enigma." And well-meaning officials and other citizens of Western countries spent a great of their time trying to explain to themselves why it proved to be so hard to get along with the Russians. One of the best of our State Department Soviet experts, former ambassador Charles Bohlen, used to say there were two classes of people he knew were lying—those who said whisky didn't affect them, and those who claimed they knew how to negotiate with the Russians.

There is a vast and arcane literature on the difficulties of negotiating with the Soviet Union, and particularly on the difficulties of negotiating arms control agreements. One branch of the literature concentrates on the Russian character and personality, and the special pressures on the Russian personality arising from the nature of the Soviet regime. Some writers of this school tell us that Russians are inscrutable Orientals, products of a mysterious culture we can never expect to understand. Others rely on the wily peasant hypothesis—that at heart Soviet diplomats are cunning Russian peasants whose natural negotiating style is that of a peasant trying to cheat his customers at a country market.

The epigraph for this chapter is taken from Bernard Lewis, "Russia in the Middle East: Reflections on Some Historical Parallels," *Round Table* 60, no. 239 (July 1970): 263.

Others still, with varying degrees of learning and insight, cite travelers to Russia since the sixteenth century who have described Russians as inveterate liars, with a hazy sense at best of the difference between truth and falsehood. In the late 1940s, Gunnar Myrdal, the Swedish economist and sociologist, predicted that we and the British would make a mess of our diplomacy with the Russians, because we would assume that Russians are gentlemen, and make agreements they would have no intention of carrying out. "What you can't believe," Myrdal said, "is what every Swede knows in his bones. The Russian culture is not a gentleman culture."

Another branch of this literature focuses on our actual diplomatic experience, especially in the negotiation of the SALT I and SALT II agreements, and the nuclear arms negotiations between 1981 and the present time. These books and articles tend to have apocalyptic titles like *Cold Dawn, Endgame, Double Talk,* and *Deadly Gambits.* Almost without exception, their thesis is that it is all our fault. The Russians are presented as Noble Savages, innocent and rather unsophisticated voyagers from a distant planet which has been overrun unnumerable times in the course of history by bloodthirsty invaders from the East, the West, and the South. As a result, we have often been told, they are preternaturally suspicious of foreigners, although kind and generous at heart, and eager to reach fair and balanced agreements with the West. If only we were more sympathetic to the natural anxieties of the Russians, more tolerant of traits and habits which writers of this school ascribe to a Russian sense of inferiority toward the West, and more ingenious and imaginative as negotiators, we would long since have sealed true détente, perhaps even genuine peace with the Soviet Union through arms control agreements which would have exorcised the nightmare of nuclear war, and allowed the two social systems to "coexist" in peace.

Neither branch of the literature is a reliable guide to the problem of living with the Russians. There is something to be learned from these books and articles, but not a great deal. Of course the Russian culture is a strong and distinct entity, not to be confused with the cultures of France, China, the United States, or any other country or groups of countries. And of course we should do our best to understand the Russian culture, both for our own sakes, and as preparation for the essential task of peaceful coexistence. The Russians are not savages, noble or otherwise, but a gifted people who have made an extraordinarily rich contribution to Western literature, art, music, and learning during the past three centuries. Their moral and religious life has deep roots, and abiding power. They are no more addicted than other people to lying, cheating, and like sins, and there are as many ladies and gentlemen among them as in the population of Western Europe and the United States. No doubt the travelers' tales are true, within the usual limits, but they only confirm the obvious—that all cultures are different, but also have much in common.

The author has known Russians all his life, and known and worked with Soviet diplomats for a good many years. Many of those diplomats, like other Russians, were cultivated and agreeable men and women, good companions and reliable colleagues. Soviet diplomats were serious professionals—intelligent, well educated, and well trained. A good many share the views one often finds among Russian students in this country or in Europe—the characteristic attitudes of the Russian intelligentsia before 1914 so well described in *Fathers and Sons* and in the essays of Sir Isaiah Berlin. The old-fashioned Russian intellectuals did not suffer from inferiority complexes. Neither does the new crop. On the contrary, they look down on Western and particularly on American intellectuals as badly educated and hopelessly naive.

Government policy, however, is not made by lay people, whether peasants or intellectuals, but by governments. And the Soviet government was an institution of a most particular character. Until the day before yesterday, it was a dictatorship controlled by the Communist Party of the Soviet Union, which evolved as a revolutionary and conspiratorial schismatic group within the Socialist movement of the last century. Forged in bitter and often violent underground struggles, its outlook was that of a guerrilla commando, equally at war with established authority and with Socialist heterodoxy. It viewed itself as the chosen instrument of the true faith, whose mission was to fulfill the apostolic prophecies of Marx and Lenin. The latter-day party included not only the few who still believed in its professed creed but careerists, power addicts, thugs, lovers of money and privilege, and other members of what Djilas called the New Class, and Russians call the *Nomenklatura*. It is not surprising that a government dominated by such a group was difficult to deal with. There is no way of dealing with it unless one understands not only Russian history and the high Russian culture of Tolstoi, Turgenev, and Dostoyevsky, but the history of the Soviet Union and the low culture so brilliantly and powerfully revealed by Solzehnitzyn, Sinyavskiy, and the other great Russian prophets of our own time.

The answer to the question Americans have put to each other so

often—"Why has it been so difficult to get along with the Russians?"—
is that the goals of Soviet and Western foreign policy have been incompatible. The obstacles to agreement were not based on misunder-
standings and could not be cured by dialogue, vodka, ingenuity in
drafting, or prolonged walks in the woods. Over the years, I have
strongly favored civil and companionable relations between Soviet and
Western citizens at many levels, personal and official. I have done my
best to further the national interests of the United States by consuming
vast amounts of food and drink with Soviet guests, hosts, and other
interlocutors. Such contacts are educational and worthwhile, but we
should never confuse ourselves by supposing that in themselves they
could have led to peace. Soviet and American officials have understood
each other's government about as well as people ever understand the
dynamics of a foreign society and government—that is to say, not very
well. But what has made the course of Soviet-Western relations so
contentious between 1945 and 1991 is far deeper and more intractable
than simple ignorance, the occasional lunacy of American bureaucracy
or politics, and the prevalence of folly, especially in the government of
the United States.

Without ever being explicit about it, Soviet diplomats expected
their opposite numbers to understand the circumstances under which
the officials of their country lived and worked. If a Western negotiator
had a reasonable familiarity with Russian culture, a clear sense of
the nature of Soviet society, and a modicum of empathy, negotiating
with Soviet diplomats was not notably more difficult than other forms
of serious negotiation. In cases where the interests of the Soviet Union
and the United States were identical, or close to being identical, it
was often easy to reach an agreement. Similarly, if the gap between
the two sides was not great, and the Soviet stake in having an agreement was strong, it was usually not too difficult to find an accommodation. For example, it was not hard to sell grain to the Soviet
Union when it wanted to buy grain, or to find common ground on
the basic ideas of the law of the sea, since both the Soviet Union
and the United States were maritime powers and had the same opinions about the international character of straits and canals. The Non-
Proliferation Treaty of 1968 was quickly achieved, because both sides
had the same interest in keeping the nuclear club small, or at least
they both thought they did.

Where the subject matter of the negotiation touched the fundamental purposes of Soviet foreign policy, however, he negotiating problem was altogether different, and proved to be insoluble. It is, in fact,

a misnomer to call such encounters negotiation in any sense. They were problems in conflict, and could be postponed or resolved in the end only by deploying the manifest reality of unacceptable risk. On issues such as these, issues which touch the nerve of sovereignty, negotiating with the Soviet Union was a bracing sport—very bracing indeed. Sir William Hayter, who served with distinction as British ambassador to Moscow, once remarked that negotiating with the Soviet Union on topics of this order was like dealing with a recalcitrant vending machine. Sometimes it helped to put in another coin. Occassionally it was useful to shake the machine, or to kick it. But the one procedure which never did any good was to talk to it. As Dean Acheson once said, one should never negotiate with the Soviet Union unless he is willing to come home without an agreement.

The earnest Western campaigners for unilateral Western disarmament deny these features of reality. They prefer to talk about the tension between the Soviet Union and the United States as "great-power rivalry" based on "mutual mistrust," and passed resolutions urging Soviet-American summit meetings. It is seriously misleading to speak of the Soviet-American relationship as if it were a normal and inevitable feature of international politics, like the rivalry of the two biggest boys in a school playground at recess. Such a view puts the two countries on the same moral plane and treats their interests as equally legitimate. But the aggressor and his victim do not stand on the same moral, political, and legal plane. Their interests are not equally legitimate. And as a practical matter the refusal to confront the profound differences between the foreign policies of the United States and the Soviet Union led to all sorts of error and naiveté in the formulation of Western policies. As President Johnson once said about a solon of his day, "that fellow would find an excuse for them if they landed in Mexico."

How to evaluate the competing claims of the Soviet Union and its Western adversaries is a question with which humanity has been struggling since the Bolshevik Revolution of 1917. It has been an intensely troubling question for people of the Western tradition, involving passionate loyalties, poignant memories, and noble dreams. But the answer to the question is no longer in doubt, thanks to the testimony which has poured out of the Soviet Union since Gorbachev took power. Where the Gorbachev revolution will end is still a mystery. But the character of the regime which preceded his is not. The Soviet Union shaped by Lenin and Stalin was a monstrous tyranny committed to the quest for dominance.

II

The scene which confronted the peacemakers in 1945 was in some ways much worse, in others much better, than that of 1919. Prospects for peace in 1945 were worse than in 1919 for two reasons:

First, the demonic shadows of Hitler and Stalin cast a pall over the Allied victory. Nothing in the First World War, ghastly as it was, compared in horror to the inhumanity of the German extermination camps and the Soviet gulag. The ghosts of the Hitler period have survived, and still have the power of nightmares. The corresponding Soviet record, extending back to Lenin's time, haunted the West's fervent hopes for a continuation of its wartime alliance with the Soviet Union. At best, that black record will not fade for many years.

The second reason why the prospects for peace seemed so poor in 1945, even as compared with those at Versailles, was that the Soviet Union under Stalin—flushed with victory, its mighty legions intact— had already embarked on an aggressive program of indefinite expansion which was soon to engulf states all around its borders in Europe and in Asia, and to threaten many others far beyond its periphery. The self-confidence and will to act of the Western powers had been weakened by the frustrations of the interwar period and the exertions of the war. They wondered fearfully if they could stop the process of Soviet expansion. As a junior State Department official in 1943 I was sent on a mission to Algiers. A distinguished assistant secretary of state and ambassador, bidding me farewell, said, "Have a good time, and don't work so hard. Nothing we do can keep Europe from going Communist."

On the other hand, the prospects for peace in 1945 were better than they were at Versailles because the United States had declared that it would not attempt to escape from world politics after the war as it had done in 1919, but on the contrary would engage in international affairs as a responsible player. True, the American armed forces nearly evaporated at the end of the war, and Roosevelt had told Stalin at Yalta that he did not think he could keep troops in Europe for more than two years: surely one of the most monumental diplomatic gaffes of all time. But Roosevelt, emulating Wilson, had made his passionate Four Freedoms speech on Allied war aims as his annual State of the Union address to Congress in January 1941, and later that year he and Churchill had issued a joint statement called the Atlantic Charter. That brief articulation of the principles on which a postwar settlement should be based became as influential a document as Wilson's Fourteen Points.

With the bravura of their courage and political leadership, Churchill and Roosevelt thus began to formulate war aims long before the United States became a belligerent, and at a time when the war news could hardly have been worse. The Germans were approaching Moscow. El Alamein, Stalingard, and the Battle of Midway were far in the future. Yet Roosevelt and Churchill expounded the war aims of the United Nations with all the assurance of chieftains on the brink of victory.

The bureaucratic development of postwar planning within the United States government began in 1942. From the beginning it was conceived and organized as a cooperative Western effort under American leadership, and the Soviet Union was regularly asked to participate. The mandate for the planners was broad. They were instructed to prepare programs for building a dynamic and reformed world economy and a new political order capable of succeeding where the League of Nations had failed. At every step of the way, the West in general, and the United States in particular, made it clear that the Soviet Union's seat at the table was being kept vacant, waiting for the day when the Soviet leadership decided that the time had come to change course.

In 1943, Jean Monnet had said that what Europe needed from America most after the war was "its energy and its optimism." As the postwar period began, the United States government and the American people provided energy and optimism galore. They also gave Europe, Japan, and the rest of the world something even more precious. America made a major contribution to the flow of ideas, plans, decisions, and actions through which the Western nations struggled first to understand and then to transform the postwar world.

These two immense flows of energy, Soviet expansion and American activism, were of course related. Some experienced American statesmen—most notably Dean Rusk—believe that if the Soviet Union had not pursued an expansionist policy during the last years of the war and the early postwar period, the American armed forces would have been withdrawn from Europe and other forward bases within a few years, never to return, and a disarmed United States would have reverted to isolationism.[1] Considering the stunning failure of Western policy in the years between the wars, it is a matter for speculation whether the United States would in fact have gone back to isolationism without the help of the frequent alarm bells announcing Soviet probes and thrusts from one end of the world to the other. There can be no

1. Dean Rusk, "Reflections on Containment," in *Containment: Concept and Policy,* ed. Terry L. Deibel and John Lewis Gaddis (Washington, D.C.: National Defense University Press, 1986), 1:41, 42.

doubt, however, that the speed, clarity, and decisiveness of the American and broader Western reaction during the Truman years was greatly influenced by the Soviet rush for power, which was like the Soviet interventions in Europe and Asia after the Bolshevik Revolution, but far more massive and extensive.

Critics of American policy after the Second World War have said that it was "reactive" rather than "proactive" or creative: that is, that the United States and its European allies adopted their policy of containment only after the Soviet Union had tried to expand so hard and so often that Western sensitivity to the risk of Soviet hegemony was alerted. This view entirely mistakes the nature of American, British, and Western European action with regard to the Soviet Union. Containment was not the first but the second Western policy toward its former ally. The first principle of American foreign policy was and is the Wilsonian goal of peace, that is, of effective worldwide peace-keeping in accordance with the United Nations Charter—by the Security Council, if possible, or through arrangements of collective self-defense like NATO, when the Security Council cannot act itself. Containment was always conceived not as a policy in itself but as the application of the policy of dealing collectively with major threats to the peace. From 1943 until 1948, when the United States offered participation in the Marshall Plan to the Soviet Union and the countries of Eastern Europe, the United States used every possible resource to persuade, cajole, or induce the Soviet Union to cooperate in the tasks both of reconstruction and of peace. Those were the years when the United States proposed the Baruch Plan to internationalize nuclear technology; agreed to admit the Ukraine and Byelorussia to the United Nations; offered the Soviet Union a loan for postwar reconstruction and urged her to become a member of the Bretton Woods institutions, the International Monetary Fund and the Bank for International Reconstruction and Development. The Soviet Union rejected all these initiatives, and others as well.

The Soviet refusal even to discuss the Baruch Plan turned out to be the most serious of these rejections, a tragic turning point in the history of the Cold War. That decision seems irreversible even in the era of Gorbachev and Yeltsin. The Baruch Plan, offered in 1946, was probably the last opportunity to achieve effective international control over the military potentialities of nuclear science. In the intervening years, the secrets of nuclear technology have spread everywhere, and the genie can no longer be put back into the bottle: any moderately industrialized country can make nuclear weapons and any rich country can get them built. The United States and its allies must therefore retain enough nuclear deterrent power to deal with such contingencies.

These persistent offers in the face of adamant Soviet rebuffs did not represent an idle or a sentimental preference on the part of the West. The Western governments were under no illusions about the Soviet Union. They were not ready to swallow Stalinism because they were duped by Soviet propaganda or controlled by Soviet moles hidden in their bureaucracies. They believed, correctly, that an organized system of peace was their highest security interest, and that the best way to reach that goal was to achieve and maintain a relationship of cooperation among the great powers in keeping the peace. What they wanted then, [and want still,] above all the other ambitions of Western foreign policy, is for Russia to become a conscientious permanent member of the Security Council of the United Nations, with all that phrase implies. A considerable degree of great-power solidarity, at least on the ultimate issues of peace or war, was the secret of the success of the Concert of Europe during most of the nineteenth and early twentieth centuries. The Concert of Europe was the model for the Security Council, and the justification for the veto power of its members.

The experience of their wartime summit meetings with Stalin reinforced that view for Roosevelt and Churchill. After their years with Stalin, the Western leaders knew that unless they succeeded in obtaining great-power solidarity, the next fifty years or so would be strenuous for the West, to put it mildly. If Japan and Western Europe—including the Western occupation zones in Germany—recovered, and became part of the Western coalition, then the West ought to be able to assure general stability without Soviet cooperation. But the chance of success would be precarious. A cooperative Soviet Union was decidedly a goal to be sought with energy and imagination.

The force of this conclusion explains why the Western leaders made so many disastrous concessions to Stalin—on Poland especially—during the closing days of the war and in its immediate aftermath. It may well be, as many have said, that they went too far, and should have drawn the line in the sand sooner than they did. They had to be sure that Stalin had really said no, and of course they shared the hopes of their fellow citizens for a harmonious relationship with the Soviet Union. It may be that psychologically it was necessary that new leaders come forward in the West to make the decisions Truman and his European colleagues made a few years later.

In fact, however, the Western leaders had little choice in 1945.

Given the size and power of the Soviet Union, there was no feasible alternative to the course that was actually followed: to work patiently for the policy of cooperation, to wait for Soviet policy to "mellow" under the influence of Russian high culture and the course of events—the word *mellow* was used by George Kennan in his influential writings of the period—and meanwhile to contain further Soviet expansion in order to prevent dangerous changes in the world balance of power. There was no real military option for the West. Only the logician Bertrand Russell advocated a Western ultimatum to the Soviet Union, backed by the American nuclear monopoly. The purpose of the ultimatum would have been to force the Soviet Union to carry out the promises it made at Yalta for free elections in Eastern Europe and to accept the policy of peace. Apart from the practicalities of enforcing such a demand, the idea of turning on an ally at the end of a war they had fought together and barely won was contrary to the nature of Western culture, and was dismissed as repulsive. The West had to continue to keep the alternative of peace visibly open; prevent Soviet hegemony; reason with Soviet diplomats and leaders; and wait.

Adam Ulam, reviewing the diplomacy of the Yalta-Postdam period and the early postwar years, concludes that Stalin's decision to reject the policy of peacetime cooperation with the Western powers was not caused by errors of Allied diplomacy or by mutual misunderstanding. Stalin had taken the measure of his interlocutors extremely well. "It would be a mistake," Ulam writes,

> to consider the Soviet attitude at Yalta as entirely cynical, or Stalin's statement, that as long as the three of them remained at the helm peace would be secure but would require great effort, as insincere. For the moment and for some months afterward, the exhilaration of victory, the relief at the almost miraculous survival not of Russia but of his own power must have inspired in Stalin some gratitude to his two partners, each with his peculiar greatness, and the wish that another war might be avoided. But whatever his feelings, Stalin could not in the long run withstand the logic of his position as the ruler of a totalitarian society and as the supreme head of a movement that seeks security through constant expansion. In these facts more than in any sins of omission or commission by the West must be seen the seeds of the growing discords and of the cold war.[2]

2. Adam Ulam, *Expansion and Coexistence: Soviet Foreign Policy, 1917–73*, 2d ed. (1968; New York: Praeger, 1974), 377.

Dean Rusk qualifies Ulam's judgment only slightly.

> I suspect that we, ourselves, bear some responsibility for launching the Cold War, [Rusk said,] because it may well be that we exposed Josef Stalin to intolerable temptations through our own weakness. [Earlier he had noted:] Just after V-J Day . . . we demobilized almost completely, and almost overnight. By the summer of 1946, we in the State Department were being told by officers on the Joint Staff that we did not have one division in our Army nor one group in our Air Force that could be considered ready for combat.[3]

The Western peoples, by and large, found it difficult to accept what their governments understood all too well: that for the Soviets the Second World War was two wars combined in one, the Allied war against Germany and Japan, and the ongoing Soviet war for the enlargement of its domain at the expense both of its allies and its enemies. The first war had a beginning and an end; the second had neither. It went back to ancient patterns of Russian behavior, reinforced by the ideology of revolution. A Russian historian once estimated that between 1462 and 1914 the Russian Empire expanded at an average rate of fifty square miles a day.[4] The Soviet regime fully maintained the record of its predecessors in this respect, at least until the volcanic events of 1989 and 1990 liberated the East European satellites and acknowledged a process of profound change which led to the disintegration of the Soviet empire.

In 1945, however, the Soviet drive for expansion was as vigorous as it had ever been in the past. It had been partly suspended by the necessities of the war against Germany, just as Anglo-Russian rivalry in Asia had been suspended between 1914 and 1918. As the end of the Second World War approached, however, it became the essence of Stalin's foreign policy to take advantage of every opportunity to renew and intensify the traditional Russian and Soviet policy of expansion, and to use force to accomplish its purpose, unless the use of force proved to be too risky. The Soviet Union never allowed any of its experiments in expansion to escalate into a general war with the Western nations led by the United States. It simply took what it could take without pushing the West to lash back in kind. Paradoxically, the American nuclear monopoly and then the great American nuclear advantage

---

3. Rusk, "Reflections on Containment," in Deibel and Gaddis, *Containment* 1:42, 41.

4. V. O. Kliushevskii, quoted in Taras Hunczak, ed., *Russian Imperialism from Ivan the Great to the Revolution,* (New Brunswick, N.J.: Rutgers University Press, 1974), 13–21. See also the Introduction by Hans Kohn.

in the early postwar years made the Soviet calculation about how far it could safely carry aggression easier than it might otherwise have been. Early in the day, the Soviet leadership came to realize the strength of Western reluctance to consider using nuclear weapons, and made that fact an integral part of its planning.

There is no ambiguity about the evidence. From the Soviet intervention in the Greek civil war and its threat to Turkey to its role in the Korean War, and literally dozens of other episodes in this cycle, the story was the same: a Soviet thrust based on the aggressive use of force or threat to use force, usually but not always defeated by the United States and its allies after a warning or a limited war. In Stalin's time and for years thereafter, the Soviet Union was simply unwilling to become a status quo power, that is, it was not yet ready to abandon the five-hundred-year-old tradition of Russian expansion. It acted as if it had been exempted from the United Nations Charter rule against aggression. Once, when the question of the Charter was put to Andrei Gromyko, the Soviet foreign minister for a generation, he replied, "You are asking us to give up a policy rooted in our nature as a society and a state." An episode toward the end of the Second World War casts revealing light on what lay behind Gromyko's remark.

In 1943, Anastas Mikoyan, then Soviet minister for foreign trade, asked Averell Harriman, the American ambassador in Moscow at the time, about the possibility of an American loan to the Soviet Union for the purpose of postwar reconstruction. The United States government reacted to Mikoyan's initiative with alacrity and enthusiasm. So did the relevant Congressional committees when the project was explained to them in due course. No American needed to be persuaded that it was important for the United States to help Stalin decide in favor of a policy of cooperation for the postwar period.

It was not possible to make loans to the Soviet Union under the Export-Import Bank legislation, because Russia was in default on loans arising from the First World War. A legal procedure was therefore worked out under the settlement provisions of the Lend-Lease Act: the United States would sell the Soviet Union for reconstruction purposes some of the materials which were in the Soviet lend-lease pipeline when hostilities ceased. The Soviet lend-lease programs were negotiated for a year at a time through a document called a protocol. If hostilities ceased relatively early in the protocol year, such a loan could have been decidedly substantial. Extremely favorable credit terms were arranged for the sale. Negotiations were continued for months, but the Soviet negotiators, having at first been insistent, became hesitant and evasive.

In the end, some time after the war, a small loan was made under the Lend-Lease Act, but the Soviets missed an opportunity for a major step toward reconstruction and cooperation. At one point during this extended negotiation, Stalin told Harriman that he appreciated what the United States was trying to do to help the Soviet reconstruction effort but added, "We have decided to go our own way."[5]

Events before and immediately after the end of the war confirmed this grim sense of Soviet policy. So did Stalin's major speech of 9 February, 1946 to the Supreme Soviet. In that formal policy statement, Stalin abandoned the Russian nationalism of his rhetoric during the war; failed even to mention the contributions Great Britain and the United States had made to the victory; and presented the defeat of Germany and Japan as the exclusive achievement of Marxism-Leninism and the Communist Party of the Soviet Union. Not even his own marshals and generals were thanked for their contributions. As for the future and the external world, Stalin talked only of "imperialist hostility" and of continuing to build the Soviet Union's scientific and industrial strength so that the country would be ready for any emergency. There was no mention of trade with the West, a topic on which he had been affable and expansive with Western visitors only a few weeks before.

Stalin's speech was delivered less than a year after the first use of the nuclear weapon had brought the war against Japan to an abrupt end. At about the same time, Churchill gave his Iron Curtain speech at Fulton, Missouri, and George Kennan sent his celebrated "long telegram" from Moscow, proposing what soon became the policy of containment.

As Hugh Thomas discovered, two foreign policy veterans, one Soviet and one American, independently evaluated the prospect for Soviet-American relations immediately after the war in almost the same words. Dean Acheson, then undersecretary and soon to become secretary of state, reported to President Truman in 1945 that if cooperation

5. The author was much involved in this episode while working in the State Department as executive assistant to Dean Acheson. Some years ago he reviewed the affair with several participants, including Secretary Acheson, Ambassador Kennan and Ambassador Harriman, who told him about Stalin's statement. His study appeared in Rostow, *Peace in the Balance: The Future of American Foreign Policy* (New York: Simon and Schuster, 1972), 111–27. Even Hugh Thomas gets the story wrong in his excellent *Armed Truce: The Beginnings of the Cold War, 1945–46,* (1986; first American edition, New York: Atheneum, 1987), 182–86. So does John L. Gaddis in *The United States and the Origins of the Cold War, 1941–1947,* (New York: Columbia University Press, 1972), 23.

between the two countries turned out to be impossible, "there will be no organized peace but only an armed truce." Maxim Litvinov, a former Soviet foreign minister, was more pessimistic. "I now feel," he remarked nine months later to U.S. Ambassador Bedell Smith, "that the best that can be hoped for is a prolonged armed truce."[6]

III

The peacemaking process began in 1945 on a completely different footing from the parallel process of 1919. The principal Allied Powers—Great Britain, the Soviet Union, France, and the United States—decided during the war that Germany and Japan should remain under military occupation until every trace of Fascism and militarism was eliminated. Then democratic governments could be formed, capable of taking their places in the new state system as responsible members of the United Nations.

These were, of course, precatory words, words of hope, not reflections of reality. The Allied governments had learned during the war how hostile Stalin was to the West, and how thin the veneer of cooperation with his allies. At Yalta, Stalin had promised free elections in the territories occupied by his troops. Long before the fighting ended in Europe, it was apparent that he had no intention of carrying out that promise. The Red Army traveled with Communist governments for the countries of Eastern Europe in its baggage trains.

From the strategic and geopolitical point of view, the most important consequence of the Second World War was that the Western zones of occupation in Germany emerged under the tutelage of the United States, Great Britain, and France, and in Japan under that of the United States. Japan and the Western zones of Germany were therefore protected from the beginning against Soviet subversion and attack. China reached something like the same protected position in 1972, when "the unnatural relation"[7] between China and the Soviet Union broke up under the strain of its own contradictions. The demarcation lines between the Soviet and Western zones of occupation turned out to be extremely sensitive Cold War boundaries. Until the Berlin Wall was torn down and the Soviet empire began to disintegrate in 1989, they were sacrosanct, except in the case of Austria.

---

6. Thomas, *Armed Truce*, vii.
7. Dean Acheson, "Crisis in Asia—An Examination of U.S. Policy," Speech of Secretary of State Acheson, made before the National Press Club 12 January 1950, *Department of State Bulletin* 22 (23 January 1950): 111–18.

IV

If one looks back at what was attempted and accomplished by the Western nations during the first decade or so of the postwar period, what is most striking is that taken together those efforts reflect the principles of a coherent and enlightened state system. The contrast between the reconstruction programs after World War I and after World War II could hardly be more vivid. The interwar years are a sour tale of little men doing mean and little things—a tale of deception, frustration, hesitation, ineptitude, childish quarreling, inadequacy, and finally of evil. The period of reconstruction after 1945, despite the vigorous opposition of the Soviet Union to the policies pursued by the West, constitutes an achievement in statesmanship which can be compared both in its vision and in its consequences only to that of the Congress of Vienna in modern times. Of course there were failures, false starts, particular activities which were misconceived or badly executed. In one area—that of nuclear affairs—the Soviet Union did succeed in blocking any significant progress toward bringing nuclear energy under effective international control. But on the whole, the United States and its colleagues of the West succeeded in adapting the architecture and dynamics of the state system they had inherited to the transformed social, political, intellectual, and economic environment. Their work was immense in scale and scope, magnanimous in spirit, and humane in its aspirations both for peace and for social progress. The ideas and methods of cooperation they launched have demonstrated their fertility for nearly half a century, and show no signs of losing their relevance and promise. And, most remarkably, the work was almost always carried on by agreement among the Allies, and with a self-confidence and energy completely unlike the passivity and defeatism of the interwar period.

The only significant exceptions to that generalization occurred during the Eisenhower Administration. One would have expected President Eisenhower to be sensitive and effective in dealing with the allies of the United States, as he had been during World War II. During his Presidency, however, the United States repeatedly pursued unilateral policies at the expense of our allies. In each case the American decision turned out to be mistaken and costly. The President had said, for example, that it would be a betrayal for the United States to reach an armistice in the Korean War without at the same time obtaining settlements of the wars in Indochina and Malaysia. We then made a separate peace with Korea, and refused to enter the war in French

Indochina at a time when France had 500,000 men in the field. After France was defeated and withdrew, Eisenhower made the SEATO treaty, guaranteeing the nations of Southeast Asia against aggression. The United States had to honor that commitment in Vietnam a few years later without the help of France.

Similarly, in the Suez crisis of 1956, we missed opportunity after opportunity to reach a coordinated allied policy for the area. Instead, when war broke out, we publicly sided with the Soviet Union against Britain, France, and Israel, a policy which led to at least two more major wars and endless lesser hostilities in the Middle East. The relationship between France and the United States has never fully recovered from the twin blows of Indochina and Suez. Eisenhower's handling of events in Cuba, Hungary, and Algeria also merit severe criticism.

V

The Western powers took initiatives in four major areas: economic policy, aid to the developing nations, social and cultural problems, and policy toward nuclear weapons and nuclear technology more broadly. They treated all four of these areas within the framework of a security policy based on the United Nations Charter supplemented by the Truman Doctrine, NATO and similar regional security treaties, and a number of bilateral security arrangements—that with Israel, for example.

The Charter of the United Nations prescribed the norms and goals of Western security policy, and the network of United Nations institutions provided a considerable fraction of the working machinery for carrying it out. A Soviet diplomat once remarked that if the San Francisco Conference on the United Nations project had been delayed for even one year, the Soviet Union would never have signed the Charter. What he meant, one would suppose, is that the Soviet Union would have refused to sign because during that period its foreign policy became incompatible with the Charter. The Charter forbids all international use of force except in individual or collective self-defense, while by 1946 the Soviet Union had embraced a principle that purported to legitimize wars to promote Socialism or national self-determination. The Soviet use of force to discipline errant Communist regimes came later.

If that is what the diplomat meant, he was far less worldly than his superiors. The character of Soviet policy during the pre-Gorbachev period was fully evident well before 1945. The Soviet Union signed the

Charter for political and tactical reasons despite the contradiction between the Charter rules and Soviet behavior. The organs of the United Nations have given the Soviet Union and many other countries excellent opportunities for propaganda and political action. And the Security Council veto gave the Soviet Union an ironclad defense against condemnation as an aggressor. The Soviet Union surely recognized the power of the political idea embodied in the Charter, that of peace through collective security. Given its ambitions, the Soviet Union could hardly have chosen to appear before the world as the declared enemy of peace.

Nevertheless, the Soviet diplomat's comment brings out the essence of world history during the past half-century: despite the Soviet thrust for hegemony, the dominant theme of that history has not been the Cold War—tiresome, noisy, and costly as it has been—but the construction of a vastly improved world order, seeking to fulfill the purposes codified in the Charter.

In Chapter 3, the Charter was analyzed as a stage in the prolonged effort to bring the phenomenon of international war under the control of law. As a matter of practical politics, that effort began with the Treaty of Westphalia in 1648, settling the Thirty Years' War in Europe, and was given enormous impetus by the Congress of Vienna in 1815. Despite setbacks and distractions, it has continued ever since, sometimes rapidly, sometimes slowly. Every major war has stimulated the quest for peace.

No country was so naive and so fervent as the United States about the potentialities of the United Nations, but the other Western nations agreed that the League of Nations had shown promise as a peacekeeping institution, and could have been made to work if it had had more authority, if it had been universal in its membership, and above all, if the great powers had backed it more strongly, with force if necessary. In any event, it was understood that with the disintegration of the European empires except the Russian empire, and the rise of many newly independent states, the world was no longer Eurocentered and that an organization like the League or the United Nations was indispensable, if only as a forum both for multilateral and for bilateral diplomacy. The increasing importance of multilateral diplomacy was evident during the League period, and accelerated steadily as the world economy became more integrated, and as governments faced the necessity for regulating more and more problems of an international character.

Because of the Cold War, many of the most important forms of

international cooperation during this period developed outside the
United Nations: NATO, for example, and other security arrangements,
Western and Eastern alike; and the O.E.C.D. and other organizations
for coordinating the economic policies of the chief capitalist nations,
especially in the economic field. But the Cold War by no means suspended the development of the peacekeeping activities or jurisprudence
of the United Nations. While the Security Council found it difficult to
function effectively in conflicts where the United States and the Soviet
Union were directly involved, even that did not prove to be a universal
rule. In the Cuban missile crisis of 1962, for example, the principal
negotiations took place directly between the Soviet Union and the
United States, but the role of the Security Council was by no means
negligible. The same observation could be made about the Suez crisis
of 1956, directly involving Great Britain and France. And in the long
series of Arab wars against the existence of Israel in which the Soviet
Union was deeply involved, the Security Council was a major instrumentality through which sharp differences among the parties and among
the major powers were defined, reconciled, and often compromised,
and then stated in resolutions which all are formally bound to accept
as consistent with the law of the Charter. While the pressures of the
Cold War surely prevented the Security Council from fulfilling the role
the Western nations intended it to have when the Charter was drafted,
it has not kept the Security Council from establishing itself as an institution capable of helping to achieve relatively peaceful outcomes for
a number of important threats to the peace where the Soviet Union
was not seriously involved, and in others as well.

Although the Security Council must decide whether parties to a
conflict have violated the Charter, and its precedents are the living law
of the Charter, the Security Council is not a court. Its arsenal includes
a wide range of political and diplomatic procedures for resolving disputes as well as its capacity to call on the nations to provide military
force for the purpose, which has not thus far been used. The diplomatic
initiatives sponsored by the Security Council to promote the peaceful
resolution of disputes and its use of its own international peacekeeping
forces to separate potential or actual combatants have been a significant
and constructive factor in international politics. While these efforts have
not always been successful, they provide the Council with tools which
could become more effective with the recession of the Cold War, and
the idea of peace enforced by collective security should become more
widely accepted.

The containment policy of the United States and its allies since the

Truman Doctrine was announced in 1947 is not in any sense a repudiation of the role of the United Nations Charter and of the Security Council in the quest for peace. On the contrary, it simply recognized that the circumstances of the Cold War made it impossible for the Security Council to mobilize in advance the forces necessary to assure adequate defense against major threats to the peace, breaches of the peace, and acts of aggression backed by the Soviet Union. The North Atlantic Treaty and other Western security arrangements are formally identified as agreements of collective self-defense within the meaning of Article 51 of the Charter. They are applications of the Charter principles in dealing with particularly dangerous situations—situations which are in effect standing threats to the peace. The Security Council has played an active role in the diplomacy of many episodes involving the Truman Doctrine throughout its history, starting with the Soviet move into Azerbaijan in 1946, and its intervention in the the Greek civil war in the late 1940s. It should be recalled that the Security Council's almost invariable practice where armed force has been used or its use threatened has been to request other states to assist the victim of the attack and to ask all states not to assist the aggressor. Mandatory "decisions" of the Security Council are rare and there have been no direct "enforcement" actions undertaken by the United Nations.[8]

VI

The second major component of the reformed state system created under the leadership of the United States and its allies in the years after 1945 was the modern worldwide capitalist economy. Planning for the reconstruction and improvement of the international economy was actively begun during the Second World War. The agreements under which the United States provided its allies Lend-Lease assistance during the war declared that both parties agreed to adopt liberal principles of international trade in the postwar period. And the first important international conference dealing with postwar economic policy, the Bretton Woods Conference, took place during the war, in 1944. That conference gave flesh and substance to the broad principles on the basis of which the Western nations proposed to reform and reestablish the postwar economy. Those principles repudiated the autarchic trade practices which had been so obstructive during the thirties, and called for

8. E. V. Rostow, "Until What? Enforcement Action or Collective Self-Defense?" *American Journal of International Law* 85, no. 3 (July 1991).

a world economy which would become integrated as rapidly as possible on the basis of low tariffs, free capital movements, and relatively stable and convertible currencies. The world in 1945 was far from those goals. There were exchange controls throughout Europe, trade barriers were high, and quotas frequent.

It soon became clear that the economic crisis of Europe had been badly underestimated. Immediate postwar humanitarian relief had been successfully carried out. Something new was needed. The gap between economic actuality and the aspirations of the new economic plans was too big to be traversed simply by changing the rules and asking the market to do the rest. Europe and Japan were cold and hungry, and their economies were limping badly. While Western Europe and Japan still had strong and responsive entrepreneurial and managerial classes, their civilian economies had been starved for capital during the war and badly injured by the fighting. Above all, as Secretary of State Marshall said in his Marshall Plan speech at Harvard on 5 June 1947, the entire fabric of the European economy had been dislocated by the events of the previous ten years, which had involved the disappearance of longstanding commercial ties, private institutions, banks, insurance companies, and shipping companies. As a result, he said, "the modern system of the division of labor upon which the exchange of products is based is in danger of breaking down." Europe needed the catalyst of outside help before it could be expected to function normally.

At the same time, the emergence of the Iron Curtain and the consolidation of Communist governments in Eastern Europe and North Korea made the task of economic reconstruction urgently political. The memories of the thirties were still fresh in the United States and Western Europe. It was generally believed that the Great Depression had put Hitler into power, and that another depression would lead to a Soviet takeover in Western Europe and Japan.

The United States reacted rapidly to the bleak economic news from Europe. (Japan was under occupation, and its problems were handled differently.) Within the government, Dean Acheson and Will Clayton were the leaders in the effort to create a program adequate to the emergency. The first public statement about the plan the United States would propose to deal with the crisis was made by Acheson, then undersecretary of state, in a speech on 8 May 1947.[9] George C. Mar-

9. Dean Acheson, "The Requirements of Reconstruction," Speech delivered to the Delta Council at Cleveland, Mississippi, on 8 May 1947, *Department of State Bulletin* 16 (18 May 1947): 991.

shall, the secretary of state, gave the Marshall Plan speech a few weeks later, one of the finest moments in American diplomatic history. He put the administration's ideas on what to do in this form:

It is already evident that, before the United States Government can proceed much further in its efforts to alleviate the situation and help start the European world on its way to recovery, there must be some agreement among the countries of Europe as to the requirements of the situation and the part those countries themselves will take in order to give proper effect to whatever action might be undertaken by this Government. It would be neither fitting nor efficacious for this Government to undertake to draw up unilaterally a program designed to place Europe on its feet economically. This is the business of the Europeans. The initiative, I think, must come from Europe. The role of this country should consist of friendly aid in the drafting of a European program and of later support of such a program so far as it may be practical for us to do so. The program should be a joint one, agreed to by a number, if not all European nations.[10]

Several features of Secretary Marshall's speech should be stressed at a time when the Western industrial democracies confront the strikingly parallel economic crisis of the nations which constituted the Soviet Union and its satellites in Eastern Europe.

In the first place, Marshall's speech was not an American initiative, but a suggestion that the Europeans take an initiative in which the United States would participate as a partner. That philosophy has characterized the American view of its relationship with its allies throughout the period since 1945. If sometimes honored in the breach, it nonetheless corresponds to an important psychological and political fact: Americans are uncomfortable in an imperial role.

Second, the speech gave official American encouragement to the European Movement. This extraordinary effort to mobilize opinion in favor of European unification was led by Jean Monnet, a remarkable French statesman and man of affairs who had been an important member of the French Provisional Government in Algiers during the war and was director of economic planning in France after the war. Monnet remained the leader of the European Movement until his death.

10. George C. Marshall, "European Initiative Essential to Economic Recovery," speech delivered at Harvard University Commencement exercises on 5 June 1947; published in *Congressional Record*, 80th Cong., 1st sess., 1947, 93: 3248; and in *Department of State Bulletin* 16 (15 June 1947): 1160.

It is by no means self-evident that a united Europe is in the interest of the United States; indeed, we have consistently opposed any attempts to achieve hegemony in Europe, as Britain did for centuries before the United States came of age. But the successive administrations of the United States since 1945 have supported the idea of a united Europe as part of an Atlantic Community including Canada and the United States. Thus far, all the principal leaders of the European movement have also been firm Atlanticists.

With the change in the scale of the state system since 1945, and the changing distribution of power within it, this view is the wisest European policy for the United States to pursue for the forseeable future, along with its parallel relation with Japan and China. While the Soviet Union survived as an expansionist power, such a conception of policy was inevitable, if only because of the state of the nuclear balance. If the Soviet Union has broken up as an empire, Russia is in itself a very large state which has for centuries been an active participant in international politics. A solid and cooperative relationship linking the industrial democracies of Europe and Asia to the nations of the Western Hemisphere should therefore remain a crucial feature of American security policy for the indefinite future. And the United States should pursue every possible means to persuade Russia to join that coalition, for the same reasons which led us to welcome Germany and Japan as allies after 1945.

Third, as Marshall's speech hinted, the United States government offered participation in the plan to the Eastern as well as the Western European governments. The Soviet Union rejected the proposal, and required Poland and Czechoslovakia, which had instantly accepted the official invitation, to withdraw. Several of Marshall's colleagues had demurred to his insistence that the United States offer its aid to the Soviet Union and East European satellites on the ground that Congress would never accept such a step, but Marshall prevailed. It was, he and Truman understood, a moral imperative, and in the long run a powerful reiteration of America's true policy toward the Soviet Union and the nations of Eastern Europe. The Marshall Plan offer to the Soviet Union and the countries of Eastern Europe has never been forgotten there.

The first reactions to Marshall's speech were indifferent, both in the press and among the European governments. But Ernest Bevin, the British foreign minister at the time, a former trade union leader and a man of great ability and force, saw at once that the American suggestion was an opportunity for Europe—and for the future of the Atlantic Community—an opportunity of the utmost importance and promise. He understood that Marshall's idea was not simply a loan but a partnership between Western Europe and America, and that its consequences could be not only economic but political and military as well. The United States was hinting that the European nations take a first step together toward the goal of forming a European polity strong enough not simply to withstand a Soviet takeover and provide a safe and constructive outlet for the energy and pride of the German people, but strong enough also to restore Europe's self-confidence and dignity after the tragedy of its long civil war. Bevin led the West European governments to respond quickly and positively to the American trial balloon. Within less than a year, Congress passed the necessary legislation, and Truman established an agency to administer the American part of the enterprise.

The driving force in the decision to offer the plan was humanitarian. As Acheson remarked after testifying for the Marshall Plan legislation before a congressional committee, "What I have said about the political and economic advantages of the European Recovery Program are all true, but they are not the real reason we should do this. That reason is that we have to shave every morning. The Europeans have been bombed and occupied during the war. We have not."

The humanitarian consequences of the Marshall Plan were remarkable. So were its political and economic effects, both for Europe and for other areas where the same methods were applied. The Europeans began the process of working together as a group, a habit which led gradually to the formation of the European Coal and Steel Community, and to Euratom, the Treaty of Rome, and the emergence of the European Economic Community, which has now become the European Community.

Recognizing that an economy integrated through trade and investment should also have an integrated monetary system, the Europeans began early to experiment with devices to coordinate national monetary policies, so as to facilitate joint action to offset the swings of the trade cycle, to enlarge trade and investment, and to stabilize exchange rates. As the process of European recovery gained momentum, the monetary authorities realized that purely regional monetary systems, like the European Payments Union, could never be more than partial solutions. European recovery was rapid, and European economic integration was proceeding more slowly, but still proceeding. The worldwide economy led by the industrialized democracies was taking shape even more rapidly, however, and generating unprecedented volumes of trade, transnational transfers, and investment. It soon became apparent that the coordination of monetary policies required at a minimum the close cooperation of the leading financial powers, and ideally, the coopera-tion of all financial authorities throughout the world.

Thus through trial and error over a period of more than forty years, the present three-tier system of monetary controls developed. There is the European monetary arrangement, evolving in the direction of a common currency for the members of the European Community; a series of more or less ad hoc committees representing the major cap-italist economic powers, whose function is to achieve the coordination of monetary policies among the members of the group, currently known as G-7; and finally the International Monetary Fund, a United Nations institution stemming from the Bretton Woods Conference of 1944, whose annual meetings involve nearly all the ministers of finance and directors of central banks in the world. The fund has not become a central bank for the world economy, but it has become a useful part of the world network of central banks. It issues Special Drawing Rights, which are supplemental reserves for central banks, increasingly used as reserves rather than gold, or holdings of dollars, deutsche marks. yen, or other currencies treated as reserves. And it has become a spe-cialist in giving economic advice to less developed countries which have gotten into economic trouble.

The developing countries have every reason to take i.m.f. advice seriously. Unless they succeed in stabilizing their economies, they can-not become loanworthy, either at the i.m.f. or at other international financial agencies, and will find their credit status seriously impaired among private banks. While these arrangements for the coordination of national monetary policies have not been so effective as those of a central bank can be, they have served about as well as could could be expected at this stage in the evolution of the relationship between national and supranational "sovereignties."

Viewed as a program, the initiatives taken by the United States and its European and Asian colleagues since 1945 have resulted in the creation of a powerful, progressive, and effective international econ-omy—as open and integrated as the world economy before 1914, and much better managed. It has avoided major recessions and offset minor recessions by coordinated governmental and central banking action. It has served the less developed nations and even the Communist and formerly Communist states well, both as a trading partner and as a source of capital and entrepreneurship. Each of the major countries has felt the stimulus of heightened competition. While the record with respect to inflation is less impressive, it is far better than that of the

1920s. The forty-seven years since 1945 have been punctuated with warfare and with sustained high levels of military expenditure all over the world, two of the most common sources of inflation. And even the best managed of the Western capitalist economies have discovered that the great increase in the scale of state activities and expenditures, especially those for welfare, are cycle-sensitive and therefore difficult to predict. The result has been the acceptance of decifit finance as common practice, and a weakening of the legal and political restraints which in the past tended to limit the natural impulse of politicans to spend public funds, but not to vote taxes to obtain them.

VII

The third dimension of the foreign policy declared by the Truman Administration and since pursued by the entire Western world has been that of providing economic assistance for what used to be called less developed countries. Most of those countries were new nations created by the dissolution of the European empires except for the Russian empire. The Soviet empire is now breaking up, as the others did, under the pressure of the principle that peoples, or at least nations, have the natural right to govern themselves.

National self-determination was proclaimed as a self-evident truth by the American and the French revolutions. It soon became an accepted part of the liberal creed, encouraging the colonized to demand their freedom and convincing the colonizers they did not have the right to rule.

While the principle of self-determination is widely cheered as a natural right, it is often inconsistent with the even more sacred principle that all states have the right to territorial integrity and political independence. Since nearly every state on earth contains more than one people, the conflict between these two principles is often acute. The second rule, that of the equality and sovereignty of states, is the foundation of international law, and is proclaimed by the United Nations Charter as the essential element in the concept of peace. Indeed, so far as the Charter is concerned, national self-determination is a right which cannot be pursued by the international use of force. As the European empires dissolved, this contradiction between the national principle and the necessities of peace often led to war and revolution, and complicated the economic and social problems of the developing nations.

When the Europeans lost or gave up control of their colonies, the new countries discovered what economists had been telling them for years but they had never believed, namely, that they had not been exploited by their masters, but heavily subsidized. With the armies, schoolteachers, road-builders, nurses, doctors, and other civil servants of the colonial governments departing, new subsidies had to be found somewhere to prevent catastrophic falls in their standards of living. In many cases, the new governments also lacked politicians, civil servants, and entrepreneurs who could manage and continue the business enterprises the Europeans had left behind, and start the new enterprises required to assure economic growth.

The record of the Western nations in helping the less developed countries is a mixed one. Some surged forward rapidly, others slowly, and others still stagnated or fell behind. In some countries, social conditions favored economic development, while in many others poverty, lack of education, political instability, and the absence of relevant work experience and work habits were serious obstacles. Moreover, many ambitious development plans, including some drawn up with the help of international experts, proved to be misguided. And in more than a few of the developing countries, more local savings were sent abroad for safekeeping in foreign banks than the total of foreign aid and investment. For present purposes, all that can be said is that a massive effort was made; a great deal was learned about the sociology as well as the economics of the development process; and the effort continues, both through bilateral and multilateral programs.

The international politics of nuclear weapons and nuclear energy more broadly will be considered in Chapter 15.

15

The Nuclear Dimension: A Case Study

While first strike calculations are important in thrashing out nuclear theory, the practical political effect of such calculations on both sides has been to confirm the curbstone judgment that there are no victors in nuclear war. The theoreticians on both sides underestimated the difficulties of designing and procuring a force that would make a first strike seem like anything but madness. The balance of terror was not at all delicate because the chief protagonists were frightened by the outcome of a nuclear war whether it was a "victory" or a "defeat." The antagonists frightened each other into their senses—a rare instance in the history of human folly.—Herbert S. Dinerstein

Ever since the first American atomic bombs ended the war against Japan in 1945, a vast literature has accumulated about the significance of the nuclear weapon in world politics. In the early years, some observers perceived the nuclear weapon as a guaranty of universal peace: any impulse toward war, they said, would be stopped at once by an admonitory shake of an American President's index finger. Others saw the new weapons as harbingers of doom. They found it inconceivable that governments might refrain indefinitely from using nuclear weapons, especially if they were close to losing a war. And they thought it self-evident that any use of nuclear weapons, however "small" and "clean," would soon escalate to general nuclear exchanges, which in turn would destroy civilization, and perhaps end all life on the planet. A small minority among the early students of the nuclear problem concluded that the new weapons were too destructive to be employed in war, and would become "flying pyramids"—spectacular technical achievements of no practical use, especially in war.

Nearly fifty years of experience with the nuclear weapon have destroyed these early theories, except perhaps the third. The nuclear

The epigraph for this chapter is taken from Herbert S. Dinerstein, *The Making of a Missile Crisis, October 1962* (Baltimore: Johns Hopkins University Press, 1976), 156.

weapon has indeed brought about profound changes in world politics since 1945, and it will almost certainly continue to do so. It has not, however, turned out to be a magic wand banishing war from the realm of human experience. Eighty wars took place during the period 1945–89, causing between fifteen and thirty million deaths; millions more were wounded and other millions forced to become refugees.[1] On the other hand, the nuclear weapon has not been fired in war since Hiroshima and Nagasaki; moreover, there have been no substantial conventional force hostilities between nuclear powers. And the early optimism about the utility of peaceful nuclear explosions has vanished. Nonetheless, the shadow of the nuclear weapon has become an inescapable factor in many situations of political and conventional-force conflict; in some of those instances, it has been a crucial factor.

The Soviet nuclear weapons program began in the late 1920s, when Peter Kapitza, then a brilliant young physicist, was sent to Cambridge to do research on atomic physics under Lord Rutherford at the Cavendish Laboratory, at that time the leading center for such studies in the world. In 1933, the Kremlin decided that Kapitza had mastered the secrets of the Cavendish, and he was denied permission to return to his post at Cambridge after a summer holiday in the Soviet Union. Some of the leading figures in British science wrote a letter of protest to the *Times* in his behalf, but Stalin was not moved.

The cut and thrust of the Cold War since 1945 and the problems of international conflict outside its boundaries test the competing hypotheses about the role of nuclear weapons in the conduct of foreign relations. The Soviet moves and American countermoves appear to have been governed by tacit rules of engagement in a limited war both sides wished to keep from going too far. The Cuban missile crisis of 1962 is perhaps the clearest and certainly the most fully documented example of a serious conflict in which the nuclear element was both visible and decisive. But the other engagements of the Cold War occurred in precisely the same framework, and were in fact dominated by the same fears and uncertainties.

II

The first Soviet experiment in expansion after the Second World War took place in Iran. British, American, and Soviet troops had been

1. Patrick Brogan, *The Fighting Never Stopped: A Comprehensive Guide to World Conflicts since 1945* (first American edition, New York: Vintage, 1990).

stationed in Iran to assure the overland flow of supplies to the Soviet Union. The three powers had promised Iran and each other that their troops would evacuate the country within six months after the end of hostilities. The British and American troops were withdrawn, but the Soviet troops remained. Their presence kept Iranian forces out of the Iranian province of Azerbaijan. When Iran protested, the Soviet government proposed that Azerbaijan become autonomous, and that a joint Soviet-Iranian oil company be formed to exploit its petroleum resources, with the Soviet Union holding 51 percent of the stock. Britain and the United States protested strongly, and filed the first complaint on the Security Council's calendar early in 1946. The issue was debated vehemently, and the United States secretly threatened unspecified counteraction unless the Soviet Union complied with the earlier agreement and withdrew its forces. Manifestly, the Security Council could not impose an outcome in the face of a Soviet veto, and Britain and the United States were hardly disposed to go to war with the Soviet Union over that issue, but the Council pressed for a solution by negotiation until the withdrawal of Soviet troops was confirmed.

Dean Rusk doubts that American nuclear power played any part in the Soviet decision to withdraw its forces from Iran, on the ground that Stalin must have known through his intelligence services that at the moment the United States did not have any nuclear weapons in inventory.[2] Whether or not the KGB knew that the American nuclear cupboard was bare, Stalin decided that Azerbaijan was not worth a conventional force confrontation with the United States, and certainly not a possible nuclear force confrontation. At that moment, immediately after the crushing experiences of the thirties and early forties, the Soviet Union was in no position for major military adventures. Stalin retreated when he was satisfied that Truman was not bluffing about countermeasures.

Stalin's decision to stand down brings out a striking feature of the tacit rules of engagement during the early Cold War confrontations: the realization, held by both the United States and the Soviet Union, that direct armed conflict between the two Cold War adversaries was exceedingly dangerous because it could escalate. Each skirmish implicated each side's total arsenal and potential, and the nuclear balance became one of the limiting factors which had to be confronted in every episode that approached the point of direct conflict. At that early date,

---

2. Dean Rusk, with Richard Rusk and Daniel S. Papp, *As I Saw It* (New York: W. W. Norton, 1990), 126.

Stalin decided to treat his move into Iran as an experiment, a feint to be given up when it was resisted. Azerbaijan remained part of Iran, the joint oil company was not formed, and Iranian troops again were stationed in Azerbaijan.

Immediately after the complaint against the Soviet Union was filed in January 1946, the Soviet Union presented the Security Council with two complaints against Britain, which had sent troops to help the Greek government deal with a Communist insurgency, and was helping the newly proclaimed Indonesian government against a variety of threats to public order, including a Communist challenge to its authority.

These moves were obviously tactical responses in part to the uproar over Soviet activities in Azerbaijan, but in Greece especially they had a long subsequent history. While the Soviet government questioned the legality of the British military aid to the Greek government, it was itself, violating international law by sending arms and guerrilla forces to participate in what became a major Communist effort to seize power.

Since Stalin had agreed to regard Greece as within the Western sphere of influence, and since Greece was a strategic position of great importance to the security of the Mediterranean, Britain and the United States reacted to the Soviet move as a fundamental threat to the possibility of peaceful coexistence. First a Security Council commission of investigation, and then two General Assembly committees, confirmed that Soviet intervention in Greece was taking place on an increasing scale from Albania, Bulgaria, and Yugoslavia. The Soviet Union blocked action in the Security Council. The affair did not end until 1948 or 1949, after Yugoslavia under Tito broke away from the Soviet Union and ceased to participate in the attack on Greece. Britain and the United States helped the Greek government defeat the Communist forces within Greece.

For the next twenty-five years or so—roughly the period in which the Soviet Union approached and then exceeded nuclear parity with the United States—the Cold War was a series of variations on the themes of the Greek and Iranian crises of the late 1940s: a Soviet thrust, apparently for limited gains; a Western diplomatic or conventional force response; and, if the Western resistance was determined, an eventual Soviet acceptance of the status quo ante. Using its own forces or those of a proxy state, the Soviet Union pursued what was more and more clearly a course of piecemeal expansion, seeking to take advantage of opportunities as they appeared, or helping to generate such opportunities by promoting Communist or Popular Front rebellions.

In the beginning, the Soviet moves were attempts to enlarge the military borders of the Soviet empire, as was the case in Czechoslovakia, Iran, Greece, Berlin, and Korea, for example. When Western resistance developed, the Soviet reaction was to flow around the obstacle, or to resume its drive elsewhere. Later, as their imperial program gained momentum, and their naval, air, and nuclear forces expanded, the Soviets chose more remote targets in Africa, the Far East, and Latin America. From the beginning, the process of Soviet expansion was not a random exercise in giantism but one guided by a clear-cut strategic goal: to gain control of Europe as a whole, and therefore of China and Japan as well, and thus decisively to change the balance of world power, isolating the United States.

As these Soviet efforts were dealt with, one by one, the situation which resulted was never in fact quite the same as the status quo ante. The Western reaction was not limited entirely to the area of the attack. True, it was soon evident that Secretary of State John Foster Dulles' declaratory policy of "massive retaliation" was stillborn. In the opening stages of each of these confrontations, the United States did not seriously consider a nuclear strike against Moscow as an appropriate way to deal with a Soviet attempt to seize a minor fort along the exceptionally sensitive frontier between the two political systems. But policy changed dramatically as the West became more and more conscious of the Soviet Union's continuous expansion through relatively small increments. The Truman Doctrine was announced in 1947, the Vandenberg Resolution, announcing the United States policy of defending Western Europe and other vital interests, was adopted in 1948, and the North Atlantic Alliance was formed in 1949. The North Korean invasion of South Korea in 1950 led to the massive rearmament of the United States and the other NATO allies and then to the rearmament of West Germany in the setting of NATO. A number of other regional security treaties and other security arrangements followed, until the United States security system formed a wide arc around the Soviet Union, contiguous to it in some areas, and at some distance from it in others. The case of China was the exception which proved the rule. The Communist revolution in China and the short-lived and uneasy Sino-Soviet alliance which followed it were understood at once as a major and most threatening development.

As American security arrangements took shape in response to the first violent push of Soviet expansion in the late forties, Soviet planners gave up any further moves directly against Western Europe and Japan, which they recognized as areas whose territorial integrity and political independence the United States considered vital to its security. Control over Western Europe, China, and Japan, however, remained the central strategic goal of Soviet foreign policy. American nuclear superiority and the American network of security agreements required the Soviet Union to pursue this objective by outflanking tactics and other indirect means. In the course of this offensive against the West, certain features of the rules of engagement for the safe conduct of the Cold War became more clearly established. Avoiding direct conflict between Soviet and American military forces remained the first rule. Thus Soviet submarines did not sink Allied ships bringing supplies to Korea or Vietnam, nor did Soviet planes shoot down the American, British, and French planes conducting the Berlin airlift.

At first, the Western powers thought that Stalin, Churchill, and Roosevelt had also established an understanding that after the war each side would respect the other's "sphere of influence." But while the Western nations refrained from sending arms or guerrillas into Eastern Europe, the Soviet Union tried to gain control of Greece in 1946, threatened Turkey as well as Iran, took over Czechoslovakia in 1948, and then blockaded Berlin. Within a few years or so, it similarly achieved dominion in Cuba and assaulted South Korea and South Vietnam—areas, its opponents thought, which were clearly in the Western sphere for reasons of geography and security. The Western Allies never challenged Soviet rule in its East European satellites, however, even when Soviet troops invaded Czechoslovakia, East Germany, and Hungary, although they never formally accepted the idea of a Soviet sphere of influence as a legal or a political principle. Instead, they insisted in each such case that the norms of the United Nations Charter applied to all countries alike, but did nothing to enforce the rule in Eastern Europe. The Soviet Union, on the other hand, attacked vulnerable targets on both sides of the supposed line with equal zest.

During the long years of debating the justification for the policy of "containing" Soviet expansion, the Western governments had to endure a great deal of criticism from well-intentioned citizens who berated them for not realizing that the Soviet Union may well have perceived things differently and were genuinely fearful of an American attack. Since 1985, when Gorbachev took power in the Soviet Union, there has therefore been some ironic satisfaction for Western policy makers in reading Russian books, articles, and speeches justifying the Western policies of containment, and sometimes criticizing the American government for not objecting more strenuously to the Soviet suppression of revolt in Poland, Hungary, and Czechoslovakia. And there is even more tangible confirmation of the Western analysis of Soviet policy in former foreign minister Eduard Shevardnadze's statement in 1990 that "until quite recently our aim was to oust the Americans from Europe at any price."[3]

The conduct of the Cold War had another element of asymmetry: the two principal actors were differently endowed with cynicism. The Soviet Union did not even pretend to respect the professed norms of international law, whereas the United States found it extremely difficult to violate them. Sometimes Soviet diplomats perfunctorily attempted to justify aggressive actions in the name of the principle of self-defense, or of a new "right" to use force internationally in order to help achieve the self-determination of peoples or the victory of socialism, or even to prevent the defection of a Socialist country from the Soviet realm.

A fourth characteristic of Cold War rules of engagement which emerged from this experience concerned the nuclear weapon itself. In all the early skirmishes and battles of the Cold War, the Soviet Union was on the offensive against the United States despite the fact that it had no nuclear weapons, or, a little later, that it had many fewer nuclear weapons than the United States. The Soviet Union planned and carried out its aggressive moves on the assumption that the United States considered nuclear weapons to be so different from even the most destructive conventional weapons that it would not actually use them except in the most exceptional circumstances. This assumption was justified by the pattern of American behavior in the cycle of early Cold War crises. The Soviets could not take it for granted, however; while it was reliable up to a point, they knew it could not be regarded as fixed. They realized that despite the inhibitions and anxieties of the Americans toward nuclear weapons, their unwillingness to contemplate the possible use of those weapons was not absolute.

Nuclear weapons had been used, after all, to terminate Japanese resistance in 1945. And under certain circumstances, Americans might be so angry and so frustrated that the nuclear taboo could be overcome again. American nuclear warnings were therefore to be taken seriously and evaluated with care. The Soviet Union could never safely ignore the American nuclear arsenal in planning its campaigns of expansion. As a campaign became a crisis, however, both parties had to consider the situation anew. Were the Americans so beset as to make a nuclear

---

3. Shevardnadze quoted from *Izvestiia,* 20 February 1990; translated and reprinted in John Van Oudenarem, "Gorbachev and His Predecessors: Two Faces of New Thinking," in *New Thinking and Old Realities: America, Europe, and Russia,* ed. Michael T. Clark and Simon Serfaty (Washington, D.C.: Seven Locks Press, in association with Johns Hopkins Foreign Policy Institute, 1991), 7.

response credible? Were the Soviets in a position to face down a nuclear ultimatum, given the state of the Soviet-American nuclear balance? The dilemma thus had two horns—a seemingly mathematical and pseudo-rational analysis of the nuclear balance, on the one hand, leading to a calculation of whether either side had the capacity to improve its nuclear position by a first strike, that is, to destroy more of its adversary's weapons than the losses it would incur; and second, a psychological judgment about whether the other side was angry enough actually to consider firing the nuclear weapon. Manifestly, the second criterion for judgment is hopelessly subjective, and the first not much better.

Two episodes throw light on the nature of the problem. In January 1968, one of the gloomiest periods of the Vietnam War for the United States, the North Koreans seized the U.S.S. *Pueblo* off the coast of North Korea, held the vessel, and imprisoned the officers and crew. The *Pueblo* was an electronic surveillance vessel. Months of bootless negotiation led nowhere, although it was known in the West that the ship was captured on the high seas, in open violation of international law.[4]

Sitting alone with Anatoly F. Dobrynin, the Soviet ambassador at the time, Secretary of State Rusk took up the fate of the *Pueblo* after a long and strenuous conversation about a number of touchy, difficult, and sensitive issues. "Tell your friends in North Korea," he said, "that we have enough on our plate. If they don't release those men, we will respond with maximum violence." Within a day or two, talks were arranged and the affair was settled. Rusk's threat was credible under the circumstances, and the Soviets took no chances with it. North Korea's behavior had been degrading and outrageous. Our nuclear position was surely strong enough to sustain a threat to North Korea, and to deter any Soviet response. And we did have enough on our plate. The Russians knew Rusk well as a highly skilled diplomatist and a disciplined, prudent secretary of state. His rage was unmistakable. They took it seriously.

The Korean War hostilities were brought to the conference table in 1951 by a comparable nuclear threat. Structurally, legally, and politically the Korean War was like the Soviet intervention in Greece a few years before, but on a much larger scale. It was started with a full-scale military invasion rather than with the infiltration of guerrillas; this factual difference is legally immaterial, however.

The Soviet Union, checked in Europe by their defeats in Greece

4. Rusk, *As I Saw It*, 393.

and Berlin and by the formation of NATO, had begun to give priority to its campaigns in Asia. According to the book which purports to be Khrushchev's autobiography, Stalin approved the North Korean plans for the invasion in advance.[5]

At the end of the Second World War, Korea had been divided into two zones of occupation, a northern zone occupied by the Soviet Union, and a southern zone occupied by the United States. The Soviet government promptly installed a Communist government in the north, and the United States encouraged the formation of the Republic of Korea in the southern zone. The United Nations Commission on the Reunification of Korea had been functioning in the south since its formation, although the North Korean government refused to receive it or to discuss with its members either the holding of an election or the possibility of reunification. Thus by chance—again as in Greece—one of its own official bodies was able to supply the United Nations with authoritative information about the South Korean elections and the subsequent formation of a government, which the commission called "the only legitimate government in Korea." It also supplied direct information about the North Korean invasion of South Korea on 24 June 1950.

The news of the invasion shocked the world. A political accident gave the Security Council a free field to act. The Soviet Union and its satellites were at that time boycotting all organs of the United Nations in which the government in Taiwan occupied the Chinese seat. The purpose of the boycott was to protest the fact that Communist China had been denied U.N. membership. The result was that the Soviet representative was absent when the Security Council took up the case on 25 June 1950.

Less than five years after the end of the Second World War, Western opinion was strongly Wilsonian. It was an article of faith that the tragedy of the Second World War could have been prevented if the Western powers had acted to defeat Japanese aggression in Manchuria in 1931 and to halt Italian aggression in Ethiopia in 1936. The result was a worldwide outpouring of support for Truman's decision both to assist South Korea's resistance to the invasion, and to protect Taiwan and the Philippines against its possible consequences.

From the beginning, the Korean War was a limited war. The forces assisting the South Korean defense were defeated in their attempt to

5. Nikita Khrushchev, *Khrushchev Remembers,* ed. and trans. Strobe Talbott (Boston: Little Brown, 1970), 368–70.

unify Korea and subsequently hostilities were confined to eliminating the consequences of the North Korean aggression. After the first few anxious days, the United States concluded that the Soviet Union had no intention of starting the Third World War. The Korean War was bitterly fought, and fought on a large scale, but fought within limits. The Chinese entered the war openly in November 1950, and from that time until General Ridgway took command in 1951, American and Allied fortunes fluctuated dramatically. By the late spring of 1951, however, the Allied military position was stabilized and much improved.

The Allied armies were straddling the 38th parallel—the demarcation line from which the war began—and would shortly be well across it. The United States started to explore the possibility of an armistice which would restore a situation close to the status quo ante, and it sought to do so through the Soviet Union rather than the United Nations or mediation by third nations. Finally, an exploratory conversation was arranged between George Kennan, then a private citizen, and Jacob Malik, the Soviet representative to the United Nations, at Malik's summer house in Long Island. Kennan gave Malik this message, as Acheson summarizes it in his memoir:

> Our two countries seemed to be headed for what could be a most dangerous collision over Korea. This was definitely not the purpose of American actions or policy. It was hard for us to believe that it was desired by the Soviet Union. Whether or not it was desired by Peking, it seemed the inevitable result of the course the Chinese were steering. If the drift to serious trouble was to be stopped, the method would seem to be an armistice and cease-fire in Korea at about where the forces were. We would like to know how Moscow viewed the situation, and what, if any, suggestions it might have. We also wished to be sure that it understood our desires and intentions. If hostilities were to end, it was a good time to set about ending them.[6]

The negotiations at Panmunjom followed soon afterwards, and have continued ever since.

The Suez crisis of 1956–57 also included a nuclear warning, but this time in the other direction. The warning was not given secretly by the United States to stop an act of Soviet-inspired aggression and expan-

---

6. Dean Acheson, *Present at the Creation: My Years in the State Department* (New York: W. W. Norton, 1969), 532.

sion. On the contrary, it was issued loudly and publicly by the Soviet Union, ostensibly to force Great Britain, France, and Israel to give up their effort to undo Nasser's seizure of the Suez Canal; to reopen the canal to the world's shipping; and, they hoped, to dethrone Nasser as well. It is immaterial that the Soviet nuclear warning was a fraud, in that it was made well after Great Britain, France, and Israel had accepted the ceasefire proposed by the Security Council and Britain and France had agreed to withdraw. It was a move of great significance, nonetheless, as evidence of what the pre-Gorbachev Soviet leadership hoped and expected their nuclear weapons to accomplish. At the time, American nuclear forces were far larger than those of the Soviet Union, and growing more rapidly. The Soviet Union did not begin to outstrip the American rate of growth until the mid-sixties. Nonetheless, the Soviet Union broadcast the claim that it had protected the Suez Canal against "the imperialist powers" by rattling its nuclear weapons. In many parts of the world, its claim was believed.

In 1973, Egypt attacked Israel with strong and large-scale Soviet support, including the help of a considerable number of Soviet officers. When, after two weeks, the tide of battle shifted in favor of the Israelis, the Soviet Union actually moved nuclear weapons to Egypt in ships, and prepared several airborne divisions for action in the Sinai. President Nixon put the American strategic nuclear forces on alert, the Israelis crossed the Suez Canal, and the Soviets backed down. They urgently sought a ceasefire, and pressed the Arab governments to accept Security Council Resolution 338, which ordered them—at American insistence—to make peace with Israel. The Soviet experiment in nuclear blackmail was not trumpeted from the housetops by the United States. Neither was it denied.

Similarly, during the early 1970s, the Soviet Union sounded out the United States government and a number of American private citizens about the position the United States would take if the Soviet Union attacked the Chinese nuclear plants. President Nixon responded to the question by secretly warning the Soviet Union not to do it. His warning was respected; the Soviets did nothing. Nixon's action was probably his most important foreign policy achievement.

III

The Cuban Missile crisis of 1962 evolved from a complex and dramatic series of revolutionary events in Guatemala and Cuba. The United States had intervened in Guatemala in 1954 to displace an allegedly Communist or near-Communist regime. Fidel Castro came to power in 1959 as the result of an apparently native revolution. The United States had withdrawn its support from his predecessor, Fulgencio Batista. A controversy persists as to whether Castro and his brother Raúl were Communists at the time they seized power. For several years Fidel Castro denied that he was a Communist, and his relations with the Cuban Communist Party were not intimate; finally, however, in 1961, he became an avowed Communist. In all probability, both Fidel and Raúl were Communists from the beginning, although Fidel Castro does not seem to have been a Party member before 1961 or 1962.

After a period of flirtation with the United States, Castro settled firmly for close association with the Soviet Union. His colleagues and rivals began to warn of the danger of American intervention: to boast that Cuba was not Guatemala, but would fight, and that Cuba would be protected by the Soviet Union and its missiles. Khrushchev joined the chorus. It was the period of Soviet optimism about soon outstripping (and then burying) the United States. Sputnik had been launched in 1957, precipitating a storm of self-reproach in the United States, and something like panic as well. Khrushchev never stopped boasting that Soviet nuclear warnings had stopped Britain and France in Egypt in 1956 and the United States in the Taiwan Straits in 1958.

While Khrushchev's nuclear exuberance was inflammatory and caused concern, he was more cautious in his practical dealings with the West. He sought economic reforms, allowed Solzhenitsyn and some other critics to be published, and preached détente with the United States. From time to time, however, he also mentioned a Soviet commitment to defend Cuba against another Bay of Pigs attempt, and talked darkly of the horrors of nuclear warfare. He kept the facts about the Soviet arsenal extremely secret, so that few in the West realized how exaggerated his claims of nuclear parity or superiority were. And he made such claims often, although he frequently said as well that nuclear war was unthinkably dangerous and that the nuclear weapon did not respect the difference between Socialism and Capitalism. It was a time when pessimism and even alarm were common in the West, and there was a sense that the Soviet Union was winning the race both economically and militarily. It was widely believed that the world balance of forces was shifting in favor of the Soviets. That fact, Khrushchev said, would determine the future of world politics.

Kennedy met Khrushchev for the first time in Vienna shortly after the Bay of Pigs fiasco and the U.S. retreat in the Soviet-American maneuvers over Vietnam and Laos. Khrushchev gave the new young

American President a psychological beating, refusing any compromises, and pressing him hard on Berlin, as well as on Cuba and Vietnam. By this time, threats that Soviet missiles would fly if the United States intervened again in Cuba had become almost routine. So had reports that the Soviet Union was planning or preparing a missile site in Cuba. In the Soviet press and the press in Latin America Communists and other spokesmen of the Left argued that because the balance of military power—especially of nuclear weapons—favored the Soviet Union, even small countries in the Third World were now shielded against the United States. The last vestiges of imperialism would soon disappear, and the revolution would triumph everywhere. Those claims seemed to be confirmed by the experience of the previous decade, which included the victory of Nasser in the Suez crisis of 1956, the defeat of France in IndoChina and its imminent defeat in Algeria, the success of the Soviet Union in suppressing rebellions in East Germany and Hungary, and the ignominious failure of the Bay of Pigs invasion, which the Soviet Union claimed had been due to Khrushchev's flat warning to Kennedy that the Soviet government "will give the Cuban people and their government every assistance necessary to repulse the armed attack on Cuba."[7]

Most students of the Bay of Pigs episode conclude that when Khrushchev's warning letter arrived Kennedy had already decided not to use American troops or air power in support of the Cuban émigré force which had landed at the Bay of Pigs. But outside the United States and some NATO capitals, Kennedy's explanation of his decision did not carry much conviction, and even at home and among our allies it left many doubts. The political fact was that the United States had bowed to a Soviet nuclear threat and forgotten the Monroe Doctrine for good measure. During the same period, in the long-drawn-out contest for Laos, Kennedy yielded again to an implied Soviet threat by agreeing to an international conference despite the Soviets' continued airlift of military supplies to the area.

It was a time of foreboding in the West. Perhaps the prophets of doom were right after all. On 28 July 1961, Castro announced that his revolution in Cuba "had chosen the Socialist path," and a few months later, on 1 December 1961, made it known that he was a Communist. His ideas, he explained, were much the same as they had been when he launched his revolution in 1953, but for some years he had concealed the full extent of his radicalism for reasons of political prudence. Now that worldwide revolutionary Communism was on the march, those

7. Khrushchev quoted in Dinerstein, *Making of a Missile Crisis,* 130.

reasons no long applied; the Cuban leader came out of the closet. In Herbert Dinerstein's wry words, Castro "was not storming an enemy position but a Soviet leadership desperate to revive the myth of world revolution by accepting this exotic revolutionary into its arms. And like many aging lovers seeking to find youth in the arms of a young admirer, money had to substitute for ardor."[8]

Castro thus became a Communist by absorbing and dominating the Communist Party of Cuba, rather than by joining it. This in itself was a heretical deviation from Leninist methods. At almost the same moment, the Soviet Union began to send much larger shipments of arms to Cuba, and Cuba stepped up its involvement in revolutionary movements all over Latin American. In July 1962, Castro made an important speech in which he talked for the first time of "a new element" that was being added to Cuba's defenses, an element that would permit Cuba "to inflict millions of casualties on the United States," and thus remove the last danger hanging over the Cuban revolution. He boasted that "direct imperialist attack would be shattered against our defenses." Dinerstein concludes that Castro was talking about deterring an attack from the United States because missiles with nuclear warheads would be on Cuban soil. In Dinerstein's view, Castro was confident that the Soviet missiles made it unnecessary to "think about retaliation."[9]

Rumors about renewed plans for an invasion of Cuba by Cuban exiles, on the one hand, and about the creation of a Soviet nuclear missile base in Cuba, on the other, began to gain currency. By the end of August 1962, eyewitnesses reported the arrival of mysterious Soviet crates and of Soviet and East European military men in Cuba. Reassuring comments from the State Department did put an end to the storm that followed. Leaks of fresh intelligence to the Senate about Soviet military activities in Cuba raised temperatures appreciably.

On 29 August, aerial photography confirmed the presence of eight SAM-2 sites in Cuba, SAMS being ground-to-air missiles used for air defense. On 4 September, Kennedy informed the nation of this discovery. We had not yet found evidence in Cuba, he said, of organized Soviet combat units or of offensive ground-to-ground missiles or other offensive capability under either Cuban or Soviet control. "Were it to be otherwise, the gravest issues would arise," the President announced, both in the worldwide context of the Soviet assault on the West, and in the more limited setting of the inter-American system. "If Cuba

8. Ibid., 149.
9. Castro's speech of 26 July 1962 is quoted and analyzed in ibid., 175–79.

should ever attempt to export its aggressive purposes by force or the threat of force against any nation in this hemisphere . . . this country will do whatever must be done."[10]

In a dramatic televised address on 22 October President Kennedy announced that the Soviets were deploying not antiaircraft missiles, but intermediate-range ground-to-ground ballistic missiles capable of reaching targets in the southeastern United States and were building bases at which they could deploy missiles capable of reaching all the cities of the United States, the Panama Canal, and most of the cities of South America. The Soviet statements that the military equipment being sent to Cuba was solely defensive were therefore false. Kennedy demanded that all further military shipments to Cuba be stopped and that all the existing missiles be dismantled and withdrawn. To stop the flow of arms to Cuba, he ordered the U.S. Navy to "quarantine" the island. To describe its action, the American government used the word *quarantine* rather than the legal term *blockade*. A nuclear attack against any nation in the Western Hemisphere, he added, would be regarded as an attack on the United States.[11]

Thus the focal point of the Cuban missile crisis of 1962—eighteen months after the Bay of Pigs affair—was a secret Soviet plan to deploy intermediate-range ground-to-ground nuclear weapons on Cuban soil. The United States had announced publicly that it would not tolerate the Soviet emplacement of "offensive" weapons in Cuba. Both publicly and through diplomatic channels, the Soviet Union had denied that it was preparing to make such a deployment. But it was doing so. With the political support of the Organization of American States (O.A.S.) and of its NATO allies, the United States assembled an expeditionary force of 250,000 troops in Florida, established a partial blockade of Cuba, and intercepted a Soviet vessel approaching the island with a load of missiles. After several rounds of hectic diplomatic exchanges, agreement was reached and the missiles were withdrawn, although Castro remained in power.

IV

Several legal questions were involved in the Cuban missile crisis. There was no armed attack on the United States and no threat of armed

10. News conferences of 29 August and 13 September 1962, *Public Papers of the Presidents: John F. Kennedy* (Washington, D.C.; GPO, 1963) 2:653, 674.
11. "Radio and Television Report to the American People on the Soviet Arms Buildup in Cuba," 22 October 1962, *Public Papers of the Presidents: John F. Kennedy,* 2: 806–09.

attack, imminent or otherwise. The nuclear balance in 1962 was so favorable to the United States that a direct Soviet nuclear attack was inconceivable. What is more, Cuba had a legal right to request Soviet assistance in defending itself against possible attack—a concern which had a certain plausibility in the aftermath of the Bay of Pigs affair. Yet the world overwhelmingly agreed with President Kennedy that the sudden, secret, and deceptive change in the Soviet-American nuclear balance, against the background of aggressive Soviet moves in Europe and in Asia, was in itself a substantial political-military threat and an illegal act of force justifying a legally appropriate American response—that is, a limited and proportional use of enough force to eliminate the Soviet breach of international law, which President Kennedy characterized as a "threat to the peace."[12]

Although President Kennedy spoke of the United States action as one of self-defense, his State Department, in presenting the case to the Security Council, the o.a.s. and the public sought to justify the American use of force in Cuba primarily under the Rio Treaty of 1947 and the action of the Organization of American States pursuant to that treaty. This legal argument is untenable. Under Article 53 of the U.N. Charter, no regional organization can authorize the use of force without the prior permission of the Security Council. No other rule is possible within the system established by the Charter, which confers primary responsibility for peacekeeping on the member states, through the exercise of their "inherent right of individual or collective self-defense" until the Security Council has effectively exercised its ultimate responsibility for peacekeeping by taking "measures necessary to maintain international peace and security."[13] The interrelationship of these complex ideas is delineated in Article 51. No regional organization can go beyond the rules of the Charter. Regional organizations cannot reduce or enlarge the states' inherent right of self-defense, any more than the Security Council itself can.

The only possible legal basis for the action taken by the United States in the Cuban missile crisis was therefore its "inherent" right of self-defense under customary international law, reaffirmed by Article 51 of the Charter. When the o.a.s. passed resolutions approving the American use and threat of force in the crisis, it was simply endorsing the American decision to use force in self-defense. Article 51 recognizes

---

12. Ibid., 806.
13. U.N. Charter, Article 51; and E. V. Rostow, "Until What? Enforcement Action or Collective Self-Defense?" *American Journal of International Law* 85, no. 3 (July, 1991).

the absolute right of every state to use force in self-defense—and to help other states in their efforts at self- defense—without the prior permission of the Security Council.

Another pertinent aspect of the law of self-defense should be noted. The language of Article 51 shows an unusual number of infelicities, even for a compromise document drafted and redrafted under conditions of diplomatic stress. For example, Article 51 seems to authorize the use of force in self-defense only in behalf of United Nations members, and only after an armed attack has actually occurred. The efforts of the Security Council and the General Assembly to defeat the North Korean attack on South Korea in 1950 make it clear that Article 2(4) is not confined only to member states: breaches of the peace and acts of aggression against nonmember states can affect the general peace. And a number of other cases which have arisen under the Charter confirm, as the Cuban missile episode does, that Article 51 should be read against the background of preexisting international law, which justifies the use of force in self-defense not only when an armed attack has already occurred, but also when a serious and forceful attack on the political independence or territorial integrity of a state is perceived—by that state—to be imminent. As Elihu Root once wrote, under international law every state has the right "to protect itself by preventing a condition of affairs in which it will be too late to protect itself."[14]

With the gloss of experience, then, and especially the experience of the Cuban missile crisis, the right of self-defense protected by Article 51 should be deemed to include threat and perceptions of threat as well as the actual occurrence of an armed attack. It includes those exercises of the right of self-defense generally accepted and recognized both by state practice and by courts, arbitral bodies, and publicists during the nineteenth and twentieth centuries. If, however, the Security Council does not or cannot exercise its "primary responsibility" for peace, the member states are entitled to take whatever actions they consider reasonably necessary to protect their security. If the Security Council decides by a majority including all five permanent members that the actions of the countries purporting to act in self-defense have gone beyond that limit, it may stop the hostilities as a breach of the peace. During the Cuban missile crisis, of course, the Security Council could

14. Elihu Root, "The Real Monroe Doctrine," *American Journal of Int. Law* 35 (1914): 427.

not be used as more than a convenient diplomatic forum, because both the United States and the Soviet Union have the power of veto.

In the history of the United Nations Charter, the decisions taken by the world community during the Cuban missile crisis embody and derive from the most extreme construction thus far of a state's inherent right of self-defense. The United States made no claim that an armed attack against it had occurred, or was imminent. Given American nuclear superiority at the time, it was clear that neither a nuclear nor a conventional-force threat by the Soviet Union to the United States was plausible. The American government did take the position that under the circumstances the secret emplacement of the missiles in Cuba was a substantial political-military threat to which the United States was entitled to respond through the use of force if necessary.

If the world accepted what Kennedy did during the missile crisis as legal—and it did—and if it therefore perceived what the Soviet Union did as illegal—and it did—then international law thereby acknowledged the altogether exceptional and sensitive character of everything to do with nuclear weapons. By the previously prevailing standards of international law, Cuba was entitled to ask the Soviet Union to deploy forces on Cuban soil to assist Cuba to defend itself against threats to its security as Cuba and the Soviet Union perceived them. That is the legal principle justifying the presence of NATO forces in Europe: a presence which includes nuclear as well as conventional weapons. And neither secrecy about military activities nor lying are such aggressive actions as to constitute in themselves violations of Article 2 (4) of the United Nations Charter. But something about the conjuncture of events in Cuba, against the background of increasing Cold War tensions in many parts of the world, led international public and governmental opinion to see Khrushchev's move in Cuba as an aggressive act of force rather than a clever diplomatic trick, and to react accordingly.

V

The first and most obvious lesson of the Cuban missile crisis is that conventional force can be used against a nuclear power only if the attacker possesses the manifest capacity—and may have the will—to respond to a nuclear attack with nuclear weapons. In 1962, the United States visibly prepared to invade Cuba with conventional forces. It addressed its diplomacy entirely to the Soviet Union as the primary actor, making it clear that it was planning its invasion of Cuba only to force the withdrawal of the Soviet missiles. Given the state of the nuclear balance between the Soviet Union and the United States, it would have been prohibitively costly for Cuba and the Soviet Union to resist an American conventional force invasion in the face of Kennedy's warning. Argentina invaded the Falklands despite the British nuclear force, gambling correctly on the judgment that Britain would not regard the fate of the Falklands as an issue justifying the use of nuclear weapons. And the insurrection in Afghanistan similarly challenged the Soviet occupation of that country on the basis of the same assumption, whose plausibility was reinforced by the long experience of limited warfare fought by nonnuclear powers against American and occasionally Soviet forces throughout the Third World. The affair of the Soviet missiles in Cuba was different, however. What made it different was that it directly concerned the central problem of the Cold War—the Soviet-American nuclear balance, an interest the United States had to consider vital.

In order to understand why the Soviet Union did what it did in 1962 in Cuba, one should begin with the distinction between the Soviet and American conceptions of nuclear deterrence, at least in the pre-Gorbachev period of the Cold War.

Both for the Soviet Union and the United States, it was clear by 1962 that the nuclear weapon is primarily a political weapon, not an instrument to be fired in war. No one can say that a nuclear war can never occur, even among the industrial powers who have had to think long and hard about the problem, but nuclear war among the present nuclear powers is the least likely of scenarios for the future. Throughout the period before Gorbachev, the Soviet Union and the United States each said it possessed nuclear weapons only to "deter" its rival, that is, to impose on it a psychological condition of paralyzing uncertainty. But each sought to possess deterrent power for quite different ends. For the United States, the goal of deterrence is to prevent conventional as well as nuclear attacks on the nation, its armed forces, and what it defines as its vital interests. For the Soviet Union, on the other hand, the goal of nuclear deterrence was to prevent the United States from defending its vital interests against Soviet attack. Nearly half a century of experience since 1945 has defined the security interests the United States deems vital: the territorial integrity and political independence of Japan, China, Western Europe, and the Middle East, as well as other areas which might become important to the balance of power. In short, for the United States nuclear deterrence is an instrument of defense; for the Soviet Union, it was the ultimate weapon of aggression.

Secretary of Defense Robert S. McNamara once told the American people that the Soviet Union had neither the capacity nor the desire to build beyond the level of nuclear parity. In the pre-Gorbachev period certainly, and perhaps during the Gorbachev period as well, McNamara's prediction was contradicted by events. The Soviet Union kept building and improving its nuclear arsenal far beyond the point of parity, or of simply maintaining a second-strike retaliatory capacity. The Soviet leadership was building a first-strike capacity, designed to paralyze any possible response to a Soviet threat or attack.

In a security environment of constant technological and political change, the goal of American nuclear policy has been to retain an unquestionable capacity to retaliate against the Soviet Union or any future aspirant for dominion in the event of an attack against its most important interests at home or abroad. Such a nuclear retaliatory capacity, we have assumed, would make it unnecessary to use the nuclear weapon. By neutralizing the nuclear force of the would-be hegemon, the United States would be able to use conventional forces at will, as it did in the Cuban missile crisis, without concern about a nuclear response.

American policy in nuclear arms control negotiations has therefore been to attain agreements based on the principle of Soviet-American equality in deterrent retaliatory capacity. Agreements which meet this standard would deny either side the capacity to alter the nuclear balance in its favor by executing a preemptive first strike, but would allow each side to protect its most vital interests by the credible threat of nuclear retaliation. It has been and remains the American and Western view that such agreements would stabilize expectations even in time of crisis and thus reduce the risk of nuclear war.

For a long time, the United States government assumed that Soviet nuclear policy was the same as our own. And even now, many Western students of the problem find it difficult to accept the fact that during the period between 1945 and the accession of Yeltsin, the Soviet notion of nuclear deterrence was entirely different from that of the Western powers. There is even more resistance to the fact that as late as 1991, the Soviet production of nuclear weapons was still going up. And there is still controversy about verifying Soviet compliance with arms control treaties. The Soviet buildup of conventional and nuclear arms and the pattern of Soviet expansion since 1945 is consistent with only one hypothesis, however: that Soviet nuclear policy has been to build a force capable of deterring any American conventional or nuclear response to Soviet aggression against American security interests, and especially to American overseas security interests. To that end, it sought to achieve a nuclear arsenal overwhelmingly superior to that of the United States, especially in ground-based ballistic missiles—the most destructive, accurate, and speedy of nuclear weapons, and the ones least vulnerable to defensive weapons. Correspondingly, their objective in the arms control talks has been to obtain American and Western acquiescence to a Soviet "right" to massive nuclear superiority, especially in ground-based missiles. The Interim Agreement on Offensive Weapons of 1972 recognized and accepted a Soviet advantage in ICBMs. Until at least 1988, the Soviet Union continued to enlarge that differential steadily.

Before Gorbachev, the Soviet arms control negotiators used two simple arguments to justify their quest for this goal: the principle of "equality and equal security," and the insistence on "equal reductions," not "reductions to equal levels." "Equal security" meant that the Soviets could have a quota equal to the sum of the American, British, French, and presumably Chinese and all other nuclear arsenals. This was the rule for British naval expenditures in the halcyon days of "Rule Britannia," and, if the Soviets were ahead, the principle of "Equal reductions" would make disparities greater. In 1981, the United States announced that it would no longer accept the Soviet version in any form. After several years in office, Gorbachev abandoned both the "Rule Britannia" policy and the claim for equal reductions. In the INF talks, he finally agreed to the principle of asymmetrical reductions to equal levels.

Gorbachev's changes in the Soviet negotiating position marked the formal acceptance of the American position that the United States and the Soviet Union should have equal quotas in arms control agreements. This is the basis for the INF Agreement of 1987, dealing with intermediate-range nuclear weapons, and for the draft START agreement, which would deal with weapons carried by delivery systems of intercontinental range.

As these pages are being finally reviewed for publication in 1992, there is great uncertainty throughout the world about the future of policy in the successor states of the Soviet Union. Will Yeltsin prove to be a new Kerensky, a weak governor who will be forced to give way to a new Napoleon, a new Stolypin, a new Stalin, or a new Hitler? Will the former Soviet Union become a society based on successful capitalism, with or without democracy, or will it continue to decline? Clearly, the states of the former Soviet Union are going through a systemic crisis and cannot continue long in their present condition.

Prudence therefore requires the Western nations to take their cue for the future of their security policy from the young Russian diplomat serving in Europe who recently said, "We are not a great power for the moment, but we shall be back."

However the revolutionary changes in Russia and the other successor states of the Soviet Union turn out, the long experience of Soviet-American nuclear rivalry will continue to be of central importance to the political life of the state system. From time to time, would-be aggressors will continue to seek nuclear superiority or its equivalent in order to paralyze successful resistance to their ambitions. And the coalitions which have come together under the American nuclear umbrella will try to retain the possibility of offsetting such threats, so that their security can be assured by conventional means.

The Soviet Union and the United States conducted the Cold War as a limited war, in accordance with certain tacit rules of engagement. On the nuclear side, the state of the nuclear balance between the two states was the crucial issue for forty years. When Gorbachev accepted the principle of deterrent equality between the Soviet and the American nuclear arsenals in the INF Treaty, he was in effect giving up the possibility of further Soviet expansion. Whether the next generation of aspirants for the mantle of Alexander the Great will be as cautious as the Soviet leadership in the face of unacceptable risks remains to be seen. Nuclear deterrence may not deter Saddam Hussein and his ilk, but thus far the state of the Soviet-American nuclear balance, in relationship to the Warsaw Pact–NATO conventional force balance, has been the decisive factor in shaping world politics, and the key issue in attempting to negotiate nuclear arms control agreements.

In 1972, when the SALT I agreements were signed, the United States and the Soviet Union had approximately the same number of warheads on intercontinental ground-based ballistic missiles (ICBMs), and the United States had a comfortable lead in sea-based and airborne forces. The American capacity for nuclear retaliation was beyond question. In 1986, the Soviet Union had a lead of more than 3 to 1 in the number of warheads on deployed ICBMs, and a lead of more than 4 to 1 in the throw-weight of these weapons. By 1990, the Soviet lead in warheads on intercontinental ballistic missiles had fallen to 2.7 to 1, primarily because of the deployment of American MX missiles. In throw-weight the Soviet lead had slightly increased since 1986. Soviet sea-based and airborne nuclear forces made comparable if less spectacular gains. This development occurred during a decade in which shifts in the Soviet-American intercontinental balance raised doubts about the ability of the United States to deter attacks against its security interests most fundamental to the balance of power—the independence of Japan, China, Western Europe, South Korea, and the Middle East.

Why did the Soviet Union build nuclear weapons at such a frantic rate for so long? Any dispassionate study of the arms control negotiations against the background of events suggests that the Soviet Union was trying to build a plausible first-strike capacity not in order to fight a nuclear war but to achieve victory without war: that is, to separate the United States from its allies both in the Atlantic and the Pacific and force it into a posture of neutrality and isolation. Clearly, in the face of a Soviet first-strike capacity which we thought might be used, the United States and the Western nations generally would have been unable to use conventional force in self-defense. That is the most obvious lesson of the Cuban missile crisis.

Henry Kissinger once asked, "What on earth can one do with nuclear superiority?" The answer to his question is now clear. The Soviet Union believed that visible nuclear superiority would be the ultimate sanction behind its program of indefinite expansion achieved by conventional means, proxy forces, terror, and insurrection aided from abroad. If the Soviet nuclear arsenal had a clear-cut first-strike capacity rather than a smaller and more ambiguous retaliatory capacity, the United States would not be able to defend its interests, and the apples would drop into the Soviet lap. De Gaulle, Kissinger, and Nixon confirmed that view of Soviet policy with their remarks to the effect that no great power commits suicide in order to protect an ally.

In this respect, Soviet nuclear strategy echoed the strategy of Germany in building its high-seas fleet before 1914. The German objective was not to fight the Royal Navy but to force Great Britain to remain neutral in the event of war on the continent of Europe. In the view of the Soviet strategists, a clear-cut Soviet first-strike capability would lead the United States to withdraw its forces from Europe, the Mediterranean, and the Far East and adopt a policy of neutrality in the event of an attack on American allies or other American interests.

The Soviet decision to sign the INF treaty is intelligible only in this context. Intermediate-range ground-based nuclear weapons—weapons with a range of between 300 and 3,000 miles—immediately threatened targets in Europe, Asia, and the Middle East at a time when the state of the nuclear balance made the American nuclear guaranty based on intercontinental or sea-based systems less and less credible. They were therefore inherently "decoupling" that is, they tended to "decouple"

America's overseas allies from the United States and thus to erode its alliance system. The INF treaty undertakes to abolish the entire class of intermediate-range nuclear warheads, deployed and undeployed.

Since the Soviet Union had some 2,000 of these weapons deployed in 1987, compared to 350 American weapons of the same range, why were the Soviet leaders willing to make so unequal a bargain? The answer is that all the targets which could have been reached by intermediate-range systems could also be reached by intercontinental weapons. No law of physics requires weapons to be fired to their full trajectory. With new Soviet systems like the SS–24 and SS–25 being deployed rapidly, the Soviets could hope to maintain or even to increase their nuclear pressure on West European, Chinese, and Japanese targets by procuring the removal of American INF weapons systems from Europe. The net effect of the treaty would therefore be decoupling, unless corresponding changes in the START treaty on intercontinental weapons and in the ABM treaty of 1972 on defensive systems could be obtained.

The pressures emanating from the Soviet-American nuclear balance were felt in the politics of all the Western countries. Helmut Schmidt talked about the "subliminal" influence of the nuclear weapon. The prospect of a Soviet capacity to destroy a large part of the American retaliatory force with 25 or 30 percent of their ICBMs alone increased the number and influence of Americans who favored the mirage of isolation and the number of Europeans and Japanese who supported the corresponding mirage of neutrality and accommodation. No one in the West had the slightest desire to discover whether the arcane calculations of a Soviet first-strike capability would prove accurate if put to the test.

The Scowcroft Commission pointed out in 1983 that "the Soviets . . . now probably possess the necessary combination of ICBM numbers, reliability, accuracy, and warhead yield to destroy almost all of the 1,047 U.S. ICBM silos, using only a portion of their own ICBM force." A first-strike capability was implicit in this Soviet posture—its ability to destroy our ICBM force, our planes on the ground, and our submarines in port with 25 percent or 30 percent of its ICBM force. The plain fact is that in the late 1980s the Soviets had the capability to destroy a range of hardened military targets and we did not. This "one-sided strategic condition" in ground-based ballistic missiles, the Scowcroft Commission report said at the time, "casts a shadow over the calculus of Soviet risk-taking at any level of confrontation with the West." We cannot safely permit that imbalance to continue, the commission added; it "must be redressed promptly."[15] No President of the United States should ever be confronted with the choice between nuclear war and the abandonment of vital national security interests. Despite the INF treaty, at least until the general collapse of the Soviet Union in 1991, the nuclear balance did not become more favorable to the United States than it was when the Scowcroft Commission Report was filed.

The experience of the Cuban missile crisis has an important corollary: the problem of extended nuclear deterrence is exactly the same as the problem of deterring attacks on the United States itself. Nuclear stability is not a matter of geography, but of the necessary relationship between the nuclear equation and the capacity of states to use conventional forces. The fact is that in order to use conventional forces in defense of Long Island, Alaska, or Japan, we need exactly the same deterrent nuclear arsenal. In other words, there is no difference between "deterrence" and "extended deterrence"—that is, between defending the American homeland and defending our national security interests overseas. If the Soviet Union or some other expansionist power had overwhelming nuclear superiority, and threatened a landing in the United States, would we fight on the beaches, or would we do what the Soviets did during the Cuban missile crisis in 1962, when President Kennedy called Khrushchev's bluff? We should of course be extremely angry if a seeker for dominion made any such threat against the United States. And we should be even more furious if it underlined the seriousness of its threat by a nuclear demonstration—destroying one of our satellites, or blowing up an American city, for example. We assume that under such circumstances we should certainly do something. But would the President really kill ten million enemy citizens in his rage, knowing that fifty million Americans would be killed an hour later?

Obviously, this fundamental lesson of the missile crisis has not yet been absorbed by American public opinion or by Congress. The inarticulate premise behind the willingness of so many members of Congress to vote for defense cuts is surely the notion that "whatever happens, we have enough to keep them off Long Island, and the rest of the world doesn't really matter after all." The brutal fact, however, is that if we do not have enough to keep "them" out of Tokyo, Paris,

15. Brent Scowcroft, *Report of the President's Commission on Strategic Forces,* April 16, 1983, 6, 16–17. See also McGeorge Bundy, *Danger and Survival: Choices about the Bomb in the First Fifty Years* (New York: Random House, 1988), 556–67; and Raymond L. Garthoff, *Reflections on the Cuban Missile Crisis,* rev. ed. (Washington, D.C., Brookings Institution, 1989).

or Rome, whoever the "them" may be, we don't have enough to keep them off Hawaii either.

If we take the Cuban missile crisis to support these four propositions together: (1) that the nuclear weapon—at least in the hands of a rational government—is primarily political, not military; (2) that the Soviet and American conceptions of deterrence have been and probably still are radically different; (3) that until Gorbachev, at least, the Soviet Union tried to achieve a nuclear first-strike capacity—that is, the capacity to improve its nuclear position by a nuclear exchange—in order to be able to keep the United States from defending its overseas interests with conventional or with nuclear weapons; and (4) that in the nuclear age there is no conceptual difference between deterrence and extended deterrence, that is, between defending the homeland of the United States and its overseas interests, it becomes apparent why Khrushchev decided to deploy some of his intermediate-range missiles in Cuba, and thus change the nuclear equation radically in favor of the Soviet Union.

Khrushchev had a number of short-range tactical objectives in mind: to acquire a big base in Latin America and incidentally to protect Cuba against another Bay of Pigs; to force the United States to abandon Taiwan, and thus gain a point in the rivalry between China and the Soviet Union; to force the United States to settle the Berlin question on Soviet terms; and to break out of the vise of the containment policy. But these were clearly secondary goals, as compared with what was at stake in his nuclear move. Indeed, success for Khrushchev in all these goals depended on his making the United States swallow his deployment of the intermediate-range missiles in Cuba. He no doubt thought that we had implicitly accepted his claims to nuclear superiority during the Bay of Pigs imbroglio in 1961. But he knew that the Soviet Union did not yet have nuclear superiority and therefore collapsed when the United States finally decided to say no.

The deployment of the intermediate-range missiles in Cuba was important to Khrushchev because of the way the Soviet and American nuclear forces had developed. The United States nuclear arsenal had far more airborne and seaborne weapons than that of the Soviet Union: While the Soviets were still well behind the United States in intercontinental ballistic missiles, they were ahead in making and deploying intermediate-range missiles carrying nuclear warheads. These missiles, ancestors of the SS-20's much discussed in connection with the INF treaty, were mainly deployed against targets in Europe and Asia—part of the basic and pervasive Soviet strategy of separating Western Europe and Japan from the United States, and neutralizing Europe, Japan, and the United States. To shift the INF weapons in large numbers to Cuba, from which they could be effective first-strike weapons against targets throughout the United States and much of South and Central America, would have been at least to double the Soviet Union's capacity to hit the United States and therefore radically change the calculus of a first-strike.

Such a move would have affected America's nuclear vulnerability in another way as well: these weapons would have outflanked the American Ballistic Missile Early Warning System and therefore threatened most American cities with little or no warning time. In their brilliant analysis of the crisis, Albert and Roberta Wohlstetter conclude:

> Cuba offered to the Russians the means for a very large and immediate expansion of the forces capable of hitting elements of the American retaliatory force based in the United States. Moreover further large increments were readily available. The effect of such a rapid increase in power on the actual military balance could not be lightly dismissed; and the political uses of even an apparent change seemed evident.[16]

Raymond L. Garthoff, who had been an important member of the American team in handling the crisis, later summed up his analysis in these terms:

> A Soviet first strike without the Cuban missiles *at best* could have destroyed four hundred or five hundred of the total of five thousand war heads in the American strategic nuclear arsenal. With the Cuban missiles, at best they could have destroyed 80 to 85 percent, still leaving something more than five hundred American strategic weapons. If that is the *best* they could have done even after a fully successful first strike, it couldn't have been very comforting to the Soviets. The balance was changed greatly by the Cuban missiles, but the end result was still the same. The United States in either case had a considerable nuclear advantage.[17]

16. Albert and Roberta Wohlstetter, *Controlling the Risks in Cuba,* Adelphi Papers, no. 17 (London: Institute for Strategic Studies, 1965), 12.

17. Quoted in James G. Blight and David A. Welch, *On The Brink: Americans and Soviets Reexamine the Cuban Missile Crisis* (New York: Hill and Wang, 1989), 32. See also Bundy, *Danger and Survival,* 445–53; Garthoff, *Reflections on the Cuban Missile Crisis;* idem, *Intelligence Assessment and Policymaking: A Decision Point in the Kennedy Administration.* (Washington, D.C.: Brookings Institution, 1984), 32–33; and Richard K. Betts, *Nuclear Blackmail and Nuclear Balance* (Washington, D.C.: Brookings Institution, 1987).

At an earlier point Garthoff had estimated that the Soviet deployments in Cuba, if completed, "would have increased the Soviet first-strike missile salvo by about eighty per cent."[18]

The effect on American security of a major Soviet military base in Cuba went far beyond the issue of nuclear stability. It would have transformed the Soviet role in the politics of South America and facilitated Soviet intervention throughout the hemisphere. It is hardly remarkable, then, that the first reaction of the American government to the missile crisis was to revive its efforts to bring the nuclear weapon under international control. The realization that the possibility of world order depended in the end on tense and subjective estimates of who was bluffing in the midst of a tumultuous crisis and who was sufficiantly enraged to consider pushing the nuclear button, made peace unbearably precarious. The United States returned to the efforts initiated by its proposal of the Baruch Plan in 1946 with a new sense of urgency.

18. Garthoff, *Reflections on the Cuban Missile Crisis,* 146; Bundy, *Danger and Survival,* 415–20.

16

The Gorbachev Era and Beyond

The First World War had transformed the United States into the holder of the balance of power; the Second World War completed her involvement by making her into one of the weights of a simple balance. But at the same time the Charter of the United Nations proposed an institution further removed from the balance of power than the League had been. The voting procedure of the Security Council was the negation of the principle of balance: giving every Great Power the right to jam the movement of the scales at will, it offered the alternatives of community of power or anarchy. Its undesigned blessing was that it was incapable of working, and the idea of the community of power had a shorter life after 1945 than it had had after 1919. It can be found in Bevin's speeches until the Communist seizure of Czechoslovakia. After that the balance of power becomes once more a respectable and indeed indispensable part of the diplomatic vocabulary, and an object of almost metaphysical contemplation by the strategic analysts. . . .

Is then the balance of power the guarantee of the independence of nations? or is it the occasion of war? The only answer is that it is both. So long as the absence of international government means that Powers are primarily preoccupied with their survival, so long will they seek to maintain some kind of balance between them. It is easy to point to instances in which the final move in the rectification of the balance has been war. It is less easy, either to remember, or to establish, how often the balance of power has averted war. For the balance of power is not the "cause" of war: the cause of war, however one chooses to identify it, lies in the political conditions which the balance of power in some degree regulates and reduces to order. The alternative to the balance of power is not the community of power: unless this means federation, it is a chimera. International politics have never revealed, nor do they today, a habitual recognition among states of a community of interest overriding their sepa-

The epigraph for this chapter is taken from Martin Wight, "The Balance of Power," in *Diplomatic Investigations*, ed. Herbert Butterfield and Martin Wight, (Cambridge, Mass.: Harvard University Press, 1966), 149, 174–79.

rate interest, comparable to that which normally binds individuals within the state. And where conflicts of interest between organized groups are insurmountable, the only principle of order is to try to maintain, at the price of perpetual vigilance, an even distribution of power. The alternatives are either universal anarchy, or universal dominion. The balance of power is generally regarded as preferable to the first, and most people have not yet been persuaded that the second is so preferable to the balance of power that they will easily submit to it.—Martin Wight

Nothing could reinforce the argument of this book more dramatically than the response of United States policy to the extraordinary changes which have taken place since 1983 in China, the Soviet Union, and the formerly Communist countries of Eastern and Central Europe, on the one hand, and the seizure of Kuwait by Iraq in August 1990, on the other. The reaction of the United States to these two seemingly distinct events was dominated by the same issue—the issue of aggression, the central problem of world peace.

As was noted in Chapter 1, this essay is an effort to test an hypothesis about the nature of the national security interest of the United States, which it defines as an interest in helping to attain and manage a system of world public order governed by the major powers in accordance with the principles of the United Nations Charter. The influence of the major powers or a decisive number of them can be asserted through the Security Council of the United Nations, through arrangements of collective self-defense like NATO, or through both kinds of institutions. Within such a system—perhaps only within such a system—it should be possible for Western civilization and its values to survive and flourish. We have seen that from its beginnings, first as British colonies and then as an independent nation, the United States has been an active participant in the life of the state system, initially as a pawn of the European States in their political manuevers and a skillful exploiter of Europe's rivalries and wars to its own advantage; then as a medium-sized power; and now as a superpower—for the moment at least, the only superpower. While the state system has self-equilibrating impulses, they are not always enough to keep the system at peace. The history of folly, miscalculation, inadequacy, and evil which characterized the coming both of the First and of the Second World Wars should persuade the most convinced skeptic that the state system is not a perpetual-motion machine, but must be guided and ultimately managed by the great powers of the day, or at least a sufficient number of them, acting in concert to maintain a balance of power. Because of the relative military strength of the United States and particularly its nuclear strength, it will be impossible to achieve and sustain such methods of management unless the United States continues to participate fully and responsibly in world affairs, as it has since the end of the Second World War.

It follows from this hypothesis that peace is a problem in the organization and uses of power, not of ideology or of economics, and that peace can be realized only if the processes of world politics maintain a balance of power among the states and enforce the legal rules necessary to their peaceful cooperation. The transformations in the Communist realm which began during the 1980s naturally aroused high hopes throughout the West for a more peaceful future, but it was soon apparent that those changes, whatever they may portend, did not bring history to an end, even in Hegel's sense of the phrase. The United States and its allies have reacted to the changes which are transforming the formerly Communist world with sympathy, prudence, and discrimination, conscious both of the opportunities and the risks which these turbulent events present.

Iraq's sudden conquest of Kuwait and its implications, in turn, demonstrated that all threats to peace do not originate in Moscow: in short, as Dean Acheson wrote in the speech from which the epigraph to Part III is taken, the problems of conceiving and conducting American foreign policy, like the pain of earning a living, will be with us for the rest of our lives. The Western nations are working to induce the Soviet Union, now Russia once again, definitively to abandon the policies of indefinite expansion which were the proximate cause of the Cold War, and take its place as a responsible member of the United Nations Security Council. Until these questions are clearly answered, however, the United States and its allies must keep their powder dry. Iraq's aggression against Kuwait, on the other hand, was treated as a serious breach of the most fundamental norm of the state system, the rule against aggression in Article 2(4) of the United Nations Charter, and dealt with accordingly. President Bush also used the episode with care and insight, and with some success, to nudge the Soviet Union further along the path to full participation in the tasks of the Security Council.

II

During the 1980s, the world was electrified by a series of revolutionary events in China, the Soviet Union, and the Communist countries of Eastern Europe. These explosions had many causes, which were autonomous but also interactive. While change in the former Soviet Union and the old Soviet bloc has continued at an accelerating pace, it has not proceeded in a straight line. Whether the tectonic plates have actually shifted or only groaned a little remains to be seen.

The revolutionary cycle began in China during the early eighties, when Deng Xiaoping announced a far-reaching program for shifting China to a market-oriented economy, and began to allow its people more freedom of speech, of assembly, and of travel than before. In the twentieth century, economic modernization is inconceivable without an educated middle class of professionals, technicians, and managers, so the number of Chinese students and professors in foreign universities rapidly increased; so did the number of foreign students and professors in Chinese universities. Soon the planes to and from China were full of European, Japanese, and American business executives, intellectuals, and ordinary tourists on holiday. Deng's reforms, especially in agriculture, began to show results quickly. When, however, the hope for and experience of more personal and political liberty in China generated large-scale demands for democratic change, Deng Xiaoping dispersed a huge demonstration in Beijing with a whiff of grapeshot, and decisively restored strict political control by the Communist Party, although the Chinese economy continued its reorientation toward pluralism.

When Gorbachev came into power in 1985, he conveyed the sense that he was leading a revolutionary movement intended to transform the Soviet Union into a free and humane society, faithful to the rule of law. The Soviet economy, he said, must be restructured to take full advantage of the dynamism of the free market. And in foreign affairs, he called for "new thinking" which would end the Cold War and permit the Soviet Union to live in peace with the Western nations. A symbol of his intentions, most people in the West believed, was his decision to return to the negotiations for a treaty on intermediate-range ground-based nuclear missile systems, an area in which the Soviet Union was far ahead of the United States. The Soviet Union had walked out of these talks in 1983, because the United States would not qualify or abandon the principle of reducing the two arsenals to equal levels.

In its first few years, the Gorbachev performance was a dazzling display of energy which, he said, sought to create a modern market economy in the country and to satisfy the yearning of the educated Soviet elite for more personal freedom, for the truth about the history of the Bolshevik regime, and for "democracy." The West responded eagerly to the tone and the promises of Gorbachev's speeches, and greeted him rapturously as a leader who would bring democracy and capitalism to Russia and "peace in our time."

During those early years, one could distinguish four characteristic perceptions of the Gorbachev phenomenon in Western public opinion. The first was exemplified by John Chancellor's exuberant comment after President Reagan's first trip to Moscow: "The Cold War is over and we have won. All that remains is to declare victory, bring home the troops, and have a parade." In 1985, that view, clearly, was euphoric nonsense. The second did not go quite so far. It saw Gorbachev as a knight in the shining armor of liberalism struggling against entrenched reactionaries to achieve progress and democracy at home and peace abroad. Members of this school urged the Western nations to help Gorbachev by giving him all the money he wanted and eagerly embracing his political and arms control proposals. If the West failed to back Gorbachev, they said, he would be replaced by a Brezhnev or a Stalin. A third view was more doubtful. It argued that the West should watch the drama unfold from the distance with sympathy and cautious hope, but do nothing to support Gorbachev, and certainly not subsidize his programs or sell him any rope. Their motto was Talleyrand's advice to diplomats: "Surtout, pas de zèle" (Above all, no zeal). The fourth school of thought, of course, consisted of the nay-sayers. A leopard cannot change his spots, they reminded us. Nothing is happening in the Soviet Union but political theatre or growing political conflict which the Russians are incapable of resolving in peace. Gorbachevism is a sham and a fraud, and we should treat the Soviet Union with suspicion and hostility, from a position of ever-increasing strength.

All these opinions turned out to be in error. Something important *is* happening in the what was then the Soviet Union and the other Communist countries, and the United States has an immense national interest in what happens next. While there was plenty of political theatre, flim-flam, and disinformation in Gorbachev's program, the processes at work were real, powerful, and even revolutionary, although they are surely not irreversible, as Khrushchev's fate demonstrates. Russian history and literature teach the reader not to expect happy endings. The West cannot do much to influence the course of events within the territories of the former Soviet Union in the interest of peace, but it can do something. Whether or not we succeed in such an effort, we should try, because our most basic security interest is engaged. The struggle between the "Westerners" and "Easterners" in Russian life, between the European and the Asian strands in Russian culture, has gone on for centuries, and will continue. It can never be resolved once and for all, but the balance between the two forces has shifted many times and will shift again.

Western opportunities in East-West relations make the next few years the most promising period for Western diplomacy since Yalta. The conjuncture of circumstance has made it feasible to seek genuinely stabilizing reforms in the structure and dynamics of world politics— reforms which take fully into account the processes of change which are occurring throughout the world. But before attempting to explain why it is possible to be relatively optimistic about the future of Western foreign policy toward the Soviet Union one should take two cautionary observations to heart:

First, Yalta is an appropriate point of reference, because the promise of the Yalta agreements was not fulfilled. Stalin committed himself there to free elections in Eastern Europe. That promise was broken, and the West acquiesced in the breach. The world has paid a heavy price ever since for America's failure to act. This time we must not settle for too little.

Second, it is equally salutary to face the fact that the weakening of empires presents as many problems for the state system as the programs of expansion through which empires are put together. One has only to recall the long cycles of war produced by the decline and fall of the Turkish, Spanish, and Austrian empires to realize how important it is for the leading powers to cooperate in influencing the end of the Soviet empire in the overriding interest of general peace. No historical analogies are perfect, and the Soviet empire is not the same as the others in geography, internal dynamism, and exposure to the rest of the world. Nonetheless, the point is one of capital importance.

The state system is suddenly more fluid than has been the case for many years. New powers are emerging, and older ones are being transformed. The European Economic Community is scheduled to become more unified in 1992. East Germany has become part of a unified, democratic German state within NATO and the other structures of the European and Atlantic communities. The Western powers have managed to preserve the fundamental balance of world power by sustaining the independence of Western Europe, China, and Japan and containing most of the secondary and peripheral Soviet campaigns of expansion without disastrous losses and without general war. The costs have been high, and the struggle has not always been well conducted, but the outcome seems clear.

By and large, the policy of containment has worked. Nonetheless, centrifugal forces are straining the security relations within the Western coalitions. The West is restless because of the apparently endless burden of the Cold War and the prospect of new troubles ahead. The influence of Muslim fundamentalism raises a question about the future orientation of Islam. Which tendency within Islam will prevail, the Westernizing forces led by Turkey, Egypt, Saudi Arabia, and Pakistan, or those symbolized by the followers of the Ayatollah Khomeini and the Muslim fundamentalists? And, as always, Americans flirt with the idea of ignoring their interests and returning to the isolationism of the nineteenth century. As for the areas of the former Soviet Union, no one in the West can yet anticipate the outcome of the struggles which are convulsing every aspect of Russian life, but one thing is certain: Russia is an enormous, highly industrialized country with a large and well-educated middle class. It will remain a major factor in world politics.

III

The Russian citizen faces an astonishing problem. He is being told by his leaders that the two most basic principles of Soviet policy have completely failed. The Soviet version of Socialism is an economic disaster, and must be replaced by a market economy—true, a "Socialist" market economy, but a market economy nonetheless. Gorbachev's effort to demonstrate his loyalty to Leninism recalls the old East European joke that the Bolshevik Revolution of 1917 made Socialism possible in every country of the world except Russia. Under Soviet Communism the state has not "withered away," as Marx promised. The Soviet Union was not an Arcadian Utopia and its citizens did not live in a state of anarchic freedom. On the contrary, the Communist Party in its more than seventy years of power produced a totalitarian police state, governed not by the rule of law but by a succession of despots, who, according to Gorbachev, have ranged from the lethargic to the satanic. It is hard to imagine the impact of these revelations on the Soviet citizen's relationship to the Russian state.

On the economic side, the program of *perestroika* was a first tentative and obviously inadequate attempt to grapple with a phenomenon which has suddenly come to the fore all over the world, in Socialist and Capitalist countries alike. The essence of the phenomenon is summed up in a story which has been going the rounds in the Communist world, to the effect that Deng Xiaoping and Gorbachev have made a new contribution to Marxist theory, the most important since Lenin. They have discovered, the story goes, that "the final stage of Socialism is Capitalism."

The sudden worldwide acceptance of the fact that Socialism, like other forms of monopoly, is a static and inefficient way to conduct economic activity can be compared in its implications only to the decline of Mercantilism two centuries ago and to the Industrial Revolution itself. The death of Socialism as an idea and an ideal has even broader consequences. It is bound to affect the moral outlook of Western societies as a group. But it is also of primary importance to the enormous task of modernizing the economies of Eastern and Central Europe. The abandonment of Socialism as a way of organizing economic life is long overdue, if one considers the increasing disparity between the standards of living and rates of growth of the Communist and the Western nations. Some parts of Eastern and Central Europe have become almost unlivable, with terrible problems of pollution as well as shortages, inefficiencies, and decrepit machinery.

In the countries of welfare-state capitalism, "pluralism," "privatization," and "deregulation" have also become familiar slogans, and the public sector is being diminished in ways which do not threaten the essence of the welfare state itself. The problem facing the Communist countries attempting to restructure their economies is more difficult, because there is no private sector to which big units of production can readily be sold. In all the Socialist countries there is of course an active black market, but so far it is largely a matter of small and shadowy operators, not a class of businessmen capable of organizing or managing large-scale companies.

For a variety of reasons, Gorbachev and Yeltsin have had more trouble than Deng Xiaoping in achieving momentum for their programing of economic reform. The statistics are so far sketchy and inconclusive, but most observers agree that the Chinese economy is moving forward more rapidly that of the former Soviet Union, both in agriculture and in industry, and that the spirit of enterprise is notably more visible in China than it is in Russia. China has not been governed by a Soviet-model state and economy for as long as the Soviet Union, nor did the slaughter of the Chinese counterparts of the kulaks reach the appalling scale of Stalin's massacres, documented by Robert Conquest and others. And China can draw on an immense resource not available to the Soviets, the brilliantly successful Chinese businessmen of Hong Kong, Taiwan, Singapore, and the rest of the world. In both China and the Soviet Union, however, economic reorientation faces the same basic problem, if in different degrees, namely, the absence of an entrepreneurial and managerial capitalist class. When Lenin introduced his New Economic Policy (NEP) in 1921, he had a considerable part of the old Russian business network available to help carry it out. That resource has long since disappeared.

For some eighty years before 1914, led by outstanding intellectuals and two generations of first-class Russian industrialists, entrepreneurs, bankers, civil servants, and merchants—and some able cabinet ministers as well—the Russian economy was a spectacular success. Its rate of growth was exceeded only by that of Sweden in Europe. But seventy years of Soviet rule drove the business leaders of the prerevolutionary economy into exile, and the experience of the Soviet system has trained an army of managerial bureaucrats for whom innovation and initiative are risks to be avoided at all costs. Considerations of personal safety, promotion, and the hope of a pension at the end of the road put a premium on doing only what has been done before. It will be impossible to break down the ossified structure of the Russian economy, and to release the energy and imagination of the Russian people in the workplace, until a considerable share of the economy is run by foreign companies providing competition, an alternative model, and apprenticeship for Soviet and East European workers, foremen, and middle-level managers.

Gorbachev was unable or unwilling to deal with this key problem. Those who rule in Poland, Hungary, and the other countries of Eastern Europe have done better, but not a great deal better. There cannot be rapid progress in the formerly Communist economies of Europe or China without Western assistance on a large scale. What is required by way of Western cooperation is not foreign credits, or foreign credits alone, but foreign direct investment, foreign entrepreneurship, and foreign management. To attract these powerful resources, the first task of the East European governments must be to restore a legal environment favorable to investment. Investors must be allowed to own the land, the plants, and the machinery they need; they must be allowed to earn and keep enough profits to induce them to put money into Russian, East European, or Chinese investments as compared with investing at home or in other foreign economies; and they must be guaranteed the right to convert their earnings into international currencies.

Thus far, the Central European countries have gagged at the prospect of direct foreign investment as "colonialism," although they are responding to the situation more realistically than the Russians. They forget that the United States, Canada, and many other new countries in the world were industrialized and modernized by foreign investment without losing control of their own political destinies. It is nearly unbelievable that seven years after Gorbachev took power, Russia is still prosecuting successful participants in the second economy as "black marketeers," "hooligans," and "speculators." The "black marketeers" should be applauded as harbingers of an economic transition the Russian leaders say they favor.

IV

Gorbachev's approach to Soviet foreign policy was dominated by his conviction that in order for his program of economic reconstruction to succeed, he must remain on good terms with the West. Initially, at least, the "new thinking" he brought to the conduct of foreign relations was tactical and not strategic. His strategic goal remained what the Soviet Union had been seeking since 1945—to get the United States out of Europe "at any price," in Shevardnadze's revealing phrase, so that Western Europe could be denuclearized, neutralized, and brought under Soviet suzerainty in the exhilirating atmosphere of *glasnost.* He understood and sought to apply the old Russian proverb that the sun is more effective than the north wind in persuading a man to take off his overcoat. In short, Gorbachev's goal during his first period in office was the same as that of his mentor and predecessor Andropov, who described the objectives of détente in these terms in a speech, at Petozavodsk in Karelia, near the border of Finland, on 5 August 1978.

Andropov argued that the task history has set for mankind is to make "détente" irreversible. Surely no American can quarrel with that goal in the abstract. Abstractly, all nations agree on the advantages of relaxing tensions and advancing their common interests through methods of peaceful cooperation. But, Mr. Andropov said, there are some in the West, particularly in what he called "warlike circles" in the United States, who question the Soviet version of détente. They should understand, Mr. Andropov said plainly, that the realities of Soviet power and particularly of Soviet nuclear power make no alternative course available. Détente Soviet-style is not simply advantageous; it is inevitable. What is détente Soviet-style? Mr. Andropov was refreshingly clear in defining the Soviet conception for the West. Here in Karelia, he said,

> One must stress the significance attached to the lengthy experience of neighborly, genuinely equal, and mutually advantageous coop-

eration between the Soviet Union and Finland. Soviet-Finnish relations today form an integral and stable system of equal cooperation in various spheres of political, economic, and cultural life. This is detente embodied in daily contacts, detente which makes peace more lasting and people's lives better and more tranquil. In the last analysis this is the highly humane meaning of the foreign policy of socialism and the foreign policy activity of our party and the Soviet state.[1]

Mr. Andropov's definition concentrates the mind. There is something breathtaking in his tone of avuncular good sense. "Things are going very well in Finland," he seems to be saying. "They could go just as well in Germany, France, Italy, Holland, Japan, China, and the United States. Each of those countries could do good business with the Soviet bloc, provided it followed Finland's example and allowed the Soviet Union a free hand elsewhere in the world."

Read with the advantage of hindsight, with the Warsaw Pact and the Soviet Union itself dissolved, and citizens in the streets from Belgrade to Vilnius demanding freedom, progress, and democracy, Andropov's confident words measure the distance the world has traveled in little more than a decade. But that is how he and Gorbachev saw the world then. Is it still the *weltanschauung* of the Russian Establishment?

Like his predecessors, Gorbachev sought to use the magnetic political force of Soviet military power as his chief instrument for accomplishing his purpose. And in his first few years in office, he continued the Soviet practice of trying to reach that goal by enlarging the lead in nuclear weapons, especially in the field of ground-based ballistic missiles, and then exploiting that advantage in diplomacy and in arms control negotiations. According to the data reviewed in Chapter 15, he tried to continue doing so until the end of his time in office, when the collapse of Soviet society made such a course impossible. It was natural therefore that Gorbachev made far-reaching changes in Soviet arms control policies soon after he took office.

His first step in 1985 was to return to the INF negotiating talks. It is significant that Gorbachev's initial move was on this subject, because the political function of the intermediate-range weapons in Soviet strategic thinking was to whip-saw the Western Allies, in order to help split the United States from its allies in Europe and Asia. This is, of course,

1. *Pravda* (Moscow), 6 August 1978, p. 2.

the idea which governed Khrushchev's tactics in the Cuban missile crisis, but on a much larger scale. In 1985, the Soviet Union was rapidly building and deploying intermediate-range missile systems which threatened targets in Europe, the Middle East, and Asia at a time of increasing doubt about the credibility of an American nuclear guaranty based on the threat to retaliate with intercontinental missiles. By 1981, the Soviet-American intercontinental balance was decidedly adverse to the United States. Many students and practitioners in the field saw the Soviet rush to build up its INF force as decoupling. In the event of a Soviet threat to Norway or Greece, would an American threat to bomb Moscow in retaliation be credible enough to deter the Russians?

The United States had started the INF negotiations in 1981 by proposing the abolition of the entire class of intermediate-range ground-based missiles and warheads. President Reagan had chosen this initial position in order to dramatize his intense desire to reduce the weight of nuclear arms hanging over the world. He often pointed out that earlier arms control treaties had led to an increase in nuclear arms. He wished to start the process of reducing them.

At the time, I was director of the United States Arms Control and Disarmament Agency and Ambassador Paul H. Nitze was our chief negotiator in the INF talks. After some eight months of formal negotiations and more personal and flexible probing, the parties were deadlocked. The United States continued to press for the zero-zero solution, as it was called—a quota of zero for each side in the category of weapon systems defined by the treaty. Meanwhile, the Soviets stood by their initial position; a treaty based on two principles, "equality and equal security," and "equal reductions" rather than "reductions to equal levels." Since the Soviet INF force was far larger than those of the Western Allies, the formula would have permitted the Soviet Union somewhat to increase its deployment of SS-20 INF systems, at the time its most advanced weapon system of its class, and denied the United States the right to deploy any modern Pershing IIs and cruise missiles at all.

Pursuant to his instructions, Ambassador Nitze had for some time been pursuing private talks with his opposite number, Ambassador Yuli Kvitsinskiy, with a view to finding grounds for a possible compromise. Kvitsinskiy was well known to the American government as a brilliant and forceful diplomat, a Pole by birth, well connected in high places, with a record which included at least one episode of floating a supposedly unauthorized trial balloon during the Berlin talks some years earlier and doing so successfully.

During July 1982, I was in Geneva on a regular visit to refresh my sense for the state of the negotiations. I arrived on a Sunday. From Geneva, Nitze had invited me to a private lunch on the day I arrived where we would have a chance to talk alone. We were old friends, as well as colleagues in this and in earlier ventures. Nitze told me that he was scheduled on the following Friday to have one of his customary private dinners with Kvitsinskiy. The Soviet ambassador had suggested that since Mrs. Nitze would be away, they might take a walk in the woods instead of dining at Nitze's apartment, and have dinner at a small country restaurant he knew and liked. Nitze gladly acquiesced, fully understanding, of course, the possible implications of the proposal to have their talk take place far from machinery for electronic surveillance. Nitze had prepared a brief sketch of a possible compromise approach which the two ambassadors might jointly present to their governments as their personal suggestion for breaking the deadlock. Nitze and I discussed and revised the paper for a couple of hours on Sunday, and again at intervals during the next two days. I departed for meetings in Vienna on Wednesday, authorizing Nitze to float the idea on Friday.

The plan which became the "walk-in-the-woods" proposal, about which much was written later on, was simplicity itself: the United States would recede from the zero-zero option to a treaty providing for low equal quotas for each side, that is, the Soviet Union would give up its quest for nuclear superiority, at least in this category of weapons. The scope of the proposed treaty would be worldwide; the Soviets had been insisting on restrictions confined to Europe. The other provisions in the proposal were of secondary importance. Kvitsinskiy studied the draft briefly while sitting on a log, suggested a few minor changes in the text, and agreed that it should be presented to each government as the personal proposal of the two ambassadors. He joked that he would put it forward as Nitze's idea, and that Nitze could submit it, if he wished, as Kvitsinskiy's.

It is often said that both governments turned down the walk-in-the-woods formula. This is not the case. After nearly two months of silence, the Soviet government did reject the plan with great vehemence, according to Kvitsinskiy's report. The United States did nothing of the sort. President Reagan took the position that the United States wished to keep the channel open and was willing to discuss the approach recommended by the ambassadors. Naturally, the United States had a number of amendments to propose by way of perfecting the ambassadors' first draft. The most important was suggested by President Reagan at the first White House meeting on the proposal in order to correct a political flaw which neither Nitze nor I had spotted. After a series of harmonious interdepartmental meetings, the United States government prepared a number of amendments to the ambassadors' plan, and got ready to negotiate on that basis. Our NATO allies were briefed on the episode, and warmly approved President Reagan's response.

The Soviet rejection was so categorical that the matter was dropped at the time, although the Soviets were informed of the President's position. During the early months of 1983, however, the United States put forward a series of provisions for low equal quotas along the lines of the walk-in-the-woods proposal. Each recommended equal quota was higher than the one before. The Soviet Union still held out for an agreement that would recognize its right to nuclear superiority, and finally broke off the talks altogether when it was convinced that the United States would not accept that principle in any form.

When the talks were resumed in 1985, the United States returned to the zero-zero option for reasons that have never been explained. By that time I was no longer in the Reagan Administration. I objected to that decision on the ground that eliminating the intermediate-range American nuclear weapons in and near Europe, Japan, and China would increase their vulnerability to Soviet nuclear blackmail. Eradicating that threat required agreement to equalize the Soviet-American nuclear balance as a whole, taking into account intercontinental weapons, tactical weapons, and anti–ballistic missile defenses, as well as the INF weapons. My objection was to no avail. The treaty was finally prepared, signed, and ratified in 1988.

Curiously, the political changes in the Soviet Union of the period before the failure of the coup attempt against Gorbachev in August 1992, seemed likely to leave the Soviet-American nuclear balance in the position against which I warned at the time, that is, with a zero-zero treaty on intermediate-range systems that would not be balanced by agreements on intercontinental and defensive weapons. As Dean Rusk had once remarked, this was a bit like building a dam across half a river. In order to determine whether a first-strike capability exists, the nuclear balance must be examined as a whole.

After some hesitation, Gorbachev agreed to use the principle of Soviet-American equality in the negotiations on the level of conventional arms in Europe and in the START negotiations on intercontinental nuclear weapons.

V

In attempting to evaluate the Soviet Union's foreign policy during the Gorbachev era one should ask first whether Soviet-force levels were really being reduced, and if so, how far. That is necessarily the point of beginning for American and Allied security policy. Gorbachev and his colleagues frequently told the world that the Soviet Union had given up its policy of expansion and was cutting both its arsenals and its military expenditures. The available evidence did not support these claims.

Since the early seventies, the United States had fallen behind the Soviet Union in terms of nearly every index of military power; until 1988, at least, that gap was widening; and, according to plans approved until the very end of Gorbachev's rule, the gap would have continued to widen, as the West cut its military budgets while those of the Soviet Union continued to increase, or at best to remain roughly stable. The statement on Soviet military expenditures of the Committee on the Present Danger (c.p.d) dated 16 May 1989 documented this pattern, and at the time foresaw only a slight decline in the rate of growth of Soviet military outlays during the period 1991–95.

The c.p.d. analysis proved to be consistent with the pattern of Soviet behavior. Soviet military expenditures remained stable at approximately the 1988 level until 1991, when they fell precipitately for the first time. Whether that decline was ordered by President Boris Yeltsin or was simply caused by the chaos of the Russian civilian economy at the moment is unknowable at this time (Spring 1992). What is confirmed, however, is that in the final days of Gorbachev's authority, Soviet military spending was projected to rise from 18–21 percent of g.n.p. to 25 percent during a period in which the military share of the American national income had fallen from 6 percent to about 4 percent, and will almost surely decline even further. In short, the future of Russian military programs and intentions was then decidedly ambiguous. All that can be said with some confidence is that the Russian military-industrial complex is the most nearly intact sector of the economy and that it encompasses the production of a large fraction of the nation's industrial capacity;[2] that its leadership is committed to mod-

---

2. A joint statement of the Atlantic Council of the United States and the Institute of World Economy and International Relations of the Russian Academy of Sciences ("The Future of Russian-American Relations in a Pluralistic World," March 8, 1992) estimates that defence industries constitute 60–80% of the Russian g.n.p. This is an astonishing figure.

ernizing the Russian arsenal and restoring Russia's "great-power" position as rapidly as possible; and, as Yeltsin has publicly remarked, that
selling arms abroad is one of the few ways in which Russia can earn
hard currency in a period of economic distress.

Before the coup attempt against Gorbachev in August 1991, experts
on Soviet military programs all over the world were arguing with each
other about whether Soviet budget decisions would actually reduce
Soviet military spending in real terms, and if so whether they were
intended to do more than reduce or even eliminate the rate of growth
which had previously been approved. Since the failure of the August
coup, the dismissal of Gorbachev, and the dissolution of the Soviet
Union and the Soviet empire, no solid evidence has surfaced to confirm
the frequent public claims of Russian officials that the Russian Republic
has in fact rejected and discarded Gorbachev's goals for the military:
to stabilize expenditure at or near the inflated levels of 1988, with a
continuing heavy emphasis on nuclear weapons. All observers agree,
however, that no prospective reductions in expenditure which the Soviet
leadership has promised or mentioned begin to compare with those the
United States is making every month under the pressures of the Gramm-
Rudman Act and rampant political euphoria. In short, the Russian
advantage in armaments is necessarily becoming greater, and will continue to do so, unless Yeltsin and his government clearly enact and
visibly carry out a program for eliminating the fantastic militarization
of the Russian economy accomplished by the Soviet regime.[3]

Furthermore, even the reductions in spending on old-style military
equipment and systems the Soviet leaders had promised during Gorbachev's last days were in all probability steps to implement the policy
of modernization vigorously and publicly advocated by Marshal Ogarkov at least since the early 1980s. Ogarkov began his campaign for
modernization after studying the sensational demonstrations of modern
military electronics by Israel in Lebanon during June 1982. His approach was adopted by Gorbachev. And the performance of United
States forces in the Gulf War surely increased the pressures for the
modernization of the Soviet forces.

Many in the West believe, of course, that the social and economic
tribulations of the Soviet Union, including its nationalities problem,
make it impossible for Yeltsin to conduct an expansionist foreign policy.
Those who take comfort from these views should recall the thirties,

---

3. Committee on the Present Danger, *Russian Military Expenditures* (Washington, D.
C.: Committee on the Present Danger, 1991).

when Stalin killed huge numbers of peasants, especially in the Ukraine—the estimates range as high as twenty million or more—and then executed a large part of the leadership both of the Communist Party and of the military forces. The Red Army defeated the Germans nonetheless. Gorbachev's bold and well-timed effort in the Security Council to defeat United States diplomacy and save Saddam Hussein at the end of February 1991, should have a dampening effect on excessive optimism, especially because in the end the United States did proclaim a ceasefire while Saddam Hussein was still in power.

Equally, despite his sensational and important retreat in Eastern Europe, there is no convincing evidence that Gorbachev abandoned the Soviet Union's long-standing policy of expansion. He did, of course, cut back a number of peripheral campaigns which were not succeeding, but he continued and even increased the momentum of others, from the Philippines and the Middle East to Scandinavia and the Caribbean. Even in Afghanistan, the Soviet puppet regime is still hanging on, with active Russian support. Moreover, Gorbachev made far-reaching security agreements both with Libya and Iran, established a naval base in Syria, and made a significant oil agreement with Kuwait.

By far the most significant feature of Gorbachev's foreign policy during the first period of his tenure, however, was its concentration on the detachment of Western Europe, Japan, and China from the United States. There was no "new thinking" in this shift of Soviet tactics. The break-up of America's security network and the isolation of the United States from its allies and associates has been the Soviet Union's main strategic goal since 1945. The striking change Gorbachev brought about in Soviet foreign policy was to make this target an immediate and urgent objective, rather than a distant and rather theoretical hope. The rhetoric of Gorbachev's approach was given an idealistic gloss. A "European House" should be created, overcoming the long and costly division of Europe; the continent should be denuclearized; and any foreign military presence in Europe should to be brought to an end.

It took Gorbachev a year or two to develop and articulate this goal, which became highly visible after 1987. He concluded that a European House was inconceivable unless the East European countries had governments their people could accept and respect as legitimate. Soviet control in Eastern Europe would therefore have to be modified and perhaps abandoned, although Gorbachev then hoped those governments would remain Socialist. The Poles, Czechs, and Hungarians hated their Soviet masters and their own puppet regimes with equal fervor.

Their governments and economies were more and more expensive for the Soviet government to maintain, and in the atmosphere created by the proclamation of *glasnost,* how could the impulses of nationalism in Eastern Europe be curbed? As former Soviet foreign minister Eduard Shevardnadze said, "A cordon sanitaire artificially created around the USSR out of shaky regimes . . . propped up by [Soviet] bayonets" could not be maintained. "What could we do?" Shevardnadze asked in another speech. "Send in the troops? Of course, we could start shooting, but then we would have to cross out everything to do with *perestroika* and democratization."[4]

In this perspective, Gorbachev's important decision not to use force to suppress the revolutions in Eastern Europe becomes intelligible. Such an attempt would have postponed and perhaps ruined Gorbachev's efforts to obtain economic help from the West. And it might well have provoked civil disorder at home and desertions or mutiny by his own troops on a much larger scale than the defection of Soviet troops in Hungary in 1956. Under certain circumstances, it could even have resulted in NATO intervention. The Soviet leadership had not forgotten that the Hungarian government asked for Western help in 1956. Did Gorbachev conclude that it was better for him to allow Eastern Europe to go free, and then trump the Western ace by denuclearizing, and therefore neutralizing the whole of Europe—East and West together?

Gorbachev's spirit was that of the resilient Foch, the great French Supreme Commander in the First World War. Marshal Foch sent a famous message to headquarters during the battle of the Marne in 1914: "My center is ceding ground, my right is recoiling. Situation excellent. I attack." Facing economic, ecological, and social catastrophe at home—earthquakes and Chernobyl; and dubious news from abroad, Gorbachev bid for the great prize, the break-up of NATO and the Finlandization of both Eastern and Western Europe. "We shall deprive you of your enemy," he said. After all, Gorbachev believed he could get all the economic help he needed from Western Europe or Japan alone, or from Western Europe and Japan together. Did he believe that if he succeeded in separating the United States from its allies in Western Europe and Asia and in liberating the Eastern European countries, he could rejuvenate the Soviet economy without paying any political and military price at all?

4. Quoted in *Foreign Broadcast Information Services Daily Report: Soviet Union* (hereafter FBIS), FBIS-SOV-90–052, 16 March 1990, pp. 23, 37, and *FBIS,* FBIS-SOV-90–078, 23 April 1990, p. 7.

This hypothesis about Gorbachev's strategy is entirely consistent with the international behavior of the Soviet government between 1985 and the Gulf crisis. It is consistent also with what Gorbachev said. And it is the hypothesis about Soviet goals which American and Western policy should prudently take as the working predicate for their own policies until persuaded otherwise by events. The United States should and does hope that the revolution started by Gorbachev and now being carried forward by Yeltsin signals the end of Soviet and Russian expansion and the beginning of a new period of democracy and international cooperation in Central Europe and Russia. We should do everything to encourage that possibility, provided the Soviet Union gives us reasonable gages that its policies have really changed. But it would be folly to assume that the policy of expansion Russia and the Soviet Union have doggedly pursued for five hundred years has already been interred.

The key to Gorbachev's ambitious planning during the early period of his rule was Germany. If Gorbachev could prevent the reunification of Germany, or allow it only on the classic terms of the Rapacki plan— reunification in exchange for neutralization—he could reasonably have hoped to snatch victory from the jaws of defeat.

The question of German reunification suddenly appeared on the diplomatic agenda during the last weeks of 1989. A reunified neutral Germany had been the policy of the Soviet Union ever since 1945, regularly floated, and categorically rejected by the NATO allies each time it came up as a patent attempt to transform the world balance of power in favor of the Soviet Union. A buffer zone of neutral East European states might be acceptable to the West, if those states themselves requested such a status after their detachment from the Warsaw Pact was fully accomplished. But the proposal to neutralize modern Germany, now deeply committed to its Atlantic and European mission, was not only frivolous, but would have been physically impossible to enforce without major war.

The neutralization of Germany—now a country of 85 million people—would destroy NATO, force the United States to withdraw from Europe into Fortress America, and leave Great Britain, France, Italy, Spain, Turkey, and the smaller countries of Europe, to say nothing of China and Japan, incapable of self-defense. Under such circumstances the American nuclear guaranty would lose all credibility. British and French nuclear forces cannot of themselves deter those of Russia, which would then be the only major nuclear power in Europe, and by far the strongest European power in conventional arms. A helot Western Europe would be the inevitable agent of Soviet economic recovery. The Gorbachev-Yeltsin springtime of liberalism would fade into autumn and winter. And a new Russian ruler would emerge as master of the Eurasian landmass from Brittany and Cornwall to Vladivostok, a leader who had finally succeeded where Napoleon, the Kaiser, Hitler, and Stalin had all failed.

Chance thwarted Gorbachev's daring bid for a denuclearized and neutral Europe, perhaps derailed it forever. As one of its first acts in 1989, the new Hungarian government tore down the barbed-wire fence between Hungary and Austria, intending only a friendly gesture in the spirit of the Hapsburg past. But suddenly East Germans began to take "vacations" in Hungary, and then to enter Austria, where they overwhelmed the German Embassy and its consulates seeking permission to enter West Germany. The movement quickly became a flood. Gorbachev tried hard to stick to his plan, but there was no chance for him to prevail without a large-scale use of force. So the miraculous unification of Germany within NATO took place, an event no student of European politics would have predicted as even a remote possibility without war.

Taking the liberation of the former Soviet satellites and the unification of Germany together, what happened between 1989 and 1991 was a major victory for the United States and its NATO allies. The military frontier of the Soviet Union was moved five hundred miles to the east—half the distance between the old Soviet border and the Atlantic Ocean. Ukraine became independent. The Baltic suddenly ceased to be a Soviet lake. Even in the age of air power and missiles, these are changes of first-rate importance to the security position of the NATO alliance.

VI

Will Gorbachev's acceptance of the reunification of Germany within NATO turn out to be the turning point or only a brief interval in the long Western effort to contain Soviet expansion and induce the Soviet Union to become a responsible member of the society of nations? The question is highlighted but not answered by Iraq's conquest and annexation of Kuwait in August 1990. Iraq has been a protégé of the Soviet Union, a major recipient of Soviet arms and military cooperation for many years, and a major instrument of the Soviet Union's longstanding campaign to control the Middle East. Despite nearly forty years of expensive failure in this effort, the Soviet Union had persisted.

For millennia, conquerors and would-be conquerors have swept across the Middle East from every azimuth, seeking to dominate what has always been a critically important part of the world. Saddam Hussein is the latest in the long line of aspirants for the laurels of Nebuchadnezzar and Ozymandias. He seized dictatorial power in 1979. Even by Middle Eastern standards, he has been a singularly brutal ruler. He has also been a vigorous promoter of Iraqi industrial development, particularly in the military sphere, and of Iraqi expansion. He first raised territorial claims against Kuwait in 1958, and was deterred from military action then by active British diplomacy, backed by the quick movement of British military forces to Kuwait. In 1979, seeking to take advantage of Iran's diplomatic isolation as a result of its holding American diplomats hostage at the time, Saddam Hussein attacked Iran. His goal was the valuable oilfields in southwestern Iran. The war that followed lasted more than eight years and cost more than a million lives.

On 2 August 1990, Iraq conquered and annexed Kuwait, and thus directly threatened the other small Persian Gulf emirates, as well as Jordan, Syria, Israel, and Saudi Arabia. Saddam Hussein was trying to become king of the Arab nation, as Nasser did. The impact of that prospect on the security of Egypt and the Maghreb, Iran, the Soviet Union, and Western Europe was self-evident. If Iraq were allowed to swallow all or any part of Kuwait, the forces determining world access to the oil of the Middle East would be transformed, and the balance of power in the region, and therefore also the world balance of power, would have been substantially changed.

Confronting these ominous events, President Bush decided promptly that Iraq's aggression against Kuwait was a major threat to the security of the United States and its allies, and had to be resisted by force if necessary. The President took advantage of Soviet dependence on Western economic help and the new orientation of Soviet foreign policy proclaimed by Gorbachev to persuade the Soviet Union and China reluctantly to support an American initiative in the Security Council of the United Nations. He obtained a series of Security Council resolutions condemning Iraq's annexation of Kuwait; assembled in Saudi Arabia a large expeditionary force supported by twenty-eight nations; and after more than five months of diplomatic efforts to persuade Iraq to withdraw from Kuwait, initiated hostilities in January 1991, shortly after the expiration of the deadline of January 15 set by the Security Council for Iraq's compliance with its resolutions. The Soviet Union was invited to send forces to join those of the Gulf coalition, but declined on the ground that its experience in Afghanistan made such action politically impossible at home.

VII

The Gulf conflict was a critical turning point in the quest for peace, like the Japanese invasion of Manchuria in 1931 and the North Korean attack on South Korea in 1950. When the great powers of the day failed to enforce the League of Nations rule against aggression in Manchuria, and then failed again in Ethiopia and the Rhineland crisis of 1936, the Second World War became inevitable. On the other hand, the successful defense of South Korea in the name of the United Nations Charter, costly as it was, strengthened President Truman's containment policy and therefore helped to produce the drastic changes of the last few years in the Soviet Union and the erstwhile Communist empire. At a minimum, it prevented Soviet control of a position vital to the defense of Japan.

Iraq's bid for hegemony in the Middle East was a threat to American security quite as serious as that posed by Japan's conquest of Manchuria in the thirties and by the Soviet Union's attempt to take control of South Korea through its North Korean proxy twenty years later. Indeed, because of the significance of Iraq's move for the world oil economy and the geopolitical importance of the Middle East, the Gulf crisis was even more threatening than those in Manchuria and Korea, if one takes into account the political fragility of the Middle East, and the implications of possible moves and countermoves by what was then still the Soviet Union. The outcome of the crisis will inevitably help to determine whether the Arab world will move forward to a Western orientation—as Turkey, Egypt, Morocco, Saudi Arabia, Indonesia, Pakistan, and other Islamic countries have done—or follow the fundamentalist policy of the Ayatollah Khomeini and his successors.

It is important to note that the war waged by the coalition President Bush assembled to defeat Iraq's aggression against Kuwait was legally a campaign of collective self-defense approved by the Security Council, like the Korean War, and not as some have claimed, an "international enforcement action" undertaken, directed, and carried out by the Security Council itself through forces under its command pursuant to Articles 42–50 of the United Nations Charter. The distinction is fundamental. No such enforcement action has ever taken place, and it is unlikely that the procedure will ever be used. To recognize the Security

Council as the exclusive instrument through which force can be used to protect states against aggression would be to strip what the Charter calls "the inherent right of individual and collective self-defense" of any meaning. Under such a rule, any permanent member of the Security Council by its veto could leave the victim of aggression naked before its enemies. That is surely not what Article 51 intended.

As Martin Wight commented in his article on the balance of power quoted in the epigraph of this chapter, treating Articles 42–50 as the only available way to enforce the Charter rules against aggression would leave the state system confronted by two alternatives—true community of power, or anarchy. Save as an occasional coincidence, true community of power on a world scale is nearly inconceivable. The diversity of the modern world and the stubborn historical reality of the national principle are much too powerful to be overcome by incantation or even by the perception of shared interest. For as far ahead as we can predict, therefore, the quest for peace in accordance with the Charter of the United Nations will depend not primarily on the United Nations institutions alone, but on the procedure used in the Korean War and in the Persian Gulf War of 1990–91: the procedure of collective self-defense, that is, supplemented where possible by the diplomatic efforts of the Security Council. If the permanent members of the Security Council cannot agree in a given case, the essential campaigns of self-defense can continue nonetheless. At this stage in the long, slow development of the state system, no more can be expected. The United Nations is not a world government, but an instrument for encouraging cooperation among the states in the interests of peace and of the other goals set forth in the Charter.[5]

VIII

President Bush's masterly handling of the Gulf crisis should help to restore the consensus in American and Western opinion behind the Wilsonian policy of collective security against aggression. That consensus was weakened by the experience of Vietnam, although no new conception of the American national interest has replaced it—or can replace it. The success of Allied arms in the Gulf should help Western opinion to realize with new confidence and energy that the classic Cold War was not the exclusive focus of Western security policy, but simply

5. The legal issue is reviewed in Eugene V. Rostow, "Until What? Enforcement Action or Collective Self-Defense?" *American Journal of International Law* 85, no. 3 (July 1991).

an example of the kind of problem the managers of the state system will have to face from time to time as the world evolves.

Great changes are taking place in the structure and the substance of world politics—changes in the division of power among the leading states, changes in the technology of war, and changes in the moral code of the society of nations. More such changes are certain to occur in the future. These changes will inevitably alter the membership in the Club of Great Powers which must dominate the Security Council of the United Nations or its equivalent as the future unfolds. One may hope these changes will also lead to changes in the content of the law the Great Powers' Club applies. The human revulsion against war—in the West at least—has rarely been expressed more strongly than was the case before and during the Gulf War. The transformations of the state system, far-reaching as they are likely to be, will not, however, alter the agenda of the Security Council or its successor. That indispensable body, whatever it is called, will face problems that would have been readily understood by the statesmen who have sought to achieve peace since Biblical times and the age of classical Greece.

The Gulf War should prove to be one of the most creative events in the long and often tragic history of the struggle for peace through collective security. Lustrous names gleam in the records of that history: Thucydides and Kant; Pitt, the statesmen of the Congress of Vienna, and Sir Edward Grey; Woodrow Wilson and both Roosevelts; Truman and Acheson. What they accomplished contributed to the emergence of the Wilsonian idea in its contemporary form and its growing influence on the modern mind. President Bush's forceful management of the Gulf crisis, coupled with the dazzling feats of Generals Powell and Schwartz-kopf and their fellows, have dramatized the Wilsonian principle and given it an altogether new vitality. In retrospect, both the Korean War and the war in Vietnam were badly handled but in the end successful. As the *Economist* concluded in 1990, "Indochina was not saved, and is today communist and wretched. Yet because America intervened, South-East Asia is free and thriving; and Indochina is being irresistibly tempted [to follow] South-East Asia's way."[6] But the public perception of the contribution the wars in Korea and Vietnam made to the cause of peace is clouded and confused by their length, their cost, and by the mistakes of the United States in conducting them. What President Bush has achieved is vividly summarized in a letter he received from A. M.

6. *Editorial, Economist,* 29 September 1990, p. 17.

Houghton, a former Navy pilot who flew 161 combat missions in Vietnam and is now a Protestant minister:

> For nearly two decades I have felt that the Vietnam years of my life were a worthless waste, [Houghton wrote]. . . . I am writing to thank you . . . for taking a stand that is bringing healing to the hearts of this and many other wounded Vietnam veterans.[7]

7. *Editorial, Washington Post,* 1 March 1991, A15.

Epilogue:
United States Foreign Policy
after the Soviet Collapse

The structure and dynamics of the state system which is taking shape in the aftermath of the Soviet revolution should be hospitable to the permanent goals of American foreign policy. That judgment is tenable, however, only if the United States and its allies take advantage of the opportunities and avoid the risks which are immanent in these turbulent flows of change. To succeed will require an American and Allied policy at least as active and probably no less expensive than the policy the Allies have pursued since the Second World War. The pattern of that policy will surely be less rigid than that of the ice age of the Cold War. And it will put a premium on flexibility, decisiveness, and above all on a shared understanding of the long-term security interests of the United States and the Western allies as a group so that the resolution of particular foreign policy crises will further those interests, or at least not do injury to them. The military component of these programs may well be less than those the United States has had to provide since 1950, when the Korean War began; in any event, it will almost certainly be different. But the overall costs can hardly be reduced much. In short, there is no "peace dividend" in sight for a compelling reason: the Allies have not yet achieved a stable peace, and, indeed, show no clear signs of having a coherent strategy for doing so. And no lesser goal can satisfy the requirements of United States and Allied security.

The closest analogy to the situation the United States and its allies confront after the collapse of the Soviet Union is the one they faced after the First World War, when, instead of working together, they fell apart. Defeated Russia was taken over by the Bolshevik coup d'état in 1917, while its hard-pressed Western allies did nothing serious to sustain the promising initiative for democracy and reform led in Russia by

The intervention of illness and the tempo of publishing schedules have combined to permit a final look at the argument of this book in light of international events between the completion of the manuscript in May 1991, and the early spring of 1992. This Epilogue summarizes my reflections on those events. (E.V.R.)

Prince Georgi E. Lvov and Alexander Kerensky. With the benefit of hindsight, there can be no doubt that the cause of peace and of humanity would have been far better served if the Western Allies had been able to rescue the first Russian republic from Lenin's putsch.

The failure of its allies to defend the Russian Republic then was surely one of the worst diplomatic blunders of the twentieth century— a period rich in such blunders. One can sympathize with the Western statesmen of the day, who had to confront the imminence of the great German offensive of the spring of 1918, reinforced by one million hardened troops from the Eastern Front, and thousands of artillery pieces. Their armies and peoples were bone-tired after three years of trench warfare. The United States had barely begun to face the realities of world politics and their untested troops were just starting to disembark in France. There had been a French mutiny. And large segments of Western opinion were dazzled by the hope that Lenin's seizure of power promised mankind a glowing future.

Giving full weight to these difficulties, it is nonetheless obvious that the Allies should have followed Churchill's advice to put down the Bolshevik regime at once. They had every legal and moral right to help a friendly Allied government defeat an insurrection. If they had acted early, the task would not have required much force. Instead, the Allies dithered and could not make up their minds. The Bolsheviks consolidated their power after a long civil war. Mussolini, followed by Hitler and lesser apostles, consciously imitated the tactics of Lenin and Trotsky, and imposed Leninist regimes on other countries. The United States retired into its cave. And Britain and France, frustrated by responsibilities beyond their strength, quarreled with each other more and more viciously, and ignored or exacerbated the portents of trouble which had surfaced even before the Armistice of 1918. The result of the folly of the Western Allies between 1919 and 1939 was the Second World War.

In 1945, the principal powers divided again, and forty-five years of Cold War ensued. This time, however, the Western Allies were forced to unite by the Soviet drive for dominant power, based on an unparalleled military buildup, especially in nuclear weapons, and a diplomacy of indefinite expansion. As a result, the Allies successfully created and sustained a considerable measure both of peace and of economic and social improvement in their half of the world.

Now the major powers, including Russia and the other successor states of the Soviet empire, have a new opportunity to cooperate in the task of consolidating and managing a condition of general peace.

The collapse of the Soviet Union and its empire and the end of Communism as a fighting faith should make it possible for them to do so, if the successor states of the old Soviet bloc remain on their westward course; if the Western Allies profit from the lessons of their previous failures and their relative success in coping with the Cold War; and above all if all the states take to heart the sermon Soviet Foreign Minister Maxim Litvinov used to preach to unwilling ears fifty years ago—that peace is indivisible.

Will the powers fail to achieve and maintain peace, as they did twice before in this century? There is no objective reason for them to fail this time. They possess all the resources required for the task. Do they also possess the insight, discipline, unity, and will without which their wealth and power will prove unavailing?

The death of the Soviet idea and of the Soviet empire, not unnaturally, has released centrifugal forces within the Western alliances. Germany, Europe as a whole, and Japan are being pressed to loosen or even break their ties to the United States. And in the United States, the apparently unquenchable American yearning for a return to isolationism has been given new life. From the point of view of the national security of the United States, the revolution in the Soviet empire is a glorious event, which should be greeted with hosannas. Unfortunately, however, it offers the nation no relief from the burden of having and carrying out a foreign policy.

For three generations, at least, world politics has been violently disturbed through profound changes in demography, geography, and technology, and in its economic, social, political, and moral life. It will take time and concerted effort to restore anything approaching the relative tranquility of the century which ended in 1914. To have any chance of success in that effort will require a hospitable welcome—and if necessary, more tangible support as well—to Russia and the other successor states of the former Soviet empire. It will also require the continued solidarity of the American alliance system and in all likelihood a broadening of its membership and an intensification of its unity as the West confronts the vast and novel changes of the years ahead.

The policy of the Western allies, and especially of the United States, toward Russia, Ukraine, and the smaller successor states of the Soviet Union has thus far been hesitant and equivocal. If this policy is not decisively reversed, and reversed with the same verve and creativeness which characterized the years of Truman and Acheson, the Western allies risk repeating the mistake they made with regard to Russia in 1917 and 1918.

The collapse of the Soviet Union offers the United States an opportunity of incalculable importance—and a threat of comparable importance—namely, on the one hand, the opportunity to bring Russia and other former components of the Soviet Union into the Western world, as we brought Germany and Japan into the Western world after 1945, and, on the other, the risk of anarchy and counterrevolution, which could result in the degeneration of the former Soviet empire into one or more powerful disturbers of the peace.

It should never be forgotten that President Truman's offer of the Marshall Plan in 1948 was made to the Soviet Union and its satellites as well as to the Western Allies. At this moment of deepening trouble, the United States has a fleeting opportunity to renew that wise and far-sighted offer, this time on behalf of all the industrialized democracies. The purpose of that offer would be what it was in 1948: to consolidate an impregnable coalition of like-minded states whose primary interest would be the functioning of the state system as a system of peace.

Facing chaos in the former Soviet Empire, the Western Allies, except for the Germans, seem almost as confused and inadequate as their predecessors after the First World War. They have none of their excuses. Today the West is rich and confident, after the triumphant vindication of the political, military, and economic policies it has pursued since the time of Truman and Acheson. The Western alliances are still firm, despite the absence, for the time being, of a visible Soviet threat, and the worldwide capitalist economy is a powerful engine for progress.

II

The Cold War of the Bolshevik era was not a matter of ideology. The United States and its allies had to contain and if possible to roll back the outward thrust of Soviet expansion not because the Soviet Union was governed by Communists, but because it threatened the world balance of power. The renewed and accelerated expansion of the Soviet Union after 1945 simultaneously challenged the independence of the coastal states and islands at both ends of the Eurasian landmass:—Japan, China, Taiwan, South Korea, Indonesia, the Philippines, and the ASEAN countries in Asia; and the NATO allies; the rest of Western Europe; the Caribbean; and the Middle East, as well. The United States and its allies therefore had to oppose the Soviet campaign for the most familiar reason which has driven nations to war throughout recorded history: the fear of an adversary which is becoming too strong.

Americans have always resisted this harsh and inescapable feature of international life. Instead of planning and implementing the adjustments of policy required to adapt Western foreign policy to the changes now taking place in the structure of world politics, more than half the Democrats in Congress, perhaps a third of the Republicans, and a large fraction of the foreign policy intelligentsia in the universities, the think-tanks, and the media are urging the nation to abandon the foreign policy tradition of Wilson and both Roosevelts, which has dominated American foreign policy since 1945, and follow the ghosts of Harding, Coolidge, and Hoover into the quagmire of the interwar period. The rejuvenated isolationists, chanting the slogans of the America First movement, seem to have forgotten that America's refusal to participate responsibly in world politics between 1919 and 1939 was the proximate cause of the Second World War, and that neither the United States nor any other country has or can have the strength to protect its security unilaterally in the multipolar modern world. Even a casual inspection of the world's demographic and economic trends for the next fifty years makes that conclusion inescapable.

What lessons have the American people drawn from their long experience with international affairs during this transforming century? Every national election since 1940 demonstrates the same pattern of American opinion about foreign affairs, which the public response to the Gulf War only confirms. The people, as distinguished from many of their leaders, have learned that Wilson was right when he proposed the League of Nations in 1919, and that the United States was tragically wrong in rejecting his advice. The United States, they have come to realize, has always been part of the worldwide state system, and in modern times is an inescapably important member of that system.

The most vital national security interest of the United States is the effective functioning of the state system as a system of general peace. Two conditions must be satisfied before that goal can be attained: First, the system must be based on a favorable balance of power; and second, it must be managed in the interest of peace by the great powers acting in concert, or at least by a decisive number of them. The American people understand that the state system is not self-regulating. It must be directed by the great powers, which alone have the capacity to do so, or it will collapse from time to time in the large-scale convulsions which lead to general war.

The notion that achieving and managing a condition of peace among the states of the world is the first duty of the major powers is a novel development which became a political reality at the Congress of Vienna in 1815. Wilson's toweringly important contribution to the quest for peace was to perceive that while the peacekeeping efforts of the Concert of Europe during the nineteenth century were an improvement over the conditioned reflexes of the balance of power principle standing alone, those efforts did not always prevail. In July 1914, for example, Germany and Austria secretly started the First World War by their response to the murder of the Austrian archduke at Sarajevo. The dominant forces in Germany, conscious of the taut network of treaties and countertreaties which defined the balance of power in Europe, feared that events in the Balkans would weaken Austria, its only ally, and thus force an end of Germany's program of worldwide expansion. The Germans knew that if and when the British foreign minister, Sir Edward Grey, learned that Austria, backed by Germany, had presented Serbia with a harsh ultimatum, he would move heaven and earth to prevent war or to end it if it had begun. Therefore the ultimatum was kept secret, and Germany repeatedly urged Austria to invade Serbia before Grey found out about it.

Wilson concluded that the Concert of Europe should be institutionalized as the League of Nations, in order to make possible constant vigilance to contain and defuse conflicts which might threaten the peace, and to initiate programs of improved international cooperation in many other areas of international life as well. And he also realized that the major powers could not hope to maintain peace through the League of Nations unless the United States was an active, indeed a leading member.

The League failed, of course, in large part because the United States refused to join, and it has been replaced by the United Nations. The Charter of the United Nations is an important part of the contemporary legal code of the international community, and is thus the only available statement of the norms which the nations have agreed should govern their behavior toward each other. Will the collapse of the Soviet Union permit the major powers to achieve greater respect for the norms of the Charter during the next half century than has been the case since 1945? Or is the United Nations Charter doomed to join the Covenant of the League of Nations in the dustbin of history, overwhelmed by the short-sightedness of mankind and the force of modern nationalism?

The answer to these questions will depend in considerable part on what the United States does and persuades others to do in carrying out the prescriptions of the United Nations Charter. For as far ahead as one can see, American leadership in the effort to vindicate the role of law in international affairs is indispensable, if only because of the nuclear element in world politics.

The American people have learned another bitter truth about their relation to the system of world public order: if the United States cannot avoid being drawn into its crises, then surely prudence requires the United States to participate in its day-to-day diplomacy, in order to help resolve conflicts before they become crises. Thus, when Iraq invaded Kuwait in 1990, American and Western opinion rallied to the proposition that aggression—at least Iraq's aggression in the Persian Gulf—was an intolerable threat to the system of world public order, and had to be defeated and undone. Enforcing the Charter rule against aggression requires not only scrutiny and conciliation efforts by the leading powers, but active and concerted Allied diplomacy, backed by the credible availability of force, to make sure that the risk of threats to the general peace is kept to a tolerable minimum. This proposition should not require the dispatch of American troops every time the Charter rule against aggression is violated or threatened. The United States is not the world's policeman, as Soviet and Chinese propaganda used to remind us frequently during the Vietnam war. But we are one of the five permanent members of the Security Council, the successors to the responsibilities of the Concert of Europe. Since the attitudes of China and Russia to these responsibilities are still equivocal and problematic, no peacekeeping efforts can be expected to prevail unless the United States, Great Britain, and France, at least, act together as the core members of the peacekeeping coalitions.

What is the foreign policy agenda facing the United States and its allies for the decades following the Soviet collapse? And why will that agenda require an Allied foreign policy at least as active and probably as expensive as was the case during the period dominated by the Bolshevik Cold War?

This Epilogue will consider two of the most important items on that agenda: the looming crisis about the proliferation of nuclear weapons and other weapons of mass destruction, and the future configuration of power within the state system.

The proliferation of nuclear weapons and other weapons of mass destruction is an urgent short-term problem which the nations must resolve in concert if any kind of order is to be achieved and maintained. The only solutions now conceivable will require change in the notion of state "sovereignty," that is, in the balance between the autonomy of the state and the claims of the state system as a whole. The future of the balance of power is a long-term problem whose resolution will be profoundly influenced by the methods which develop for dealing with nuclear proliferation and other short-term problems. Many difficult and important issues of international concern are already visible over the horizon—environmental issues, for example, and those of water supply. How the nations deal with the two problems selected for examination here, nuclear proliferation and the future of the balance of power, will go far toward deciding whether the state system will be able to resolve the other issues on its agenda, or be overwhelmed by chaos.

III

The evolution of international policy toward the nuclear weapon is a text book confirmation of Montesquieu's famous dictum that the laws of society are determined, like the laws of the physical universe, "by the nature of things," in this case, by the nature of nuclear power and by the moral code of the society of nations. By invoking Lucretius' "De Rerum Natura" the great French philosopher was not suggesting a monistic theory of social determinism, like that of Marx. On the contrary, Montesquieu's view of the social process recognized the influence of all aspects of social experience in determining the course of its evolution, and above all the influence of what he called "the spirit of the laws," the moral code of each society, and its aspirations for the future.

From the beginning of the nuclear age in 1945, sober opinion throughout the world has recognized the nuclear weapon as a terrifying object, something qualitatively different from even the most destructive conventional weapons. The possibilities of permanent radiation and the other difficulties of dealing with nuclear waste intensified the sense of mystery and awe which enveloped the subject from the first announcement of the bombing of Hiroshima and Nagasaki. The nuclear accident at Chernobyl has confirmed and intensified those fears.

At the same time, it was also clearly understood that if a potential adversary possessed nuclear weapons, the threatened states had to find protection from the menace through alliances or nuclear weapons of their own, or through reliable and enforceable changes in international law.

Americans can be proud that their government, then the sole possessor of nuclear weapons, proposed in 1946 to make nuclear science and technology an international monopoly, controlled by an agency of the United Nations. The idea had been developed and put forward by Dean Acheson and David Lilienthal, and reviewed by a committee headed by Bernard Baruch. President Truman formally proposed what is generally called the Baruch Plan in 1946. Stalin's rejection of the proposal, even as a basis for study and negotiation, was one of the tragic turning points of the Cold War. It made clear Stalin's decision that the Soviet Union "would go its own way," to recall his comment to Ambassador Harriman in 1944 on an American offer of a loan for postwar reconstruction.[1]

The United States and other nations did not take Stalin's rejection of the Baruch Plan as final, and they pursued a variety of agreements which aimed to limit nuclear weapons and to reduce the dangers the use of nuclear technology poses to health and to the environment. As the nations groped forward in these efforts, nuclear energy was more and more widely used for peaceful purposes: in medicine, for example; in the generation of electrical energy; and in the engines used to propel ships.

The most important of the efforts to minimize nuclear risks was the series of international agreements seeking to confine the possibility that nuclear weapons would be used again in war—first, the Non-Proliferation Treaty of 1968; then the bilateral nuclear arms treaties between the Soviet Union and the United States negotiated and signed during the last twenty years; and finally the treaties establishing Nuclear Free Zones. These treaties together reflected the way in which nuclear arsenals had developed in the first period after 1945, and the way in which the states perceived the problem.

In the Non-Proliferation Treaty of 1968, the nuclear states which were party to the Treaty—the United States, the Soviet Union, and Great Britain, initially—undertook not to transfer such weapons, directly or indirectly, "to any recipient whatever," and each nonnuclear state which is party to the treaty agreed not to receive the transfer of such weapons from a nuclear state, directly or indirectly, and to accept international safeguards of its compliance. All parties agreed to cooperate in the peaceful uses of nuclear energy, and to pursue negotiations in good faith on measures to terminate the nuclear arms race at an early date and to achieve nuclear disarmament. While France did not sign the Non-Proliferation Treaty, it declared that it "would behave in the future in this field exactly as the states adhering to the treaty."

The Non-Proliferation Treaty has another extremely important dimension: the security obligations it implies on the part of the nuclear

---

1. I reviewed the history of the postwar loan project in E. V. Rostow, *Peace in the Balance* (New York: Simon and Schuster, 1972), chap. 4.

powers toward nonnuclear states which are objects of nuclear aggression or of other threats by nuclear powers. Great Britain, the United States, and the Soviet Union supported a Security Council Resolution adopted in March 1968 which provided that nuclear aggression or the threat of nuclear aggression against nonnuclear states would create a situation requiring immediate action by the Security Council, and especially by its permanent members. The members of the nuclear club should be deemed to have responsibility for the security of states which have agreed to forgo membership for themselves. The extent of that responsibility has not yet been tested, but such a test is not far off.

At first, despite general anxiety about the hazard of nuclear clouds, nuclear weapons were treated by the nations as legitimate weapons of war, simply another form of aerial bombardment. If nuclear weapons were recognizably different from ordinary bombs and shells, they were legitimate weapons nonetheless. And it was within the sovereign right of every state to make them and indeed to use them, as the United States had used them in 1945. But the states were always uneasy about this proposition. It was assumed and recognized that nuclear weapons were in a class apart. And there was recognition too of the fact that the widespread proliferation of nuclear weapons would make world politics almost unpredictable, and therefore extremely volatile. General Gallois, Herman Kahn, and others argued plausibly that nuclear proliferation would made it impossible for any state to use nuclear weapons, and therefore would make for stability. No one was quite convinced. After all, what if they turned out to be wrong? Thus there was a shock to opinion around the world when the Soviet Union became a nuclear power, and lesser shocks when Great Britain, France, and China revealed that they too had nuclear weapons. The Soviet Union moved rapidly to catch up with the United States in nuclear science and in nuclear strength. It had probably begun to work on nuclear weapons before the United States, once Peter Kapitza was forced in 1933 to return home after several years at the Cavendish Laboratories in Cambridge. The Soviet nuclear weapons program was accelerated after the Second World War and soon approached and then outstripped that of the United States.

Since 1945, neither the United States nor the Soviet Union has in fact exploded nuclear weapons in situations of conflict, although nuclear hints or even threats were made during several of the crises of the Cold War. When such threats were objectively credible, they were heeded. Each side purported to have nuclear weapons only for purposes of deterrence, but the Soviet and the American doctrines of deterrence were altogether different. The purpose of American deterrence was to prevent the Soviet Union from using or threatening to use either conventional or nuclear weapons in pursuit of its programs of expansion. Hence the United States refused to make a "no first-use" pledge. In the American view, it would be ridiculous or worse to neutralize nuclear weapons in order to make the world safe for aggressive war based on the use of conventional weapons. Thus the American position has rested and should continue to rest on the proposition that the nuclear weapon cannot be tamed unless aggression itself is tamed. It reserved the right to use nuclear weapons if necessary to resist, for example, a massive conventional force attack in Western Europe, and it forced the Korean War to an armistice by telling the Soviet Union it could not predict or control the consequences unless an armistice in place was promptly reached.

The Soviet nuclear doctrine has been entirely different. It was designed to paralyze the United States by reaching at least the position of nuclear superiority the United States had had at the time of the Cuban missile crisis of 1962. The Soviet leaders believed that overwhelming Soviet nuclear superiority against the United States, especially in accurate, swift, and extremely destructive land-based intercontinental weapons, would make it impossible for the United States to use either conventional or nuclear forces at all in defense of Europe, Japan, the Middle East, or other vital American interests, which could then be brought under Soviet control without a shot of any kind being fired.

This was the reasoning which controlled events in Cuba in 1962, when President Kennedy assembled 250,000 troops in Florida, and prepared to invade Cuba with conventional force. The Soviet-American nuclear balance at that time was so favorable to the United States that the Soviet Union had to back down once it was clear that Kennedy would in fact invade Cuba with conventional forces if necessary. The Soviet Union would have been unable to match United States conventional forces in Cuba, and could not then match our nuclear forces either.

On certain assumptions, then, the Soviet view of deterrence was all too convincing. As de Gaulle once asked, "Who can believe that the United States is willing to risk bombs on New York in order to defend Paris?" Unless the United States has a second-strike nuclear capacity, de Gaulle's question has only one possible answer, even at the level of abstract analysis.

The experience of the Cuban missile crisis led the United States to press the Soviet Union for nuclear arms agreements, especially those affecting intercontinental nuclear weapons, which would make it impossible for either side credibly to threaten the use of nuclear weapons against the other. Until late in Gorbachev's period of rule, the Soviet position in those negotiations was that agreements should be based not on the principle of Soviet-American equality, which the United States favored, but on a standard of "equal security," by which they claimed the right to have an arsenal equal to the combined arsenals of every other nuclear power in the world. This was the formula Great Britain used in planning its naval building programs during the nineteenth century, in order to make sure that Brittania "ruled the waves." It took twenty-three years before the Soviet Union was ready even nominally to accept the principle of agreements providing for nuclear equality as a guaranty that neither side could use nuclear weapons. Even so, the series of treaties designed to assure this result is not yet complete.

Thus the familiar Cold War nuclear array of the powers emerged: there were two nuclear superpowers, the United States and the Soviet Union, with extremely large and diverse arsenals; France and Great Britain, allied to the United States, each with much smaller nuclear arsenals; China, an increasingly active nuclear power, pursuing a more and more independent foreign policy; India, which has exploded "a nuclear device," and is capable of quickly becoming a nuclear power, if it has not already done so; Israel, which is generally considered to be nuclear-capable and perhaps has a small stock of such weapons to be used in situations of extreme danger; and a number of other countries which are believed to be in earlier stages of secret nuclear development: Brazil, Argentina, Pakistan, Iraq, Iran, North Korea, and some others.

At the moment, Russia and the other successor states of the Soviet Union seem to be agreed that only Russia will be a nuclear power in the future, and Yeltsin has announced plans for radically and unilaterally reducing its nuclear arsenal. Since nuclear technology has escaped from the laboratory, and any moderately industrialized state can make nuclear weapons, it seems clear that the present nuclear powers will almost surely retain some nuclear weapons, as a safeguard against the possibility that outlaw states will manufacture or purchase nuclear weapons or other weapons of mass destruction.

For nearly thirty years that configuration remained roughly constant. There are many fewer nuclear powers in 1992 than many observers in 1968 had feared would be the case. The present candidates for membership in the nuclear club seem to have read the lesson of the Cuban missile crisis differently. They regard Khrushchev's Cuban ploy of 1962 not as a failure, but as a success, because Castro still reigns in Cuba. Iraq, Iran, North Korea, and other expansionist or revanchist states are not aspirants for world domination, as the Soviet Union was in 1962. Their aims are more limited. They want to use force to conquer some of their neighbors without interference from the United States or its allies. From their point of view, Khrushchev succeeded in 1962, because Kennedy did not throw Castro out of Cuba. In order for Saddam Hussein to have kept Kuwait in 1991, all he needed, they think, was a small arsenal of nuclear weapons. The United States would not have exposed 500,000 American and allied troops to Iraqi nuclear weapons even though it had the power to destroy Baghdad with nuclear weapons in response. They believe that if Khrushchev had waited a few years, until Soviet nuclear superiority over the United States was apparent, the United States would not have dared to force the Soviet nuclear weapons out of Cuba. Iraq cannot dream of matching the nuclear strength of the United States or of Russia. But in attacking Kuwait, it gambled on the hypothesis that if Iraq had any nuclear weapons, the United States would not risk a nuclear war to defend Kuwait or even Saudi Arabia, that is, that the notion of "extended deterrence" is dead, at least against regimes as reckless as that of Iraq in 1990. After all, Iraq attacked Iran in 1979, and the United States did not lift a finger.

The prevalence of thinking of this kind is why the United States and its allies must enforce the cease-fire agreement in the Gulf War, which is embodied in Security Council Resolution 687.

It is important to be clear about the legal character of the Gulf War. It is often described as an exercise of the Security Council's extraordinary powers to enforce the rule of the Charter against aggression on its own motion. This is not the case. The extraordinary enforcement powers of the Security Council have never been used, and and probably never will be used. They conflict too deeply with ancient principles of national sovereignty to be accepted. The legitimacy and legality of the Gulf War do not arise from the votes of the Security Council. The Security Council did not "authorize" the war. The war was expressly fought as an action of collective self-defense, legitimated by what Article 51 of the Charter calls "the inherent right of individual or collective self-defense," and approved by the Security Council. The Security Council's role in the Gulf War was thus exactly the same as the role it played in the Korean War—that of blessing the campaign of self-defense waged by a state (there, South Korea) and its allies under customary international law and the law of the United Nations Charter.[2]

The cease-fire agreement codified in Security Council Resolution 687 recognizes a new and most important development in the international law regarding nuclear weapons and other weapons of mass destruction: the formal acceptance of the proposition that certain states cannot be allowed to possess such weapons. International law generally, and the United Nations Charter in particular, rests on the principle of the sovereign equality of states. Resolution 687 declares that some states are more equal than others. It is difficult to exaggerate the radical character of the cease-fire agreement in the Gulf War and of Security Council Resolution 687.

The proposition that certain countries cannot be allowed to possess nuclear weapons has been gaining in strength for a long time. It was the heart of the American position in the Cuban missile crisis, which the world community accepted, but did not formally approve. On the surface, the Security Council criticized Israel's attack on the Iraqi nuclear plant at Osirak in 1981, but it secretly welcomed the action. During and since the Gulf War, high officials of both the Soviet and American governments have publicly praised the Israeli bombing of Osirak. But Resolution 687 takes a long step forward by acknowledging a far-reaching restriction on the sovereignty of some nonnuclear states and mobilizing the entire Security Council behind it.

The idea was faced, but not definitively settled, when the Non-Proliferation Treaty of 1968 was negotiated and ratified. Should the Gulf War be regarded as an action to enforce the Non-Proliferation Treaty—that is, as an authoritative decision that the world community, led by the nuclear powers, will enforce the Non-Proliferation Treaty, which Iraq, Iran, and North Korea, among others, have signed, and are now believed to be violating?

The Non-Proliferation Treaty cannot be enforced by paper resolutions alone. If a signatory country has been devoting huge amounts of money, brains, and energy for years to secretly building a nuclear weapons capacity, better inspection arrangements or more "transparency" cannot alone be expected to accomplish the task of enforcement. Detecting concealed nuclear activities is difficult. Detecting the manufacture of chemical weapons by nonintrusive methods is virtually impossible. As coercion, economic sanctions would be no more effective

---

2. The issues are more fully discussed in E. V. Rostow, "Until What? Enforcement or Collective Self-Defense?" *American Journal of International Law* 85, no. 3 (July 1991).

in such situations than in any other—that is, not effective at all. Military occupation, perhaps United Nations trusteeship, may well be needed in some cases to enforce the emerging rule. The threat of nuclear weapons or other weapons of mass destruction in the hands of rulers like those of Iraq, North Korea, or Libya is too serious to be dealt with only by the methods of peaceful diplomacy. The Security Council's Resolution 731 of 22 January 1992 demanded that Libya surrender to the United States and Great Britain two men who were sought for trial in those countries for blowing up the Pan American plane which fell on Lockerbie in Scotland in 1987. Some of the votes in favor of Resolution 731 were obtained by asking delegates whether their governments preferred the international law against state-supported terrorism to be enforced by the Security Council and British and American courts or by unilateral great-power military action in self-defense.

How far this trend in the law will go depends on many factors, particularly the behavior of the outlaw states in pursuing their secret nuclear programs. Surely there will be deep resistance to the qualification of sovereignty as an abstract principle. But it is not unreasonable to anticipate that if sufficiently pushed the nations may return to the ideas of the Baruch Plan of 1946 and seek to adapt them to the political situation of the 1990s. Can the nuclear nightmare and the nightmare of state-supported terrorism be dispelled by less drastic methods?

IV

American foreign and security policy will have to be concerned with many problems beyond those of terrorism and nuclear proliferation in the years ahead. Of these, the most important is the future relationship of the great powers and the great-power constellations which will dominate world politics in the future as they have in the past. Many in the West naively believe that the United States will remain the only great power indefinitely, and that the United States can stand aloof from the changing pattern of great-power combinations. Nothing could be further from the truth.

Objectively, the prospects are neither unfamiliar nor unduly threatening. The Soviet Union has collapsed, and the state system is adapting itself to that fact. The problem is not novel. Empires have collapsed before. In recent years, the British, French, Belgian, Dutch, and Portuguese empires have been dissolved, and on the whole the consequences of these events have been absorbed rather peacefully within the framework of the state system. Certainly recent adjustments of this kind have led to fewer wars than the dissolution of the Spanish Empire during the nineteenth century and the end of the Turkish Empire during the nineteenth and early twentieth centuries.

The dissolution of Turkey and the quarrels of rivals over its remnants gave rise to a long series of wars, including the pre–1914 Balkan Wars and the First World War itself, as well as the war between Greece and Turkey in the early postwar period. Nothing comparable has happened after the Second World War except for the massacres which occurred when Great Britain withdrew from India, and India was divided into two states, India and Pakistan. Perhaps the fate of South Africa and of the British mandate for Palestine will prove to be exceptions to this generalization. But thus far, at least, the worst has been avoided.

The collapse of the Soviet empire and the economic condition of the formerly Communist states present the world political system with a challenge which will have to be watched and managed carefully in order to avoid the emergence of a new and unstable balance of world power, a balance decidedly unfavorable to the security of the United States. Russia and the former Soviet satellites in Eastern Europe will surely recover economically, and recover rather quickly. For the next ten years or so, success in their recovery programs will depend on the extent to which the industrialized democracies of the West cooperate intelligently in their effort. Whether the experiment of democracy in Russia and the other former members of the Soviet bloc will succeed is uncertain, perhaps even unlikely. But these countries will recover their economic and military strength, as Russia did after 1917.

Obviously, humanitarian assistance will be required for a year or two in order to provide food and medicine for large populations in dire need. But humanitarian assistance cannot begin to address the larger problem. The ex-Communist countries need capital and entrepreneurship in almost unlimited qualities. Once they establish a legal and monetary environment favorable to foreign private and public investment, their recoveries should go forward almost as rapidly as the post–1945 recoveries of Western Europe and Japan. The analogy is by no means perfect, but it is surely relevant. The Western economies in 1945, weakened as they were by warfare, occupation, and years of inadequate capital maintenance, had the infrastructure of effective capitalist economies, and an ample supply of native managers and entrepreneurs. For a decade or so, the ex-Communist economies will have to depend heavily on foreign entrepreneurship for a large part of the leadership and energy which their situation demands. China may need less foreign entrepreneurship than Russia and Eastern Europe, but China's need for foreign private investment will remain high nonetheless.

Under appropriate political conditions, it is greatly in the interest of the Western industrialized countries that the economic recovery of the former Communist states take place as quickly and as successfully as possible. Anything like a return to dictatorial, militaristic, and xenophobic government in these areas would be a major catastrophe, and a threat to the possibility of a reasonably stable and progressive peace. It should not be forgotten that in the interwar period, the economy of the Soviet Union moved forward rapidly, despite several years of famine and chaos. It obtained a great deal of foreign investment in the 1920s both under its secret military arrangements with Germany and under Lenin's New Economic Program. During the thirties and forties the Soviet Union confronted world politics with a military establishment which more than held its own against Germany and, in the late thirties, against Japan as well. As was pointed out earlier, the Western governments must not consider repeating the mistakes they made with regard to Russia after 1917. For reasons of their own vital interests, they should cooperate actively with the peoples and governments of the successor states of the Soviet Union and the nations of Eastern Europe to assure their economic, political, and social integration into the Western world.

It should be the deliberate decision of the governments concerned that in organizing and encouraging such recovery programs, the Open Door principle should be the rule: that is, that businessmen from all the capitalist countries should be allowed freely to participate in the process. From the point of view of the security interests of the United States, the most dangerous possible scenario for the future would be the economic modernization of Russia and Eastern Europe accomplished in a nearly exclusive partnership with Western Europe, or even with Germany alone, and the modernization of China accomplished in an exclusive or nearly exclusive partnership with Japan.

It is, however, to the equal interest of every nation, and emphatically to the interest of the United States, that the former Communist countries become part of the integrated capitalist economy and polity whose creation and development has been the finest achievement of Allied foreign policy since World War II. That interest is not only economic; it is a political and a security interest as well. The further integration of the world economy is no guarantee against war: the British, French, and German economies were interdependent to a high degree before 1914 and 1939. But a division of the world economy into rival blocs would tend to strengthen ancient impulses and ancient fears which have already shown themselves much too strongly for comfort in the relations among the Western allies, and in China's behavior since the collapse of the Soviet Union.

Since 1945, the United States has strongly supported the development of a united Europe within the Atlantic community. There were excellent reasons for that policy, and those reasons remain persuasive. More than ever, however, the Atlantic dimension of our European policy deserves special emphasis. Western Europe standing alone is already bigger and richer than the United States. Unless Europe, the United States, and Canada maintain their political solidarity, the European Community could not only neutralize but even oppose the United States in the long run. Its political leadership will not always be as cooperative as has been the case since 1945. If Russia and Eastern Europe should combine with the European Community, moreover, they would constitute a single entity embracing the entire Eurasian landmass. We have fought in two wars and struggled for more than forty years with the Cold War in order to prevent any such outcome. That must continue to be the first principle of American national security policy. As Jefferson said of Napoleon's attempt to conquer Russia, "It can never be in America's interest to have all Europe united under one monarch." And Gorbachev appropriately quoted Palmerston after his first meeting with Reagan at Geneva in 1985: "Great nations do not have permanent friends: they have permanent interests."

The United States will (and should) always prefer a concert of power to an uneasy balance among the major powers. If it is impossible for the powers to agree, however, a favorable balance of power is preferable to chaos, although it is definitely second-best as a solution to the problem of peace.

Exactly the same principle applies to our relations with other parts of the world. In the communiqué issued after Nixon's visit to China in 1972, China and the United States set forth their separate views on a number of issues. They agreed on only one: that each country "opposes any hegemonic power in Asia." Japan later endorsed that statement, despite the vigorous and threatening opposition of the Soviet Union.

Opposition to hegemony is hardly the whole of a nation's security policy. But it is the necessary starting-place for such a policy. Twice in this century the Western nations and Russia have had to fight terrible wars because they allowed drives towards German hegemony to develop unchecked until it was too late to do anything else.

At this point in the post-Gorbachev era, it is too soon to predict with any confidence what the map of world politics will be like twenty years hence. Will Yeltsin fail, as Kerensky and Gorbachev did? How will China and India fit into the world political system, both enormous industrialized countries with large and well-educated elites? Will there be aspirants for dominion, and alliances designed to achieve it, regionally or on a world scale? However these questions are answered, what is certain is that problems of this order will arise, and that how they are resolved will directly affect the vital interests of the United States. It should therefore be America's policy that such threats to the general peace be dealt with, insofar as it may be possible to do so, by bringing the concerted influence of the society of nations, or of a decisive number of them, to bear on the conflicts out of which they developed. This is not a formula for rigidly preserving the status quo, like the policy of the Holy Alliance early in the last century. It is, however, a policy for confining the forces of change to peaceful channels.

It should be noted also that in the round, contracting, and interdependent modern world there are few if any real buffers between the major powers, so that radical change in the structure of power is much easier to accomplish quickly than was the case in earlier centuries. In the age of missiles, the oceans and the Arctic and Antarctic icecaps are not the barriers they once were. There are no longer 300 independent states between Russia and France. And Japan is no longer a remote island, aloof from the world's affairs. The glittering prospect of hegemony will be especially tempting in a world where political and geographic barriers to hegemony are no longer available.

There are several institutions through which the United States should seek concert among the nations, depending upon the nature of the problem. Bilateral diplomacy remains the most important of those institutions. Some write of multilateral agencies as alternatives to bilateral diplomacy. The fact is, however, that multilateral agencies are no more than forums and catalysts for bilateral diplomacy, which is the indispensable component of whatever action multilateral agencies may be persuaded to take. Some do useful work. But it is an illusion to think of them as a substitute for national diplomacy and national action. The unanimous Security Council votes of the Gulf War period were not exclusively the product of reasoned debate in the Council chamber. Those votes were obtained principally by bargaining in the capitals.

Of necessity, the United States will continue for some time to bear the responsibilities which Great Britain had to meet during the century before 1914 in leading the Concert of Europe. There is no other power which can discharge those obligations. The instrument through which the United States should seek to carry out its task in the first instance is the North Atlantic Alliance. Until the state system is far more stable and unified than is the case today, the NATO alliance, backed by its strong military forces in being, should be a far more effective institution of conciliation, at least for conflicts arising in or near the Atlantic Basin, than the Security Council of the United Nations. The Security Council has been a useful forum for diplomacy during and since the Gorbachev era, but it is handicapped by a fundamental structural flaw for which there is no remedy: it can undertake "enforcement actions" to defeat aggression only when the permanent members agree. As a result, the U.N. Charter offers the state system the unpalatable choice between unanimity and chaos in attempting to deal with threats to the peace. Under its Harmel Resolution of 1967, reaffirmed five years later, the members of the North Atlantic Alliance are no longer strictly bound by a rule of unanimity, at least in conflicts arising outside the treaty area. For the crucial tasks of peacekeeping, therefore, the state system will continue to rely on arrangements of collective self-defense like those of NATO, blessed where politically possible by the Security Council, but used without that blessing when necessary.

The veto provisions of the Charter are indispensable if there is to be a Security Council at all: at this stage in the development of the state system, they reflect the true balance between the principles of national sovereignty, on the one hand, and of fidelity to law, on the other. There is no possibility that the veto can or should be given up.

For the foreseeable future, therefore, "enforcement actions" by the Security Council cannot supplant individual and collective self-defense as methods for assuring compliance with the rule of the Charter against aggression. Useful as the Security Council sometimes is, it is not and cannot be a substitute for measures of self-defense sanctioned by Article 51.

The way in which the Korean and the Persian Gulf wars were handled brings out the nature of the problem, both legally and politically. Both wars were fought as wars of collective self-defense under accepted principles of customary international law. As was pointed out earlier, Article 51 of the United Nations Charter provides that "nothing in the charter shall impair the inherent right of individual or collective self-defense until the Security Council has taken measures necessary to maintain international peace and security," that is, the Security Council does not have to give its permission before a nation can use force in self-defense.

United States policy toward the secession crisis of 1991–92 in Yugoslavia illustrates the way in which these considerations interact. That crisis was precipitated by the attempts of Croatia and Slovenia to secede from Yugoslavia, a patchwork state precariously cobbled together by the peace conference after the First World War. The United States, anxious to avoid another conflict which promised to be more difficult than the Gulf War, preferred to leave the issue to the European Community, and then to the United Nations Security Council. This was a costly mistake, It should have been American policy to take the matter up in the NATO Council from the beginning. Neither the European Community nor the United Nations Security Council has the military forces required to make any peacemaking initiative in the Balkans plausible. The strong preference of the United States should have been to use NATO as the forum for devising a peaceful solution of the crisis because of its overriding interest in preserving and enhancing Alliance solidarity and the peace of Europe.

The implacable implications of nuclear proliferation—and of cognate problems of international concern, like those of the environment, the drug plague, fisheries, and others—will do much to determine how closely the Western powers, the successor states of the Soviet Union, China, and other important countries (Brazil and Argentina, for example, and India and China) will find themselves committed to a degree of solidarity which now seems utopian. That solidarity, once achieved, may permit the states to prevail in their long-term plans for converting the balance of power into a concert of power. At any rate, that, I submit, should be the central goal of United States foreign policy in the years ahead.

The twentieth century has destroyed two related articles of the nineteenth-century creed: the idea of perpetual progress, and the conviction that enough energy coupled with enough will can fulfill the millenary dreams of Utopia in the here and now.

Like other works of art, Utopias play an important role in the evolution of social philosophies. They help to define the hopes and aspirations of human societies, and therefore the future policies they pursue. But Utopias can never be used as architectural drawings. Isaiah Berlin chose the title for his recent collection of essays in the history of ideas from Kant: "Out of timber so crooked as that from which man

3. Isaiah Berlin, *The Crooked Timber of Humanity* (New York: Alfred A. Knopf, 1991). The original reads: "Aus so krummem Holze, als woraus der Mensch gemacht ist, kann

is made, nothing entirely straight can be built."[3] The Socialist Utopias of the past two hundred years helped make modern capitalism more humane than its predecessors. Socialist states became instruments of tyranny only when prophets and demagogues imposed their teachings by force, without respect for the traditions and rules of civil society.

The idea of perpetual progress has never been defined in ways which commanded general agreement. Is progress simply making people richer? Better? Better educated? More cultivated? Achieving a society capable of fraternity as well as liberty and equality, or, indeed, of fraternity despite the absence of liberty or equality? The Victorians and Edwardians never decided what they meant by progress, but they were possessed nonetheless by a sense of Darwinian optimism which dominated their consciousness. There were always agnostics among them: Nietzsche and Schopenhauer, for example; Brooks Adams, Spengler, and Carlyle. But people of their outlook were a minority. The prevailing view, especially in Great Britain and the United States, was that mankind and its social environment were improving steadily, decade after decade, at an average rate of 2½% a year, or thereabouts.

Utopianism is, of course, Darwinian optimism raised to the tenth power. If the evolution of men and society propelled by science, improved morality, and social reform is moving man slowly toward perfection, why not speed up the pace by revolutionary action? Isn't cooperation more civilized, after all, than cut-throat competition, and equality morally superior to the division of society into the rich and the poor? So movements as innocent and gentle as Guild Socialism, with its stress on arts and crafts, vegetarianism, and Morris dancing, gave way to the unspeakable violence of Communism and Fascism. The restraints of civilization, built up over the centuries, were overwhelmed, for the moment at least, by the triumphant surge of the aggressive instinct. Mankind has had to witness and endure the Terror of the French Revolution over and over again, but on a gigantic, prolonged, and Orwellian scale.

The end of Darwinian optimism has not, however, destroyed man's stubborn hope for social improvement. It would be difficult to find a contemporary who has not noticed that societies decline at least as often as they improve, however "improvement" is measured. But twentieth-century man has also noticed that some societies do not improve, or even decline. The prevailing conviction as we approach the end of

---

nichts ganz Gerades gezimmert werden." (Immanuel Kant, "Idee zu einer allgemeinen Geschichte in weltburgerlicher Absicht" [1784]).

the century is that neither rise nor fall is ordained by the stars. Within limits, the efforts of men and women can influence the process of social change, which is the function of many variables, autonomous but interactive. While efforts to achieve reform often fail, they are not necessarily futile. The web of traditions, habits, and beliefs which constitute a culture defines the goals it aspires to reach through political action, and sets limits on its capacity to achieve change. If those limits are respected, however, a good deal can be done.

In no realm of social international action is this austere observation more pertinent than in the quest for international peace. The history of that effort since 1815 can be viewed as a struggle between the proponents of two ideas. The first is the notion that the state system endures cycles of more or less acute anarchy, and that mankind must accept frequent small wars and occasional big wars as the order of nature. The rival idea is the Wilsonian thesis that anarchy is not the order of nature, and that peace therefore is not a chimera entertained only by unworldly philosophers and clerics. Those of the Wilsonian persuasion believe that a considerable degree of peace is an altogether practical goal for politicians to seek—in fact, that they must do so seriously, because modern warfare threatens civilization itself.

This is not to suggest, however, that mankind is likely soon to achieve and sustain peace, without war to enforce its rules. Both the inertia and the momentum of history make it impossible—and probably dangerous as well—to expect or even to seek perfect peace. On the other hand, a prudent degree of social continuity does not condemn mankind to live forever in a state of unmitigated anarchy.

In his *Thoughts on Perpetual Peace,* Kant dismisses the idea of world government as not only impracticable but morally wrong. "For states in their relation to each other there cannot according to reason be any other way to avoid the lawless condition which contains nothing but war than to give up (just like individual men) their wild and lawless freedom, to accept public and enforceable laws, and thus to form a world state of nations. . . . But states do not want this, as not in keeping with their idea of a law of nations, and thus they reject in fact what was true in theory. Therefore, unless all is lost, the positive idea of a world republic must be replaced by the negative substitute of a union of nations which maintains itself, prevents wars, and steadily expands."[4]

---

4. Immanuel Kant, *Thoughts on Perpetual Peace,* reprinted as appendix to *Inevitable Peace* by C. J. Friedrich (Cambridge, Mass.: Harvard University Press, 1948), 257.

Index